Love Is a Journey

Love Is a Journey

The Inspiring Life and Legacy of Pope John Paul I

Mo Guernon

Foreword by Loris Serafini

A SHEED & WARD BOOK

ROWMAN & LITTLEFIELD

Lanham • Boulder • New York • London

Rowman & Littlefield
Bloomsbury Publishing Inc, 1385 Broadway, New York, NY 10018, USA
Bloomsbury Publishing Plc, 50 Bedford Square, London, WC1B 3DP, UK
Bloomsbury Publishing Ireland, 29 Earlsfort Terrace, Dublin 2, D02 AY28, Ireland
www.rowman.com

British Library Cataloguing in Publication Information available

Library of Congress Cataloging-in-Publication Data
Names: Guernon, Mo, 1952- author. | Serafini, Loris, writer of foreword.
Title: Love is a journey : the inspiring life and legacy of Pope John Paul I / Mo Guernon ; foreword by Loris Serafini.
Description: Lanham : Rowman & Littlefield, [2025] | "A Sheed & Ward Book." | Includes bibliographical references and index.
Identifiers: LCCN 2024055799 (print) | LCCN 2024055800 (ebook) | ISBN 9781538190708 (cloth) | ISBN 9781538190715 (epub)
Subjects: LCSH: John Paul I, Pope, 1912-1978. | Popes—Biography. | Catholic Church—Clergy—Biography.
Classification: LCC BX1378.4 .G84 2025 (print) | LCC BX1378.4 (ebook) | DDC 282.092 [B]—dc23/eng/20250124
LC record available at https://lccn.loc.gov/2024055799
LC ebook record available at https://lccn.loc.gov/2024055800

For product safety related questions contact productsafety@bloomsbury.com.

In loving memory of my parents,
Alice Henault Guernon
and
Eudore A. Guernon,
who always gave more than they received.

This story shall the good man teach his son.
—Shakespeare, Henry V[1]

NOTE

1. William Shakespeare, *Henry V*, Project Gutenberg, March 1, 2023, https://www.gutenberg.org/ebooks/2253.

Contents

Part III: Allure

Part IV: Finale

Acknowledgments

"Don't judge a book by its cover" is a cliché whose truth I never fully realized until researching and writing this book.

This author's solitary name appearing on the cover conveys the misleading impression that I am the sole creator of the volume in your hands. In reality, this work—like every book, I suspect—was a collaborative effort.

I am, therefore, beholden to a host of people who contributed to the book's completion and enhanced it far beyond what my modest skills alone would have wrought. To each of the following I owe a debt of gratitude that words cannot adequately convey and that never can be repaid in full.

My wife, Elizabeth Kelley, always has been my most perceptive, exacting, and reliable editor. All my published work has benefited immeasurably from her keen insights and wise recommendations. From the dubious onset of this book project to its sometimes seemingly unattainable culmination, her faith in my eventual success never faltered (or, if it did, she was considerate enough never to vocalize her misgivings). For more than a decade she tolerated without a single complaint my recounting endless anecdotes (many repeated ad nauseam) to whoever would listen about Albino Luciani. Her unfaltering help, patience, and encouragement sustained me throughout the prolonged process of finalizing this opus. As the manuscript submission deadline loomed with considerable work yet unfinished, she undid my heavy burdens by cheerfully working twelve-hour days, seven days a week, for more than a month, assisting in the completion of tasks that made publication possible. Whenever I felt overwhelmed or suffered setbacks (all-too-frequent occurrences), she came to my rescue, providing unfailing affection and selfless acts of kindness that provided me the impetus to surmount daunting impediments. For that, and so much more, I am forever grateful.

To Bruce Daigle, my friend and brother in spirit for more than four decades, I offer my abiding appreciation for his genuine enthusiasm and vital support for this project from its inception to its completion. A humble man and writer of uncommon skill, his unvarnished editorial critique of the entire tome enriched the quality of this narrative beyond measure. He, too (at his insistence), lent indispensable succor, doing yeoman's work particularly during the final stretch of preparing the manuscript. Every day, for weeks, whenever our doorbell rang in the morning, there was no mystery as to the identity of the caller. All his painstaking and often tedious work he completed tirelessly with unfailing professionalism and tension-reducing wit. After completing one task, he generously would insist on doing more. The extent of my gratitude is matched only by my admiration and depth of affection for him. No one has been blessed with a better friend. To his kindhearted wife, Monica, who prepared meals for us despite the paucity of time available to her during our most feverish period of labor, much love. My wife and I are blessed to embrace the Daigles as family.

The pivotal figure in making this book a reality is Loris Serafini, a gentle and generous man. Our mutual admiration for Albino Luciani brought us together in the most unlikely circumstances. Since we first met in 2010, he has selflessly guided me throughout my research sojourns in Italy, at times when I would have been hopelessly lost. I repeatedly tapped into his vast knowledge of the pope's life for enlightening anecdotes and facts (a slew of them that he learned about directly from the pope's brother Edoardo), as well as validation of my research. The wealth of information he provided over more than a dozen years through conversations, interviews, correspondence, and sharing primary documents and recordings was indispensable. All his efforts on my behalf—far too many to enumerate—he provided beyond what I had any right to request, and he did so despite his overwhelming professional and family responsibilities. Author of the delightful book *Albino Luciani: Il Papa del Sorriso*, he is director of the Pope Luciani Foundation and Museum of Canale d'Agordo, Italy, and one of the world's foremost experts on Pope John Paul I. I'm honored that he agreed to write this book's foreword. My wife and I treasure our friendship with him and his wife, Inna. *Gli devo centomila ringraziamenti, perché senza di lui questo libro non sarebbe stato realizzato.*

Without the labors of Elizabeth, Bruce, and Loris, completing this book would have been impossible.

Our children—Greg, Alexandra, and Shayla—were also supremely supportive in every conceivable way. They are the substance of all my life's dreams come true. To my sons-in-law, Andre Loli and David Wilson, who came to my rescue whenever technological crises derailed my work, I am deeply obligated. And to our grandchildren, Aiden, Adeline, Cameron, and Jack endless love for reminding me (especially by some of their interruptions when I was absorbed in my work) what makes life truly meaningful.

Important contributions also came from a variety of other individuals I gladly acknowledge:

For granting me in-person, phone, and/or Skype interviews besides additional information through subsequent correspondence, I extend an abundance of gratitude to Pia Luciani and Dr. Lina Petri, two of Blessed John Paul's nieces; bishop emeritus John Magee, John Paul's personal secretary at the Vatican; don Diego Lorenzi, Luciani's personal secretary as patriarch of Venice for two years and subsequently during his pontificate; Rev. Silvio De Nard, a Belluno, Italy, native whose parents knew Albino Luciani; and other intimates of the pope's who shared their knowledge of him but who wished to remain anonymous.

I would be remiss if I did not acknowledge the assistance of the following individuals as well: my friend Adrianna Cillo, who patiently devoted countless hours to translating lengthy interviews that I had conducted in Italian; Laura Busin, who served as my interpreter, tour guide, and occasional driver through the remote hinterlands of northern Italy; and Claudia Tancon at the Papa Luciani Museum and Archives for her cheerful, competent, and timely exertions in securing rights to various sources on my behalf.

I am indebted to Lauretta Seabeck and her late husband, Ray, who have been an inspiration for the three decades of aid they supplied to the poor of Haiti through the organization they founded, The Missionary Servants of Pope John Paul I. Our conversations about Papa Luciani and the research materials they supplied me were invaluable. More noble people I have never met.

The following individuals also contributed in significant ways: Ray Flynn, former United States ambassador to the Vatican; Louis Gelineau, bishop emeritus of the diocese of Providence; Robert Evans, my former pastor and auxiliary bishop emeritus of the diocese of Providence; Msgr. Francis Kelley, cousin and friend; Dr. Suzanne Fournier, professor of English at Providence College; and Roger Guernon, my brother.

Also, I am beholden to the following who passed away prior to the publication of this book: Dr. Lori Pieper, founder of the Pope John Paul I Association in New York and translator of many of Pope John Paul's writings, some of which are recorded in her book, *A Passionate Adventure: Living the Catholic Faith Today*; Msgr. Francesco Taffarel, personal secretary to Albino Luciani when he was bishop of the diocese of Vittorio Veneto; and Rinaldo De Rocco, mayor of Canale d'Agordo, for his hospitality during my initial stay.

Finally, thanks to my literary agent, Anne Devlin of the Max Gartenberg Agency, for her sound advice, successful advocacy of this book, and consummate professionalism throughout our partnership. To Richard Brown, my acquisitions editor at Rowman & Littlefield Publishing Group, for his passion and support of this project, for believing in the ability of a first-time author to complete an endeavor of this magnitude, and for his unfailing kindness, I offer heartfelt appreciation. To Victoria "Tori" Shi, assistant editor at R&L, goes a tip of the cap for her forbearance and graciousness in counseling a fledgling author who was often in need of guidance. She was a lifesaver. To Meaghan Menzel, my production editor, thanks for providing technical guidance.

My delight in acknowledging all who contributed to the success of this venture is tempered by my consternation that I might have inadvertently excluded someone. If that is the case, I offer a thousand inadequate apologies for the oversight. Should the book undergo a subsequent printing, I will be relieved to rectify my omission.

This entire undertaking has been a labor of love. I pray that I have done justice in this work to the memory of Albino Luciani, Blessed Pope John Paul I, who touched my life profoundly.

Any errors contained in this book are my sole responsibility.

Foreword

Recommending this important biography of blessed John Paul I (Albino Luciani) by Mo Guernon is indeed a special honor for me.

I first met Mo in 2011 when he visited Canale d'Agordo, the pope's birthplace, to learn more about him and the environment in which he was raised. His admiration and affection for Albino Luciani were evident immediately. During his stay he interviewed me and some of the pope's relatives. He also conducted research in the Papa Luciani archives. From this visit began a friendship and collaboration that has continued since. The following year Mo and I were speakers at the centenary conference of John Paul's birth held in New York City.

I was struck by his tenacity in researching and writing this Luciani biography despite the extensive travels involved to conduct interviews and visit Luciani sites in Canale d'Agordo, Agordo, Feltre, Belluno, Vittorio Veneto, Venice, Rome, and in the Vatican State to become acquainted with the places where Albino Luciani lived and served the Church.

In 2022 Mo returned to Italy to attend John Paul I's beatification presided over by Pope Francis. There we were reunited for several days in Rome and afterward in Canale, where Mo did more research at the pope's museum archives. The result is this biography.

Love Is a Journey is an important, unique, and masterful book.

It is one of the few biographies of John Paul written in English and provides the most up-to-date information available. The book is also much more than a chronological presentation of facts. In that regard it avoids repeating the patterns of many Luciani biographies, particularly of those written by some Italian authors.

It raises awareness of Blessed John Paul I while giving readers an accurate account of his inspiring life and countering the widespread distortions, especially about his death. So much misinformation about this holy man has tarnished the real man's image. Mo Guernon here reveals the true personality and humanity of a great man who is worthy of admiration.

The book captures beautifully the essence of a humble and holy man who had a heart full of love for all humanity and served the Church with a lifelong devotion. *Love Is a Journey* reveals the author's affection for the pope, but it doesn't idealize him. Here the reader meets Albino Luciani as he was, venerable but not perfect, as all saints are, through his words and actions.

Mo reconstructs the major events of Albino Luciani's life in an original and fascinating manner that gives the reader rare insights into the pope's character through the skillful use of facts and anecdotes from a variety of sources, documents, and conversations with people who knew him well.

The book portrays real events, essential ones—told in the manner of a master storyteller who faithfully relied on facts found in a variety of dependable sources in both English and Italian.

I am pleased to have been one of those many sources. Since we first met, Mo has questioned me about my knowledge of Albino Luciani, which I gained from so many conversations over the years with his friends and family and through research I had conducted for my own book, *The Smiling Pope*.

Singer Patti Smith—a great admirer of John Paul—repeatedly called him "a man who was able to transmit love to everyone, believers and nonbelievers, all over the world and in just a few days."

She is right, and her opinion is shared by everyone who remembers John Paul's papacy. His achievement amazed everyone. *Love Is a Journey* captures the passion that Pope John Paul I produced everywhere. Historians would have a difficult job finding a man who was able to accomplish this wonderful success in so short a time.

Mo Guernon catches the excitement, happiness, and hope that people everywhere felt during the thirty-three days that Albino Luciani was pope. Readers of this book will share in those emotions, too. People everywhere lost a beautiful religious leader who was a friend to all when John Paul I died. Those who were alive when he was pope were fortunate. Now, because of Mo Guernon's passionate telling of his life story, others can relive those days.

This is a book that all English-speaking people should read. They will be better for it.

On behalf of the entire community of Canale d'Agordo, Albino Luciani's birthplace and home, I sincerely thank my friend Mo Guernon for having written this exceptional work about our most beloved townsman.

Loris Serafini
Director, Museum Birthplace of Blessed John Paul I
Canale d'Agordo, May 31, 2024

Preface

Genesis—To Begin Anew

As the British historian Edward Gibbon once admitted about his own attempt at writing a book, I had the audacity to pen this biography though my formal training as a writer is negligible: a single semester high-school course. My skills in composition—such as they are—were honed over time by writing research papers in college and graduate school; then later working as a journalist for a small newspaper, crafting a column for Rhode Island dailies and weeklies, and ultimately publishing freelance work in magazines. But writing a book was a substantial leap from composing short pieces of prose.

Nevertheless, the idea itself dated back to the nineties. After reading one of my columns while vacationing in Rhode Island, a New York City literary agent called me to determine whether I had any interest in composing a book. I was flattered and intrigued, but the timing was not propitious. My wife and I were then raising three small children, both of us were teaching full-time, and I had the additional demand of completing my weekly column. As a result, the proposition withered. But a seed of aspiration had been planted.

A confession is in order at this point. Though raised a Catholic by devout parents, I was religiously adrift by 1978, indifferent to others and unmindful of the spiritual perils of my heedless ways.

"The unexamined life is not worth living," Socrates wisely taught ages ago.[1] It was a lesson I resisted for decades. Looking back, I suspect I dared not engage in genuine introspection, unconsciously fearing the dreadful truth I would discover about myself. Considering that reality, what transpired in late summer of 1978 is inexplicable.

On August 26, I was watching television when a newscaster announced that a pope had been elected to succeed the recently deceased Paul VI. Out of casual curiosity, I awaited the revelation of the new pontiff's identity. Not surprisingly, I was unfamiliar with Cardinal Albino Luciani, who took the name John Paul I. No matter. The new pope would have no bearing on my life. Or so I thought.

To my utter astonishment, almost immediately after he emerged on the central balcony of St. Peter's Basilica, I was awestruck. John Paul flashed a benevolent smile that immediately penetrated my heart and stirred my soul. There was a transcendent luminosity about the man that I had never encountered in any other person. He radiated gentleness, serenity, and love. For the first time in my life, I was beholding a glimpse of God in a man. The pope uttered not a word other than chanting the traditional blessing. Nevertheless, his appearance alone was transformational. His fleeting presence held me spellbound. My epiphany at that moment was less dramatic than Saul's, the persecutor of Christians who, Scripture tells us, was suddenly struck by the dazzling light of Christ on his journey to Tarsus and became a convert as a result. Still, my experience was so intense as to eventually alter the trajectory of my life.

A mere thirty-three days later, a seemingly vibrant John Paul died unexpectedly. The news rocked the world.

The tragedy was personally distressing to me and led to prolonged disillusionment. Before long, I instinctively resumed my wayward ways. The hope that I would devote myself henceforth to emulating the pope's virtues died with him. Yet his memory lingered deep in the recesses of my subconscious.

Far too many years after Albino Luciani's departure from this world, I rediscovered my faith (before harboring doubts again later, though my admiration of John Paul remained undiminished), and the notion of reviving his memory by writing his biography became a mission I could not resist. Ironically, my work would honor a man who had embodied humility and spurned ambition—the very antithesis of who I had been. Thanks to John Paul's example, my desire to pursue a life of noble purpose ultimately prevailed, though whatever degree of humility I've since acquired is lamentably meager. Each day continues to be a struggle to make a modicum of progress. Meekness is an elusive virtue—problematic to attain and challenging to sustain. As Luciani, himself a paragon of humility, once publicly admitted, "I have conducted my pride's funeral a hundred times, convinced I was burying it six feet underground . . . and a hundred times, I have seen it rise again, more sprightly than ever."[2]

Prior to my retirement from full-time employment in 2010, I started learning Italian and researching the pontiff's life. I was oblivious to the hurdles of the quest that beckoned me. "Writing books involves endless hard work, and that much study wearies the body," *Ecclesiastes* warns.[3] That truth became all too apparent shortly after I embarked on the project. I encountered formidable obstacles, discouraging setbacks, and secret qualms. Because I had wholly underestimated the magnitude of the labor, my opus evolved sluggishly, intermittently, and exasperatingly over more than a decade into the volume that you now hold.

Any rational person, I suppose, would have called the project a fool's errand from the start. I had no experience researching or writing a book; I knew virtually nothing about the publishing industry; I found Italian to be a daunting language to master; and I had not even the remotest connections to the late pope's intimates, making the prospect of conducting interviews with them implausible.

The more I learned about Albino Luciani in the ensuing months and years, though, the more captivated I became by his humility, wisdom, simplicity, and sweetness of character. Because his exemplary life increasingly inspired me, I was undaunted by countless impediments and proceeded with my long-deferred labor of love.

Deep into my research, I connected with a former U.S. ambassador to the Vatican, Ray Flynn, who advised me to bring John Paul's personality back to life. It was sage counsel. Albino Luciani could soften even the most hardened hearts. Countless people in our broken world could morally mend from knowing a man whose life embodied the triumph of love over hate, tenderness over cruelty, forgiveness over retribution, and humility over arrogance. Concomitantly, I thought it imperative to introduce the man to generations who were deprived of the wonder that was John Paul I. One doesn't have to be Catholic or even religious to be transformed by this uncommon man; his prescription for living a life of fulfillment is universally applicable.

This book is by no means a comprehensive biography. Instead, imperfectly imitating a portrait painter, I've attempted to capture the essence of the man; in doing so I've selectively depicted events in the pope's life that I believe best shed light on his character. Doing so is unavoidably subjective. There is no pretense of detachment on my part; I freely offer my own interpretations about the significance of Albino Luciani's words and deeds. Further, the narrative itself sometimes reads more like a novel than a work of nonfiction as I sought to capture the ambience of the unfolding drama of his life in a compelling way by using some techniques of the novelist without, I hope, compromising factual integrity.

From childhood we've all been fascinated by stories. It's been true of all peoples, in all places, at all times. Some tales are whimsical, others authentic, but stories of all genres endure because they are essential to cultural vitality and to a fundamental human need: They help us understand our world and ourselves.

President Kennedy, a devotee of biography, once astutely observed that what makes biography fascinating is "the struggle to answer that single question: What's he like?"[4] In this book I attempt to answer that question about Albino Luciani. Doing so was demanding. The chapters on his pontificate presented a unique conundrum. Because of the brevity of his papacy, his words often overshadowed his accomplishments, and thus his homilies, speeches, and informal talks became the primary means of conveying insights into his temperament. But utterances aren't as dramatic as action, so I toiled arduously to depict a genuine sense of the wonder that his public addresses engendered.

There is an ever-present frustration in writing about Luciani. His saintliness and universal appeal defy adequate capture in prose. Language has limitations. Written accounts of his deeds, as well as manifestations of his personality, are deficient in capturing the entirety of the man. They do provide a hint of who he was but fail to resurrect him. Photographs help to augment the written word, but they, too, are inadequate. Video is essential to accomplish the goal. Only through this medium can we experience Luciani's mystique. Only through this means can we see him as he was in life; observe his mannerisms and facial expressions; hear his voice: soft, consoling, at times dramatic, always entrancing; witness his genial but sometimes shy interactions with people; marvel at the fervor generated by his charisma; feel the gentleness of his personality; gaze at that mystic smile and sparkling eyes; experience the holiness that he radiated. Fortunately, snippets of film are easily accessible on YouTube. Watching them is an unforgettable experience.

This book is only one version of Albino Luciani's life. I have made every effort to adhere to the truth throughout. Unfortunately, truth is often difficult to ascertain. In those instances where conflicting accounts of events were impossible to untangle, I have presented all credible sides that I'm aware of, unless the preponderance of evidence supports a particular version as the factual one. People are complicated, though, leading both private and public lives. Penetrating the personas that we all adopt when interacting with others is problematic. To depict a person with perfect precision, therefore, is beyond the scope of a writer's ability. A biographer's best hope is to render with fidelity as many facets of a subject's character as possible by exploring both his virtues and shortcomings. This account is no exception.

Perspective is added by integrating recollections of those who knew him best—family members, friends, colleagues, neighbors, students, superiors, and subordinates. Although their perceptions are indispensable, they are not infallible. Memories fade over time, and those recollections that were recorded during Luciani's life or shortly thereafter probably tend to be more accurate than those that were elicited through interviews and testimony decades after his death. In addition, some tend to overlook Luciani's flaws. Still others provide self-serving, counterfactual accounts. Yet, despite these limitations, the details of his intimates' personal experiences with Luciani remain invaluable despite the passage of years.

John Paul made us yearn to become better individuals, to become more like him. Those who have forgotten him, as well as those who weren't alive when he was pope, deserve to encounter a holy man whose story can provide them with hope as well as the longing and wisdom to lead more righteous and fulfilling lives.

Albino Luciani's exceptionality is that he was a part of but apart from this world. His faith was profound and abiding; thus, much of his life was steeped in the spiritual world. As a result, he was an individual of transcendence who astounded us. All who make blessed John Paul I's acquaintance, even retrospectively, will discern divine attributes in an unassuming man. The power of that experience cannot but be transforming, inspiring us to progress on our own journey of love, and that can make all the difference in our lives and in those we touch.

NOTES

1. Plato, *Apology*, Project Gutenberg, October 4, 2020, https://www.gutenberg.org/ebooks/1656.
2. Albino Luciani, *Illustrissimi,* trans. William Weaver (Boston: Little, Brown, 1978), 50.
3. *The Jerusalem Bible*, *Ecclesiastes* 12:12 (Garden City, New York: Doubleday, 1966), 990.
4. Ben Bradlee, *Conversations with Kennedy* (New York: Pocket Books, 1976), 57.

Prologue

Transfiguration (August 6, 1978)

> Jesus took with him Peter and James and his brother John and led them up a high mountain, by themselves. And he was transfigured before them, and his face shone like the sun, and his clothes became dazzling white.
> —Matthew 17:1–2 (NRSVCE)

The enfeebled old man confined to his bed was dying. For weeks he had discerned death's stealthy shadow stalking him, and there were moments when he almost welcomed looming death's deliverance from his earthly woes.

Advanced age and debilitating ailments alone did not account for the man's inclination to surrender to his mortality. For fifteen years, the octogenarian had been battered by bitter controversies; he had agonized over his every decision and was tormented by the derision and discord that often ensued.[1] The seemingly endless turbulence that traumatized him had taken a staggering toll that sapped his strength, darkened his mood, and eroded his will to live.

The past several months had been fraught with encumbering emotional, psychological, and spiritual torment that he endured stoically. With a single exception, he bore the suffering patiently and privately; even so, the anguish was plainly etched on his face.

The recent brutal murder of his lifelong friend had plunged him into deep depression, if not outright despair. He had never prayed more ardently, begging God for former prime minister Aldo Moro's safe release from the bloody hands of the Red Brigade terrorists who held him captive. Inexplicably, the Almighty, to whom he had been a devoted servant throughout his life, had dismissed his entreaties: Moro's bullet-riddled body was discovered stuffed in the back of a car like a discarded sack of trash.[2]

In response to his spurned solicitations, at Moro's funeral mass on May 13, 1978, in St. John Lateran, the soft-spoken man had virtually scolded God in a publicly shocking, desperate cry of nearly unendurable suffering. "Lord, listen to us," he demanded in a chastening tone. "You did not hear our plea for the safety of Aldo Moro, for this good, gentle, wise, innocent, for this friend."[3]

And so, for him, the dread of his approaching end diminished; he was inclined to embrace it as liberation from the unrelenting sorrows of earthly life. Now, as he felt the frosty breath of death upon him, he could relinquish all the crushing burdens and the seemingly endless personal vilification. This saintly man had done his best, always conscientiously devoted to his sacred mission, and yet, he was the victim of a vortex of voluble dissent that caused him unbearable self-doubt and self-flagellation. Perhaps he feared for his legacy; certainly, he worried about the future of his beloved Church that now found itself in limbo—caught between the irreconcilable forces of progress and retrenchment.

Around the time of his eightieth birthday, he had confided to an associate, "I go from challenge to challenge, I never have a moment's respite, never a moment's rest. And it will go on like that until my death."[4] To another, while examining old photos of his closest friends, he bemoaned, "They've all gone, all gone, leaving me alone, and at my age I feel this solitude. When the friends of your own age, your contemporaries, your classmates are no more, you are really alone."[5]

When the time of his own demise was imminent, however, he no longer readily welcomed death as an emancipator. In his final hours, in fact, he became agitated. Like Jacob wrestling mightily with the mysterious angel in the night, it was as if the elderly man's soul were struggling fiercely to take flight from its physical captivity but encountering stubborn resistance from its mortal coil.

Providentially, unlike Aldo Moro, he was not alone in his final moments the evening of August 6, 1978. He took some consolation in that. Ministering to him in the dim bedroom of the dwelling in the Alban hills to which he had fled Rome's wilting heat only a few short days before, virtually certain that he would return as a cold corpse, were men whose devotion to him was akin to that of dutiful children to their beloved father. They were not, in fact, his sons but faithful personal assistants whose admiration and affection for him knew no bounds. For years, both had walked by his side each day like guardian angels or courtiers to a king: always at his elbow, ready to respond promptly to his every wish. They were here now to cater to his final needs and to offer whatever small consolation they could as he prepared himself for his final journey into the mystery of eternity.

Both men were priests. Msgr. Pasquale Macchi had been the dying man's gatekeeper and protector for years; John Magee, the "junior" associate, still in awe of the man he served, functioned now as a veritable nurse.

This Sunday was the feast of the Transfiguration of Christ, the miraculous moment of the Messiah's glorification shortly before He divulged His approaching passion to His disciples.

Confronting the end of his life, the patient asked pardon of "all those to whom I have not done good," and he delivered a parting blessing: "I close my eyes on this sad, dramatic and magnificent world, calling God's charity down on it once more."[6]

So, it was on this solemn feast day that Giovanni Montini received a sliver of solace from his assistants as the light of his life gradually dimmed. These selfless men hovered by the patient's bed, monitoring his every labored breath, offering whatever comfort they could. It was a grueling undertaking. Emotionally drained and physically exhausted, Magee ministered to his elder with a heart aching with sorrow.

Near the patient's bed was one of his few personal possessions, an outdated alarm clock, the unfailing mechanism he had relied on to wake him daily. It had been permanently set for 6 a.m. decades before.[7]

The first undeniable sign that the end was approaching came suddenly, around three o'clock in the morning when both priests, awakened by the sound of a bell indicating the patient was in distress, raced to the ailing man's bedchamber. They found him sitting precariously on the edge of his bed gasping for breath. They moved him into an armchair. Magee gently slipped an oxygen tank's clear plastic tube into the struggling man's nostrils. While Machi summoned the doctor, Montini's labored breathing almost immediately eased with the infusion of the oxygen. Enveloped by the darkness of night, Magee nonetheless suffered from the unrelenting sweltering heat.[8]

It was not yet the end, only the first stage of failure. But to be sure, the deathwatch now commenced in earnest. For the next eighteen hours or so, the inexorable slide into eternal slumber took its laborious course. Magee held the dying man's hand for hours as he alternately faltered and then rallied.[9]

Three decades later Magee vividly recalled, "I held his hand all the time he was dying—for hours. Thirteen times that day as I was holding his hand he would attempt to get out of his bed, and I would help him up and put him in a chair, and no sooner was he there than I had to move him back again into the bed. And on the thirteenth time I was so exhausted, the perspiration dropping down off me onto him." A frustrated Magee asked him what it was that he wanted. He opened his eyes and said calmly, "A little patience." They were the last words he ever spoke to Magee.[10]

The time ticked by ever so slowly. In the afternoon, as the vigil continued, others filtered into the sick room in silent prayer to bid their final farewell.

At 6 p.m. Macchi began celebrating the Mass of the Transfiguration in the chapel adjacent to the patient's bedroom. The dying man listened intently.

Magee, still by his side, clasped his hand as if he were a child needing reassurance. After the consecration, Montini received Holy Communion. Several minutes later, coinciding with the conclusion of the Mass, he abruptly sustained a crippling heart attack. Yet for three more hours he tenuously clung to life, now surrounded by a nephew, Magee, and Macchi along with his doctors who were helpless to do anything for him other than to monitor his temperature and blood pressure as nature took its inevitable course.[11]

The stricken man managed to open his eyes about an hour later. Though his condition was grave, he could speak softly though lucidly. "We have arrived at the end. We thank—" Unable to finish the thought, he shut his eyes.[12]

Later, regaining consciousness once more, Montini in a feeble voice began reciting the Our Father. At the foot of his bed, his secretaries joined him, the three men of God united in prayer, an earthly trinity. They began to pray the rosary, but as they proceeded to a recitation of the Hail Mary, the dying man insisted on repeating the Our Father; just the Lord's Prayer, the one the Savior Himself had bequeathed to His followers. In unison they intoned: "Our Father who art in heaven, hallowed be thy name, thy kingdom come . . . Our Father who art in heaven, hallowed be thy name . . . Our Father who art in heaven . . . Our Father—" The repetition was like the steady rhythm of a healthy beating heart and induced in the exhausted petitioners a nearly trancelike state as they battled physical and emotional exhaustion.[13]

This continued until 9:30. Then slumber overtook the old man yet again. All the while, Magee, still holding the patient's hand as his last connection to the living, felt his pulse ebbing. Ten minutes later the doctor declared the man dead. The time was 9:41 p.m.[14]

Mysteriously, at that very moment the alarm of the dead man's old-fashioned clock, still set for 6 a.m., pierced the air, startling the men surrounding the bed.[15]

Giovanni Battista Montini, known to the world as Pope Paul VI, had died.

That he should have expired on August 6 was ironic, for it was a date that had held personal significance for him. It was on the sixth of August 1964 that he had published his first papal encyclical. More momentous, on August 6, 1968, he had issued his controversial encyclical, *Humanae Vitae*, banning artificial birth control. According to Magee, Paul VI had told him once that "the transfiguration of the Lord was a feast day that he looked forward always to celebrating." And then he confided to Magee one day, "You know I believe that I shall see that transfigured person on the sixth of August."[16]

That same day, some 330 miles north of Castel Gandolfo, the sumptuous papal summer residence where Paul had escaped the sullen bonds of earth, an unassuming little priest with a grand title—patriarch of Venice—took solitary strolls on a sliver of island beach known as the Lido, a seven-mile-long sandbar less than two miles from Venice.

Cardinal Albino Luciani had arrived on the morning of July 25, unaccompanied by his personal secretary don Diego Lorenzi who took the rare time off to visit his native village.

The cardinal was hosted by nuns who operated a small hospital on the isle. His accommodations were spare, perfectly suited to his penchant for austere living.

The Lido was an idyllic destination, affording him the peaceful solitude that he always cherished. His doctor had advised him to leave his residence in Piazza San Marco as hordes of tourists invaded, to embark on a walking regimen without the encumbrance of curious sightseers. Walking would be therapeutic for his swollen ankles.[17] Compliantly, Luciani ambled along the seashore. Daily, he rose with the ascending sun to saunter along the tranquil beach, a routine he faithfully repeated as dusk approached, when he pursued the shimmering sun sliding leisurely from the heavens to caress the western horizon.

Not only was this activity a boon to Luciani's physical health, but it was also nourishing for the soul, providing him with opportunities to pray, to meditate, and to read in tranquility. He found the exercise and the serene surroundings so beneficial that he extended his stay into August.

Prior illnesses had beset the diminutive priest at various periods of his life, and now, in his mid-sixties, he was on a regimen of medications to treat a condition that he dismissed as little more than a nuisance. The spiritual leader of the prominent Venetian diocese, Albino Luciani had what he considered more pressing concerns.

Undoubtedly, the pious but cerebral cardinal was absorbed either in silent conversation with God, pondering solutions to problems in his diocese, or engaging in enticing intellectual speculations as he strolled along the shifting sands by the restless sea. Whatever dominated his thoughts during those placid moments, it surely was not the passing of the pope, an event of which he was yet unaware. The pontiff's death was, however, a momentous event that would abruptly abbreviate Luciani's restorative island retreat and would drastically alter his life. He could not possibly have imagined as he faithfully traced the arc of the sun each day that he would soon depart for the Vatican, never again to return home.

NOTES

1. Kenneth L. Woodward, "Choosing a New Pope," *Newsweek*, August 21, 1978, 48.

2. "Former Italian Prime Minister Aldo Moro Is Found Dead," https://www.history.com/this-day-in-history/aldo-moro-found-dead.

3. Paul Spackman, *God's Candidate: The Life and Times of John Paul I* (Herefordshire: Gracewing, 2008), 113.

4. Peter Hebblethwaite, *Paul VI: The First Modern Pope* (New York: Paulist Press, 1993), 694.

5. Hebblethwaite, *Paul VI*, 695.

6. Woodward, "Choosing a New Pope," 55.

7. John Magee (bishop emeritus, diocese of Cloyne, Ireland), in discussion with the author, February 17, 2010.

8. Hebblethwaite, *Paul VI*, 709.

9. Magee, discussion.

10. Magee, discussion.

11. Magee, discussion.

12. Hebblethwaite, *Paul VI*, 710.

13. Magee, discussion.

14. Hebblethwaite, *Paul VI*, 710.

15. Magee, discussion.

16. Magee, discussion.

17. Spackman, *God's Candidate*, 118–19.

Part I

ADVENT

• 1 •

Pontiff—Week I/Charisma

A Divine Smile (August 26–September 2, 1978)

Be the living expression of God's kindness; kindness in your face, kindness in your eyes, kindness in your smile. —Mother Teresa[1]

SATURDAY, AUGUST 26

In a flash the world would fall in love with a total stranger, though not a soul had any inkling of it. Not just yet. Smoke signals, of all things, delayed the onset of that mystifying moment.

A two-thousand-year-old institution, the Roman Catholic Church clings to tradition like a magnet to iron even when a custom has long outlived its practicality. As a result, the Vatican insists on preserving an obsolete means by which it alerts the world of a new pope's election.

In a centuries-long preoccupation with secrecy, the Church adheres to strict protocols for concealing the proceedings of papal elections. The cardinal electors, literally incarcerated in the Sistine Chapel and its immediate vicinity (they now have accommodations at St. Martha's House, a guest house for clergy, located near St. Peter's Basilica) burn all the ballots in a crude, temporary stove. The practice serves a dual purpose: the fire destroys written records of what has transpired, and the color of the smoke it produces informs the world whether a new pontiff has been selected. Not lacking in symbolism, black smoke indicates that the balloting has been inconclusive whereas white smoke signifies that a pope has been chosen.[2] Seems so simple. But not this time.

Representatives of the world's media had converged on Rome to cover Pope Paul's funeral and remained to report on the election of his successor. According to *NBC Nightly News*, multitudes started gathering in St. Peter's

Square early in the day. They stayed until noon when black smoke spilled out of the makeshift chimney poking through the roof of the Sistine Chapel. The crowds then dispersed, a great many returning later in the day when another emission would indicate the results of the afternoon voting. But few, if any, Vatican experts had expected the cardinal electors to conclude their business on this first day of voting. Such a swift conclave was unusual.

At 6:18 p.m. smoke curled into the sky from the flue. A steady stream of billowing smoke ensued, initially appearing light gray but then darkening. Vatican Radio reported the color to be black, and Italian reporters rushed to announce the news to their audiences: "*E nera*!" ("It's black!") As a result, disappointed spectators started drifting away. Almost simultaneously, however, a blast of smoke, like the billows of ash erupting from a volcano, turned gray, then white, and then gray again. The result was mass confusion. Frenzied reporters from around the world along with perplexed spectators tried deciphering the meaning of the smoke signals.[3]

While the smoke continued swirling into the early evening sky, St. Peter's Square once again filled with onlookers whose curiosity was aroused anew. The scene became chaotic as scores of taxis arrived, dropping off additional spectators. As the piazza gradually swelled and with anticipation mounting once more, the key Church figures in this unfolding drama were hidden inside St. Peter's Basilica, preparing the traditional public formalities following the election of a pope.[4]

Finally, after forty-six long minutes, a disembodied voice blaring from a public address system advised the confounded crowd to focus its gaze on the central balcony of the basilica. In the throng was don Diego Lorenzi, a Don Orione priest, who had been personal secretary to the patriarch of Venice for two years. Standing next to him was a Swedish family who inquired about his occupation. "I am in Rome for a few days. I work in Venice," he replied vaguely.[5]

Revelation

Finally, at 7:20 the ponderous glass doors of St. Peter's slowly swung open and Pericle Felici, the senior cardinal deacon, garbed in royal scarlet robes and matching biretta, strode onto the terrace perched high above the spectators. Silently, he peered down at the packed piazza, tantalizing the increasingly restive audience with his genial silence. Finally, looking pleased and speaking in a stentorian voice, the cardinal uttered the ritual Latin words: "*Annuntio vobis gaudium magnum: Habemus papam*!" ("I announce to you a great joy: We have a pope!") Then, teasing out the remainder of the ancient formula with dramatic pauses, he revealed the name of the victor, Albino Cardinal Luciani. The enthralled spectators roared their approval even though the name was unfamiliar to most; the new pope was an obscure figure to virtually everyone except for those from northern Italy. Before reentering the basilica, Felici announced that Luciani had decided to be called John Paul I, a history-shattering double papal name.[6]

As soon as she heard her brother's first name proclaimed, Luciani's sister, Nina, watching the developments on television at home some 350 miles from Rome, knelt and wept.[7]

Upon the announcement of the victor's identity, Diego Lorenzi became emotional, turned with glee to the family next to him, and revealed that he was secretary to the new pope.[8]

Shortly after Felici's declaration, four Vatican employees attired in crisp, black suits unfurled the enormous tapestry displaying the papal coat of arms and secured it to the balustrade.[9]

Apparition

Figure 1.1. "Habemus Papam!" John Paul I makes his first public appearance as pope on the central balcony of St. Peter's Basilica. At far left is Secretary of State Jean Villot, and at far right is Cardinal Sebastiano Baggio, who had entered the conclave as a papal frontrunner.

Moments later at 7:30, the 263rd pope, wrapped in a red silk mozetta (a short cape) adorned with the richly embellished papal stole, stepped forward, his palms pressed against each other with little fingers crossed, a pious gesture from his days as an altar boy half a century before. For the first few seconds, he looked solemnly at a mostly hushed crowd. From far below John Paul appeared tiny and fragile against the imposing basilica's facade.[10]

And then, without forewarning, it happened: that spellbinding moment when the new pontiff broke out in a spontaneous smile, what would forever afterward be known in Italian as "*il sorrisso di dio*"—the smile of God. It was as if a divine luminosity had cast its rays on all the gathered faithful and instantaneously penetrated their hearts and souls, an inexplicable phenomenon that left the multitude entranced. John Paul exuded pure benevolence, as if he were an angelic emissary of God. Even those watching the proceedings on television were transfixed.

The new pope lifted his right arm briefly in acknowledgment of the now deafening cheers. Then, in an impulsive gesture, he extended both arms, bent at the elbows, palms inward, shaking them vigorously in greeting to his new flock. The crowd erupted again in a raucous response: deafening applause and extemporaneous exclamations of exultation echoed throughout the cavernous piazza, handkerchiefs fluttered in the air, fathers hoisted their children on their shoulders. The atmosphere was euphoric.[11]

In a single precious moment, an inscrutable conversion had transpired: John Paul, a stranger mere minutes before, was now a favored figure. The swift metamorphosis from unknown to intimate was not attributable to stirring words, for the pope remained silent. He had wanted to speak but demurred when advised that it was not customary to do so. Following protocol, he simply delivered his "Urbi et Orbi" blessing "to the city [Rome] and to the world." His singing voice was weak and tremulous, perhaps a sign of nervousness or exhaustion, or both. As soon as the microphone was removed and while the faithful below were still responding in a solemn chorus of "Amen," the pope was beaming again and waving robustly. In response, the crowd erupted once more in cheers and applause.[12]

An American woman living in Rome who had seen five popes in person described the sensation: "It was like an electric charge, a spiritual electric current from the loggia to the square. It was a current of love . . . and he, the pope, so simple, so gentle, almost boyish." She said it was like nothing she had ever experienced.[13]

The astonishing emotional bond that was to last decades beyond John Paul's death was forged with the speed and power of lightning by his luminous appearance and his tender gestures of humility. Those who watched him discerned something profoundly ethereal about the man. He exuded pure kindness, and the joyous multitude savored the ecstasy as if they were witnessing a vision from heaven.

Observed Msgr. Giulio Nicolini, "Unending applause filled with enthusiasm and affection thundered from the square. It was unforgettable. I was convinced that I was witnessing an amazing historical event."[14]

And then, to the disappointment of all, he suddenly vanished. His appearance was all too brief, as would be his pontificate. But his sway was to linger. The affection he had already engendered among those who now reluctantly departed from the enveloping arms of Bernini's colonnade had provided them with pure joy. And they were stunned by that bewildering occurrence.

Back to the Chapel

Now reunited with the cardinals inside St. Peter's, John Paul made an unpopular decision: extending their stay.[15] Though they acquiesced without protest, none seemed thrilled with being confined in their stark, dormitory-like rooms for another night. The pontiff, however, wanted to consult with his colleagues, to pray with them, to seek their advice, to absorb their encouragement and reassurance, to share his hopes for his pontificate. It was an opportunity he might never have again with this collection of 110 cardinals.

At dinner that evening John Paul took the seat at the table that he had been assigned during the conclave. Conversation flowed easily. At the conclusion of the meal, a cardinal who was suffering from acute nicotine withdrawal sheepishly asked the pope permission to smoke even though that practice was prohibited. Cardinal Joseph Suenens of Belgium later divulged that John Paul, appearing serious, replied without hesitation, "Eminence, you may smoke on one condition: the smoke must be white!" Those in the immediate vicinity chuckled.[16]

In the evening the pontiff returned to his cell, deciding that the message he would deliver immediately following the next morning's Mass would be televised. He recognized the importance of sharing his plans with the largest audience possible. The Secretariat of State provided John Paul with a text of this speech, but during the sleepless night, he spent hours revising it.[17]

DAY 1/SUNDAY, AUGUST 27

Taking Charge

At 9:30 the next morning, the pope concelebrated Mass with the cardinal electors. In a gesture of respect for the sixteen cardinals who had been barred from voting because they were over the age of eighty, he invited them to join him in the Sistine Chapel.[18]

At the conclusion of Mass, John Paul, sitting on a high-backed chair before the chapel's altar and wearing miter and green vestments, read his first official message in Latin. Above and behind him stood a massive crucifix.

Looming in the background was Michelangelo's colossal Renaissance masterpiece, *The Last Judgment*, a stark reminder of the divine verdict that awaits even cardinals and popes in the afterlife. His audience, attired in gold vestments, sat at rows of tables, as they had during the just concluded conclave.[19]

Surprisingly Bold Leadership

If the cardinals assumed that they had elected a simple, acquiescent pastor with parochial views, John Paul's first speech must have startled them. The humble pontiff, whose foreign travels were limited, had in fact a keen understanding of the universal Church's challenges as well as the complexity of world affairs.

Always gracious, John Paul began by thanking the electors for the faith they had demonstrated in him barely fifteen hours before, which he described as "absolutely unexpected and also unmerited" and modestly asked for their prayers. He confessed to being "overwhelmed." It was vintage Luciani: unassuming and candid.[20]

Then he turned to the urgency of attitudinal change within the highest levels of Catholicism's leadership. He advised the princes of the Church to put aside their ideological differences and to focus instead on unifying the Church, which at the time was split asunder between reformers and arch conservatives, a direct result of the Second Vatican Council. "Let us give the world a show of unity, even by sacrificing things now and then," he implored.[21] This, too, was typical of John Paul, the realist whose overarching aim was softening rigid individual opinions for the benefit of the Church. It was an objective that just might be realized, not so much by persuasion as by the power of his congenial personality.

The new pope then outlined an ambitious agenda for his pontificate. It was a six-point program of continuity, renewal, and change. Of paramount importance was ongoing implementation of the Council's reforms; strengthening collegiality with other bishops in decision-making; revising canon law that governed the hierarchy and administration of the Church; rededicating the Church to "its first duty" of evangelizing; promoting ecumenical reunion by dedicating "prayerful attention to everything that would favor union . . . without diluting doctrine but, at the same time, without hesitance." His final objective was the pursuit of constructive dialogue with all: "men should know one another, even those who do not share our faith."[22]

The pope's priorities made it difficult to define him as a conservative or liberal, but the illusion that he was malleable vaporized as he revealed an assertive style of leadership: "We must avoid an approach that is hesitant and fearful."[23]

The pope also delivered a message of caution to those who sought accommodation with secular trends to modernize the Church. "Overcoming internal tensions which can arise here and there, overcoming the temptation of identifying ourselves with the ways of the world or the appeal of easily won applause, we are, rather, united in the unique bond of love which forms the inner life of the Church."[24]

The pope then segued to the secular world. He referred to all people as "friends and brothers." He greeted families and extended a special blessing "to all who are suffering, to the sick, to prisoners, to exiles, unemployed, or who have bad fortune in life."[25] They had always been his ministry's primary constituency.

John Paul painted an unsettling picture of the world that modern man had created: "The world . . . by research and technology has already reached a peak, beyond which yawns the abyss, blinding the eyes with darkness. It is the temptation of substituting for God one's own decisions."[26]

"The danger for modern man is that he would reduce the earth to a desert, the person to an automaton, brotherly love to planned collectivization, often introducing death where God wishes life," he asserted. The pope characterized the contemporary world as "both troubled and magnificent" and one that "thirsts for love and for truth."[27] It was a grim assessment but not unpromising.

The pope specifically saluted young people, referring to them as "the hope of tomorrow—a better, a healthier, a more constructive tomorrow . . . A dawn of hope spreads over the earth, although it is sometimes touched by sinister merchants of hatred, bloodshed, and war with a darkness which sometimes threatens to obscure the dawn." Thus, he pledged himself to "seek for the world the dawn of a more serene and joyful day . . . [to be] at the service of truth, of justice, of peace, of harmony, of collaboration within nations as well as rapport among peoples."[28]

"The Church . . . intends . . . to safeguard the world, that thirsts for a life of love, from dangers that would attack it . . . We will do so until our last breath."[29]

It was clear that John Paul envisioned for himself an active role in global affairs now that he was pope. The speech reflected a deep understanding of the consequences of man's fallen nature: the perils of existence in the nuclear age, including war, poverty, and inequality. He acknowledged a disturbing devaluation of the dignity and rights of individuals, an increasing preoccupation with the accumulation of wealth in the advanced countries of the world, social trends that deviated from Church teachings, and a decline in faith. It was a sophisticated analysis.

John Paul sounded more like an experienced diplomat than the bishop of a small diocese. And yet the talk was suffused with his characteristic humility as evident in his closing in which he asked "all our sons and daughters for the help of their prayers."[30]

Charm

Figure 1.2. The unassuming new pope, flashing his winning grin, charms the crowds in St. Peter's Square at his first Angelus.

Every Sunday, as tradition dictates, the pope delivers the Angelus, usually from his study window to those assembled in the square. It is an invitation to prayer and meditation and includes suitable remarks. This one was unique in style and substance, enhancing the popularity John Paul had earned the evening before.

At noon the new pope again appeared on the basilica's central loggia instead of the study window in the papal apartments. He was now dressed entirely in white, his *zucchetto* (skull cap) slightly askew. The papal cassock needed alterations, the long sleeves nearly swallowing his hands, and the sash drooping to his left at the waist. He had not yet had time for a haircut either. An unruly gray forelock peeked out from under his zucchetto.[31]

John Paul seemed to have accepted God's will regarding his election with swift serenity. He gazed down at what some estimated to be two hundred thousand people crowded into St. Peter's Square,[32] his broad grin eliciting from the faithful the deafening cheers usually reserved for entertainment superstars.

To nearly everyone's surprise, John Paul spoke spontaneously and from the heart. His informal discourse in Italian further endeared him to his flock as he broke with tradition by using the first-person singular pronoun "I" rather than the royal pontifical "we." Such informality from a pope was unprecedented. He began: "*Ieri mattina*" [yesterday morning], but the crowds drowned out his high-pitched voice. Gently gesturing to his listeners to end their applause, he began anew.[33]

He spoke animatedly, fervently, teasingly, and humbly about his election, providing insights into what had transpired behind the locked doors of the Sistine Chapel, though he, like all the other electors, had sworn an oath of secrecy. The pope's talk was surprisingly candid, even intimate. Wild cheering punctuated his remarks, especially when he admitted his shock at the outcome of the conclave. John Paul indicated that he had entered the Sistine Chapel calmly. He confided that he became fearful as the "danger" of his election drew near. As it became clear that he was about to become pope, two nearby "colleagues" whispered words of encouragement to him. Despite his profound sense of unworthiness, Luciani accepted out of a sense of responsibility—not his will but the Lord's will be done.[34]

The pope spoke fondly of his two immediate predecessors, John XXIII and Paul VI, and decided to honor them by taking the name John Paul. Applause erupted at his mention of the beloved Pope John, now dead for a decade and a half. He recounted good naturedly an incident involving Paul in Venice that had caused him embarrassment at the time: "Pope Paul not only made me a Cardinal, but some months earlier . . . in St. Mark's Square, he made me blush to the roots of my hair in the presence of 20,000 people, because he removed his stole and placed it on my shoulders. Never have I blushed so much!"[35]

The pope concluded his brief address with humility: "I have neither the 'wisdom of heart' of Pope John, nor the preparation and culture of Pope Paul, but I am in their place. I must seek to serve the Church. I hope that you will help me with your prayers."[36]

Msgr. Francesco Taffarel, his personal secretary when he was a bishop, noted years later that the pontiff's unassuming comparison to his predecessors was misleading, as the world would soon discover. John Paul was a man of great warmth and empathy, vast learning and wisdom, and a towering intellectual.[37]

The performance was a tour de force. The crowd interrupted him with cheers and applause six times in four and a half minutes. Self-effacing, Luciani had just brought to the office a personal style of informality that contrasted sharply with the prim Paul VI. "The new Holy Father has conquered the Romans with his modesty, his smile, and his evident candor. And yet until yesterday he was virtually unknown here," marveled a monsignor in attendance.[38]

Lorenzi was among the crowd listening to the Angelus. At its conclusion he overheard a little girl perched atop her father's shoulders tell him, "Papa, I understood everything!" Luciani had demonstrated to the world his mastery of the art of reaching his entire audience—young and old, unschooled and well-educated. "That was his gift, to put complex things in a way that a little girl could understand," Lorenzi remembered years later.[39]

There was something else remarkable about the event. Something counterintuitive. The rare attribute known as charisma, which John Paul clearly exuded, is almost exclusively associated with individuals of striking good looks, glamour, panache, eloquence, and relative youth. The Holy Father, nearly sixty-six years old, enjoyed none of those qualities. He was neither statuesque nor handsome by conventional standards. Short and slight of build, his facial features were imperfect: a creased forehead, jowls that revealed a five o'clock shadow, dark and bushy eyebrows. His thin lips appeared slightly lopsided when pursed, and his teeth were yellowed with age and stained by his substantial consumption of coffee. Lined bifocals embedded in an inexpensive metal frame perched on a prominent hooked nose.

Ah, but those russet eyes glowing with warmth and the irrepressible smile combined to transform his flawed features into a handsome countenance. As Leo Tolstoy once observed, "what we call beauty in a face lies in the smile."[40]

Settling In

The pope took possession of the papal apartments, escorted by his new retinue with whom he engaged in conversation.[41] He seemed remarkably self-possessed, a stark contrast from the distraught new pope described by his colleagues shortly after his election.

In the afternoon the pope phoned the Sisters of the Holy Child of Mary requesting that they continue their service at the Vatican as they had previously in Venice and Vittorio Veneto.[42] At dinnertime, one of the sisters in the papal service alarmingly discovered that the kitchen cupboards were bare, no doubt because Paul VI had been at Castel Gandolfo when he died. With the apartments inaccessible after his death, no one had thought to stock the refrigerator. Scurrying to a convent across St. Peter's Square, the nun searched for provisions. She scooped up leftover minestrone as well as some bread, cheese, and a little wine. John Paul, an abstemious eater, contentedly dined on donated reheated soup for his first meal as pope in his new quarters.[43]

Figure 1.3. The new pope arriving at the Apostolic Palace with an entourage. In the rear, wearing glasses, is his secretary from Venice, don Diego Lorenzi.

The Wolf

Maffeo Ducoli, Belluno's bishop, tried reaching the pope, who was in his private chapel at the time. As soon as he was available, John Paul, an inveterate caller, personally phoned his old friend. He poked fun at himself for continuing the habit even as pope. "Excellency, you see the wolf has changed his clothes but not his nature!" Surprised to be speaking directly with the new pope, Ducoli told him of the great joy in Canale d'Agordo, his birthplace, and Belluno, where he had attended seminary, taught, and administered the diocese. Ducoli inquired about how he felt. John Paul responded, "Well, I didn't sleep last night . . . It was so unexpected and so sudden."[44]

The bishop asked for the pope's permission to speak of their conversation to his townsmen. John Paul readily agreed, lamenting that he would no longer return to his hometown. He asked Ducoli to send his blessings to his relatives and friends and to ask for their prayers.[45]

John Paul's remark about never again returning to his birthplace was a simple acknowledgment that his new circumstances would make visits there impractical. It also might have been an intuition that his life would run its course without an opportunity ever to return.

Installation News

An official Vatican announcement designated the date for the new pope's installation—Sunday, September 3. This would mark the official commencement of John Paul's pontificate. He rejected the use of the *sedia gestatoria*, the portable papal throne and the elaborate fanfare including a procession accompanied by ostentatious ostrich feathers. His investiture would be dignified by its simplicity.[46]

DAY 2/MONDAY, AUGUST 28

Hometown Villagers

Ducoli went to Canale to celebrate a Mass of thanksgiving. Arriving there, he was greeted by a tumultuous crowd that packed the tiny town square. Augmenting the locals were journalists from around the globe. They and curious visitors besieged the new pontiff's relatives. The pope's brother Edoardo was irritated by the intrusive reporters: "It is difficult to be pope—but it's even more difficult to be the pope's brother. I can't get any work done with all these journalists pestering me from morning till night. I would like to send them all to the devil, but what would my brother the pope say? He's landed me in a fine mess."[47]

Status Quo

In Rome, perhaps the most significant decision that the pope made on this day was to reappoint French Cardinal Jean Villot as secretary of state. He noted the primacy of his position as the pope's most constant collaborator and expressed his "deep admiration, the sincere appreciation, and the paternal goodwill" he felt toward Villot. The document confirming Villot's continuation in office was in the form of a personal, handwritten letter.[48]

The pope also reappointed all his predecessor's key officials.[49] The action might have been in part a fulfillment of his promised continuation of the late pontiff's program, but it likely was reached largely because of his unfamiliarity with the makeup of the Curia. Presumably, he reserved the right to make personnel changes after he became acquainted with the individuals who headed the various departments. Continuity at this early stage of his pontificate was essential to his mastering the internal workings of the bureaucracy, including its politics, and the status of the policies currently guided by existing personnel. It was an opportunity for him to evaluate the key individuals with whom he would work, to assess their abilities and compatibility.

Automatic Pilot

If the new occupants of the palace were overwhelmed by their circumstances, they soon discovered that the Vatican administration continued to function autonomously. The Secretariat of State, the dominant department at the Vatican, moved swiftly to seize control of developments. For example, a representative from that office dictated that the pope's two secretaries would rotate sitting by John Paul's side on a weekly basis during general audiences.[50]

Confusion and Control

Lack of preparation to assume their new roles left John Paul and Lorenzi largely at the mercy of the bureaucracy. Lorenzi confessed, "[W]e barely had time to look around. Our suitcases had arrived from Venice, but we had not even had time to unpack them. None of us by that stage had any idea what we were in for. I needed time to get my bearings."[51] The pope found himself largely dependent on the bureaucrats to guide him, and he recognized the urgent need to become as knowledgeable as possible about the key leaders and operations of the organization so that he could assert control over developments. He did not wish to become a prisoner of the establishment. As Rev. Thomas Reese has written, "a newly elected pope . . . can be intimidated by the strangeness and the complexity of the internal operations of the Vatican."[52] John Paul, like some of his predecessors, certainly was.

It was mainly for this reason that Rev. John Magee, at the new pope's personal request, was retained as papal secretary. The Irishman had been preparing to leave, his immediate future uncertain, so he promptly acceded to John Paul's wishes.[53] Magee had been packing Paul VI's books when the new pope recognized him and asked how he could get a cup of coffee. Magee fetched it himself. Shortly thereafter, the pope made his proposal.[54] The veteran Vatican figure could provide the new pontiff with a wealth of knowledge about the functioning of the papacy, the major Vatican personnel, and the internal politics at the highest levels of the Church. It was a recognition by John Paul of his need to familiarize himself with the demands of his new role.

Establishing Routines

A daily routine was being established already. After celebrating daily Mass, the personal secretaries would breakfast with John Paul. As they ate, the pope perused some Italian newspapers and press clippings supplied by the

Secretariat of State. After a series of morning papal appointments, the three would again meet for lunch. At night the Venetian nuns who prepared the meals would serve a light dinner while John Paul caught up on television news. The pope followed developments in Italian politics with avid interest.[55] Before retiring for the night, John Paul would go to the kitchen to thank the sisters for dinner and to wish them a good night.

DAY 3/TUESDAY, AUGUST 29

Venice, Sisters, and Books

The new pope, concerned about the leadership vacuum in the diocese that he had suddenly vacated, wasted no time in appointing an apostolic administrator to replace him temporarily. In addition, John Paul sent a message to the citizens of Venice to whom he had not the opportunity to bid farewell.[56]

Sr. Vincenza Taffarel, his friend and household assistant since his tenure in the diocese of Vittorio Veneto where the pope had once been bishop, agreed to resume her duties in the papal apartments.[57] The two were delighted to be reunited; her presence was of considerable comfort to the pope. Several other nuns from Venice joined the team of housekeepers and remained for the duration of the pontificate. The nuns were soon to learn that the pope considered them valued members of his household. Unlike Paul VI, John Paul treated them more like friends or members of his family, even inviting them to daily Mass in his private chapel.[58]

Installation Planning Continues

Plans for what had previously been a coronation were modified substantially. The pope insisted on a simple ceremony of investiture in which he would don a plain pallium of lamb's wool instead of being crowned with the papal tiara, a fixture in coronations since the third century. Pope Paul's tiara, a triple crown shaped like a beehive, was embedded with jewels including diamonds, rubies, and sapphires.[59] The humble new pope could not abide donning the accoutrement of a king. Like Pope Paul's installation ceremony and Mass, however, John Paul's would be held outdoors in St. Peter's Square.

DAY 4/WEDNESDAY, AUGUST 30

Straight Talk to the Cardinals

John Paul met with the cardinals on this day in Consistory Hall. The pontiff delivered his address to the cardinals in Italian, a version that was different from the “official” text released to the public. The new pope’s talk created a stir among the press corps because of its informality and spontaneity; John Paul discarded the written text, something Paul VI had never done.

“I would like to apologize in some way, because I saw in the press that I almost reproached the Sacred College,” he began. There had been some misinterpretation of what he had said following his election when he had exclaimed to the cardinals, “May God forgive you for what you have done!”[60]

“I wasn’t scolding you at all!” he asserted. “[I]t came spontaneously, from the memories of school . . . the reaction that St. Bernard had when he heard that Eugene III, one of his own, had been made pope.” In an unguarded moment, John Paul had reached back into his phenomenal memory and plucked out that quotation from his reading as a student. He then thanked the cardinals for the faith they had in him, which he described as “absolutely unexpected and also undeserved.”[61]

He lamented his new isolation that would prohibit the continuation of pastoral activities. “In a way, I am sorrowful that I cannot return to the life . . . which I enjoyed so much. I always had small dioceses . . . so my work was . . . pastoral. I won’t be able to do this work anymore.”[62]

John Paul told the cardinals that they needed to think not only about their own dioceses but also about the “universal church.” He then went beyond that: “[T]oday there is a great need for the world to see us united . . . We have to work together.”[63]

The Holy Father could not have been more sincere about his desire for collegiality with the cardinals. “Have mercy on the poor new pope, who truly did not want to ascend to this place. Try to help him and try together to give the world a show of unity, even sacrificing a few things at times.”[64]

Then came the moment for bestowing the apostolic blessing, and he felt self-conscious about doing so. “To tell you the truth, it feels a little strange to give apostolic blessings . . . Somewhat courtly language. Bear with me.” And then either doubt or a note of self-effacement: “Should I give the blessing?”[65]

After the speech, all the cardinals assembled in a receiving line to greet the pope, embrace him, and offer words of fealty, congratulations, encouragement. Cardinal Giovanni Benelli of Florence, the man who had orchestrated Luciani’s election, greeted the pope with a smile of supreme satisfaction. The pope held both hands of some cardinals. With others he held their chins with his left hand.

Afterward John Paul approved the third general conference of the Latin American bishops to be held in Puebla, Mexico, October 12–28, less than two months away. Though the pope received an invitation, he politely declined. John Magee related a strange exchange with the Holy Father after he received a facsimile ticket to the event. The pontiff, without explanation, gave the ticket to Magee, instructing his secretary to pass it on to his successor. It left Magee baffled.[66]

DAY 5/THURSDAY, AUGUST 31

Peacekeeper

The main event of this day was the pope's meeting with the diplomatic corps.[67] It was a get-acquainted session that emphasized John Paul's determination to use whatever powers inherent in his office to maintain and promote peace among nations. The Holy Father knew some of the diplomats by name from reading newspapers and watching television news. They, in turn, knew virtually nothing about him. In the reception line Vatican Secretary of State Villot, on the pope's left, made personal introductions. The pope greeted each with his trademark smile. John Paul's address to foreign diplomats from fifty-one countries was delivered in French, the international language at the time.

"We have not previously had the honor of making your acquaintance," he began. "But now, in this See of the Apostle Peter, our mission has indeed become universal and places us in relationship . . . with all peoples, with their qualified representatives, and more particularly with the diplomats of the countries that have established relations on this level with the Holy See. On these grounds we are very happy to receive you here and to tell you of our esteem for you, our trust in you and our understanding of your noble role."[68]

For the past ten years, Vatican City had been a permanent observer state, not a member, of the United Nations.[69] John Paul appreciated the organization's role in preventing and helping to settle wars. He pledged to continue Pope Paul's initiatives in promoting human rights and world peace. But he went beyond that. Now he explicitly committed himself to the pursuit of détente, disarmament, and justice in the world.

The pope said he looked forward to meeting with the "civil leaders" of their nations in a spirit of collaboration. He committed himself to promoting "real brotherhood between peoples." He defined the foundations of such an effort: "[R]espect for one's neighbor, for his life and for his dignity, care for his spiritual and social progress, patience and the desire for reconciliation in the fragile building of peace." However, he acknowledged the fact that "Our possibilities for diplomatic interventions are limited and of a special character."[70] The papacy no longer wielded temporal power as it had throughout most of its history.

The session was conducted only hours after release of a scathing report about the Vatican Bank by *Il Mondo*, Italy's most prominent economic weekly, accusing the financial institution of ignoring laws prohibiting the transfer of capital abroad and unspecified "speculation in unhealthy waters." The publication specifically urged the pope to insist on "order and morality" in the church's financial dealings.[71] The pope did not comment publicly on the story, but he was aware that he would have to intervene in rectifying irregularities and even scandalous practices at the bank. He had had prior unsatisfactory dealings with the financial institution, and there is little doubt that reforming it would soon become a top priority. There was precedent for his resolving unsavory behavior within the Church in a transparent and decisive way during his bishopric. He found improprieties and illegalities inherently intolerable but also because they were inconsistent with the purity of the Church's mission. Action in this case, however, would have to wait.

DAY 6/FRIDAY, SEPTEMBER 1

Meet the Press

The pope held a press conference of sorts attended by a thousand media representatives from countries on all continents in the massive Hall of Benedictions. "I would . . . like to assure you of the esteem I have for your profession and of the care I will take to facilitate your noble and difficult mission."[72]

In particular, he thanked the reporters for the professional work they had completed in the previous several weeks in covering the dramatic events at the Vatican: the death and funeral of Paul VI, the interregnum, the conclave, his election, and the immediate aftermath. He emphasized that he was aware of "the increasingly important function that the media . . . have come to assume in the vitality of modern man."[73]

Although John Paul was laudatory of the media representatives, he also respectfully reminded the reporters of the importance of their focusing on substance. He stated his concern directly, though diplomatically, saying he had the "impression that sometimes reporters lingered on completely secondary things of the Church." He also recognized that the press had a responsibility to comment on his "humble ministry . . . I hope you will do so with love of truth, with respect for human dignity, for such is the purpose of all social communication."[74]

"Please understand," he informed the press, "the profound reasons why the Pope, the Church, the Pastors of the Church must sometimes ask, in the performance of their apostolic service, for a spirit of sacrifice, generosity, renunciation in order to build a world of justice, love, and peace." For his part, he pledged to conduct "frank, honest and effective cooperation with the instruments of social communication, which you here worthily represent." The suggestion was that a new era of openness was about to be inaugurated between the Vatican and the mass media.[75] The transparency he was promising was as welcome and as refreshing as it was innovative to the international press, if not high-ranking Vatican bureaucrats.

This group, composed primarily of skeptical veteran journalists who were assigned to cover an institution that closely shielded its business from public scrutiny, had a challenging and often frustrating assignment. Now they were dealing with a pope who was open and, further, admitted that, had he not become a priest, he would have been a journalist—one of them. His pontificate had the potential to transform the entire nature of their jobs. Besides that, John Paul had been stunningly charming. Following his address, as the Holy Father slowly made his way toward the exit, these hardened correspondents besieged him. They were giddy with excitement, their faces beaming, their bodies straining against the railing and their arms stretching out eagerly to touch him, to shake his hand. It was as if they had never been in proximity to a pope or any other famous individual, political or otherwise. Theirs was like the reaction of young fans beholding their favorite celebrity in person. The pope gently touched the cheek of one ecstatic aging reporter with his left hand while the man's colleagues, in a long row, glowed with excitement as they gazed at the pope, hoping to make physical contact with him, too.

Ratzinger and Liberation Theology

Though meeting the press was the highlight of his day, it was not the only item on the pope's agenda. Notably, he dispatched Cardinal Joseph Ratzinger to represent him in Latin America, where liberation theology was becoming increasingly popular.[76] It was a cause of concern for the pope, who perceived dangers in priests becoming political activists. He had dealt decisively with a similar problem in Venice when he was patriarch, and he sought to intervene in these developments in the hope of thwarting the movement.

Final Installation Plans

The finishing touches on the inauguration ceremony to be held on Sunday were completed. A quarter million spectators and dignitaries were expected to attend. The central part of the ceremony would be the celebration of Mass, which had been a fixture of papal coronations for twelve hundred years.[77]

DAY 7/SATURDAY, SEPTEMBER 2

Family Reunion

Figure 1.4. A joyous John Paul with brother Berto, sister Nina, and grandnieces.

This was a jubilant day for John Paul, who met with members of his family for the first time since becoming pope the week before. He was serene but evidently ecstatic to be surrounded by his family. In the library of the papal apartment, John Paul glowed in the presence of his siblings and his nieces and nephews. Their young children entertained themselves at his feet, unaware of the grand personage before them, and his broad smile expressed his enjoyment of their playful interactions.[78]

Later in the day he met with his siblings in private. He insisted that Edoardo bring a large ivory crucifix home. At this point his brother explained that he would be branded a thief if he was seen carrying such an enormous object out of the apostolic palace. About an hour later, one of the pope's domestic employees delivered the crucifix to Edoardo, who grew to treasure it.[79]

The pontiff told his sister, Antonia, who was concerned about his new burdens, not to worry about him because he himself was tranquil. He reassured her that she should not worry about him and that she should feel free to visit him as she had done in Venice. The siblings said they would see each other again in several weeks to celebrate John Paul's sixty-sixth birthday.[80]

When his sister wistfully said to the pope, "If only mama could be here now," his thoughts must have wandered back nostalgically to the days of his youth, a time when his pious, devoted mother was the central figure in his life.[81]

NOTES

1. The writings of Mother Teresa of Calcutta © by the Mother Teresa Center, exclusive licensee throughout the world of the Missionaries of Charity for the works of Mother Teresa. Used with permission.
2. "How Is a New Pope Chosen?" United States Conference of Catholic Bishops, https://www.usccb.org/offices/general-secretariat/how-new-pope-chosen.
3. "Conclave A.D. 1978—Election of John Paul I," *Caeremoniale Romanum: Liturgia et Mores Curiae Romanae*, video, 7:17, https://www.youtube.com/watch?v =8d1TSlDnc1c.
4. "Conclave."
5. Paul Spackman, *God's Candidate: The Life and Times of Pope John Paul I* (Herefordshire: Gracewing, 2008), 137–38.
6. "Conclave."
7. Dr. Lina Petri (niece of Pope John Paul I), in discussion with the author, Rome, July 6, 2011.
8. David Yallop, *In God's Name: An Investigation into the Murder of Pope John Paul I* (New York: Penguin, (1984), 73.
9. "Conclave."
10. "The Election of Cardinal Albino Luciani as New Pope," August 16, 1978, https://www.youtube.com/watch?v=ZaSpHn-p1MA.
11. "Election."
12. "Urbe et Orbi following JPI election," video, 1:23, https://www.youtube.com/watch?v=jf87gZbPM8I.
13. Raymond and Lauretta Seabeck, *The Smiling Pope: The Life and Teaching of John Paul I* (Huntington, IN: Our Sunday Visitor, 2004), 58–59.
14. Seabeck, *Smiling Pope*, 56.
15. Seabeck, *Smiling Pope*, 57.
16. Spackman, *God's Candidate*, 139.
17. Spackman, *God's Candidate*, 139.
18. Seabeck, *Smiling Pope*, 59.
19. Albino Luciani photograph 252.JPG, Foundation Papa Luciani of Canale d'Agordo (Belluno-Italy).
20. "Urbi et Orbi," speech delivered to the Sacred College of Cardinals broadcast on radio and television, August 27, 1978. Collection of recordings of the original speeches and statements of Blessed Pope John Paul I of the Archives of the Foundation Papa Luciani of Canale d'Agordo (Belluno-Italy).
21. "Urbi et Orbi."

22. "Urbi et Orbi."
23. "Urbi et Orbi."
24. "Urbi et Orbi."
25. "Urbi et Orbi."
26. "Urbi et Orbi."
27. "Urbi et Orbi."
28. "Urbi et Orbi."
29. "Urbi et Orbi."
30. "Urbi et Orbi."
31. Albino Luciani photograph 200.JPG, Foundation Papa Luciani of Canale d'Agordo (Belluno-Italy).
32. Spackman, *God's Candidate*, 147.
33. Speech delivered prior to Sunday Angelus, August 27, 1978. Collection of recordings of the original speeches and statements of Blessed Pope John Paul I of the Archives of the Foundation Papa Luciani of Canale d'Agordo (Belluno-Italy).
34. Seabeck, *Smiling Pope*, 92.
35. First Angelus.
36. First Angelus.
37. Msgr. Francesco Taffarel (personal secretary to Bishop Albino Luciani, diocese of Vittorio Veneto, Italy), in discussion with the author, Tarzo, Italy, July 11, 2011.
38. Paul Offmann, "Pope John Paul Promises to Continue 'Ecumenical Thrust,'" *Bangor Daily News*, August 28, 1978, 4.
39. John Allen, "The Word from Rome," *National Catholic Reporter*, September 5, 2003, http://www.nationalcatholicreporter.org.
40. "Childhood, Boyhood, Youth Quotes," Goodreads, https://www.goodreads.com/quotes/search?utf8=%E2%9C%93&q=tolstoy+%22what+we+call+beauty+in+a+face+lies+in+the+smile.%22&commit=Search.
41. Stefania Falasca, *The September Pope: The Final Days of John Paul I* © 2017, PIEMME; 2020, Libreria Editrice Vaticana. English translation published by Our Sunday Visitor, 2021, 158.
42. Gordon Thomas and Max Morgan-Witts, *Pontiff* (New York: Doubleday, 1984), 265.
43. Allen, "Word from Rome," 4.
44. Seabeck, *Smiling Pope*, 59.
45. Loris Serafini (director, Foundation Papa Luciani and Museum Albino Luciani of Canale d'Agordo), in discussion with the author, Canale d'Agordo, Italy, July 11, 2011.
46. "Easy-Going Style Likely," *Bangor Daily News*, August 28, 1978, 4.
47. Spackman, *God's Candidate*, 145.
48. Chirograph of His Holiness John Paul I for the Nomination of the Secretary of State. Dicastero per la Comunicazione—Libreria Editrice Vaticana, https://www.vatican.va/content/john-paul-i/en/speeches/documents/hf_jp-i_spe_27081978_chirograph.html.

49. Fr. Victor Feltes, "Retentions, Reactions, & Regalia," August 6, 2014, www.johnpauli.wordpress.com.
50. Allen, "Word from Rome," 5.
51. Allen, "Word from Rome," 5.
52. Thomas J. Reese, *Inside the Vatican: The Politics and Organization of the Catholic Church* (Cambridge, MA: Harvard University Press, 1996), 7.
53. John Magee (bishop emeritus, diocese of Cloyne, Ireland) in discussion with the author, Cobh, Ireland, February 17, 2010.
54. Magee, discussion.
55. Magee, discussion.
56. Falasca, *September Pope*, 158.
57. Falasca, *September Pope*, 158.
58. Yallop, *In God's Name*, 167–68.
59. "Pope Paul Donates His Jeweled Tiara to Poor of World," *New York Times*, September 14, 1964, https://www.nytimes.com/1964/11/14/archives/pope-paul-donates-his-jeweled-tiara-to-poor-of-world.html#:~:text=Estimates%20of%20its%20intrinsic%20value,the%20opinion%20of%20observers%20here.
60. Speech to the Sacred College of Cardinals, August 30, 1978. Collection of recordings of the original speeches and statements of Blessed Pope John Paul I, Archives of the Foundation Papa Luciani of Canale d'Agordo (Belluno-Italy).
61. Speech to College of Cardinals.
62. Speech to College of Cardinals.
63. Speech to College of Cardinals.
64. Speech to College of Cardinals.
65. Speech to College of Cardinals.
66. Magee, discussion.
67. Fr. Victor Feltes, "Greeting the Peacemakers," August 6, 2014, www.johnpauli.wordpress.com.
68. Speech to the diplomatic corps accredited to the Holy See, August 31, 1978. Collection of recordings of the original speeches and statements of Blessed Pope John Paul I, Archives of the Foundation Papa Luciani of Canale d'Agordo (Belluno-Italy).
69. "The Holy See Celebrates 54 Years as Permanent Observer to the United Nations," *Permanent Observer Mission of the Holy See to the United Nations*, https://holyseemission.org/contents//mission/5ac79b91753bc.php.
70. Speech to the diplomatic corps.
71. "Solutions Sought by Pope," *Victoria Advocate*, September 1, 1978, 2D.
72. "Pope Asks Press to Focus on Substance of Church," *St. Petersburg Times*, September 2, 1978, 6.
73. Speech to the international press corps, September 1, 1978. Collection of recordings of the original speeches and statements of Blessed Pope John Paul I, Archives of the Foundation Papa Luciani of Canale d'Agordo (Belluno-Italy).
74. Speech to the international press corps.
75. Speech to the international press corps.
76. Fr. Victor Feltes, *Meet the Press*, August 6, 2014, https://johnpauli.wordpress.com/.

77. "Simplicity Will Mark Installation of Pope," *Observer-Reporter*, August 29, 1978, A9.

78. "Albino Luciani," photograph 397.JPG, courtesy of Foundation Papa Luciani of Canale d'Agordo (Belluno-Italy).

79. Serafini, discussion.

80. Serafini, discussion.

81. Serafini, discussion.

• 2 •

In the Beginning

Blessed Are the Poor (1912–1923)

Albino Luciani's birth was a harrowing event.

October 17, 1912, was a bitterly cold day, unusually so for the fall season. Snow already blanketed the morning meadows as the elderly midwife, a relative named Maria Fiocco, trudged to the Luciani home to assist in the delivery. There, to her dismay, she found Bortola, the expectant mother, pale, exhausted, and distressed.[1]

The delivery itself was arduous, but worse, the baby's condition was critical. As was all too common at that time and in such remote places, giving birth was a perilous experience. The infant mortality rate was frightfully high. Rare was the family that did not experience the heartbreak of losing an infant, often several in succession, in the birthing bed or soon thereafter.[2] Mothers often bled to death, and newborns routinely faced a dreadful diversity of life-threatening complications.

The midwife shuddered as the baby's head emerged; the umbilical cord was tightly coiled around his neck like a noose threatening to asphyxiate the newborn before he could draw his very first breath. Relying upon her experience and essential skills, she worked rapidly to loosen the cord that stifled his breathing, yet the infant remained disturbingly feeble, his life still in peril. Maria considered the boy's condition so precarious that she feared his death was imminent. Only a miracle, she thought, not ordinary human hands like hers, could preserve his life. Despite her own dread, Maria reassured the emotionally distraught mother, telling her she should not fear because God would help her.[3]

Confronting a likely tragedy despite her frantic efforts to avert it, the midwife performed an emergency baptism. For Catholics, the administration of this sacrament was necessary to assure an infant's entry into heaven.

In those days the Catholic Church taught that unbaptized babies who died were eternally consigned to limbo, a place where they did not suffer but also could never see God because they were tainted by Original Sin. When, as in this instance, there was no time to summon a priest, it was acceptable for a lay person in dire circumstances to perform the sacrament.[4]

Maria procured holy water from beside the wooden bed and prepared to christen the boy. She asked the mother what name she wanted to give her son. "Albino," she replied weakly though without hesitation. The name was at the insistence of her husband, who had wanted to honor the memory of a close friend and coworker who had died in a blast furnace accident at work.[5] The father was absent during his son's birth because he was working in France; no employment was available near home.[6]

Then the midwife sprinkled the water on the baby's head while reciting the unadorned words, "I baptize you in the Name of the Father and of the Son and of the Holy Spirit." Bortola looked on, her eyes glistening with emotion, her heart filled with foreboding as well as a hint of hope. Now, the two women were helpless except to wait and pray for the newborn's survival. The minutes ticked by agonizingly. Hours later the crisis passed as the baby breathed more freely and gradually gained strength. Despite the formidable odds against the frail Albino's survival, Bortola's prayers had been answered, and the miracle that Maria had sought occurred. Decades later some of the local faithful would intimate that Albino's survival was in fulfillment of a divine plan for his future role in the Church.[7]

Two days following the birth, Achille Ronzon, the curate of the local church, formally baptized the infant in a traditional ceremony at the baptismal font that is still used in San Giovanni Batista, the town's fifteenth-century church.[8]

In the first months of his life, Albino was visited by a friend of his mother's named Giuditta Zus, who acted as wet nurse. Luciani, forever grateful to her for having kept him alive in his infancy, always visited her whenever he came home, both as priest and bishop.[9]

THE VILLAGE

Luciani was born and raised in Canale d'Agordo, known at the time as Forno di Canale, a tiny fourteenth-century village in a narrow valley of northeastern Italy's towering Dolomite Mountains, some of which soar to the breathtaking height of roughly ten thousand feet.[10] Dominating the landscape, they are the most striking natural feature of the area. Like all majestic natural wonders, they take the breath away, engendering feelings of awe because of their sheer size and beauty. Canale is embraced by these peaks. Even in summer their crowns are sometimes topped by pristine caps of snow, like the white skull caps that adorn the heads of popes.

Historians tell us that geography has helped shape the course of human events throughout the centuries. Emerson, the eminent American transcendental contrarian, insisted, however, that there is no such thing as history; there is only biography. If that is true, then it is reasonable to conclude that geography contributes to the molding of men and their character. This was certainly so with Albino Luciani, a child of the mountains. As a priest, Luciani often said that we must feel small before God.[11] Surely the grand summits surrounding his hometown, in addition to inspiring wonder, made him feel tiny.

From the heavens, where angels purportedly hover in watchful protection of humans, who are imbued with a glimmer of the divine, the town must seem to be an ever so slight laceration in the earth's skin. Isolated from virtually all that is necessary to sustain beating human hearts, subject to the daunting vicissitudes of nature, this geological fissure seems as inhospitable to life as a lunar crater. Especially in winter, Canale looks forsaken, brutally hostile to existence, particularly of the precarious human variety. The winters are long, harsh, unforgiving. Temperatures often drop precipitously with snowfall accumulating as high as ten feet.[12] Its remoteness and rugged topography make one wonder why anyone would hazard establishing a life there. The answer lies in the indomitable human spirit.

Man has always been an intrepid creature whose innate curiosity, sense of adventure, and determination to survive know no bounds. And the pioneers who first settled there were among the boldest and heartiest of men and women, willing to suffer almost unbearable travails in their quest to endure. Their physical, emotional, and spiritual strength—transmitted to subsequent generations—is a testament to the resolute human will that is sustained by an unshakeable faith. These discoverers overcame seemingly insurmountable hurdles to create a community there, one that has survived against all odds for centuries. A modern visitor to this village cannot but be impressed with the stamina and relentless determination of the people who subdued nature to make this their home. The roots they established there are as durable as the sturdy foundations of the mountains they scaled to build Canale.

From ground level, Canale assumes an entirely different aspect: a vibrant, picturesque little village of singular beauty. A rustic wooden bridge spanning a sometimes-restless stream conveys pedestrians and vehicles into the town square that beckons just ahead. That piazza is now named after Albino Luciani, the town's most famous and beloved son. The center of the village features the Church of St. John the Baptist. The other structures surrounding the piazza are modest but attractive buildings, some adorned with vibrant flowers. They include most prominently the rectory, the town hall, and the Papa Luciani Museum.

Today, local pedestrians often linger in Canale's hub, sitting on benches to while away the long summer hours in quiet comfort and genial conversation with their fellow townspeople. Some assemble at outdoor tables to enjoy a glass of wine or a cold beer on a sweltering afternoon, while incongruously, the pinnacles of the neighboring Dolomites still sport their wintry white wigs.

At a leisurely pace, you can walk the length of the sleepy village's main road in about twenty minutes or less. On many days, it is virtually clear of cars. An occasional leather-skinned man of advanced age is sometimes spied tending his vegetable garden, and elderly women conspicuously lean out their windows to hang laundry. In the morning a few solitary villagers take a stroll before the blistering afternoon sun saps them of energy. It is an enchanting setting, providing visitors with the welcome sensation they have traveled back to a simpler time. Canale traces its roots to the Middle Ages and was known for its production of butter and cheese.[13] Located in the Valle del Biois in the province of Belluno, it is currently the home of some twelve hundred inhabitants.[14]

At the time of Albino Luciani's birth it was the religious, economic, and social nucleus of the Valle del Biois and the focal point of merchants hawking their wares.[15] Attractive homes scattered on the hillsides coexisted with dense clusters of pine trees.[16] It was also a farming community but with a short growing season. Domesticated farm animals shared the rough roads of the village with their owners. On Sundays, faithful worshippers from all over the valley would crowd the ancient square.[17]

The first several generations of villagers deservedly developed the reputation of being hardy and industrious; they had to be if they were to survive, particularly those who engaged in the backbreaking labor of tilling the region's rocky soil while others, confronting a lack of jobs, reluctantly left their families for extended intervals to seek a living in distant lands.[18]

Brawny men felled the towering trees and rolled the logs down the river. Lumber was such a precious commodity that a saucy saying spread: "You can touch my wife, but keep your hands off my wood!"[19]

ALBINO'S PARENTS

Giovanni Luciani was born in Canale on May 27, 1872.[20] The future pope's father was a handsome man sporting a thick mustache. He was a pipe smoker, perhaps one of the few pleasures available to a poor man who wandered ceaselessly, searching for gainful employment, a reality that took him long distances away from his family much of each year.[21]

Figure 2.1. Giovanni Luciani (sitting on the wheelbarrow, center) and fellow laborers. The pope's father was a staunch advocate of workers' rights, a cause his son Albino would later embrace.

A bricklayer by trade, Giovanni, like so many other locals, accepted employment requiring diverse skills in other European nations.[22] At various times, the elder Luciani toiled as a stonemason, metalsmith, and glassworker.[23] He labored intermittently in various western European countries. In Germany he encountered socialists and became involved in their quest to ameliorate the plight of laborers. Eventually, he became a committed socialist himself.[24]

Giovanni was a widower whose wife had died young, leaving him with two little daughters who were both hearing impaired.[25] They too were born in Canale, Amalia in 1900 and Pia nearly two years later.[26] Their mother, Rosa Angela Fiocco (1877–1906), also had given birth to three boys, all of whom passed away within days of their nativity.[27] Giovanni's love for the friend who had lost his life in the blast furnace tragedy must have been extraordinary, for he named each of the boys Albino.[28] (It is remarkable that, following the premature deaths of his first three sons, he still insisted that his first born by Bortola be called by the same name.)

Figure 2.2. A young Bortola Tancon, Albino Luciani's mother.

Bartolomea Tancon, known as Bortola, also from Canale, was born in 1879. Although her formal schooling was limited to three years, that was more education than typical Canale girls completed.[29] She was industrious and strong willed. At one time she toiled as a scullery maid.[30] Prior to becoming a kitchen worker at the hospital of Saints John and Paul (the names her son would take as pope) in Venice in 1911,[31] she held numerous other jobs including working as a domestic for a Jewish family, which perhaps indicated her lack of bigotry at a time when anti-Semitism was on the rise.[32] She even labored in Switzerland for a few years.[33] In addition, Bortola was employed for eleven years by a Venetian religious group.[34]

Giovanni's sister Angela finally advised him that he needed help raising his children, insisting that he should remarry because his young ones needed a mother. She asked him if he knew Bortola Tancon, who she vouched was a good woman. Not entirely convinced that the idea was practical, Giovanni nevertheless decided to act on his sister's suggestion.[35] As a result, he went to work in a Murano foundry near Venice, the city where Bortola was employed at that time.[36]

The plan succeeded. The two met in the city of canals, the future home of their son Albino. When Bortola met Giovanni, she was almost thirty years old. They were married on December 2, 1911. The groom was thirty-nine and the bride seven years younger.[37]

In one respect they were an unconventional couple: he, a lackadaisical Catholic; she, exceptionally religious. Bortola attended daily Mass.[38] Reportedly, Bortola insisted on one condition before marriage: Any children would be raised in the Church. Ultimately, Bortola lured her lapsed Catholic husband back to the faith. She became a loving mother to her two stepdaughters, whom she treated with as much affection as if they were her biological children.[39]

HOME AND FAMILY

Figure 2.3. The humble Luciani home, birthplace of the future pope, as it appeared in 1912, the year he was born in Forno di Canale, now Canale d'Agordo, a town dwarfed by the Dolomite Mountains.

Albino Luciani was not born in a manger, but the place of his nativity was a meager upgrade. The primitive structure was incorporated into a hayloft.[40] The house, such as it was in 1912, today would be considered little more than a hovel. To call it rustic would endow it with charm that its crudeness precluded. The glacial winters' howling winds penetrated the walls of the ramshackle abode, driving its inhabitants to huddle together in a corner by the heat of their wood-burning stove, a location that became the center of family life.[41]

The pope's birthplace later became the permanent home of his brother Edoardo and his family. The house was significantly expanded to accommodate his large brood. Today, the structure—open to the public—does not resemble in the least the house in which Albino and his siblings grew up but family mementos abound.

The Lucianis had four children of their own besides Giovanni's daughters from his first marriage. Albino was the couple's firstborn. Their second child, Tranquillo Federico, was born September 2, 1915, and died nine weeks later of pneumonia.[42] Edoardo, named after one of his father's brothers who had been killed in an avalanche, was born on March 26, 1917.[43] He was nicknamed Berto. As an adult he became known as Maestro in town because he taught school.[44] Finally, a girl named Antonia but known as "Nina" was born on February 3, 1920.[45]

Growing up, the girls shared a room adjacent to the one occupied by the boys. In the center of the original home was the room that served both as the parents' bedroom and the "sitting room" in which the stove was located.[46]

The premature death of the second Luciani child had a chilling impact on his siblings. Berto revealed that his mother was scrupulous about making sure that the windows and door remained closed to preserve the baby's health. Albino dreaded that his brother had died because of some unspecified carelessness on his part, an unbearable burden for a three-year-old. He was persistently haunted by the thought. Berto recalled years later about Albino: "He said to me that he often woke up during the night and he thought, 'Perhaps I have been the cause of my little brother's death.'"[47]

The winter following Albino's birth, his mother cared for the infant while reciting the rosary in the long evenings. The pious mamma offered thanks to God for this precious gift. She lit the oil lamp, sat next to the cradle, and sang a lullaby to the baby.[48] Bortola was a loving mother who had the primary responsibility of raising the children. Giovanni was in Canale for part of that winter, but he had to leave again to work abroad—a reality that robbed him of precious time with his young family.[49]

Resilient bonds of love existed between mother and son, and Luciani's devotion to her manifested itself throughout her life. She had a major impact on his character formation as well as his piety. Bortola beckoned young

Albino to her lap and taught him beautiful prayers about acts of faith, hope, and charity—prayers he would remember and recite all his life. He was especially fond of one, and he often referenced it publicly as an adult. It was profound in its simplicity and guided him throughout his life: "Lord, take me as I am, with my faults and with my sins, but make me become as you wish."[50]

Bortola at one time had contemplated entering the convent. Each of her days revolved around morning Mass, where she received the Eucharist; and in the evenings, she unfailingly recited the rosary.[51]

Bortola taught the children the catechism, which she knew by heart, when she washed and dressed them in the morning as well as when she put them to bed at night. She also taught them all their prayers. Her children would learn from her the virtues of humility and rectitude.[52] They were

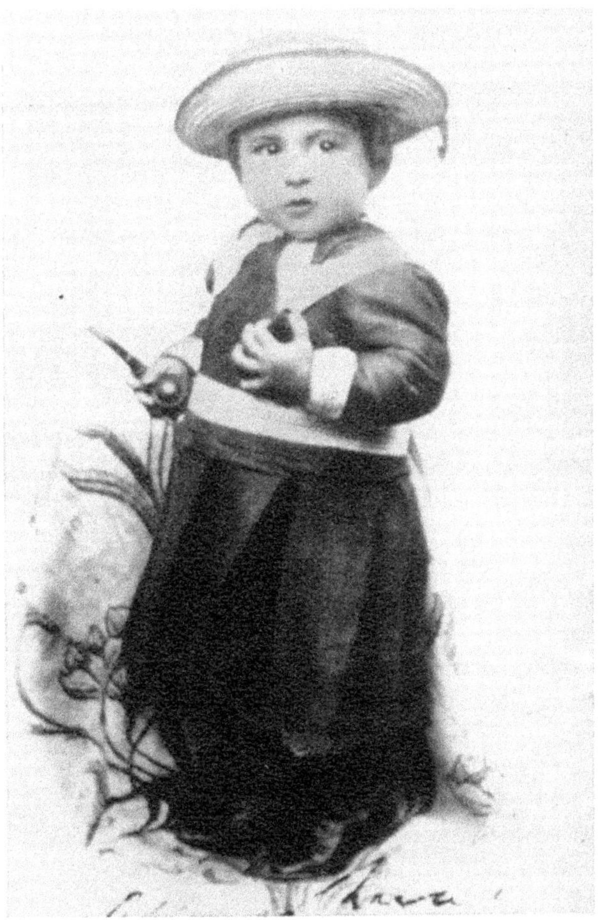

Figure 2.4. Albino at age three poses for the camera, clutching his father's pipe.

profoundly influenced by her spiritual devotion as evidenced by her recitation of the rosary and her frequent reception of Communion.[53]

Pia was a second mother to Nina, spending considerable time with her. Although she could not speak well, Pia taught Albino to read and write when he was six.[54] Even though the young Albino was attached to Pia, he was ecstatic about having a younger brother as a companion. As the years wore on, a close bond of friendship developed between the two that would last throughout Albino's lifetime.

PINCHING POVERTY

The Luciani family were rich in their poverty. They suffered physical misery but simultaneously experienced emotional bliss, thanks to boundless maternal affection and devotion. Love and loyalty prevailed among the siblings and between the parents and children. Above all, their faith provided them with sustenance and hope, thereby mitigating their tribulations. Poverty and its accompanying deprivations, therefore, did not bring debilitating misery to the Luciani family. According to Berto, "Our family had very, very little money, but . . . all of us always had smiles on our lips and we knew the most joyous and carefree childhood. My father, when he was working at home, used to whistle from morning till night."[55]

Nevertheless, the children were reminded of their poverty daily. In winter they wore rubbers and outdated hand-me-down jackets that were inadequate to keep them warm as they braved the harsh elements, including stomping through snow in their twice-daily trek to and from school.[56]

There was often a paucity of food in the Luciani home. As any parent can imagine, this was both excruciating to the famished youngsters and the source of anguish for the mother who often had to resort to boiling roots for dinner. Albino occasionally accompanied his mother to the countryside to gather herbs.[57] The future pope's lifelong compassion for the poor stemmed at least in part from his own family's grinding poverty.

At age eight, Albino once did chores for a woman who rewarded him with a piece of white bread, a much-coveted commodity by the poor of Canale. (They consumed dark bread only.) Despite the urgent temptation to devour the treat himself, Albino demonstrated surprising selflessness and self-discipline by giving it to his young brother instead. Apparently, Berto's hunger was so acute that even in the latter years of his life he still remembered his brother's kindness.[58]

Paradoxically, the harshness of his early life produced the gentleness that was inherent in Albino's character throughout his existence. It is quite probable also that the paucity of food in his childhood contributed to Albino's preference for meager meals in adulthood.

THE CRUELTIES OF WAR

When news of the outbreak of World War I reached Bortola, she wondered what would happen to her and her family. Would the enemy kill the husbands and children of the village? Her worst fear did not materialize, but the enemy occupation of the area during World War I was ruinous to the local population and resulted in more widespread hunger in the aftermath of the conflict. Even bread became scarce.[59]

As the war continued, life became increasingly difficult in Canale, in part because of the lack of men to defend the women and children. Unlike Giovanni, who was spared military service (presumably because of his age and young family), most of the other local men had gone to the battlefields. Enemy soldiers were constantly coming and going, and many locals feared an attack by the foe, who prowled in the vicinity. Their fears were justified. In 1917 the Austrians invaded the valley, and in that year of famine they confiscated the cows and stole the few potatoes that were ready to be harvested.[60]

These were grim years for the Luciani family. They suffered from persistent hunger. The foes plundered the town, leaving the inhabitants with virtually nothing. Albino, who was five or six years old, never forgot those grueling times. The family's situation was so dire that the hungry children would cry when they saw their plates covered only with grass and nettles. Once, with his sister Pia, Albino resorted to begging for food, an episode that caused Bortola embarrassment.[61]

The war was a source of personal trepidation for the boy. Whenever he heard the din of Austrian soldiers outside, he would hide within, trembling with fear. In April 1918, the six-year-old Albino witnessed Austrian soldiers taking down church bells and shattering them under the gaze of the indignant Msgr. Luigi Cerutti.[62] The enemy, in danger of losing the war, collected bronze in the Bellunese territory from which they made ammunition. It was shocking to the boy, as it was to the other villagers.

Years later his mother recalled how one winter Albino had escaped from the house barefooted, and he was drenched by the time she reached him. Shortly afterward, he became sick. Medical treatment was unavailable, and the mother feared his condition would deteriorate. Fortuitously, a medical official who was passing by as part of a military patrol silently examined the sick boy and left. He returned with medicine but warned the mother that the boy's prospects were dismal. Astonishingly, however, Albino soon recovered.

Despite the conflict, progress came to Canale. One night toward the end of the war, as Albino was approaching home, he was surprised to see an unusual light emanating from a window. The family now had electric lighting. Out went the old oil lamp for good—in the kitchen at least. Because the other rooms were used sparingly, it was considered a waste of scarce financial resources to install electric lights there. But now the entire family could pursue their nightly ritual of reciting the rosary under the comparatively bright electric light.[63]

The war finally ended, but the deprivation for the family continued. Fortunately, Albino's health and strength were good now, enabling him to endure the ongoing suffering.

A RAMBUNCTIOUS CHILD

Albino was known for being affectionate. Even so, his brother remembered that he was not always an obedient child. By 1917 when his vigor had returned, Albino displayed nearly boundless energy. The child enjoyed running in the nearby fields and woods. He also was a mischievous, though harmless, prankster known to engage in fisticuffs with schoolmates and pulling girls' hair. Once he deliberately tripped a companion.[64]

"I . . . was involved in 'battles': snowballs in the winter season; blows and punches and the like in every season of the year. Sometimes I was on the receiving end, but I also gave a few, trying to balance the ledger," Luciani recalled with a chuckle as an adult.[65]

When he went out to the woods to work, he would sometimes run away with other children. He enjoyed playing ninepins, a version of bowling, which his mother—perhaps overly protective—considered dangerous. She scolded him when he participated in the game, even administering a spanking to the future pope on one of these occasions.[66]

The young Luciani enjoyed organizing amusements. One time, in collusion with a cousin, he managed to rig a contest in which he "won" the first prize of chocolate and biscotti without the other children noticing that they had been swindled. Albino acted on his imagination, too, and constructed a pool of sorts in the mountains where he and his companion, Giulio Bramezza, played. He also loved to play cards with his friends.[67]

Like Saint Francis, Albino loved animals, particularly birds. He spent a substantial amount of time catching them. "Sometimes we played hooky to catch birds. Albino loved birds, and we would climb up into the mountains with birdlime to catch them, in order to raise them and hear them sing. Then we let them go. If we caught goldfinches, then our day was a great success," reminisced Giulio decades later.[68]

"We always remained friends. Anyway, it was impossible to quarrel with him; he always managed to convince me to do what he wanted to do, even if I didn't want to. He had a way of saying things that made one quickly give in to him. He even succeeded in teaching me doctrine and was always there when I needed help. He never changed," recalled Bramezza.[69] Apparently, even early in Albino's life, there were signs of leadership skills and the gift of persuasion to augment his generosity of spirit.

The tenuous nature of life was a fact the young Luciani became acutely aware of in 1919 when forty-two of his fellow villagers, including some of his friends, succumbed to the "Spanish Flu" pandemic. Then, only months later, the village rumbled when it was struck by an earthquake.[70]

With a single major exception, the summer of 1922 was a happy one for Albino, now ten. He often occupied himself playing with his younger brother. On one occasion when his father had instructed him to watch after Berto, Albino was distracted from his responsibility by playing with his cousins. Much to his chagrin, his little brother vanished. An adult search party was formed that initially was unable to find the child. A frightened and miserable Albino wept bitterly. There was water nearby with a current that posed a danger to youngsters. Eventually, the young boy was discovered sleeping near a fir tree, unaware of the frantic commotion that his disappearance had created. The next morning his mother went to church to light a candle in thanks to Saint Anthony for having found her lost son.[71]

Even at that young age, chores curtailed Albino's playtime, for youngsters like him were charged with responsibilities including babysitting younger siblings, putting cows out to pasture, and assisting their mothers with domestic work. He tended his family's goat and cow when he was not in school. While he was a student, his summers were spent working in the fields.[72] Together, the Luciani children would leave Canale at dawn to cut grass by hand with a scythe, a hand tool that demanded stamina to wield. At night they would load all the grass they had cut on a wagon and pull it back to town. He discharged these duties barefooted; in winter he wore wooden clogs.[73]

AN ABLE BUT UNRULY STUDENT

Albino was precocious, and his love of books was insatiable. The boy had an advantage over his classmates in mastering all subjects, thanks to having learned to read early. Books appealed to his intellect and ignited his imagination. Fiction enabled him to escape the confines of Canale and travel to exotic lands. The scope of his literary interests was already extensive, ranging from science fiction to classical literature and devotional works. He read and enjoyed Dickens's Christmas Books "because they are filled with love for the poor and a sense of social regeneration."[74] His mother made an early impression on Albino by giving him a copy of Saint Francis de Sales's *An Introduction to the Devout Life*, an edition specially intended for children. It launched a lifetime of esteem for de Sales and his teachings.[75]

The seeds of Albino's interest in writing were planted in the primary grades. He had a natural talent for crafting prose, likely attributable to his extensive reading. His devotion to Bortola was evident in an essay titled "My Mother" in his fourth-grade notebook. In it he boasted that she was able to read and write as well as do some arithmetic.[76]

Albino provided composition ideas to his friend, Giulio, who later became a carpenter in Canale. Sitting next to his companion in class, Bramezza, who was less skillful in composition than Albino, would raise the ire of his teacher by looking at his friend's notebook.[77]

Albino was so mischievous and performed pranks so often that his teachers found it necessary to inform Bortola. One of them would reassure his mother that he was not a bad boy, just lively.[78] Albino's brother added, "In the first years, he was surely anything but a model student . . . often, his teachers could not do other than to request his mother to visit the school for a 'chat.' It was not that the boy was . . . a villain towards his companions but, simply, he could not remain quiet on his bench."[79] Having heard those stories about her uncle as a youngster, Pia Luciani, daughter Edoardo ("Berto"), many years later suspected that he had ADHD, a hyperactivity disorder that remained undiagnosed in the early twentieth century.[80]

The most astonishing of his "offenses" took place in 1922, and it so incensed his elderly teacher that she paid a visit to the Luciani home. Early in the school year the teacher had asked Albino if he would allow a needy fellow student to borrow a book he no longer used. The nine-year-old readily agreed. However, at the conclusion of the academic year, Albino asked the teacher to return the book, but she balked. He responded impetuously by calling her a thief! There is no record of what discipline he received for this breach of respect,[81] but at the beginning of each year Albino resolved to improve his behavior. However, like all new resolutions, it was easier to make them than to keep them.

DISCOVERING HIS VOCATION

On the evening of October 11, 1919, a ferocious storm with biting wind accompanied by rain and snow assailed Canale. It was the kind of inclement weather to which Albino and his young friends seemed impervious. At the time they were playing at the site of a brewery that featured huge beer barrels that he and his comrades would climb when the owners were absent. One of the boys who was standing guard suddenly saw a figure in black approaching. The stranger carried a worn-out suitcase and was followed closely by a boy who was overloaded with bundles. Looking exhausted, the two climbed the stone stairs leading to the rectory. The boy standing watch warned Albino and his friends to run. They immediately exited through the rickety wooden gate of the garden and hid by the corner of the church where they could glimpse the outsider, who shook the snow off his cloak before stepping into the rectory. The mysterious man turned out to be the new parish priest, don Filippo Carli, eagerly awaited by the parishioners for the past three years. His arrival was momentous, for Carli became the most important spiritual influence on Luciani.[82]

According to his own recollection, Luciani as a youngster was drawn to the Church as if it were a lodestone whose attraction he was unable to resist. It became a salve for his poverty, an escape from the deprivations of daily life, a source of hope, a dispenser of dignity, a great equalizer, a refuge, and a source of individual inspiration.[83] He later wrote of attending Mass as a youth, "I forgot my usual poverty and had the impression that the organ was welcoming especially me and my little companions as if we were princes. From this first vague intuition came the strong conviction that the Catholic Church is not only something great, but also makes great the little and the poor, honoring and ennobling them."[84]

It became his daily habit to get up early to serve at the five o'clock Mass. This was a special joy after his sister was born, because before leaving the house he would steal a few moments admiring the baby who was sleeping soundly. Then he would rush into the darkness to reach the church.[85]

Despite his growing religious fervor, Albino was not without flaws, but his conscience was well-developed. On March 5, 1923, he composed a letter to his mother in which he confessed a sin, expressed his remorse, and promised to make reparation. It provides a poignant insight into his character at that early stage of his life. He wrote, "Dear Mamma, you sent me to Cencinighe to buy medicine and you gave me 12 lire. On the way I lost two lire and I told you it cost seven lire instead of five. I never had the courage to confess that I lost two." Since the incident, however, his conscience had been troubled by the deception. He expressed his hope that his mother would forgive him and promised to restore the missing lire, though he did not explain how he would acquire the money to do so.[86]

The earnestness of Albino's religious fervor was evident in what Giulio recalled about his friend's deportment on a special day: "We made our First Holy Communion together when we were seven or eight. I remember it so well because usually he was very vivacious and playful, but on that day, he was different, less carefree, more pensive. That day and for some time after, we spoke less, nor did we confide in each other. Albino seemed to be thinking of things he could not explain."[87]

Albino knew his vocation as early as age ten when he attended a Capuchin mission, but his mother, along with his parish priest, insisted that he wait a year before attending what was then called "minor seminary."[88] Shortly before that time arrived, Albino had his tonsils removed. During his convalescence, he was told that in a few days he would be able to return home. He, however, insisted that he wasn't going home; he was on his way to the seminary.[89]

The boy had not the haziest notion of the struggles that awaited him.

NOTES

1. Loris Serafini (director, Foundation Papa Luciani and Museum Albino Luciani of Canale d'Agordo), in discussion with the author, Canale d'Agordo, Italy, July 14, 2011.
2. "The First Years of Albino Luciani, Part I" (1912–1948), video, https://www.albino-luciani.com/index.php?id=270&L=3.
3. Serafini, discussion.
4. "First Years, Part I," https://www.albino-luciani.com/index.php?id=270&L=3.
5. Serafini, discussion.
6. Pia Luciani (Pope John Paul I's niece), in discussion with the author, Canale d'Agordo, Italy, July 6, 2011.
7. Serafini, discussion.
8. "John Paul I—Timeline of His Life," https://www.ewtn.com/catholicism/library/john-paul-i-timeline-24637.
9. Serafini, discussion.
10. "The Dolomites," UNESCO World Heritage Convention, https://whc.unesco.org/en/list/1237/.
11. Serafini, discussion.
12. Paul Spackman, *God's Candidate: The Life and Times of Pope John Paul I* (Herefordshire: Gracewing, 2008), 5.
13. Serafini, discussion.
14. *Italy Magazine*, Edgartown, MA, http://www.commune.canaledagordo.bl.it/.
15. Serafini, discussion.

16. "First Years, Part I."
17. Serafini, discussion.
18. Raymond and Lauretta Seabeck, *The Smiling Pope: The Life and Teaching of John Paul I* (Huntington, IN: Our Sunday Visitor, 2004), 11.
19. Serafini, discussion.
20. Spackman, *God's Candidate*, 1.
21. Serafini, discussion.
22. Seabeck, *Smiling Pope*, 11.
23. Serafini, discussion.
24. Spackman, *God's Candidate*, 4.
25. Seabeck, *Smiling Pope*, 11.
26. Spackman, *God's Candidate*, 2.
27. Spackman, *God's Candidate*, 2.
28. Spackman, *God's Candidate*, 2.
29. Spackman, *God's Candidate*, 1–2.
30. David Yallop, *In God's Name: An Investigation into the Murder of Pope John Paul I* (New York: Penguin, 1984), 3.
31. Albino Luciani, *A Passionate Adventure: Living the Catholic Faith Today*, trans. Lori Pieper (New York: Tau Cross Books, 2013), 9.
32. Peter Hebblethwaite, *The Year of Three Popes* (Cleveland, OH: Collins, 1979), 89.
33. Serafini, discussion.
34. Seabeck, *Smiling Pope*, 11.
35. Serafini, discussion.
36. Hebblethwaite, *Three Popes*, 89.
37. Seabeck, *Smiling Pope*, 11.
38. Spackman, *God's Candidate*, 4.
39. Seabeck, *Smiling Pope*, 12.
40. Serafini, discussion.
41. Kenneth L. Woodward, "The 34 Days of John Paul I," *Newsweek*, October 9, 1978, 73.
42. Spackman, *God's Candidate*, 2.
43. Spackman, *God's Candidate*, 3.
44. Spackman, *God's Candidate*, 37.
45. Spackman, *God's Candidate*, 3.
46. Serafini, discussion.
47. Spackman, *God's Candidate*, 3.
48. Serafini, discussion.
49. Spackman, *God's Candidate*, 3.
50. Spackman, *God's Candidate*, 5.
51. Serafini, discussion.
52. Spackman, *God's Candidate*, 4.
53. Spackman, *God's Candidate*, 4.
54. Spackman, *God's Candidate*, 6.
55. Seabeck, *Smiling Pope*, 12–13.

56. Serafini, discussion.
57. Seabeck, *Smiling Pope*, 12.
58. Seabeck, *Smiling Pope*, 12.
59. Loris Serafini, in discussion with the author, Canale, d'Agordo, Italy, July 14, 2011.
60. Serafini, discussion.
61. Luciani, *Passionate Adventure*, 10.
62. Serafini, discussion.
63. Serafini, discussion.
64. Serafini, discussion.
65. Albino Luciani, *Illustrissimi: Letters from Pope John Paul I*, trans. William Weaver (Boston: Little, Brown, 1978), 73.
66. Serafini, discussion.
67. Serafini, discussion.
68. Seabeck, *Smiling Pope*, 13.
69. Seabeck, *Smiling Pope*, 14.
70. Spackman, *God's Candidate*, 9.
71. Serafini, discussion.
72. Spackman, *God's Candidate*, 8.
73. Serafini, discussion.
74. Luciani, *Illustrissimi*, 3.
75. Seabeck, *Smiling Pope*, 19.
76. Serafini, discussion.
77. Seabeck, *Smiling Pope*, 13.
78. Spackman, *God's Candidate*, 6.
79. Spackman, *God's Candidate*, 6.
80. Luciani, discussion.
81. Spackman, *God's Candidate*, 7.
82. Serafini, discussion.
83. Spackman, *God's Candidate*, 4.
84. Seabeck, *Smiling Pope*, 12.
85. Serafini, discussion.
86. Spackman, *God's Candidate*, 5–6.
87. Seabeck, *Smiling Pope*, 13.
88. Seabeck, *Smiling Pope*, 14.
89. Serafini, discussion.

• 3 •

Student and Seminarian

Austerity and Obedience (1923–1935)

AN UNCERTAIN FUTURE

Albino's aspiration to become a priest was in jeopardy from the outset.

The most immediate impediment worried him unremittingly. While his mother was elated at the prospect of her son's future in the Church, the boy's father was not likely to share Bortola's enthusiasm. And without Giovanni's permission, Albino was destined for a secular life.

Giovanni had compelling reasons for objecting to his son entering the priesthood. For one thing, the elder Luciani was affiliated with a socialist political party that had anticlerical tendencies. Moreover, as the eldest son in a family mired in poverty, Albino could otherwise assist in the economic support of the household if he were employed. Attending seminary would not only deprive the Luciani family of his monetary assistance but would further strain its limited financial resources because of the expenses the theological institute required. And indeed, Giovanni was initially opposed to his son becoming a priest despite his sister's plea to give his consent.

Young Albino wrote to his father informing him about his longing to enter the seminary and asking for his blessing. Because his father was working in France at the time, Albino knew there would be a delay in receiving an answer. The uncertainty about his future and the anxiety it produced prompted young Albino to dash to the local post office each day in hopes of receiving an affirmative reply.[1]

Surprisingly, Giovanni enthusiastically responded to his son's wish. His own personal commitment to improving the conditions of exploited laborers was a major factor in his decision. "I hope that when you are a priest you will take the part of the poor and the workers, because Christ took their part," he wrote. It was advice that the young Luciani would forever heed. So precious was this letter to Albino that he kept it in his wallet for the remainder of his life.[2]

FALSE ALARM

In preparation for his fall studies, Albino took lessons with a teacher who resided in the local rectory. One summer afternoon shortly before departing for the seminary, young Albino took his notebook of lessons to the pasture. Absentmindedly, he left it next to the cow's saltlick as he sauntered off to play with other boys. Upon returning, he discovered that the cow had chewed it to shreds. Panic seized him. Rather than facing the consequences of his lapse of responsibility alone, he asked his mother to accompany him to the rectory. There he was the victim of a ruse. The instructor, finding the situation involving the cow humorous, decided to pretend it was a serious offense. "Since the cow has eaten his lessons, Albino won't be able to go to the seminary," he asserted in mock seriousness. The boy's response to this news was immediate and predictable: a thunderstorm of tears. Don Filippo Carli put his hand on Albino's head and reassured him that his place in the seminary was secure. "Now, now, there are other notebooks, and you will still be able to go to the seminary."[3]

ON HIS WAY

On his eleventh birthday, Albino took his first step on the road to the priesthood and the journey that fifty-five years later would lead to his improbable election as supreme pontiff of the Roman Catholic Church.[4]

Feltre, site of the minor seminary that Albino would attend, is only thirty-eight miles south of Canale d'Agordo. To a boy his age who had not trekked far beyond the confines of his birthplace, it must have seemed a remote destination. If his departure from home, family, and friends caused him anxiety, it was not evident. He displayed pure glee when embarking on this long-awaited venture. Perhaps he took comfort in his mother's advice. She had assured him that although she would be honored if Albino became a priest, he should not feel obligated to continue in the seminary if he was not happy there. A change in his attitude toward a priestly vocation was sufficient reason, Bortola believed, to leave the seminary. She didn't want her son to continue on the path to the priesthood simply because he was worried about disappointing his mother.[5]

Carrying a crude wooden "suitcase" with a metal handle along with his initials carved on the lid, Albino boarded a small wagon left over from the war. His sister, who was only three at the time, wouldn't remember him leaving home, but it was a painful parting for Berto who never forgot the smile on Albino's face. As the lorry departed, the little boy cried to see this unfamiliar vehicle carting his older sibling away to an unknown destination.[6]

MINOR SEMINARY

Figure 3.1. A studious eleven-year-old Albino in minor seminary, Feltre.

When the wide-eyed youngster arrived at the Feltre seminary, awaiting him was a reassuring surprise: a young man he already knew by sight, Giuseppe Strim of Falcade. Much to Albino's delight, the boys spoke the same dialect. In time, Strim became one of Albino's dearest friends. They studied together for ten years at Feltre and then in Belluno.[7] From the start he would not be a stranger in a strange land, a source of relief for the boy from Canale. The transition to his new life also was eased by the assistance of a young priest named Giulio Gaio, who befriended the boy and guided him.[8] Gaio turned out to be the most important influence on Albino as a young seminarian. Thanks to these two individuals, the youngster felt relatively comfortable in his new surroundings almost immediately. After meeting the rector, he gladly took a tour of the seminary that was to be his home for the next five years.[9]

Very early the following morning, Albino awoke to the shouting of older seminarians instructing the initiates to get out of bed immediately. Still groggy from the sudden summons from slumber, he was confused regarding his whereabouts and instinctively sought his mother, but he soon gained his bearings. He was beginning the daily drill: washing his face hurriedly using a basin filled with frigid water (on some winter days it would turn to ice); he then received a book from which he read aloud with his peers during the morning meditation. Afterward, it was off to Mass. Classes started punctually afterward and ended in the early afternoon. In the evenings, the boys went to chapel to pray the rosary.[10] The strict regimen was akin to boot camp for youths.

Life, even at a minor seminary in those times, was spartan. One of the most difficult adjustments Albino had to make besides separation from his home and family was the restrictions on his personal freedom and the rigidity of the schedule to which he now was fettered. His new home more closely resembled a barracks than a domestic domicile. Here eleven-year-old Albino began his study for the priesthood still harboring high hopes,[11] but a photo of him at this time depicts an unusually serious demeanor for one so young.[12]

The boy was an industrious student who completed his assignments thoroughly and achieved mostly notable grades, especially in geography and history.[13] Even so, he sometimes vexed his seminary teachers, one of whom once noted, "Albino Luciani [is] too exuberant. He has such an original personality, only God knows how he will turn out."[14]

MAJOR SEMINARY

In October 1928, five years after beginning his studies in Feltre, Albino entered the Gregorian Seminary in Belluno for what was in essence his high-school education. It was located fewer than nineteen miles from his previous school. He remained there until shortly before his ordination. Albino wrote home weekly and always asked his family to say a Hail Mary for him and his fellow seminarians.[15] Although he prospered there, in various photos he looks solemn, with little hint of the infectious smile for which he would later be famous.

At his new school Albino received a classical education. He excelled in biblical exegesis, history, and Latin, but mathematics was the bane of his academic experience.[16] Albino had a capacity for learning languages easily.

Fellow students who found Greek and Latin challenging discovered an eager source of assistance in Albino.[17]

In addition to his studies, he also was passionate about singing in the choir. "I can still see him, happy and content, singing with 'gusto' with the characteristic twist of his mouth, which we used to tease him about," recalled a fellow seminarian.[18]

At this time, a daily ritual that was to persist for a lifetime had its origins. Before going to sleep, he would put away his black seminarian's habit with great care, and each morning prior to dressing, he would kiss it reverently.[19]

The seminarians slept on simple but sturdy beds of iron. The rules there were as firm as the bunks they slept in. Luckily for Albino, he could escape the ruggedness of his new existence by resorting to his beloved pastime: reading. His appetite for literature continued to be ravenous, and it was here that he became intimately acquainted with an array of illustrious authors. His prodigious memory would be his faithful friend during examination periods: he could recollect with astounding accuracy dates, names, facts, and concepts from literature as well as philosophy. His recall was so impressive that it amazed his teachers.[20]

REQUEST DENIED

In time he became attracted to the Jesuit life of obedience and dedication to academics. Two of his seminary friends had entered the order. Albino requested permission to join them, but he was rebuffed by the bishop who wanted him to serve in a parish. His disappointment was profound.[21] (A delicious irony is that had Luciani become a Jesuit he, not Cardinal Jorge Bergoglio who took the name Francis, would have become the first pope from the Society of Jesus.)

DISCOVERING A SAINT

Albino first read the autobiography of Saint Thérèse of Lisieux, *The Story of a Soul*, as a seventeen-year-old seminarian. The book had a substantial impact on his thinking. "It was like a bolt from the blue," he remembered.[22] Saint Francis de Sales had influenced Thérèse as he would Albino. The seminarian would later dedicate one of the letters in his book *Illustrissimi* to Saint Thérèse.[23]

Influenced by her *Little Way*, in which she revealed a simple, childlike relationship with God, Saint Thérèse, who died at age twenty-four, did not attempt grand moral feats but, instead, committed small acts of service to others. Albino mirrored her thoughts and beliefs when he preached, "Let us trust above all in the mercy of God, Who, knowing that we are poor and little, is happy with our sincere desires and daily efforts to grow in holiness."[24]

A SPONTANEOUS ACT OF COURAGE

Shortly following his election as pope, a prominent magazine suggested that Albino Luciani seemed to have some mettle in him.[25] The writer's assessment of the new pope's character was accurate. The docile seminarian had hidden reserves of virtues including valor.

Returning to the seminary from a country outing one night, Albino and his companions spotted dancing flames illuminating the black sky in the distance. Approaching, they discovered a blazing barn and heard the echoes of panicked animals trapped within. Without hesitation, he and his friends rushed in despite the danger posed by the scorching fire that was rapidly consuming the wooden structure. The owner of the property was away at the time of the incident and was grateful when he learned that the seminarians had risked severe injury, perhaps even death, to rescue all his animals from the conflagration.[26]

MONETARY WOES

The seminary depended on tuition revenue to sustain itself, and that created hardships for many families whose sons attended. That was certainly true of the Lucianis. Albino's parents sacrificed enormously to pay for a portion of his expenses. Every two months they sent money to the seminary for fees. The only way Bortola and Giovanni could pay their sons' financial obligations was for Nina to be employed. As a result, at age eleven she left school to work. Keenly aware of his sister's selflessness, Albino would frequently say to his mother that he appreciated the great sacrifice that Nina had made to make possible his dream of becoming a priest. Albino was forever grateful to her.[27]

The seminarian would come home for Easter and in summer, remaining from June to early October. Even Giovanni would rest briefly from his punishing labors for a time but needed to leave Canale again because of debts that taxed the family sorely. Her husband's long absences from home over the years had distressed Bortola. In anguish, she visited don Carli, who advised her to trust in divine providence. At long last her husband found a job locally as a night watchman near Canale. Besides enjoying the company of his family now, Giovanni could relax in his own home.[28]

What truly eased both the anxiety and financial woes of the Lucianis was the generosity of strangers. A well-to-do Jewish couple in Belluno, who had converted to Catholicism, donated money to the seminary. Beyond that, they inquired whether any deserving seminarians were in need of tuition assistance. Albino became one of the recipients of their generosity.[29]

HOMECOMING

Spending summers in Canale, reunited with his family and neighbors after undergoing three seasons of arduous academic demands, must have seemed like paradise to Albino. This was the land and people he loved. These were the fields where he had played as a child. For him, summer was a time to rejuvenate from his virtually military-like lifestyle in the seminary. Work, including haymaking, became part of his routine. Every morning, he would arise early and attend Mass before taking his scythe to the fields, where he worked diligently.[30] Warm memories of happy times enjoyed during the innocence of Albino's youth crowded upon his consciousness. He could recapture some of those pleasures, but summers for seminarians were not occasions to be devoted solely to indolence and games, and so the real world and its responsibilities intruded on his nostalgia.

PASTOR AND MENTOR

The work of preparing for the priesthood was a year-round commitment. Filippo Carli was an influential priest in Canale from 1919 to 1934. Whenever Luciani spoke of vocations later in life, he often mentioned Carli.[31] The pastor provided Albino with a form of priestly internships during summers at home. Under Carli's tutelage Albino made excursions within the parish, during which he gained intimate perspectives on how conscientious priests comforted the sick, encouraged struggling families, conducted services, and administered the sacraments.[32]

Carli, an early role model, made a permanent impression on the young Albino. Among the chores assigned to him were maintaining the church, teaching the catechism, working with the choir, and even engaging in clerical work such as bookkeeping.[33] One reason Carli kept the seminarian busy was to combat idleness. He even assigned Albino mundane tasks such as typing articles for the parish bulletin and helping the sacristan adorn the altar with flowers and fresh linen.[34]

"Once I tried to teach myself bookbinding and he [Carli] encouraged me. Another time I collected stamps and took up typewriting," Luciani recalled later in life. During one leisurely day, Carli assigned Albino the task of repairing an alarm clock, apparently without an instruction manual or even rudimentary training. The result was a bust. "The clock never worked again once it got into my hands!" Albino would remember with a chuckle.[35]

As an older seminarian, when Albino returned to Canale for vacations, he always relished teaching students the catechism. Carli had the utmost confidence in the seminarian's ability to succeed in this endeavor and enthusiastically entrusted him with this vital task. Indeed, Albino had a gift as a catechist and always considered this role as central to his priesthood. The importance he attached to it was evident years later when he wrote the book *Catechism in Crumbs*.[36]

It was a habit of the pastor to bring Albino and other seminarians with him when he traveled far from Canale. Once Albino accompanied Carli to the Madonna of Pietralba near Bressanone, a slog of about sixty-five miles. It was his first time there.[37] The stunning basilica is known as the Cathedral of the Dolomites. It owes its existence to a hermit who witnessed an apparition by Mary in 1553 and built a chapel there in commemoration of the supernatural event.[38] (The site continues to be a destination for pilgrims, the most famous of whom was Pope John Paul II in 1988.)[39] In later years Luciani would think back with fondness to the pleasant walks he took with don Filippo.

A PROFILE IN COURAGE

Albino's faith and love of Christ instilled in him the tenacity and fearlessness of a martyr. These attributes would be displayed repeatedly throughout his life whenever he encountered threats to innocent people and to his beloved Church. This was especially true during World War II. An early instance was an encounter with a bold fascist who had mounted a box in Canale's village square in front of the church on a Sunday afternoon, encouraging young people to join the movement. Fascists, of course, were virulently anti-Catholic. Albino intervened immediately by approaching the man and insisting that he depart. It is not known whether the man was armed nor specifically what Albino told him, but the priest succeeded in removing the intruder and nullifying his potential influence on the youth who had listened to him.[40]

BOOKS, BOOKS, AND MORE BOOKS

In his final years as a seminarian, Albino indexed and cataloged the entire ancient and valuable collection of four thousand books in the parish library housed in the rectory. (The volumes remain on the shelves exactly the way he organized them.)[41] It was a joyful task. The library even contained books in a variety of foreign languages, a veritable treasure to a young man whose thirst for knowledge was unquenchable. Berto observed with wonder how his older brother would breeze through books at an astounding pace.[42]

According to an old friend, Giuseppe Strim, SJ, "One day I went to visit him at Canale, and I found him reading as usual, his cassock stained with grass as he had been haymaking all day. He looked up, smiling. 'What a workhorse you are,' I said to him, 'do you want to go crazy with your books?' 'Don't worry,' he replied, 'this is the last book in the library, and since I have no money to buy books, I'll start reading them all over again!'"[43] Albino did much of his reading when he was in the meadows tending the family cows.[44] There he would enjoy learning in the tranquility of the countryside.

Carli, though, had major concerns about Albino's reading habits, and so he attempted to steer the young seminarian to more religious works. "I am glad that you read, but I want you to read only the books in the rectory," he told Albino. "You read too many novels," don Filippo complained. "Be more moderate and read some lives of the saints." Recollecting his pastor's advice in later years, Luciani revealed that he did not completely comply. "That was easy; the library has a collection of very good novels," he said. Nevertheless, when Albino was a seminary professor, he acknowledged the wisdom of Carli's advice, for he similarly admonished one of his own students. "Do you know that I risked losing my vocation when I was your age, by reading unsuitable books?"[45]

DEATH OF A FATHER FIGURE

In September 1934, Carli was hospitalized in Padua for treatment of a life-threatening malady; nevertheless, he remained serene. He wrote reassuringly to Albino that though bedridden he was not suffering. It was to be his final letter. In October Carli died, and a heartbroken Albino was unable to leave the seminary to attend the funeral of his old mentor. Albino relied on a close friend to provide him with details of the service and interment.[46] The death occurred just a few months prior to Albino's ordination.[47]

ACHIEVEMENT OF A DREAM

Against imponderable odds, Luciani's dream was about to come true. His ordination was imminent. The time to begin his life's work was at hand. Though he had a vision of what that mission would be, the destinations that lay ahead of him were beyond belief.

NOTES

1. Raymond and Lauretta Seabeck, *The Smiling Pope: The Life and Teaching of John Paul I* (Huntington, IN: Our Sunday Visitor, 2004), 14.
2. Seabeck, *Smiling Pope*, 14.
3. Seabeck, *Smiling Pope*, 15.
4. Seabeck, *Smiling Pope*, 15.
5. Loris Serafini (director, Foundation Papa Luciani and Museum Albino Luciani of Canale d'Agordo), in discussion with the author, Canale d'Agordo, Italy, July 11, 2011.
6. Serafini, discussion.
7. Serafini, discussion.
8. Seabeck, *Smiling Pope*, 16.
9. Serafini, discussion.
10. Serafini, discussion.
11. Seabeck, *Smiling Pope*, 16.
12. Albino Luciani photograph 5.jpg., Foundation Papa Luciani of Canale d'Agordo (Belluno-Italy).
13. Paul Spackman, *God's Candidate: The Life and Times of Pope John Paul I* (Herefordshire: Gracewing, 2008), 11–12.
14. Seabeck, *God's Candidate*, 17.
15. Serafini, discussion.
16. Spackman, *God's Candidate*, 18.
17. Seabeck, *Smiling Pope*, 19.
18. Seabeck, *Smiling Pope*, 19–20.
19. Serafini, discussion.
20. Serafini, discussion.
21. Spackman, *God's Candidate*, 22.
22. Seabeck, *Smiling Pope*, 19.
23. Albino Luciani, *Illustrissimi: Letters from Pope John Paul I*, trans. Lori Pieper (Boston: Little, Brown, 1978), 146.
24. Seabeck, *Smiling Pope*, 19.
25. "Compassionate Shepherd," *Time*, September 4, 1978, 62.
26. Seabeck, *Smiling Pope*, 19–20.
27. Serafini, discussion.

28. Serafini, discussion.
29. Serafini, discussion.
30. Serafini, discussion.
31. Serafini, discussion.
32. Seabeck, *Smiling Pope*, 16.
33. Seabeck, *Smiling Pope*, 16.
34. Serafini, discussion.
35. Seabeck, *Smiling Pope*, 16–17.
36. Serafini, discussion.
37. Serafini, discussion.
38. "Madonna di Pietralba Pilgrimage Site," Weinstrasse.com., https://www.weinstrasse.com/en/highlights/sights/churches-andmonasteries/madonnadipietralba-pilgrimage-site/.
39. Serafini, discussion.
40. Seabeck, *Smiling Pope*, 20.
41. Spackman, *God's Candidate*, 12.
42. Serafini, discussion.
43. Seabeck, *Smiling Pope*, 20.
44. Serafini, discussion.
45. Seabeck, *Smiling Pope*, 17.
46. Serafini, discussion.
47. Seabeck, *Smiling Pope*, 20.

• 4 •

Priest and Promotions

Home and Away Again (1935–1958)

THE MOST MEMORABLE DAY: ORDINATION

A man's ordination to the priesthood is akin to marriage. When couples are blessed with enduring love, their wedding day is one of unmatched bliss, and for the remainder of their lives the vivid memory of that occasion neither fades nor loses its exceptionality. The same is true of deacons whose undying passion for Christ leads to their consecration as priests. And so it was for Albino Luciani. The realization of his fondest desire was the culmination of a decade of personal asceticism, intense study, and religious devotion. For the remainder of his days, he treasured the occasion of his ordination more than any other—even his elevation to bishop, cardinal, and pope.[1]

Luciani's consecration as a priest took place on July 7, 1935, and was officiated by Giosue Cattarossi, bishop of Belluno-Feltre.[2] At age twenty-two, he was young to enter the ranks of the clergy. In his day, to be ordained prior to the age of twenty-four required a papal dispensation, which Luciani had been granted at the request of his superiors, who recognized his readiness to carry out the pastoral responsibilities of a clergyman.[3]

The site of his consecration was the Church of St. Peter in Belluno, one that had personal significance for him. Adjacent to the Gregorian seminary, it was a house of worship where he often engaged in communal prayer. Franciscan friars had built the edifice in 1326. Nearly four centuries later an earthquake compromised the structural integrity of the historic church, requiring its demolition. It was completely rebuilt in 1750; yet the exterior, at least, preserved the appearance of antiquity.[4] Its drab brick facade with a solitary window elevated above a wooden door conveyed its ancient origins while creating the erroneous expectation that its interior was equally unrefined. Not so. Upon entering the nave, one is pleasantly surprised by its ornate baroque style, sublime and suitable for the celebration of the venerable rite of consecration.

Ordination is a sacrament that always takes place within the context of the Mass. At his ordination, like all others, Deacon Luciani promised obedience to the diocesan bishop and his successors, for, as a priest, he would be under their care, supervision, and direction. As part of the ritual, he prostrated himself before the altar, a symbol of his submission to the will of God. The essential ritual of the sacrament—the moment when the actual ordination takes place—is the laying on of hands. Bishop Cattarossi placed his hands on Luciani's head while calling upon the Holy Spirit. The bishop then anointed the newly minted priest's hands with sacred chrism.[5]

The priesthood was a lifetime commitment based on holy vows that he was not in the least hesitant to make and to maintain. He would be a priest for the next forty-three years; it was the calling for which his character, personality, piety, and profound love of God and man were perfectly suited.[6] Reminiscing years later about receiving the sacrament of Holy Orders that prepared him for his life's vocation, Luciani said, "My priestly ordination and my first Mass seemed to pass in a dream."[7]

NO PLACE LIKE HOME

There was bustling activity in the usually sleepy village of Forno di Canale on July 8, and it seemed to involve all the inhabitants of that hamlet. They were preparing a warm welcome for the local boy they loved who in their estimation had become a man of distinction. Many had known Albino Luciani since his childhood. It was a source of pride that a native son was returning home as a priest. In anticipation of his arrival, the villagers had adorned the public square with elaborate decorations. The piazza featured numerous signs of salutation. An assortment of flowers of dazzling colors graced the door of the rectory that would now be don Albino's home.[8]

The young priest entered the piazza like a celebrity; Luciani's family and friends honored his homecoming with a flourish. The church bells pealed jubilantly as villagers in the square chatted excitedly. A band played lively tunes as a large, black car carried the new priest across the timeworn bridge leading into town. A young girl approached the guest of honor after he disembarked from the automobile to recite a welcoming poem, and a smile lingered on Luciani's face as he carried his black biretta in hand. The procession included friends of the priest, altar servers, and the new archpriest of the parish, Augusto Bramezza, along with Msgr. Angelo Santin. Everyone of note in Canale was present with the conspicuous exception of the late don Filippo Carli. Luciani remembered him on this occasion with warm words of affection and gratitude, the pain of his mentor's loss still fresh in the young priest's heart. As his siblings, Berto and Nina, gazed with pride upon their older brother's shining countenance, his parents, Bortola and Giovanni, were overjoyed.[9]

Figure 4.1. A formal picture of Albino Luciani as a young priest.

FIRST MASS AND CELEBRATION

It was ironic that Luciani's initial assignment was to be curate (assistant pastor) in the parish he knew best and loved most. On that day, Luciani sang his first Mass at his old local church, San Giovanni Batista (St. John the Baptist). It was the church where Luciani had been baptized, received his first Holy Communion, served as an altar boy, sang in the choir, and devotedly attended Mass during his youth. It was there also that the seminarian had spent so much time when he returned home during vacations. His service in that parish under don Bramezza, and subsequently under Msgr. Luigi Cappello, was to be brief, from July to December.[10] Neither he nor his townsmen could know that on this day of jubilation.

THE MISSION BEGINS

Luciani advocated frequent confession, a sacrament that Catholics of that era received more commonly than today. He believed that the soul needs to be cleansed frequently through repentance and the absolution of sins granted by the priest through the intercession of God so that people could begin their moral lives anew, unencumbered by previous transgressions. Though a virtuous man himself, he was very cognizant of man's moral frailty, including his own, and frequent confession was an integral part of his own life. (As a bishop he would go to confession weekly.)[11] He fervently trusted in the capacity of people to improve their spiritual lives through prayer combined with a determined effort to avoid the snares of sin. Throughout his long ministry, Luciani persistently preached God's tender mercy for even the most detestable sinners should they earnestly seek forgiveness.

In the ensuing days and weeks, he immersed himself in his parish duties. He was always readily available to all who needed him, a practice he did not abandon even when he was a cardinal. This was the service to others that he had longed to perform and for which he had assiduously prepared. The experiences provided him with indescribable satisfaction as he performed God's work.

From the start, Luciani had a flair for preaching; he sprinkled his sermons with amusing anecdotes and relevant examples to illustrate whatever his core message happened to be at the moment. It was the same strategy that he employed so successfully in teaching children, and it was effective with adults, too.[12]

In his sermons he frequently referenced both St. Thérèse Lisieux and St. Francis de Sales, both noted for their advocacy of the simple virtues.[13] Luciani often spoke of joy, which he counseled was a Christian obligation. He, of course, was a man who consistently displayed signs of joy, as always, teaching by personal example. Biographically, Luciani shared salient similarities with de Sales: they both grew up in the mountains, de Sales in the Alps and Luciani in the Dolomites; both were bishops who lived austere lives and scorned accolades; and both were authors of some repute. In fact, de Sales is the patron saint of "Catholic writers and journalists." They were also strikingly similar in virtues and temperament. Both were admired for their gentleness, kindness, compassion, humility, powerful intellect, and breadth of knowledge. What Fr. John C. Reville wrote about de Sales applied to Luciani: "There is a winged grace in his words, a twinkle, a joyance, subdued and tender in his eyes."[14]

PRAYER

Not surprisingly for a priest, Luciani ardently believed in the efficacy of prayer; in addition to celebrating daily Mass, he prayed silently at every opportunity and unfailingly prayed the rosary daily.[15] Often up by 5 a.m., Luciani's days were spent in a constant conversation with God. It was a complete abandonment of self. In addition, he habitually asked others to pray for him, especially to say a Hail Mary on his behalf.[16]

SEEKING GREATER PIETY

Luciani was eager to become a member of an organization that promoted commitment to prayer. In 1936, he joined the Apostolic Union of the Clergy, an association, international in scope, consisting of priests whose priority was to devote themselves to "intense Eucharistic piety and prayer." He was inducted as a member following a six-month probationary period and the completion of "the Promise" that all members were required to make. He wrote a letter to Msgr. Angelo Santin, the seminary rector, in which he expressed the importance of membership to his personal and religious life: "I want very much to make the Promise because the Apostolic Union does me so much good. I consider it a grace from Our Lord to belong to it."[17]

UNSOUGHT PROMOTIONS

Figure 4.2. Monsignor Luciani with a friend, his beloved mountains in the background.

Albino Luciani was not destined to fulfill his modest ambition of a career as a parish priest. He loved pastoral work, relished being a catechist, and he would have been content to finish his ecclesiastical calling as he began his vocation: a simple country parish priest administering to his flock. His niece Pia Luciani revealed that he privately harbored an idyllic vision of becoming pastor of a little parish on a lake where his beloved mother and father would live out their lives in hard-earned tranquility.[18]

His superiors, however, recognized rare qualities in him that launched him on an administrative track that he neither foresaw nor sought. He swallowed his disappointment (and perhaps apprehension) to obey their orders. Luciani had learned the hard lesson of obedience in seminary, and it was a practice that he adhered to throughout his career, a sure sign of his core belief in the legitimacy of the hierarchy of the Church. Prior to becoming a bishop, he received a flurry of promotions in the diocese of Belluno. Not only was Luciani entrusted with an array of responsibilities, but this experience proved indispensable to his preparation for becoming an effective administrator as a prominent Church leader in the future.

First, Luciani headed back to the Gregorian Seminary. In July of 1937, he became vice rector, appointed by rector Msgr. Santin, and his affection for the institution that, in effect, had become his home never diminished. His responsibilities included ensuring that the seminarians followed rules, counseling them, spending time with those who were ill, and engaging them in recreational activities. He was devoted to his charges and always stayed close by them.[19]

In 1947, Luciani began his lengthy diocesan administrative career by becoming Episcopal pro chancellor of the diocese of Belluno. (In that capacity he managed the administrative offices and was responsible for the official archives of the diocese. Often a bishop adds other responsibilities, and the chancellor may end up being, in fact, executive director of the diocesan office.) On December 16 of that year, Pope Pius XII designated him a monsignor, an honorary title bestowed on a priest who has distinguished himself by providing exceptional service to the Church.[20] It has no effect on the priest's duties or ministerial assignment, however. The recognition is typically granted upon the recommendation of the priest's diocesan bishop.[21]

The designation meant little to Luciani, who was not enamored of titles and never would be. On one occasion a fledgling seminarian addressed him as "don" rather than "Monsignor." Some of his peers upbraided the student for being disrespectful, but Luciani himself in a private moment shortly thereafter assured him that he did not feel slighted: "You see, these titles are a farce."[22] Few of his fellow members of the clergy shared his attitude.

On the day that Luciani became a monsignor, he was appointed secretary of the Diocesan Synod at age thirty-five.[23] A diocesan synod is an assembly that includes pastors, religious administrators, and the laity who assemble to discuss important matters of the faith, which were often helpful to the bishop. (Bishops' synods, held every few decades, are often transformative, resulting in renewal of the life of the Church.) It was only the beginning of the myriad responsibilities that would be entrusted to him. From then on, the promotions in Belluno followed in rapid succession.

On February 2, 1948, he became pro-vicar general, a position he held until February 6, 1954,[24] when he was promoted to vicar general of the diocese by Bishop Gioacchino Muccin.[25] The vicar general is a priest who acts in the name of the bishop in administering the diocese. As an executive authority within the diocese, he is intimately involved in its day-to-day pastoral and secular administration.

Then, in 1949 Luciani became assistant to the diocesan young women's section of Catholic Action, a group of laymen and laywomen advocating for greater Catholic influence in secular society.[26] That same year he organized the Diocesan

Eucharistic Congress and served as director of the Catechetics Center.[27] These demands required an abundance of energy and a significant commitment of time. Luciani fulfilled all his obligations faithfully, capably, and ardently.

Finally, on June 30, 1956, Luciani became canon of the cathedral of Belluno, a position that made him responsible for administering the imposing church.[28] A week later he impressed a prince of the church, and that would alter the entire trajectory of his life. July 6 was a fateful day for him because it was then that he made the acquaintance of Cardinal Angelo Roncalli with whom he attended a conference of theology teachers.[29] Together they toured an orphanage and had many opportunities for conversation. Roncalli swiftly developed a liking for Luciani, and, as a direct result, the vicar general's future was sealed—and not in a way he would have wished.

FASCISM, WAR, AND HEROISM

In late 1922, Benito Mussolini, leader of the fascist movement, came to power in Italy and established a dictatorship largely through the magnetism of his temperament. With the national government now exercising control of the economy, it outlawed labor unions and strikes. Not a few members of the Italian clergy were enthusiastic about Mussolini and fascism itself. A cult of personality had developed around "*Il Duce*" (The Leader), and he received almost universal public adulation from Italians. Luciani, though, wasn't a fan, and he fearlessly urged his students to renounce both fascism and Nazism. He also assisted members of the Resistance.[30]

One morning in Canale, Luciani's mother, Bortola, opened the door of her home to discover a woman kneeling at the doorstep. She was begging for help for her husband, a teacher, who had been whisked away and sentenced to death by the fascist regime. Her hope was that don Albino would intercede on her spouse's behalf. The entreaty was a sign of the esteem his fellow citizens had for the priest as well as a testament to his valor and efficacy in dealing with the opposing military. He came from Belluno without hesitation and persuaded the authorities to release the man.

These were ominous times for Italy. During World War II (1939–1945) intense suffering afflicted the country because of the harsh domestic regime and its Nazi allies. In September of 1939, German troops occupied Italy in search of the Resistance. Many refugees hid in the mountains. Luciani's brother, Berto, became a leader in the local opposition movement.

His sister, Nina, herself acted as a veritable spy, responsible for notifying Resistance members of the enemy's movements. During this period, she met often with Albino. Berto would send her to Belluno to solicit their brother's advice. There were perilous moments for her; it was all too easy to make a mistake and be discovered by the enemy. If caught, the consequences could have been catastrophic. She listened to Albino's advice and returned to report to Berto.[31]

In March of 1945, Bishop Bortignon famously confronted German soldiers who manned machine guns as they were about to hang Resistance fighters. He defiantly climbed the stairs of the gallows to administer the last rights to the victims. Accompanying him on this mission was Luciani. Whenever the subject came up in later years, Luciani shifted the focus to the bishop's extraordinary courage. But Bortignon acknowledged his younger accomplice's bravery. The bishop's admiration led him to recommend to Pope John XXIII that Luciani be consecrated a bishop. It didn't take much persuading; the pope was the very same Cardinal Roncalli with whom Luciani had established an amiable relationship.[32]

Luciani's old school friend Bramezza recalled a poignant incident during World War II when Luciani came to his aid once again. "In 1945 I was a prisoner of war in a German concentration camp. My wife had not heard from me for over a year, and in desperation, she went to don Albino who was then teaching in the seminary. Shortly afterward, two German soldiers brought me to a radio and said, 'You may speak. Your wife is listening.' Somehow, Albino had succeeded in finding me." What Luciani did to secure that favor is unrecorded.[33]

Even in the aftermath of the war in Italy, life was rife with dangers. Among the perils was vigilantism. The urge to redress grievances without the sanction of law motivated members of the Resistance, who had long been hiding in mountain outposts, to visit their wrath on those who were suspected of having been Nazi collaborators. One day a group of these vigilantes erected a scaffold, intending to hang twelve people presumed to be guilty. Luciani caught wind of the plan and convinced the would-be avengers to abandon their retribution because justice would not be served by their intended action; that, in fact, they were engaged in an atrocious act of revenge that was morally repugnant and contrary to their Christian beliefs. In so doing he saved twelve lives.[34] Forgiveness, even of men who had committed atrocious deeds, was a Christian responsibility because it was God's command. The professor's ingenuity and persuasiveness were becoming legendary.

NOTES

1. Raymond and Lauretta Seabeck, *The Smiling Pope: The Life and Teaching of John Paul I* (Huntington, IN: Our Sunday Visitor, 2004), 45.
2. Seabeck, *Smiling Pope*, 248.

3. Paul Spackman, *God's Candidate: The Life and Times of Pope John Paul I* (Herefordshire: Gracewing, 2008), 22.

4. Marco Perale, https://www.belluno-turismo.it/en/project/s-pietro-church/.

5. "Rite of Ordination," Roman Catholic Diocese of Syracuse, accessed September 22, 2024, https://syracusediocese.org/rite-of-ordination.

6. Seabeck, *Smiling Pope*, back cover.

7. "Priest in Agordo and Belluno," *Humilitas* 9, no. 3 (December 1995).

8. Loris Serafini (director, Foundation Papa Luciani and Museum Albino Luciani of Canale d'Agordo), Gloucester, Rhode Island, October 10, 2012.

9. Serafini, discussion.

10. Seabeck, *Smiling Pope*, 20.

11. Msgr. Francesco Taffarel (personal secretary to Bishop Albino Luciani, diocese of Vittorio Veneto, Italy), in discussion with the author, Tarzo, Italy, July 11, 2011.

12. Serafini, discussion.

13. Seabeck, *Smiling Pope*, 19.

14. Saint Francis de Sales, *An Introduction to the Devout Life* (Rockford, IL: Tan Books and Publishers, 1994), xvii.

15. Seabeck, *Smiling Pope*, 26.

16. Seabeck, *Smiling Pope*, 60.

17. Seabeck, *Smiling Pope*, 21.

18. Pia Luciani (niece of Pope John Paul I), in discussion with the author, Canale d'Agordo, Italy, July 11, 2011.

19. Seabeck, *Smiling Pope*, 22.

20. Highlights of the Life of His Holiness John Paul I, http://www.vatican.va/holy_father/john_paul_i/biography/documents/hf_jp-i_bio_01021997.

21. Rev. Silvio De Nard (pastor, Sacred Heart Parish, East Providence, Rhode Island), in discussion with the author, East Providence, May 14, 2011.

22. Seabeck, *Smiling Pope*, 25.

23. De Nard, discussion.

24. Highlights of the Life of His Holiness John Paul I.

25. Serafini, discussion.

26. Seabeck, *Smiling Pope*, 249.

27. Seabeck, *Smiling Pope*, 25.

28. Spackman, *God's Candidate*, 264.

29. "The First Years of Albino Luciani, Part I" (1912–1948), video, https://www.albino-luciani.com/index.php?id=274&L=3.

30. Albino Luciani, *A Passionate Adventure: Living the Catholic Faith Today*, trans. Lori Pieper (New York: Tau Cross Books, 2013), 20.

31. Spackman, *God's Candidate*, 32.

32. Serafini, discussion.

33. Seabeck, *Smiling Pope*, 14.

34. Seabeck, *Smiling Pope*, 24–25.

Part II

ACQUIESCENCE

• 5 •

Pontiff—Week II/Faith

Servant of Servants (September 3–13, 1978)

We walk by faith, not by sight. —2 Corinthians 5:7 (NRSVCE)

Clothe yourselves, all of you, with humility toward one another. —1 Peter 5:5 (RSVSCE)

[T]he Son of Man did not come to be served, but to serve. —Mark 10:45 (NRSVCE)

"Why me?"

During the first several days of his pontificate, John Paul privately posed this question on occasion to Rev. John Magee.[1] Such a preoccupation with his unworthiness for the papacy had the potential to undermine the efficacy of his leadership. Somehow it didn't. Almost certainly, the query underscored his undiminished astonishment at his selection, but it might also have indicated that his humility was, in these instances, obscuring his recognition of the God-given gifts that made him fit to be pope. Also plausible is that it reflected his personal disappointment that his own will had been thwarted by his colleagues in conclave. In fact, he had precedence for this self-doubt; when he was appointed bishop, he had protested vigorously and only reluctantly agreed to the promotion when the pope insisted that Luciani comply with his wishes. Also, according to don Diego Lorenzi, prior to the conclave he had asked what Luciani would do if elected; the patriarch said he would refuse.[2] This rejoinder was either a reflexive reaction that revealed his sense of unworthiness or, paradoxically, a flash of hubris. If, as the cardinals believed, they were guided by the Holy Spirit in their choice of a pope, Luciani's rejection of his election would have been tantamount to rejecting God's will, a shocking anomaly in his life of humble obedience.

John Paul's humility, in all its manifestations, is what won him unparalleled public acclaim so swiftly, and it's an essential virtue that the cardinal electors had sought in a new pope. Then again, his humility, as he publicly admitted, did not come effortlessly and was subject to lapses. Paradoxically, John Paul—the embodiment of the servant of servants—who often shocked visitors with the greeting "How can I serve you?" reigned with apparent composure despite his misgivings.[3]

DAY 8/SUNDAY, SEPTEMBER 3

Reunions

On the morning of what was to be his first official day as pope, John Paul met separately with visitors from his former dioceses of Belluno, Vittorio Veneto, and Venice. The Holy Father reminisced nostalgically about his years in each location. His mood was ebullient as he spoke with fondness to these admirers who had traveled considerable distances to see their former local leader as pontiff. He pointed out individual members of each delegation whom he recognized and had cheerful personal remarks for each. Both he and the members of the assemblies were overjoyed.

Another visitor arrived, the pope's longtime physician, Antonio Da Ros. Whether this was a social or medical call is not clear. On two other occasions, the doctor traveled a long distance to visit John Paul, who had not yet been assigned to a Vatican physician.

Silvio Luciani, who had immigrated to America fifty years before, returned to Italy to attend his cousin's investiture. He did not arrive at the Vatican in time to participate in the gathering that John Paul hosted for his family members, but he and his daughter received communion directly from the pope at his inaugural Mass.[4]

Born in the same town as the pope, Silvio was the son of the pope's paternal uncle. The elder cousin recalled his impression of the pope when he was young, describing him as "a small, smiling boy with big eyes." Because of their significant age difference, Silvio being some fourteen years older, the two men had barely known each other. Silvio had immigrated to the United States when Albino entered the minor seminary.[5] Nevertheless, they had met in Italy on three previous occasions. Silvio said of his cousin the pope, "He is Christ-like. When we had dinner with him, there was little we had in common to talk about. But it was the little things, his concern, the real kindness was there in his eyes and face." Their last meeting had taken place in Venice two years before.[6]

The elder Luciani claimed that in 1976 he had predicted his cousin would be elected pope. "I've been telling people around here the last two years, but nobody would take me seriously. They never heard of my cousin. But they heard about him today," he said proudly on August 26. "Oh, my arms and legs were shaking when they said Albino Luciani was the new pope," he told a reporter.[7]

Saint Gregory the Great

At noon John Paul noted in his Angelus remarks that he was officially beginning his pontificate on the date that Saint Gregory the Great had been elected pope. His distant predecessor was significant to him for a few reasons: the seminary in which John Paul had studied for seven years and remained as a professor for twenty more was named after Saint Gregory. Like John Paul, Saint Gregory did not want to be pope, and he noted that even then the papacy was a burden. He reminded his audience that he needed their prayers.[8]

The Tradition of Monarchical Ceremonies

In effect, a man becomes pope the moment he accepts his election, but his pontificate does not officially begin until he is inaugurated. It is an almost indispensable formality for a man assuming an office as noteworthy as the papacy. As such, John Paul recognized the importance of retaining the initiation rite, but he would do it his way: stripping it of its regal features.

The coronation of popes was a centuries-old tradition. The ostentatious papal tiara originally had been worn by Persian and Babylonian kings. Its use by newly elected popes dates to Pope Constantine in the early eighth century,[9] signifying the supreme pontiff's secular as well as ecclesiastical authority. Because modern vicars of Christ no longer wielded temporal power, a coronation seemed inappropriate, yet the practice continued until 1963 with the investiture of Pope Paul VI. The practice was also unseemly. Jesus had worn a crown of thorns; how improper, then, for his vicar on earth to adorn himself with a symbol of wealth.

Traditional papal coronation ceremonies had other majestic aspects. Like a conquering king of old in triumphant procession before his adoring subjects, the pope sat on his ornate portable throne (known as the *sedia gestatoria*), which was hoisted on the shoulders of formally clad underlings. He was accompanied by other attendants who carried ostentatious ostrich feathers shaped in half-moons. The triple tiara awaited the pope on the altar. Proceeding to a high-backed throne positioned prominently on a temporary stage, the pope sat with his head bowed, and the beehive-shaped crown was ceremonially placed on his head. At the conclusion of the event, the crowned pope, once again settled in the *sedia gestatoria*, departed, acknowledging the adoring crowds by blessing them.[10]

Terminating Traditions

John Paul eliminated hallmarks of the traditional rite, most notably the crowning but also the fanfare. It was inconsistent not only with his modesty but with his view of the papacy as one of service. In dispensing with this time-honored custom, he insisted simply on celebrating an installation Mass outside the basilica.[11] "He abolished the 1,000-year-old ceremony with the tiara and relegated it permanently to the trash heap. It will be impossible to go back to this triumphalism of the past," noted Church historian John Jay Hughes.[12] He was right: John Paul's successors followed his example.

St. Peter's Square Transformed

Nearly ten thousand law enforcement officers were present to protect dignitaries and secure the site.[13] The pope had been in office just over a week and yet his life had already been threatened.[14] Prior to the commencement of the ceremony, violence broke out between demonstrators and the police. The protesters opposed the presence of delegations from repressive South American governments. In particular, their anger was directed at strongman Jorge Videla, president of Argentina. Videla was responsible for countless human rights abuses, including widespread political arrests, imprisonment, torture, and executions of suspected dissidents.[15]

Almost 120,000 people assembled in St. Peter's Square to witness the new pope's historic installation. Dignitaries galore occupied reserved seats in a section to the side of the altar. Among them were kings and queens, presidents, prime ministers, ambassadors, and religious authorities of non-Catholic denominations.[16] In the front row sat the pope's siblings, their children and grandchildren numbering about forty behind them. "The whole world is here," Vatican Radio announced hyperbolically.[17]

Before the proceedings began, Luciani visited the tomb of Saint Peter, considered to be the first pope, whose bones are interred beneath the main altar of the basilica. Giovanni Lucchetta, a priest from Luciani's region who had predicted his election, was surprised by what he saw as a portent in the sky. Writing to the archpriest of Canale he described the sign, a rainbow appearing though it didn't rain.[18]

The public function began shortly after the pope's supplications at the tomb concluded. Preceding the pope out of the basilica were most of the cardinals. Then, wearing a tall, elaborate miter and clad in splendid gold vestments decorated with red crosses, the pope entered the square on foot. As soon as he appeared, he was greeted by vigorous applause, the jubilant clanging of the bells of St. Peter's, and the Sistine Chapel choir singing the Litany of the Saints. In his left hand, John Paul held a simple silver crozier, the staff of a bishop, symbolic of a shepherd's crook and a sign of a bishop's pastoral authority. John Paul's was topped by a small crucifix, the crossbeam slightly curved downward, from which hung the emaciated body of Christ, his arms hideously elongated to emphasize his excruciating suffering.

The pope walked to a temporary, pyramidal-shaped stage atop five steps that allowed the guests to view the new pontiff, who sat placidly in a high-backed, unadorned chair facing the altar and the attendees. The cardinals arranged themselves on either side of the altar; behind them sat an assembly of bishops. The service was elegant in its simplicity.[19]

Making It Official

Figure 5.1. His zucchetto characteristically askew, Pope John Paul I receives the pallium from Cardinal Pericle Felici at his installation ceremony.

Pericle Felici, the senior cardinal deacon, had the honor of adorning the pope with the pallium that represented the episcopal authority of the Church. Felici approached the solemn-looking pope and draped the strip of white lamb's wool over his collarbone. It was ornamented with a half dozen black crosses, as it had, since at least the fourth century. The choir erupted into the "*Tue es Petrus*," Latin for "Thou art Peter." And so, it was done. John Paul now wore the simple symbol of his status as the vicar of Christ. Rather than being a religious monarch, he would be the humble shepherd of a global flock.[20]

Princes of the Church in Procession

Figure 5.2. The archbishop of Kraków, Poland, Cardinal Karol Wojtyla, who was to succeed Luciani only a few weeks later and take the name John Paul II in his honor, pays obeisance to the new pontiff.

Then the gilded clad cardinals in their flowing garments formed a long line and individually approached the pope, knelt and kissed both his cheeks as a sign of peace. To each, a beaming John Paul shared a few private words. When his two immediate successors, Cardinals Karol Wojtyla and Joseph Ratzinger, paid their obeisance, no one suspected what lay in store for them.[21]

Curiously, when Wojtyla approached, he whispered something in the pope's ear, eliciting a smile, and the two talked briefly. Wojtyla kissed John Paul's hands twice in quick succession after exchanging the kiss of peace. Then John Paul leaned in close, forehead touching forehead. Wojtyla listened to the pope's words and then nodded. What the pope whispered to the man who would replace him in a mere month is lost to history. The official Vatican photograph was later released with the title, "The secret of two popes."[22] As the Pole rose to leave, John Paul, still clasping one of the cardinal's hands with his left, clenched his right fist and gently tapped his heart twice—the very heart that would stop beating twenty-three days hence and shortly thereafter result in Wojtyla's surprise election as Pope John Paul II.[23]

Humility with a Twist on Display

Unlike his relaxed talks at general audiences, on this occasion the pope read a formal address. There was another difference: he used "we" instead of "I."[24] Perhaps he thought the occasion called for it because he and his flock were now formally joined as one Church. Yet it seemed out of character, especially on an occasion that he insisted should be unassuming.

The pope began speaking in Latin (the official language of the Church), segued to Italian, then French (still the international language at the time), and finished in his native Italian. He echoed publicly, without embarrassment, his continued perplexity regarding his election: "God has raised us to the Chair of blessed Peter by his own design, which human reasoning cannot explain. The words of Saint Paul the Apostle come spontaneously to our lips: 'How unsearchable are his judgments and how inscrutable his ways!'"[25]

John Paul already was implementing his plan to use the mass media to communicate with the world: "[W]e embrace" those that are "watching us and listening to us at this moment through the modern media of social communication."[26]

He was all inclusive in his welcome, pointedly embracing non-Catholics and hinting that in some ways he was more of a sibling than a father to them all: "We greet all . . . We regard them and love them as our brothers and sisters."[27]

His papal motto being *Humilitas*, the pope again demonstrated the remarkable humility that had gained him such ardent admiration: "With surprised and understandable trepidation, but also with immense trust in the powerful grace of God and the ardent prayer of the Church, we have agreed to become Peter's Successor in the See of Rome, taking on us the yoke that Christ has wished to place on our fragile shoulders."[28]

He acknowledged with gratitude the outpouring of love for him by millions: "From the moment we were elected throughout the days that followed, we were deeply struck and encouraged by the warm manifestations of affection given . . . by those sending us from all over the world the expression of their irrepressible jubilation."[29]

The pope once more emphasized his ambition to establish dialogue with other denominations to achieve unity among all Christians; "we think . . . of all those who endeavor to be disciples of Jesus Christ, to honor God, and to work for the good of humanity . . . we greet affectionately and with gratitude Brethren not yet in full communion."[30]

During the Mass the epistle was sung in Latin and the gospel in Greek. Other readings from Scripture were delivered in nine different languages. After the consecration of the host and wine, Felici administered Communion to the pope before John Paul did the same to his relatives. Two hundred priests fanned out into the square to distribute Communion to the crowd.[31]

Leave-Taking

Felici delivered the benediction in Latin. No one could discern the irony of his words: "May you reign gloriously through many years of earthly light until, called by your Lord, you will be reclothed with the stole of immortality in the Kingdom of Heaven."[32] How surprisingly soon the Almighty would provide John Paul his eternal garments.

As the Mass proceeded, St. Peter's was slowly enveloped in the blanket of twilight; the ceremony reaching its culmination in harmony with the setting sun as if it had been choreographed. With dusk descending on the square, the pope blessed those assembled, and another flood of applause swept the square.[33] John Paul turned toward the basilica, again on foot, with the cardinals in tow. The unique ceremony was over, and the Church itself would never again be quite the same. Inside St. Peter's, the cardinals crowded around the pope, glee bursting forth on every countenance. All were eager to touch him just one more time as if to reassure themselves that John Paul was not a mere illusion. They were convinced that they had chosen the best among them.[34]

DAY 9/MONDAY, SEPTEMBER 4

The pope delivered a speech in flawless French about the nature of Vatican diplomacy to delegations of statesmen who were in Rome for his investiture. He informed them that the Vatican was preeminently concerned with "the human causes that the temporal power is intended to advance."[35] Subsequently, John Paul held private audiences with heads of state.[36]

He also met with a group of Italian bishops followed by a private audience with Cardinal Bernadin Gantin, president of the Pontifical Commission for Justice and Peace.[37]

DAY 10/TUESDAY, SEPTEMBER 5

Portent: A Fatal Meeting

The pope had a private audience with Nikodim, the Orthodox metropolitan of Leningrad.[38] It was a highly anticipated meeting. Nikodim was an open-minded man, someone John Paul believed he could count on as a partner to foster unity within Christianity. As an advocate of ecumenism, he had established contacts with the Catholic Church.[39] Nikodim also expressed his hope for the continued development of positive relations between the two churches, which had begun under Pope John XXIII, even to the point of joint service in the pursuit of peace in the world. Without warning, Nikodim suddenly collapsed into the pope's arms. He died instantly of a massive heart attack, foreshadowing John Paul's own fatal coronary just three weeks later. Nikodim lay on the floor with his eyes partially open. The pope knelt and gave him absolution in Latin. Shortly thereafter a doctor arrived and declared Nikodim dead. "My God, my God, even this has to happen to me," the pope exclaimed.[40]

This spontaneous reaction by the Holy Father revealed his continuing unease with what had happened to him in the Sistine Chapel less than two weeks before. It was a lamentation that bordered on self-pity. Despite this emotional outburst, however, John Paul, demonstrating amazing self-discipline, quickly composed himself and adhered to the remainder of his schedule. Other delegations were waiting to see him, and he was determined to fulfill his commitment to them. He subsequently met with the apostolic nuncios to Thailand, Sri Lanka, and Australia before conferring with high-level government officials from Brazil and Egypt.[41]

He sent a telegram of sympathy to Patriarch Pimen and met with a Russian delegation, just two days later, in the same room where the metropolitan had been stricken with his sixth and fatal heart attack.[42] In a public statement John Paul spoke of his conversation without revealing any details. "Two days ago, Metropolitan Nikodim of Petersburg died in my arms. I was answering his address. I assure you that in my life I have never heard such fine words for the Church as those spoken by him. I cannot repeat them, it remains a secret. Truly I was impressed . . . I believe he suffered a lot for the Church."[43]

DAY 11/WEDNESDAY, SEPTEMBER 6

First General Audience: Humility

Figure 5.3. The new pope entering Nervi Hall on foot for his first general audience.

The pope walked down the central aisle of the cavernous Nervi Hall to the roar of the attendees. Another first—no riding on a portable throne. He was grinning, always grinning, and surrounded by a sea of faithful enraptured by his presence. John Paul was greeted by twelve thousand giddy visitors hoping to catch a glimpse of the bishop in white. But he was relatively short and surrounded by bishops and monsignors, most of them taller than he. Consequently, only those fortunate enough to have an aisle seat could see him. The others strained unsuccessfully. He exchanged pleasantries and clasped the hands of hundreds (a pope shaking hands was also a novelty) in the half hour it took him to wend his way to the stage. Before taking his place on a high-back wing chair on center stage, he faced the audience and joyously lifted both arms spread apart, then clasped his hands before tentatively waving in a self-conscious manner. His shyness seemed to have been transformed into embarrassment because of the adulation that he was receiving. Yet his smile lit up the auditorium. Also on stage with him were some one hundred bishops and forty cardinals.[44]

His formal talk—though delivered informally—was titled "God, Neighbor, and Ourselves." John Paul spoke animatedly, with fervor, and without notes; yet the talk was seamless. His "extemporaneous" speeches were painstakingly prepared, and he memorized verbatim what he had written in advance.

A New Form of Papal Talk

From the outset the pope held his audience captive. He began by paying tribute to Pope Paul: "I will try to imitate him in the hope that I, too, will be able, somehow, to help people to become better." "We must feel small before God," he asserted. "When I say, 'Lord, I believe,' I am not ashamed to feel like a child before his mother. One believes in one's mother. I believe in the Lord, in what He has revealed to me."[45]

He followed with homey stories, including one from Andrew Carnegie that amused and instructed at the same time. (This was yet another departure from the staid discourses that popes delivered at their general audiences.) John Paul was a master at immediately capturing the interest of his listeners and then regaling them with sometimes humorous but illuminating anecdotes that captivated them. He had been so all his adult life. The only difference now was that he had the entire world for an audience. Magee, among others, was impressed.

The pope made an implicit comparison between Carnegie's poverty in his early life with his own. Carnegie once said, "I was born in poverty, but I would not exchange the memories of my childhood with those of a millionaire's children. What do they know of family joys, of the sweet figure of a mother who combines the duties of nurse, washerwoman, cook, teacher, angel, and saint?"[46]

Then John Paul surprised the assembly again by calling a young Maltese altar boy named James De Bono to the stage. The pope as a priest and bishop had done this a thousand times before. But this audience wasn't aware of that.

James stood to the pope's left, John Paul holding his hand. The boy was visibly nervous and responded to the pope's questions hesitantly, in a barely audible voice. Thus went the chat:

"James . . . have you ever been ill?"

"No."

"Ah, never?"

"No."

"Never been ill?"

"No."

"Not even a temperature?"

"No."

"Oh, how lucky you are!" (And the pope laughed good-naturedly before guiding the boy.) "But when a child is ill, who brings him a little broth, some medicine? Isn't it his mother? Afterwards you grow up, and your mother gets old . . . and your mother, poor thing, will be in bed, ill. Well, who will bring the mother a little milk and medicine?"

"My brothers and I."

"Well said! I like that."

And with a smile, the pope patted the boy's head. The audience was both amused and charmed by the exchange. No pope in memory had ever sought to illustrate a point by having a conversation with a child.

John Paul then reinforced the need for people to show compassion with a story of his own.

"As Bishop of Venice, I sometimes went to homes. Once I found an elderly woman, sick."

"How are you?"

"Well, the food is all right!"

"Are you warm? Is there heating?"

"It's good."

"So, you are content?"

"No." She almost began to cry.

"But why are you crying?"

"My daughter-in-law, my son, never come to see me. I would like to see my grandchildren."

The pope had clearly conveyed his message. But he wasn't finished.

"As bishop, I was very close even to those who do not believe in God," he admitted. And then the Holy Father arrived at the heart of his message: the need for people to become humble. In doing so he made a controversial assertion: "I will just recommend one virtue so dear to the Lord. He said, 'Learn from me who am meek and humble of heart.' I run the risk of making a blunder, but I will say it: the Lord loves humility so much that, sometimes, he permits serious sins. Why? In order that those who committed these sins may, after repenting, remain humble."

His official message concluded, John Paul offered a compliment to a group in attendance and a plea to the entire audience. To members of the Seventh International Congress of the Organ Transplant Society, "We owe a special greeting . . . We pray to God, the Author of life, to inspire you and assist you in these magnificent and formidable responsibilities." Although the Church was not opposed to organ transplants, its support was conditional.

And before departing, a plea for peace: "Now, if you permit, I should like to invite you to join with me in prayer for an intention that I have much at heart . . . the success of the Camp David meeting: that these talks may pave the way towards a full and just peace."[47]

DAY 12/THURSDAY, SEPTEMBER 7

This day's schedule would test the pope's stamina: a speech and meetings with patriarchs of Eastern Rites, Rome's vicar general, and a philologist.[48]

Straight Talk from a Gentle Man

As the bishop of Rome, the pope wanted to become familiar with the sprawling diocese. He was happy with the briefing he received from the bishops and had much to say to the Roman clergy, especially about their responsibilities, particularly when they were unhappy with their circumstances. John Paul referred to the priests in the hall as his brothers. He admitted to not knowing many among those in attendance, but he pointed out a couple whose acquaintance he had made decades earlier and said good-naturedly, "I hope I did not give them a bad example in those years."

And then came the hard lessons he wished to imprint on them. Alluding to bishops, including himself, the pope quoted St. Augustine, saying, "[W]e bishops preside, if we serve" and that the same applied to priests. He impressed upon the clergy in attendance that they must "dialogue with God without forgetting men and to dialogue with men without forgetting God."

The priesthood required discipline, he preached, and that meant sacrificing one's personal wishes for the greater good of the flock and the Church. Even priests are not always happy in their vocation, he acknowledged. "Apart from those who are fully resigned to God's will, everyone would like to change his own condition to that of others," the pope observed.

He warned, "[L]et the pastor avoid the temptation to desire to be loved by the faithful instead of by God or to be too weak for fear of losing the affection of men . . . I have been a bishop for 20 years: I confess to you, several times I have suffered, really suffered, from not being able to reward someone, who really deserved it; but, either there was a lack of a place or I did not know how to replace the person or adverse circumstances arose."

Fearing that he had spoken too long, the pope was almost apologetic toward the end. "Another component—and I'm done, don't be afraid—of priestly discipline is the love of one's place. I know: it's not easy to love the place and stay in it when things are not going well, when you feel like you are not understood or encouraged . . . But don't we work for the Lord? Do we not work for the Church?" He concluded on a positive note: "I can assure you that since I became your bishop I love you very much. And it is with a heart full of love that I impart to you the Apostolic Blessing."[49]

He also had an audience with Cardinal Ugo Poletti, the vicar of Rome.[50] Because Poletti, in this official capacity, was responsible for managing the day-to-day activities of the Vatican City State, the two men presumably discussed practical matters. Whether the conversation also included a report on some initiative or a tutorial on the functioning of the bureaucracy is unknown.

Forging ahead with his plans for eventually uniting the Church, John Paul met with patriarchs of three Eastern rites: Armenian, Chaldean, and Maronite.[51] Their differences were significant and difficult to resolve. Issues relative to the Holy Spirit and the pope having supreme authority were partly responsible for the divide, but beyond those differences, practices including divorce and married priests posed further complications. The various hurdles toward unification demanded ongoing, forthright discourse and, eventually, mutual concessions. Unification, if possible, lay in the future, perhaps the distant future. Neither side expected a quick resolution, but John Paul had taken the first step in the process.

Interestingly, the pope also met privately with Vittore Branca, a philologist—an authority on the history of language.[52] Branca was a prominent professor at several universities. He had dedicated much of his life to the study of Boccaccio, the famous Italian author of *The Decameron*, and was known for his many translations. Branca oversaw numerous book collections and magazines and presided over many cultural organizations.[53] The pope's wide reading and his fondness for Italian culture and Italian authors likely prompted this meeting, which must have been a source of intellectual satisfaction for him.

DAY 13/FRIDAY, SEPTEMBER 8

On this day and the next, the pope worked in the privacy of the Apostolic Palace. The Holy Father led an intense prayer life. In addition to celebrating morning Mass each day, he devoted hours to silent prayer and recitation of the rosary. It's likely that when his schedule was light, he devoted even more substantial time to praying, reading, and writing. Also, he still had much to learn about his new role and undoubtedly reserved time to further his practical knowledge on how to manage the bureaucracy.

John Paul commissioned Cardinal Johannes Willebrands, president of the Pontifical Council for Promoting Christian Unity, to represent him at Metropolitan Nikodim's funeral in the Soviet Union.[54] Demonstrating his interest in reaching out to all peoples of the world, the pope had an audience with the apostolic nuncio in Pakistan, an overwhelmingly Muslim country.[55] In the evening, he hosted Cardinal Antonio Poma, president of the Italian Bishops' Conference, for dinner.[56] It was during meals that John Paul most enjoyed conversation. The pope also wrote a letter celebrating the eighty-fifth German *Katholikentag*.[57]

DAY 14/SATURDAY, SEPTEMBER 9

No official audiences appeared on the pope's calendar on this day. The only recorded activity he engaged in was sending a message of gratitude and congratulations to Cardinal Silvio Oddi in commemoration of the twenty-fifth anniversary of his ordination.[58]

DAY 15/SUNDAY, SEPTEMBER 10

Angelus and Courting Controversy

As was traditional for delivery of the weekly Angelus, John Paul spoke from his study window on the third floor of the Apostolic Palace to an overflow crowd assembled in the piazza. Once again, he talked fervently without referring to notes, both of his hands braced on the windowsill. Peace was on his mind.

"At Camp David, in America, Presidents Carter and Sadat and Prime Minister Begin are working for peace in the Middle East. All men are hungry and thirsty for peace, especially the poor, who pay more and suffer more in troubled times and in wars." Deeply concerned about the need for peace in the Holy Land, the pope again urged his flock to pray for the success of the Camp David talks that the American president was mediating between two neighbors whose enmity was ancient: Israel and Egypt. (The talks did succeed, leading to a historic accord between the former enemies.) In speaking of the three leaders, the pope quoted from the Old and New Testaments as well as from the Koran. (For a pope to recite a passage from the sacred book of Muslims was highly unusual.)

Then he spoke of God's love: "[W]e are the objects of undying love on the part of God. We know: he always has his eyes open on us, even when it seems to be dark. He is our father; even more he is our mother . . . He wants only to do good to us, to all of us.[59] If children are ill, they have additional claim to be loved by their mother. And we too, if by chance we are sick with badness, on the wrong track, have yet another claim to be loved by the Lord."[60]

The reference to God as a mother was a risky thing to say; there is no "God, the Mother" in the Holy Trinity. Some within the Vatican hierarchy would find this assertion foolish or improper. People, particularly archconservatives, might even interpret this as apostasy. Yet John Paul used the metaphor deliberately. Nothing is more tender than the love of a mother for her children. How appropriate, then, for God's love for His children to be described in this way. It was a surprising, even startling, statement but one that caused many of his listeners to understand the Lord's love in a more profound way.

The smiling pope was breaking barriers, reaching people and teaching them. They were listening intently and responding positively. His personality drew people of all sorts to him: heads of state, high-ranking clergy, persons of other faiths, atheists and agnostics, workers, serious sinners, the disillusioned, just about everyone. Already he was changing lives for the better by his personal example, the power of his words, and the appeal of his beliefs. The possibilities for what he could accomplish in the years ahead seemed almost without limit.

DAY 16/SEPTEMBER 11

On this day, classified details about what had transpired in the conclave that elected Albino Luciani were published in a highly respected magazine with a worldwide circulation. *Time* ran a cover story titled "How Pope John Paul I Won," in which it revealed privileged information about the events that had occurred within the confines of the Sistine Chapel and the portions of the Apostolic Palace where the electors dined and slept.[61]

Despite all the precautions taken to ensure the confidentiality of the conclave's proceedings, several cardinals in their exuberance over the election's winner made indiscreet revelations to reporters. Others who were present to assist the electors overheard at least snippets of conversations among the cardinals and undoubtedly couldn't resist revealing secrets of the proceedings.

All cardinals participating in the conclave had sworn an oath of secrecy in which they solemnly agreed to protect the "secrecy regarding everything that in any way relates to the election of the Roman Pontiff and regarding what occurs in the place of the election."[62] Those who violated their oaths did so at great peril (at least in theory), for excommunication was the prescribed penalty for anyone divulging what transpired though, with the cardinal electors at least, it is difficult to imagine how that punishment could have been imposed.[63] Ironically, John Paul himself in his first public remarks the day following his election shared private details.

The ruckus that resulted from the revelations among some in the Vatican had no apparent impact on the pope, who adhered to his typical daily schedule. He consulted with the cardinal archbishop of Guatemala,[64] a poor nation in Central America with a large Catholic population. Because of the Holy Father's conviction that the rich nations of the world, along with the church itself, had an obligation to help reduce poverty wherever it was rampant, he often granted audiences to numerous emissaries from the Third World. Doing so provided him with knowledge that would help shape the policies he would implement to provide succor to the suffering people of those countries.

He also met with the general secretary of the Synod of Bishops and the apostolic nuncio to Spain.[65] As a bishop, John Paul had participated in synods (assemblies to discuss issues of significance in the Church) and recognized their value. The pope also intended to familiarize himself with the status of the church globally, and he thought it imperative to learn as much as he could about the political and religious climate in as many nations as possible. Not having traveled widely prior to assuming the papacy, John Paul had a paucity of personal knowledge about the internal affairs of most countries around the world. He would rely on discussions and briefings with heads of state, ambassadors, papal nuncios, as well as bishops to develop a degree of expertise that would inform his decisions. Papal nuncios are repositories of knowledge about the countries to which they are assigned by the pope. In effect they serve as ambassadors to nations that maintain official diplomatic relations with the Holy See. Their responsibilities include promoting reliable relations between the government and the Vatican and reporting to the pope on the condition of the Church in their respective countries.[66]

In addition to his audiences, the pontiff appointed a new director of the Vatican Museums.[67] This was not an insignificant act. The museums house a collection of some seventy thousand artistic masterpieces, twenty thousand of which are displayed to the public. They include famous Roman and Renaissance artistic masterpieces collected over centuries.[68]

DAY 17/SEPTEMBER 12

On the one-month anniversary of his predecessor's funeral, John Paul descended into the grottoes of St. Peter's to pray at Pope Paul's burial site.[69] Paul was on his mind; the pope had previously noted publicly how the late pontiff had suffered for the Church, and now John Paul had inherited the crushing burdens that had caused Pope Paul such anguish.

The Holy Father launched other initiatives on this day. For the first time, the new pope acted on behalf of the Vatican in foreign affairs. He opened diplomatic relations with the Fiji Islands by creating an Apostolic Nunciature there despite its small number of Catholics, which consisted of less than 10 percent of the entire populace. Most of the inhabitants were Christian (primarily Methodists), but there were also Hindus and Muslims among them. Establishing closer ties with the people there would provide opportunities for evangelization.[70]

At a private audience with John Paul, Cardinal Mario Casariego of Guatemala invited the pope to visit his country in 1979. Although the Holy Father expressed his appreciation, he made no commitment. He was still an apprentice pope who had to master the intricacies of his job before traveling to foreign countries.[71] Subsequently, he was briefed about conditions in two other nations of interest. He met with the apostolic nuncios to India and Rwanda, continuing his education about far-off lands in all parts of the world.[72]

Ugo Poletti, Rome's vicar general, called on the pope to discuss matters relating to the Vatican. John Paul was getting acquainted both with the leaders of the church and the issues of paramount importance to the institution. As the figure who oversaw the daily operations of the Vatican City State, the vicar general was an indispensable source of essential information.[73]

DAY 18/SEPTEMBER 13

The Holy Father received another visit from Dr. Da Ros, the second in ten days. It is reasonable to conclude that the physician, who was intimately familiar with the Holy Father's health history, made the trip to examine his patient. Perhaps he wanted to check on John Paul's swollen ankles, an ongoing concern of his. No longer in close proximity to the pontiff, Da Ros could not ascertain from afar whether the walking regimen he had prescribed was being followed, and, if so, whether it was having the desired effect.

The pope also met privately with the metropolitans of the Orthodox Church of Cyprus. Then he hosted the treasurer of the archdiocese of Venice for lunch. He was relieved to see crates of his books and personal papers finally arrive from Venice.[74] Then he was off to teach and preach.

USING THE THRONE AT A GENERAL AUDIENCE

John Paul made what for him was a major concession at his second general audience: he reversed his decision to abandon use of the ornate *sedia gestatoria*.[75] An ostentatious symbol of the majestic papacy of yore, the portable throne was incompatible with the pope's papal motto, *Humilitas*. The tradition of being carried on the chair, which he had originally discarded, stretched back more than a millennium.[76] For the remainder of his papacy, he, like his predecessors, would be transported on the shoulders of twelve attendants known as *sediari*, the Italian word for chair bearers. His reluctance to use the throne, though, was an act of humility; he was simply responding to the letters of disappointed spectators who entreated him to use it because they had been unable to see him as he walked down the aisle at the previous general audience. To please them, he put aside his distaste for this method of transport and never publicly complained about it.[77]

As he entered the packed Nervi Hall, he was greeted with a hearty ovation by an ecstatic crowd. Flashes from cameras sparkled like shooting stars from all directions while people waved white handkerchiefs and hats. As he was carried down the central aisle, the smiling pope turned from side to side alternately waving and blessing the throng.[78]

After the *sediari* lowered the throne, John Paul climbed the steps to the platform from which he would deliver his address. Lorenzi, this time, sat to the pope's right. During the talk Lorenzi looked bored, as if he had heard this spiel before, and perhaps he had, because the pope was fond of recycling prior talks. Lorenzi alternately looked up at the ceiling, then down in his lap. The other accompanying prelates stared straight ahead as the pope spoke again extemporaneously and with passion.[79]

At this audience the pope wanted to focus on the virtue of faith. He began self-deprecatingly as he laughed, "Who knows if the Holy Spirit will help the poor pope today?" Then he told amusing stories about the Italian poet Trilussa, Saint Paul, Pope John XXIII, and Augustine to drive home his message about faith.

As always, his homely homily reached the simple as well as the sophisticated. He defined faith as "surrendering to God, by transforming our own lives. Something that is not always easy." His clear message was that humans are capable of moral improvement so long as they have faith.

Hearkening back to previous Church scandals and presaging the paroxysm of future sex scandals involving countless priests and bishops that would rock the Church, the pope asserted, "Christ is good; the Church must also be good; she must be a mother to everyone. But what if by chance there should sometimes be some wicked people in the Church . . . even if in the Church there are—and sometimes there are—some defects and some failings, our affection for the Church must never fail . . . Let us try to improve the Church by becoming better ourselves."

The pope didn't minimize the obstacles to maintaining faith. "It is also difficult to accept some truths, because the truths of faith are of two kinds; some pleasant, others unpalatable to our spirit. For example, it is pleasant to hear that God has so much tenderness for us, even more tenderness than a mother has for her children, as Isaiah says. How pleasant and congenial it is . . . Other truths, on the contrary, are hard to accept. God must punish, if I resist. He runs after me; he begs me to repent and I say: 'No!' I almost force him to punish me. This is not agreeable. But it is a truth of faith.

"We must accept the Church, as she is . . . When the poor Pope, when the bishops, the priests, propose the doctrine, they are merely helping Christ. It is not our doctrine, it is Christ's; we must just guard it and present it . . . The first thing I did, as soon as I was made Pope, was to enter the private Chapel of the Pontifical Household. Right at the back Pope Paul had two mosaics made . . . St. Peter dying, St. Paul dying. But under St. Peter are the words of Jesus: 'I will pray for you, Peter, that your faith may never fail.' Under St. Paul, on whom the sword falls: 'I have run my race, I have kept the faith.'"

Then he turned personal, invoking his mother's words. "My mother used to tell me when I was a boy: 'When you were little, you were very ill. I had to take you from one doctor to another and watch over you whole nights; do you believe me?' How could I have said: 'I don't believe you, Mamma? Of course I believe, I believe what you tell me, but I believe especially in you.'" A readily understandable example of faith.

"The Church is also a mother . . . if by chance there should sometimes be bad people in the Church? We have our mother. If mother is sick, if my mother by chance should become lame, I love her even more. It is the same, in the Church. If there are, and there are, defects and shortcomings, our affection for the Church must never fail."[80]

Shortly before the end of his talk, as if he felt he was imposing on the time of his listeners, he reassured them that his brief discourse was nearly done.[81]

At the conclusion of his formal remarks, he had words of encouragement for the sick in attendance, and he congratulated some newlyweds there, drawing laughs by telling a story in which marriage was described as a snare.[82] Then, more seriously, he said of the couples, "They have received a great sacrament. Let us wish that this sacrament which they have received will really bring not only goods of this world, but more spiritual graces . . . marriage is not a trap, it is a great sacrament!"[83]

He hadn't lost his touch in connecting with the faithful in ways that were meaningful to their lives.

NOTES

1. John Magee (bishop emeritus of diocese of Cloyne, Ireland), in discussion with the author, Cobh, Ireland, February 17, 2010.

2. Don Diego Lorenzi, "Giovanni Paolo I: nel Ricordo di Don Diego Lorenzi," *Messaggi di Don Orione*, 2000, 63.
3. Mo Guernon, "The Forgotten Pope," *America: National Weekly*, October 24, 2011, 19.
4. "American Cousin Recalls Pope as a 'Smiling Boy,'" *Toledo Blade*, September 3, 1978, 1.
5. "American Cousin Recalls Pope as a 'Smiling Boy,'" 1.
6. "Cousin Predicted Pope's Election," *Argus Press*, August 28, 1978, 2.
7. "American Cousin Recalls Pope as a 'Smiling Boy,'" 1.
8. Speech delivered prior to Sunday Angelus, September 3, 1978. Collection of recordings of the original speeches and statements of Blessed Pope John Paul I of the Archives of the Foundation Papa Luciani of Canale d'Agordo (Belluno-Italy).
9. Joseph Braun, "Tiara," *Catholic Encyclopedia*, vol. 14 (New York: Appleton, 1912), http://www.newadvent.org/cathen/14714c.htm.
10. "Coronation of Pope Paul VI," *Caeremoniale Romanum*, video, 59:01, https://www.youtube.com/watch?v=KNOedla1cm4.
11. Gordon Thomas and Max Morgan-Witts, *Pontiff* (New York: New American Library, 1984), 260.
12. "The September Pope," *Time*, October 9, 1978, 79.
13. "John Paul I Inaugurates Reign," *Bangor Daily News*, September 4, 1978, 1.
14. Thomas and Morgan-Witts, *Pontiff*, 267.
15. Fr. Victor Feltes, "Inauguration Day September 3," Pope John Paul I Papacy—Day by Day, johnpauli.wordpress.com.
16. "John Paul I Inaugurates Reign," *Bangor Daily News*, 2.
17. Thomas and Morgan-Witts, *Pontiff*, 261.
18. Loris Serafini (director, Foundation Papa Luciani and Museum Albino Luciani of Canale d'Agordo), in discussion with the author, Gloucester, Rhode Island, October 12, 2012.
19. "The Papal Inauguration Mass of John Paul I," *Caeremoniale Romanum*, video, 4:35, https://www.youtube.com/watch?v=6Pjb7mDK4GI.
20. "Papal Inauguration."
21. "Papal Inauguration."
22. Serafini, discussion.
23. "Papal Inauguration."
24. Homily delivered at the Initiation Mass, September 3, 1978. Collection of recordings of the original speeches and statements of Blessed Pope John Paul I of the Archives of the Foundation Papa Luciani of Canale d'Agordo (Belluno-Italy).
25. Homily.
26. Homily.
27. Homily.
28. Homily.
29. Homily.
30. Homily.
31. Paul Spackman, *God's Candidate: The Life and Times of Pope John Paul I* (Herefordshire: Gracewing, 2008), 166.

32. Spackman, *God's Candidate*, 164–65.
33. Raymond and Lauretta Seabeck, *The Smiling Pope: The Life and Teaching of John Paul I* (Huntington, IN: Our Sunday Visitor, 2004), 61.
34. Albino Luciani, photo 285JPG, Archives of the Foundation Papa Luciani of Canale d'Agordo (Belluno-Italy).
35. Speech delivered to members of official delegations, September 3, 1978. Collection of recordings of the original speeches and statements of Blessed Pope John Paul I of the Archives of the Foundation Papa Luciani of Canale d'Agordo (Belluno-Italy).
36. Spackman, *God's Candidate*, 167.
37. Stefania Falasca, *The September Pope: The Final Days of John Paul I* © 2017, PIEMME; 2020, Libreria Editrice Vaticana. English translation published by *Our Sunday Visitor*, 2021, 159.
38. Falasca, *September Pope*, 159.
39. Spackman, *God's Candidate*, 168–69.
40. Spackman, *God's Candidate*, 169.
41. Falasca, *September Pope*, 159.
42. Spackman, *God's Candidate*, 169–70.
43. "Nights of Sorrow, Days of Joy," National Catholic News Service, 1978, 102.
44. Spackman, *God's Candidate*, 170–71.
45. "General Audience: Humility," September 6, 1978. Collection of recordings of the original speeches and statements of Blessed Pope John Paul I of the Archives of the Foundation Papa Luciani of Canale d'Agordo (Belluno-Italy).
46. "General Audience: Humility."
47. "General Audience: Humility."
48. Falasca, *September Pope*, 159.
49. Conversation with the Roman clergy, September 7, 1978. Collection of recordings of the original speeches and statements of Blessed Pope John Paul I of the Archives of the Foundation Papa Luciani of Canale d'Agordo (Belluno-Italy).
50. Falasca, *September Pope*, 159.
51. Falasca, *September Pope*, 159.
52. Falasca, *September Pope*, 159.
53. "Vittore Branca," Fondazione Giorgio Cini, https://www.cini.it/en/who-whe-are/staff/vittore-branca.
54. Falasca, *September Pope*, 159.
55. Falasca, *September Pope*, 159.
56. Falasca, *September Pope*, 159.
57. Falasca, *September Pope*, 159.
58. Falasca, *September Pope*, 159.
59. Speech delivered prior to Sunday Angelus, September 10, 1978. Collection of recordings of the original speeches and statements by Blessed Pope John Paul I of the Archives of the Foundation Papa Luciani of Canale d'Argordo (Belluno-Italy).
60. Speech delivered prior to Sunday Angelus, September 10, 1978.
61. "Religion: How Pope John Paul Won," *Time*, September 11, 1978, https://content.time.com/time/magazine/article/0,9171,946069,00.html.

62. Nicole Winfield, "Conclave's Rituals, Oaths and Secrecy Explained," *San Diego Union-Tribune*, February 16, 2013.
63. Fr. Victor Feltes, "Telling Time," Pope John Paul Papacy—Day by Day, https://johnpauli.wordpress.com.
64. Falasca, *September Pope*, 160.
65. Falasca, *September Pope*, 160.
66. "Region," *Brittanica*, https://www.britannica.com/topic/nuncio.
67. Falasca, *September Pope*, 160.
68. "Inside Vatican Museum," Detailed Guide, 2024, https://www.thevaticantickets.com/inside-vatican-museums/.
69. Falasca, *September Pope*, 160.
70. "Fiji," Geography and Travel, *Britannica*, https://www.britannica.com/place/Fiji-republic-Pacific-Ocean.
71. Fr. Victor Feltes, "To the Ends of the Earth," Pope John Paul Papacy—Day by Day, https://johnpauli.wordpress.com.
72. Falasca, *September Pope*, 160.
73. Falasca, *September Pope*, 160.
74. Falasca, *September Pope*, 160.
75. "Pontiff Makes Use of Throne," *Sarasota Herald-Tribune*, September 14, 1978, 5A.
76. Serafini, discussion.
77. Fr. Victor Feltes, "Faith in our Mother," Pope John Paul Papacy—Day by Day, https://johnpauli.wordpress.com.
78. Feltes, "Faith in our Mother."
79. John Cornwell, *A Thief in the Night: Life and Death in the Vatican* (New York: Penguin, 1989), 95.
80. "General Audience: Faith," September 13, 1978. Collection of recordings of the original speeches and statements of Blessed Pope John Paul I of the Archives of the Foundation Papa Luciani of Canale d'Agordo (Belluno-Italy).
81. Seabeck, *Smiling Pope*, 102.
82. Seabeck, *Smiling Pope*, 103.
83. "General Audience: Faith."

• 6 •

An Intelligible Intellectual

Talented Teacher and Admired Author (1936–1976)

Albino Luciani possessed a brilliant mind. His powers of analysis were astonishing. His memory was photographic. His knowledge was vast and unfathomable. His wisdom was renowned.

But that was both a blessing and a burden. The advantages were abundant. His intellectual prowess allowed him the pleasure of satisfying his natural curiosity. His ability to recall details, even verbatim passages, was convenient in writing, teaching, and preaching. His capacity to remember the particulars of conversations endeared him to people he encountered. His understanding of innumerable domains of knowledge allowed him to synthesize information and make connections among disparate concepts, to reach a more cohesive view of life and the world. His wisdom provided him astute insights into the human condition, making him a persuasive advocate of the tenets of Christianity. However, being intellectually superior to most also can lead to the deadly sin of pride and a penchant for being condescending toward others who are less rationally formidable. According to Luciani's niece Pia,[1] he was acutely aware of that. His humility, therefore, was a virtue he had to cultivate through daily prayer and practice. Ultimately, he would attribute whatever degree of meekness he acquired to the grace of God. For, as Luciani admitted, conquering pride was a struggle even for him.

Brilliance is not omniscience. Like all mere mortals, Luciani was prone to errors in judgment. He was at times a prisoner of the zeitgeist of his era. But even when he was hampered by a limited vision of social issues, he also seemed prescient at times.

FORESIGHT

Albino Luciani's striking depiction of the perils of his own times often presaged many that would plague the world half a century into the future—and beyond. A small sample of his disturbing observations from the seventies identifies evils that would impede the unadulterated dissemination of truth by a multitude of media in free societies of the twenty-first century, producing a post-fact culture where millions confuse veracity with propaganda to the detriment of society:

> Through the press, radio, television, people do not come into contact with events themselves, but with a version of events, interpreted by different people in different ways. And thus, there is insinuated into the mind the pernicious idea that the truth can never be reached, but only opinion.[2]
>
> [C]ertain hard heads . . . cling to mistaken opinion in the teeth of all evidence to the contrary.[3]
>
> [T]here are those who deliberately set out to deceive with their words . . . and nasty human passions come into play.[4]

For the most part, Luciani was perceptive in his assessment of the prevailing moral, social, political, and religious realities of his age. Some of his written ruminations were ominous. And yet he was no cynic but, rather, a champion of hope. He perceived a fundamental solution to the problems he described: a united humanity guided by God. This remedy was not entirely original; he borrowed the motto expressed by the heroes of *The Three Musketeers*, a novel he had enjoyed in his youth: "All for one and one for all!" Luciani transformed the maxim into a formidable formula. "If we would avoid grave mishaps, the rule must be this . . . Insist on what unites us and forget what divides us."[5] Striving for unity was a guiding principle throughout his life and became the cornerstone of his papal agenda.

Luciani's depth of understanding of the human condition, his unremitting curiosity, his relentless probing of ideas, and his resolute hopefulness—all were evident in both his teaching and writing. To understand the man, then, an exploration of his career as a professor and scribe is essential.

A NATURAL IN THE CLASSROOM

A lover of people and books, Luciani inevitably was drawn to the classroom and to writing. He excelled at both. His training as a teacher and writer began in earnest when he was a new curate, and his expertise in both professions became more sophisticated as he gained experience.

In July of 1937, at the age of twenty-five, Luciani became a professor and vice rector at the Belluno seminary despite his lack of a licentiate in theology, which he would not receive until 1942.[6] The range of courses he taught is illustrative of his unusual breadth and depth of knowledge, particularly for one so young.[7] Luciani sporadically taught a diversity of subjects that few accomplished scholars would dare attempt. They included administration, art history, canon law, catechetics (principles of Christian religion), dogmatics (incontrovertibly true principles), eloquence (preaching), history, liturgy, patristics (early Christian theology), scholastic philosophy, sacred art, and pastoral theology.[8]

A former seminarian under Luciani's guidance described him as a strict disciplinarian but one who stood out from the other teachers for being exceptionally patient and considerate. According to this student, "When I did not understand him in class, I went afterwards to his study to ask for explanations. He always listened to me very willingly, and since he never showed the least sign of impatience with me, I kept going back to him, never dreaming that I might be asking too much or wasting his time."[9]

Luciani enjoyed augmenting his classroom lessons with field trips, especially to acquaint his students with artistic masterpieces, some dating back to ancient Rome. Architecture, frescoes from the sixteenth to the eighteenth centuries, paintings, and sculptures were the objects of fascination, which Luciani shared with his students. He theorized,

> Beauty is not truth, but the radiant expression of truth. One cannot judge the artist only by his technical ability because the artist must have above all, spiritual and moral qualities . . . Art must be neither pure realism, nor exaggerated idealism which devalues truth and sacrifices reality . . . Nature must be seen with the eyes of a poet . . . The artist retouches nature in such a way as to bring it back to that purity and holiness which it had at the beginning of the kingdom of goodness and innocence in which we would all like to live . . . entering into the kingdom of art, each one should become better.[10]

As inspiring a teacher as he was, Luciani did not always succeed in sustaining the interest of all his students. According to one account, he once recommended certain readings about God while some distracted students eagerly awaited recess. He tried personalizing the importance of these books by revealing his own experience. "At your age, when I got these volumes, I read them right through, and I was so struck by them that for some days I was incapable of thinking about anything except God." Not all his seminarians were motivated by this anecdote.[11]

If Luciani felt frustrated by a lack of enthusiasm of some students, it was understandable. Being an intellectual colossus—as he was—could be a curse for an instructor: Students with average intelligence might not share his fascination with certain esoteric subjects; even if they attempted to read about them, their failure to understand the texts could easily lead to frustration. Fortunately for them, Luciani had the gift of explaining in comprehensible terms the most complicated ideas. In later years, many of his students would recollect his talent for explaining intricate concepts that easily facilitated their understanding. They also inevitably recalled his signature virtue, humility, which apparently manifested itself even in the classroom.[12]

Professor Luciani, a realist, at least once gave voice to a version of the adage that education is wasted on the young. "The misfortune of a young student is not so much scant memory as scant willpower."[13] Self-discipline was essential to achieving academic excellence, but he found that was a relatively rare virtue among students.

Luciani devoted twenty-one years to instructing seminarians, leaving in 1958 to become a bishop. Otherwise, it's likely that he would have continued teaching there indefinitely.

But in reality, he would never stop teaching. For the remainder of his life, Luciani instructed a wider audience of all ages via homilies, informal talks, personal conversations, speeches, letters, published newspaper and magazine articles, and books. Even at his general audiences as pope, he was teaching. And he employed his trademark method: speaking informally but with passion; interacting with members of the audience, especially children; sprinkling his addresses with illuminating stories, often humorous and sometimes personal.

CONTROVERSIAL PEDAGOGICAL VIEWS

As an enthusiastic teacher for decades, Luciani had developed concrete ideas about what constituted sound educational practices. He wrote about these perspectives over a period of time and in a variety of venues. Regarding pedagogy, he was not an ideologue but a pragmatist. His writing about teaching and learning provides insights into the kind of instructor he was.

Luciani was critical of the instructional methods prevalent in the seventies, though he didn't condemn them altogether. On student-centered discovery of knowledge, his disapproval was based on practicality: "if one does not benefit from others' teaching, one loses a great deal of time in seeking truths that are already known. It is not possible always to make original discoveries."[14] He criticized the elimination of competition among students for academic achievement and the trend toward group assessment of mastery of content and skills: "Attention to the weaker members of the class is a fine and positive thing. But it can be achieved still without losing a certain amount of competitiveness. School is a preparation for life, which is made up of inequalities."[15] "The words that today . . . are extremely fashionable are group work, 'open classroom' schools, socially and democratically directed, enriched with assemblies and demonstrations," he lamented. Nevertheless, he conceded that some of these innovations were not useless, if they were integrated with proven traditional methods of instruction.[16]

He vigorously defended the value of lecturing by instructors who were authorities in their specialties: "It should not be believed that, in listening to a professor, the student remains purely passive or receptive."[17] A successful student in a lecture-oriented classroom had to listen actively, develop sustained concentration, process information, discriminate between essential and less consequential facts, and make logical connections among ideas. While defending teacher-centered instruction, Luciani found fault with at least one feature of traditional teaching methods: "in the past the schools exaggerated on the side of rote learning."[18] This approach contradicted one of his fundamental tenets: "joy is the atmosphere necessary for every effective system of education."[19] "Love books, you will be in contact with the great men of the past," he advised students, yet at the same time he was critical of some texts that took the pleasure out of learning.[20] "History, as recorded in textbooks, seemed to me a distillation of noise, as Carlyle said, all made up of dates, wars, armistices, treaties."[21] He, on the other hand, viewed history as drama, captivating, suspenseful, and incorporating all the other disciplines.

EARNING A DOCTORATE—UNCONVENTIONALLY

Luciani's endless quest to acquire knowledge led him to pursue postgraduate studies. In 1941 he registered at the Gregorian Pontifical University,[22] a prestigious institution established in 1551 by Ignatius Loyola,[23] founder of the Society of Jesus, a religious order more commonly known as the Jesuits. There was a major obstacle to his admission, however: He had a commitment to continue teaching at the Belluno seminary. The university was situated in Rome, nearly four hundred miles away—an obvious impediment to his attending classes. Through the intercession of influential superiors, though, Luciani received a dispensation from this requirement.[24] His intellectual prowess, combined with his self-discipline, guaranteed his success despite his demanding teaching load.

Luciani wrote his doctoral dissertation on a nineteenth-century priest and philosopher named Antonio Rosmini-Serbati, who was suspected at one time of being a heretic. That controversial fact did not deter Luciani from investigating the man's thinking. In fact, Luciani was sympathetic to Rosmini and initially sought to rehabilitate his reputation.[25] As his research progressed, though, he reassessed his view about the validity of Rosmini's philosophy, a sure sign that his research was not intended to support any preconceived notions.[26]

The title of his thesis was "The Origins of the Human Soul According to Antonio Rosmini." Luciani successfully defended his thesis in February of 1947, and he did so with distinction. His work earned accolades from the Congregation for Seminaries and Universities, now the Congregation for Education.[27] On February 27, 1947, he received his doctorate in sacred theology magna cum laude. Three years later he published his treatise.[28] Given its esoteric nature, the book was not intended for mass consumption.

THE ROOKIE WRITER

Even during his years as a seminarian, Luciani demonstrated a talent for writing. From his vast reading of eminent authors, he had absorbed an elegant style that he made his own. But his intellectualism often hampered his ability to reach a broad audience, especially because it consisted of individuals with widely varying degrees of literacy. He had to simplify his writing, but Luciani didn't recognize the necessity of doing so on his own. As a seminarian who spent summers back home, he wrote for the parish bulletin. Reviewing one of Luciani's articles, don Filippo Carli, his pastor, complimented the work but insisted that it was too sophisticated. The seminarian, he emphasized, should remember his reason for writing—to reach all his readers, the unlettered as well as the erudite:

> It is well written but reeks of a sermon and it is too long and difficult to understand. Think of some poor old peasant woman trying to read your article, full of long words and complicated sentences. Poor old lady! Imagine her looking at those words full of "isms" and trying to understand those long sentences! Do it again, stick to the point, write short sentences with simple ideas. Illustrate your ideas with word pictures. Think of that old peasant woman![29]

The lesson of the priest would not be lost on the aspiring cleric. From then on, all his popular written work was simple in style even when complex in content.

GETTING PUBLISHED

During his adult years at the seminary, Luciani wrote prodigiously for various newspapers but primarily Belluno's diocesan newspaper, the popular *L'Amico del Popolo* (Friend of the People). Often, he argued against the socialists, and at other times he was an apologist for the social teachings of the Church.[30] Early on, his articles were anonymous, par for the course for a humble man who shied away from the limelight. The articles without a byline engendered good-natured fun among the family. After reading the paper, Berto would place bets on which articles were written by his brother.

Years later, Luciani wrote occasionally for *Il Gazzettino* (On Wings of Hope), Venice's daily newspaper.[31] His articles, wherever they appeared, were popular among readers. He had perfected, at last, the "common touch." Luciani loved writing so much he would admit publicly that had he not become a priest, he would have been a journalist.[32]

Though he would continue to write short pieces until he became pope, Luciani also became an author of books.

LUCIANI'S OPUS

The one book for which he is most famous is an intriguing volume titled *Illustrissimi* (The Illustrious Ones) that he wrote while he was patriarch of Venice.[33] The book is a compilation of forty imaginary letters to famous people, both real and fictitious. The missives initially appeared monthly for the *Messenger of Saint Anthony* from 1971 to 1974.[34] The reason he published them in serial form and later collected them in a book was to reach a much wider audience than he could by preaching at St. Mark's.[35] The book was first published in 1976 and was later translated into twelve languages—a testament to its popularity.[36] In one of his final acts, Luciani reviewed and revised the fourth edition.[37]

It seems inconceivable that a cardinal would publish a letter to Pinocchio or to an Italian legendary bear, or to historical figures whose bones had long been laid to rest. But Albino Luciani did so with relish. Only the foolish dared ridicule him for it; from the wise he received widespread acclaim for his fanciful but thought-provoking epistles.

A cardinal publicly expressing his convictions about spiritual and social matters in this whimsical manner is amusing and unique. Beyond voicing his opinions in the book, Luciani also provided insights into his character, personality, and experiences while revealing his love of literature from which he drew fundamental life lessons. His homely anecdotes, appealing particularly to the unsophisticated, are simply charming and resonate to this day. "The idea was a delight, the book even more so," observed two journalists based in Rome.[38] Wrote American Cardinal John Wright in an introduction to an English edition, "his writings radiate joy."[39]

The self-revelatory work is the closest thing to a Luciani autobiography available. Here the cardinal shared an abundance of information about himself without vanity or self-consciousness: youthful impressions, likes and dislikes, sincere opinions about timeless controversial issues, self-doubts, and personal shortcomings. Here, both his wisdom and shortsightedness are exposed. Here the tension between his traditionalist inclinations and his yearning to free himself of the shackles of stale thinking become distinct. Here he sometimes boldly advances nuanced progressive ideas but also reveals that he was a creature of his time, committed to notions that current readers could find outdated and, in some cases, offensive.

But Luciani's endearing personality sparkles throughout the book. He didn't succumb to the temptation of concealing the less admirable aspects of his character—something all too common in autobiographies. In fact, Luciani freely revealed his imperfections. What is stunning is the specificity with which he divulged his flaws, especially his confession to being guilty of pride, the deadliest of all sins, an astonishing revelation considering his well-earned reputation for humility. Paradoxically, this admission in itself was an act of humility in that he laid bare to the public an embarrassing character defect. Luciani made no excuses for his moral lapses, using them as an opportunity to teach his readers that everyone—including cardinals—succumbs to temptation.

Beyond that, the reader inevitably discerns the nobility of Luciani's character and the attractiveness of his personality. He comes across as a man with firmly held convictions but with a willingness to consider opposing beliefs. He displays a compassionate understanding of human frailty. He addresses contemporary problems with candor and self-confidence. He is always polite and considerate even to those with whom he disagrees vehemently. He uses humor freely and effectively to engage the reader.

The letters were an innovative tool for addressing contemporary matters of consequence that also were subjects of interest to the recipients of his letters when they were alive. These were "conversations" that took place across time. The people with whom he corresponded were all famous to various degrees, and they were figures of influence in some fashion: fourteen authors, seven saints, six fictitious characters, three religious individuals, three secular leaders, two biblical luminaries, a musician, a scientist, and assorted others. The group was eclectic, including Charles Dickens, Mark Twain, King David of the Old Testament, Figaro the Barber, Pinocchio, Hippocrates, Saint Luke the Evangelist, and Jesus Himself.

He tackled a wide range of topics, offering his individual assessments—many controversial both then and now. In some cases, the titles of the letters themselves are intriguing: "Beautiful without All This Nonsense," "When You Get a Crush on Someone," "Vacation Fever," "The Time of Imposters," "Words, Words, Words," and "I Write in Trepidation."

A HOST OF CONCERNS

No explanation is given for the order of recipients of the author's letters or the order of importance of the subjects discussed. Some topics are addressed to more than one recipient, allowing Luciani to elaborate. Throughout, the patriarch didn't shy away from being critical of institutions, groups, ideologies, and movements that were certain to generate a public backlash.

The Catholic Church

Surprisingly, Luciani didn't spare the Catholic Church from criticism; he was at times blunt about its failings. "Made of sinners, in fact, the Church is also perforce a sinner."[40] "It cannot be denied that in the Church today there are serious problems and even errors against the faith."[41] Besides those fundamental realities, he found the carping within the highest echelons as damaging to the institution and its mission. "On the right, they shout impiety and sacrilege every time an old ritual is abandoned for a new one. On the left, vice versa, novelty is indiscriminately hailed for the sake of novelty, the whole edifice of the past is merrily dismantled."[42] As was typical, Luciani sought a reasonable middle ground.

He acknowledged that "the hierarchy has in the past been wanting and can also be wanting now."[43] Nevertheless, he defended with vehemence the institutions that trace back to Christ, including the primacy of the pope[44] and the autocratic structure of the institution. "In the Church, either hierarchy . . . or anarchy."[45]

Morality

Luciani lived when secularism was on the rise, and, as a priest, that trend caused him grave apprehensions. He lamented the tendency of society to embrace a "broadly permissive morality. Even admitting that in the past there was too much severity on some points, the young must not accept this permissiveness."[46]

Some of his views would be denounced today as anachronistic, sexist, and homophobic. For example, he objected to "unrestrained contraception, abortion at a mother's wish, all the divorce you like, premarital relations, homosexuality, use of drugs."[47] All the while he expressed compassion for those whose practices he regarded as wrong.

God

Luciani confronted atheists boldly, making logical arguments to contradict their conviction that a supreme being is fictional. To the cardinal, it was inconceivable that a beneficent creator of the universe did not exist. God, in his view, was essential to human progress and to the rehabilitation of a fallen humanity. "Today the whole world, which has such need of God, is a poor abode!" he lamented.[48] And the deplorable state of the world was attributable to the sinfulness of man who was dependent on God's mercy: "We will always see goodness in God and wretchedness in ourselves. We will see divine goodness well disposed toward our wretchedness."[49]

Christ

Like every good Christian, Luciani believed that salvation for mankind resulted from Christ's death on the cross. The crucifix was an omnipresent fixture in his every abode, and as bishop, cardinal, and pope, he wore a pectoral cross. Jesus was the central figure in his life. The Savior's words and example guided his ministry. And yet his letter to Jesus is the very last in the book. He admitted in this epistle that he had been criticized for writing to all sorts of figures except Christ. Luciani was reluctant to do so; he felt unworthy and diffident. This letter is in stark contrast to all the others in tone and content. "[H]ere is the letter. I write it in trepidation," he confessed.[50] He concluded it with an admission of inadequacy. "I have never before been so dissatisfied with my writing."[51]

Faith

Though Luciani's faith was unwavering, he recognized that even those individuals who are devout struggle at times with their belief in the Almighty. During times of personal tribulation in particular, doubt can arise and even thrive, eventually overpowering a person's faith. The cardinal was sympathetic to those who struggled with preserving their faith. He acknowledged that it is the rare individual who never experiences a crisis of faith. He concluded that "the journey of faith proves to be . . . a journey at times difficult, at times dramatic, and always mysterious."[52]

Goodness, Sin, and Redemption

Luciani reminded us that, in the Gospel, Christ is referred to as a friend of sinners.[53] He, like Christ, understood the temptations that individuals faced and the difficulty of avoiding sin. "[W]e are all exposed to temptations."[54] "Life is always very complex; even the good have failings, even the bad have virtues."[55] Though he added, "[R]epeated sins become habits, chains that are harder to break."[56] "[S]in becomes willy-nilly, the master of the sinner . . . the sinner remains its slave."[57]

He believed fervently in redemption and encouraged repentance regardless how sordid a person's past. "[N]o tempestuous past should frighten us. The storms, which were evil in the past, become good in the present if they drive us to remedy, to change."[58] But, at the same time, Luciani warned that personal reform should begin as soon as possible: "He who takes the road of later ends then on the road of never."[59]

He recognized that personal character traits can be inherited, yet if they are negative, they, too, can be overcome through diligent effort. "[Y]ou can become saints, whatever your family history may have been, the temperament and blood inherited, your past situation!"[60] But, he admitted, that path, too, is difficult—even for Christians. Despite receiving the sacraments, attending Mass, engaging in prayer, and doing good works, Christians, like all other people, are weak. "[H]umans, Christians, have a hard time changing!"[61] Luciani added, "To be good is a great and beautiful thing, but difficult and arduous."[62]

Pride

The cardinal shed light on a basic snare besetting us all. "When we are shown a group photograph in which we posed, which is the likable, attractive face we look for at once? Sad to say, it is our own. Because we are vastly fond of ourselves, above all others. Loving ourselves so much, we are naturally led to enlarge our own merits, to play down our transgressions, to judge others by different standards from those used to judge ourselves," he wrote.[63]

He confessed his own shortcomings in this regard. "I still dislike criticism, while I like praise, on the other hand, and I am concerned about what others think of me."[64] Luciani elaborated: "those who are higher attract us, we want to overtake them, putting our equals below us . . . We would like to shine, to be in first place, through recognition, advancement, promotions."[65]

Satan

He clung to a notion that today is regarded by multitudes as a laughable medieval superstition: the existence of the devil. He wrote about this topic at length to Christopher Marlowe, author of *The Tragical History of Doctor Faustus*. According to Luciani, the devil "tries to move through this world completely incognito; he leads men to deny his existence so that he can bring them to foment the revolution against God which he himself began; and now, to some extent, he has succeeded."[66] Surprisingly, according to one public opinion survey conducted in 2023, Luciani's belief is still shared by 58 percent of Americans, though he and Pope Paul were belittled for publicly expressing this view.[67]

Confession

Luciani admitted that Catholics in ever greater numbers were avoiding confession, but he expounded on its benefits to those individuals who take advantage of the sacrament of reconciliation: "Will the soul become soiled again after confession? It is quite likely. To keep it clean now, however, can do nothing but good, because confession not only removes the dust of sins, but instills a special strength to avoid them and reinforces our friendship with God."[68]

Love

"Joy is mingled with Christian love," according to Luciani.[69] He was a living example of that truth. At the same time, he admitted that loving our neighbor is often challenging.

In his letter to Maria Theresa of Austria, he praised her for loving her husband and mourning his death despite his repeated infidelities.[70] "Anyone who truly loves Christ cannot refuse to love mankind, for all are Christ's brothers. Even if they are ugly, bad, or boring, love must transfigure them a little," Luciani preached.[71]

"To help others as best you can, to avoid losing your temper, to be understanding, to keep calm and smiling on these occasions (as much as possible!) is loving your neighbor . . . in a practical way."[72]

The Defects of Capitalism

Luciani, who always deplored injustice and inequality, expressed stern criticism of the excesses of capitalists in their relentless pursuit of profit and the detrimental cult of materialism that it produced. "[T]he frantic race for creature comforts, the exaggerated, mad use of unnecessary things, has compromised the indispensable things: pure air and pure water, silence, inner peace, rest."[73]

In his letter to Dickens, he traced the origins of the labor movement, which he viewed as a necessary means of ameliorating the capitalists' abuse of workers. His sympathy for those who were exploited no doubt stemmed in part from the work experiences of his socialist father. Although Luciani himself didn't embrace socialism, he sharply attacked capitalism, which "was, and in some instances still is, a 'wicked system.'"[74]

He used Dickens's portrayal of hideous working conditions in his novels to shed light on the ongoing plight of the poor. "[T]hese delicate creatures are bound to the powerful noisy machine, to the physically and morally unhealthy environment, and driven often to seek oblivion in alcohol or to attempt an escape through prostitution."[75] Though he was an ardent critic of Marxism, he gave it some credit "for having made many people realize the sufferings of workers."[76]

He lamented the plight of Third World nations mired in poverty and criticized the advanced countries for ignoring their suffering. Luciani disparaged what he considered the preventable disparity of wealth in the world: "in one-third of the world there is an extraordinary abundance of everything and a shameless squandering; in two-thirds of the world there is a poverty that is increasing all the time. It would suffice to cancel the insane expenditures for arms and reduce certain luxuries."[77]

Luciani went beyond that, deploring the widespread poverty, unemployment, and job insecurity that existed even in developed countries.[78] He didn't advocate the elimination of the free enterprise system but promoted its reform: "Capitalism . . . should be profoundly modified. The wealth produced is good; provided that the heart does not become too attached to it, that it can be shared among as many people as possible, and that it no longer creates the serious inequities of today."[79]

Women

Luciani applauded certain advances in women's rights. "[W]omen have made some conquests! Conquests that, for the most part, are positive."[80] "[T]oday you find women in political contests, in sports competition."[81] "In itself it is good," he concluded—but conditionally.[82] "My wish . . . is that women may achieve new conquests, but just and lofty ones."[83] Unfortunately, he didn't specify what those were.

In those respects, Luciani was "modern" in his views toward women; nevertheless, he was a sexist by today's standards, particularly regarding the restricted roles permitted to women in the Catholic Church. In his letter to the Old Testament figure, Lemuel, author of the poem "Ideal Woman," he began by admitting to being blindsided by a child: "The other day a little girl in the fifth grade put me in an awkward spot by stating: 'Is it fair that Jesus created seven sacraments and only six of them are available to women?'" She was referring, obviously, to Holy Orders to which only males are admitted.[84] The cardinal's response that this is compensated by the gift of motherhood seems to the modern individual as unconvincing, as by implication, it was to him. Why should priesthood and motherhood be mutually exclusive?

Modesty

Luciani seems prudish to the modern reader. "Now everything is dared: in dress, in songs, in writing, in photography, in shows, in behavior."[85] He went on to complain about "Lilliputian" (mini) skirts and shorts popular with women of the sixties and seventies.[86]

Sex

Likewise, he found that promiscuity debased the sex act. He enjoined young couples in love to reach for a higher love than the mere sensual: "As long as you are engaged, love should procure not so much sexual pleasure as spiritual and sensitive joy, manifested in an affectionate way, of course, but correct and worthy."[87] It's a quaint sentiment, one unlikely to have altered the sexual behavior of very many young people. Casual sex, a consequence of the sexual revolution, spurred in part by the ready availability of various forms of birth control that freed women from the fear of unwanted pregnancies, drew his criticism, if not outright condemnation. He inveighed against "the frantic cult of sex."[88] His view was out of step with the prevailing trends of his time, as it is today, but Luciani was never deterred from speaking his mind simply because his views might be unpopular.

Abortion

Luciani's uncompromising opinion of abortion earned him criticism during his lifetime and would be deplored perhaps more stridently today. He was unalterably opposed to abortion at any time in a pregnancy, by any means, and for any reasons. He viewed abortion as "abominable."[89] In maintaining this position Luciani was adhering to the teachings of the Church (still in effect today), but there is no doubt that he believed in the evil of abortion to the depths of his soul. His rationale? Life is precious, a gift from God. Human life begins at conception, and, therefore, taking the life of the unborn is evil, tantamount to murder. What undoubtedly would rankle many today is his apparent silence on the moral quandary of opting for abortion as the lesser of two evils in instances where the fetus would die at birth or when it suffered from serious biological abnormalities that would make its life unbearable, or when the life of the mother was in danger. Apparently, in his view even victims of rape or incest who became pregnant as a result didn't justify having an abortion.

Marriage

Luciani recognized that marriage is difficult and that "numerous obstacles . . . stand in the way of conjugal love."[90] In particular, he cited the proclivity for extramarital affairs, especially when there are tensions between spouses. "Venus appears, or Adonis, in the form of a fellow-employee at the office, and you find you have more ideas in common with him or her than with your spouse," he observed.[91] And infidelity undermines the sacrament of marriage, often leading to divorce (also opposed by the Church) with dire consequences, especially for children.

Students

Luciani looked favorably on young people, seeing them as the hope of the future. "[T]he students of today . . . are good, likable young people."[92] He informed Figaro the Barber that "millions of young people are doing . . . what you did two centuries ago . . . they rebel."[93] He was amused. "Many of these young men wear a pigtail as you did and worry about their hair . . . All these beards! And sideburns and mutton chops!"[94]

"We must also allow the young to be different from us older people in their way of judging, of behaving, of loving, and praying. They also have—as you, Figaro, had—something to say worth listening to, worth the world's respect," Luciani insisted.[95] "We must share with them the task of making society progress."[96]

At the same time, he worried that they would become the pawns of societal forces more powerful than they. He feared their exploitation. The young "invoke the name of spontaneity, nonconformity and originality; actually, canny 'clothing industrialists' manipulate the field."[97] He sees youth as having good intentions but unaware of being manipulated by others for profit.

Luciani moves from the problems to potential solutions and always expresses hope. "It would be best for us to show that we are very open and understanding toward the young and toward their mistakes. Mistakes, however, must be called mistakes . . . The young . . . like to be told the truth."[98] He is gentle and honest with them.

The cardinal admired their idealism. He found goodness in so many of them, those who "show pity for the poor, the outcast, the underprivileged. They declare themselves opposed to all social barriers, against all discrimination by class or race. This is beautiful and generous."[99]

He cautioned against extremism, however, in their challenge to the status quo. Some "preach a complete break with the past, rejecting, with one swoop, society, family, marriage, school, morality, and religion."[100] He conceded that significant numbers abandoned the Church, and that saddened him.[101] Despite all of this, however, Luciani maintained that ongoing dialogue with the young is essential because not all of them were extremists and even those who were might be influenced to moderate their views.[102]

The Environment

Luciani was prophetic about the unintended consequences of modern scientific progress such as environmental disasters. In particular, he expressed concern about the dangers of nuclear power. "[N]uclear energy . . . involves the risk of radioactive wastes, dangerous to man and his environment."[103] His fears were justified. The year following his death a nuclear power plant in Pennsylvania had a partial meltdown of a reactor; seven years later a more serious accident took place at the Chernobyl nuclear power plant, leading to the release of radioactive material into the atmosphere that affected hundreds of thousands of people.[104] Then, in 2011, three reactors at the Fukushima, Japan, power plant were damaged, causing radioactive materials to contaminate the air.[105]

Society and Advancement

Luciani analyzed modern civilization and saw it beset with tribulations. That situation he attributed largely to the decline in religious practice. He claimed "there is a terrible moral and religious void. Today all seem frantically directed toward material conquests."[106] Echoing Dante's famous statement that the deepest circles of hell are reserved for those who in times of moral crisis do nothing, Luciani clearly articulated the duty of people of conscience: "the Christian must concern himself, and effectively, with the great social problems . . . one must lend a hand in establishing justice on earth."[107]

He expressed incredulity that human progress could occur in a world in which God was marginalized. Luciani warned, "[T]his vaunted progress is not everything that was hoped; it also brings with it missiles, bacteriological and atomic weapons, the current process of pollution: things which . . . threaten to bring catastrophe on the whole human race."[108]

But regardless of the apparent intractability of human problems on a vast scale, he was hopeful, though not necessarily optimistic, about the future. Why? It was fundamental to his view of humanity: "We are the children of hope." And hope was inseparable from God.[109]

Peace

It is fitting that Luciani, a disciple of Jesus Christ, the Prince of Peace, should promote universal human harmony. In the nuclear age he deemed it essential to the survival of our species while lamenting the perseverance of hatred and its offspring: atrocities and war. He was not naive about the colossal effort that achieving peace would require, but neither did he see it as an impossible goal. In this respect, he was in accord with a Catholic world leader who had previously expressed his belief that peace was feasible. Both men were realists. From Luciani's perspective, though, human efforts alone were inadequate. In this respect, they differed.

When President John F. Kennedy delivered the commencement address at American University in 1963, his focus was world peace, a goal he believed could be achieved. "Our problems are manmade—therefore, they can be solved by man . . . No problem of human destiny is beyond human beings."[110] In contrast, Luciani maintained that peace was impossible without God. In his letter to St. Luke he wrote, "Peace . . . has a price: it is not made with words, but with sacrifices and loving renunciations by all. Nor is it possible to obtain it with only human efforts. God's intervention is required."[111]

Beguiling Comments by a Gentle Man

Luciani's meekness and consideration of others led him to apologize to the long-dead Charles Dickens for troubling him with his letter. Luciani chose to reach out to Dickens because of his Christmas books, which engaged him as a youngster, particularly because they expressed love for the poor and "a sense of social regeneration . . . Here I am taking the liberty of disturbing you" as if he were writing to a live person.[112]

He told Mark Twain—as if he were instructing him—that St. Francis de Sales, "a bishop like me and a humorist like you, wrote: 'We blame our neighbor for the slightest faults, and we condone the greatest ones in ourselves . . . What we do for others always seems a great deal, what others do for us seems nothing.'"[113]

In his letter to Saint Bernardino, he saw a kindred spirit, addressing him as "Dear Smiling Saint."[114] He also wrote to his favorite role model, Saint Francis de Sales. In his salutation, Luciani called him "Gentlest of saints."[115]

De Sales was an advocate of catering to the sick and the poor, two of Luciani's own favored constituencies.[116]

He admitted a special fondness for Pinocchio. His letter oozes enthusiasm from his youth. "I was seven years old when I read your Adventures for the first time . . . how many times I have reread them since . . . in you, I recognized myself as a boy, and in your surroundings, I saw my own."[117] But he lamented, "I . . . have grown old . . . I no longer recognize myself in you."[118]

Despite his dedication to writing the letters and compiling them in a volume, Luciani wondered about the efficacy of his words.[119] He concluded one letter almost in defeat. The cardinal spoke openly about the effects of his writing: "I may have irked my readers. Some will have found me romantic, ingenuous, and out of date . . . others will have broken off their reading as soon as they caught a whiff of 'moralism.' One of the many risks of my job."[120]

Illustrissimi is notable for its creative format and content, and it became a best-seller after Luciani's election as pope.[121] Eventually, it was translated into twelve languages.[122]

The book is timeless.

SECONDARY WORKS

Catechetica in Briciole (Catechetics in Crumbs)

Luciani's passion for catechetics never waned. He had enjoyed success in teaching the catechism to the young, and it always remained one of his priorities. It's no wonder, then, that he wrote a book devoted to the formation of catechists.[123]

Published in 1949 and dedicated to the memory of his mother (his first catechist), who had died the previous year, *Catechetica in Briciole* focused on the fundamental mission of the catechist. He characterized that work as vital, insisting that the benefits to pupils are receptivity to God's grace and reverence of the sacraments as well as development of a genuine Christian attitude toward God and people.[124] Luciani also described a catechist's work as difficult because he or she often encounters resistance or indifference to the teachings.[125]

In the initial section titled "The Mission of the Catechist," Luciani wrote,

> There is a painting by Murillo called "The Children of the Seashell." In a tranquil and serene background, while angels from on high are looking on and smiling, the boy Jesus is giving little John the Baptist some water in a shell drawn from a limpid brook which is flowing at their feet. This is

> the mission of the catechist: to take the place of Jesus and give, with the catechism, the water of eternal life to children.[126]

Luciani knew that instruction in the faith was indispensable to developing devout, lifelong practicing Catholics.

Though the subject matter of the book appealed to a limited audience, by the time Luciani became pope, the book was in its seventh printing.[127] Following his election, he rejected a proposal to republish the text because its methods were outdated due to the extensive revisions of the catechism resulting from the Second Vatican Council. Nevertheless, following his death, Italian publishers printed a new edition.[128] In the aftermath of John Paul's passing, anything associated with Albino Luciani was in great demand.

A Booklet for Priests

As a bishop, Luciani was in almost constant communication with clergymen. He valued the work that parish priests performed daily in administering the sacraments, in counseling those who needed guidance, in consoling the suffering and the grieving, in spreading the Good News of the Gospels.

Compendium

A collection of the bulk of Luciani's published work, including articles, homilies, and letters, has been compiled in a nine-volume work consisting of more than fifty-three hundred pages known as *Opera Omnia* (Latin for Complete Works).[129] They were essential in the process of determining Luciani's suitability for canonization decades later.

ASSESSMENT

Albino Luciani was obviously a man of many talents. A gifted teacher and writer, he was also a riveting public speaker, able administrator, accomplished pastor, wise counselor, and a singular role model. Long before he became pope, he contributed to improving the lives of countless people from children to whom he taught the catechism, to seminarians he supervised and instructed, to priests whom he guided, to the Catholic laity to whom he administered the sacraments, to the downtrodden to whom he provided succor. The cardinal electors in the August 1978 conclave who knew him or of him recognized that these qualities would benefit the universal church, and that undoubtedly played a pivotal role in his election. Only as pope, did the entire world come to realize just how special he was.

Albino Luciani was mortal, but his inspiring vision for the future of all humankind will never die.

NOTES

1. Pia Luciani (niece of Pope John Paul I), in discussion with the author, Canale d'Agordo, Italy, July 6, 2011.
2. Albino Luciani, *Illustrissimi*, trans. William Weaver (Boston: Little, Brown, 1978), 117.
3. Luciani, *Illustrissimi*, 69.
4. Luciani, *Illustrissimi*, 68.
5. Luciani, *Illustrissimi*, 8.
6. Albino Luciani, *A Passionate Adventure: Living the Catholic Faith Today*, ed. and trans. Lori Pieper (New York: Tau Cross Books, 2013), 12.
7. Raymond and Lauretta Seabeck, *The Smiling Pope: The Life and Teaching of John Paul I* (Huntington, IN: Our Sunday Visitor, 2004), 23.
8. Seabeck, *Smiling Pope*, 248–49.
9. Seabeck, *Smiling Pope*, 22.
10. Seabeck, *Smiling Pope*, 24.
11. Seabeck, *Smiling Pope*, 23.
12. Seabeck, *Smiling Pope*, 22–23.
13. Luciani, *Illustrissimi*, 100.
14. Luciani, *Illustrissimi*, 201.
15. Luciani, *Illustrissimi*, 201.
16. Luciani, *Illustrissimi*, 200.
17. Luciani, *Illustrissimi*, 201.
18. Luciani, *Illustrissimi*, 202.
19. Luciani, *Illustrissimi*, 124.
20. Luciani, *Illustrissimi*, 97.
21. Luciani, *Illustrissimi*, 202.
22. Seabeck, *Smiling Pope*, 249.
23. Gregorian University Foundation, https://gregorianfoundation.org/#aboutus.
24. Paul Spackman, *God's Candidate: The Life and Times of Pope John Paul I* (Herefordshire: Gracewing, 2008), 26.
25. Luciani, *Passionate Adventure*, 13.
26. Luciani, *Passionate Adventure*, 13.
27. Seabeck, *Smiling Pope*, 25.
28. Spackman, *God's Candidate*, 28.
29. Seabeck, *Smiling Pope*, 17–18.
30. Luciani, *Passionate Adventure*, 14.
31. Luciani, *Passionate Adventure*, 20.

32. David Yallop, *In God's Name: An Investigation into the Murder of Pope John Paul I* (New York: Penguin, 1984), 148.
33. Seabeck, *Smiling Pope*, 47.
34. Seabeck, *Smiling Pope*, 47–48.
35. Seabeck, *Smiling Pope*, 47–48.
36. Seabeck, *Smiling Pope*, 47.
37. Luciani, *Illustrissimi*, xv.
38. Merill Sheils and Loren Jenkins, "A Man of the People," *Newsweek*, September 4, 1978, 42.
39. Luciani, *Illustrissimi*, x.
40. Luciani, *Illustrissimi*, 182.
41. Luciani, *Passionate Adventure*, 31.
42. Luciani, *Illustrissimi*, 208.
43. Luciani, *Illustrissimi*, 93.
44. Luciani, *Illustrissimi*, 93.
45. Luciani, *Passionate Adventure*, 73.
46. Luciani, *Illustrissimi*, 79.
47. Luciani, *Illustrissimi*, 195.
48. Luciani, *Illustrissimi*, 8.
49. Luciani, *Illustrissimi*, 52.
50. Luciani, *Illustrissimi*, 254.
51. Luciani, *Illustrissimi*, 258.
52. Luciani, *Illustrissimi*, 29.
53. Luciani, *Illustrissimi*, 27.
54. Luciani, *Illustrissimi*, 79.
55. Luciani, *Illustrissimi*, 182.
56. Luciani, *Illustrissimi*, 26.
57. Luciani, *Illustrissimi*, 163.
58. Luciani, *Illustrissimi*, 25.
59. Luciani, *Illustrissimi*, 26.
60. Luciani, *Illustrissimi*, 26.
61. Luciani, *Illustrissimi*, 172.
62. Luciani, *Illustrissimi*, 52.
63. Luciani, *Illustrissimi*, 10.
64. Luciani, *Illustrissimi*, 50.
65. Luciani, *Illustrissimi*, 51.
66. Luciani, *Illustrissimi*, 185–86.
67. Julia Shapero, "Belief in God, the Devil Falls to New Low: Gallup: Belief in God and Other Spiritual Entities Is Highest among Those Who Attend Regular Religious Services," https://thehill.com/changing-america/respect/diversity-inclusion/4107968-belief-in-god-the-devil-falls-to-new-low-gallup/.
68. Luciani, *Illustrissimi*, 232.
69. Luciani, *Illustrissimi*, 151.
70. Luciani, *Illustrissimi*, 19
71. Luciani, *Illustrissimi*, 150.

72. Luciani, *Illustrissimi*, 150.
73. Luciani, *Illustrissimi*, 7.
74. Luciani, *Illustrissimi*, 6.
75. Luciani, *Illustrissimi*, 4.
76. Luciani, *Illustrissimi*, 209.
77. Luciani, *Illustrissimi*, 207.
78. Luciani, *Illustrissimi*, 7.
79. Luciani, *Illustrissimi*, 209.
80. Luciani, *Illustrissimi*, 242.
81. Luciani, *Illustrissimi*, 243.
82. Luciani, *Illustrissimi*, 243.
83. Luciani, *Illustrissimi*, 246.
84. Luciani, *Illustrissimi*, 121.
85. Luciani, *Illustrissimi*, 22.
86. Luciani, *Illustrissimi*, 23.
87. Luciani, *Illustrissimi*, 79.
88. Luciani, *Illustrissimi*, 179.
89. Luciani, *Illustrissimi*, 246.
90. Luciani, *Illustrissimi*, 56.
91. Luciani, *Illustrissimi*, 57.
92. Luciani, *Illustrissimi*, 97.
93. Luciani, *Illustrissimi*, 61.
94. Luciani, *Illustrissimi*, 61.
95. Luciani, *Illustrissimi*, 64.
96. Luciani, *Illustrissimi*, 64.
97. Luciani, *Illustrissimi*, 62.
98. Luciani, *Illustrissimi*, 64.
99. Luciani, *Illustrissimi*, 180.
100. Luciani, *Illustrissimi*, 178.
101. Luciani, *Illustrissimi*, 179.
102. Luciani, *Illustrissimi*, 180.
103. Luciani, *Illustrissimi*, 7.
104. "Assessments of the Radiation Effects from the Chernobyl Nuclear Reactor Accident," United Nations Scientific Committee on the Effects of Atomic Radiation, https://www.unscear.org/unscear/en/areas-of-work/chernobyl.html.
105. "Fukushima-accident," https://www.britannica.com/event/.
106. Luciani, *Illustrissimi*, 179.
107. Luciani, *Illustrissimi*, 193.
108. Luciani, *Illustrissimi*, 15.
109. Luciani, *Illustrissimi*, 28.
110. John F. Kennedy, "Commencement Address at American University," June 10, 1963, John F. Kennedy Presidential Library and Museum, https://www.jfklibrary.org/archives/other-resources/john-f-kennedy-speeches/american-university-19630610.
111. Luciani, *Illustrissimi*, 197.

112. Luciani, *Illustrissimi*, 3.
113. Luciani, *Illustrissimi*, 11.
114. Luciani, *Illustrissimi*, 96.
115. Luciani, *Illustrissimi*, 103.
116. Luciani, *Illustrissimi*, 104.
117. Luciani, *Illustrissimi*, 72.
118. Luciani, *Illustrissimi*, 73.
119. Luciani, *Illustrissimi*, 102.
120. Luciani, *Illustrissimi*, 138.
121. Francis X. Murphy, *The Papacy Today* (London: Weidenfeld and Nicolson, 1982), 166.
122. Seabeck, *Smiling Pope*, 47.
123. Seabeck, *Smiling Pope*, 25.
124. Seabeck, *Smiling Pope*, 25–26.
125. Loris Serafini (director, Foundation Papa Luciani and Museum Albino Luciani of Canale d'Agordo), in discussion with the author, New York, October 12, 2012.
126. Seabeck, *Smiling Pope*, 25–26.
127. "Compassionate Shepherd," *Time*, September 4, 1978, 62.
128. Seabeck, *Smiling Pope*, 25.
129. Seabeck, *Smiling Pope*, 8.

• 7 •

The Reluctant Bishop

Humility (1958–1970)

Now a bishop must be above reproach . . . temperate, sensible, dignified, hospitable, an apt teacher . . . and no lover of money. —1 Timothy 2.1 (RSVSCE)

"I am the little one of once upon a time, I am the one who comes from the fields, I am pure and simple dust, on this dust the Lord has written the episcopal dignity of the illustrious Diocese of Vittorio Veneto . . . I desire only to enter into your service and to put at your disposal all my poor strength, the little I have and the little I am."[1]

With those touching self-revelatory remarks, Bishop Luciani introduced himself to his new flock in the diocese of Vittorio Veneto. The audience was taken aback. Bishops didn't speak that way about themselves. As men of status, they were above and detached from the faithful they led; their public addresses, therefore, were formal and often patronizing. The humility Luciani demonstrated in his initial public words in Vittorio Veneto signaled that he would be a radically different kind of bishop. The diocesan clergy and their parishioners would now be served by a man who viewed himself as a simple priest whose primary responsibility was pastoral in nature. The underlying message to his flock was that he was one of them.

AN UNWELCOME APPOINTMENT

Saint Isidor of Seville profoundly influenced Pope John XXIII's view of a bishop's fundamental role. According to the saint, a bishop is primarily a virtuous teacher and role model. "Every bishop should be distinguished as much by his humility as his authority," wrote Isidor. The Holy Father recognized in

Luciani's meekness of character and devotion to spreading the Good News of the Gospels a priest who was superlatively suited to be a bishop.[2]

The Holy Father personally informed the forty-six-year-old seminary professor that he was naming him a bishop.[3] Luciani respectfully demurred, but the pope rejected his objection out of hand. Undaunted, Luciani again attempted to decline the appointment based on his precarious health, citing respiratory problems. John cleverly neutralized the issue immediately. "Excellent!" he responded to a deflated Luciani. "If that's all it is, I'll send you to Vittorio Veneto. The bishop's palace there is high on a hill; the air is wonderful and will do you good!"[4] And so it was settled.

Luciani's promotion was unusual because he had never demonstrated any interest in ecclesiastical advancement. "He said a hundred thousand times, 'I haven't moved a finger to be the Bishop of Vittorio Veneto. The Pope made me and I said yes. I haven't moved forward a pawn [alluding to a minor chess move] so that they would make me a bishop. I was fine in Belluno,'" he confided to Msgr. Francesco Taffarel, who would later work for him.[5]

Luciani's elevation to the episcopate was attributable to the pope's personal affinity for him as well as the enthusiastic recommendation of two influential church leaders, Belluno's Bishop Girolamo Bortignon and his successor, Msgr. Gioachino Muccin, both of whom held Luciani in high esteem.[6] The pope had met Luciani in 1954 when the latter oversaw Belluno's Diocesan Eucharistic Congress. The patriarch of Venice at the time, Cardinal Angelo Roncalli, would become Pope John XXIII in 1958.[7] "He [Roncalli] came to see the Bishop of Belluno. I kept him company for a half day bringing him down the Dolomites," Luciani eventually told a confidant.[8] As a direct result of that meeting, Pope John XXIII nominated Luciani as bishop of Vittorio Veneto on December 15, 1958.[9]

AN EXTRAORDINARY CONSECRATION

Pope John himself consecrated Luciani in St. Peter's Basilica. At the pivotal moment of the ceremony, the Holy Father embraced Luciani tightly. The newly minted bishop, in turn, thanked the pope and pledged his obedience and devotion. Afterward, he borrowed a cape for the official photo with the pontiff because he didn't have one of his own at the time.[10] He looked uncomfortable; his serious gaze was almost grim, and his garment was so long that it swept the floor.[11] Pope John, however, could hardly contain his enthusiasm for Luciani; following the consecration, he advised a monsignor, "Watch that little bishop, you will see . . . you will see."[12]

Several days before the ceremony, the pope summoned Luciani to a private meeting. The two conversed with ease as they had before at the Eucharistic Congress in Belluno. At the end of the audience, the pope advised him to preach in simple, clear terms; Luciani had heard this counsel from an earlier mentor and had faithfully and effectively followed the advice ever since.[13]

Not surprisingly, Luciani chose *Humilitas* as his episcopal motto, the very same one he would select later as patriarch and pope. In doing so, he was emulating Saint Charles Borromeo for whom Luciani had exceptional admiration. His coat of arms bore a representation of his beloved Dolomite Mountains with three stars representing the theological virtues of faith, hope, and charity. They were the subjects of his discourses at the general audiences he would conduct two decades later as pope.[14]

CANALE CELEBRATES

On January 4, 1959, Luciani's hometown held a festival in his honor.[15] As the new bishop entered the ancient church in Forno di Canale that had been the center of his life from his youth to his days as a new priest, his thoughts turned to his parents, now both deceased. How he wished they could be here at this moment. His mother had died on March 2, 1948, in a Belluno hospital at the age of sixty-eight of "bronchopneumonia." Luciani personally cared for her.[16] During her illness, he celebrated Mass on four occasions.[17] On March 2, he wrote in his diary simply, "mama dead at 2:50 a.m." He accompanied her body from Belluno to his hometown, where she was interred. His father passed away on January 9, 1952, in his home at age seventy-nine. The death certificate identifies "palpitations" as the cause.[18]

Sometime after the loss of his parents, Luciani confided in his brother that he regretted not having visited them more often. Apparently, he was so dedicated to fulfilling his responsibilities as a priest that he neglected to pay adequate attention to his family. If his later visits to his family during his years in Vittorio Veneto and then in Venice are any indication, he had learned from his regrets, for he visited Canale more often.[19]

Now his fellow townsman greeted him and kissed his ring. Approaching the first bench, Luciani spied his siblings, who became emotional. Nina attempted to kiss his hand, but Albino moved away, whispering to her that it was not acceptable for siblings to act in that manner.[20]

A SON OF CANALE DELIVERS A SERMON

Luciani began his homily by addressing his audience as equals: "My dear fellow villagers," he intoned. In his sermon he reflected on hope, advising the congregation, "Never despair!" He followed with a startling example in which he showed pity even for Christ's betrayer: "Look at Judas, he made a serious mistake. Poor man, he betrayed the Lord! But his real mistake was not that; his real mistake was when he no longer had hope; when he said, 'My sin is too great.' No sin is too great, no sin is greater than the boundless mercy of the Lord."[21] The bishop's description of Judas, the most notorious villain of the New Testament, must have shocked those in attendance. However, Luciani had succeeded in conveying an indelible lesson about God's boundless clemency. He concluded with a practical piece of advice: "Let's try to be good at the cost of any effort, at the cost of any sacrifice. The Lord will give a recompense, and He will reward us."[22]

> I know that you have been kind enough to take an interest in this event; they've told me that you have rung the bells, and you have sent a delegation to Rome. What's more, at considerable sacrifice, you decided to give me a gold pectoral cross. Thank you; you have done too much for me. When I wear this cross, I will feel that I am wearing something that will stimulate me to do good, to work for souls and not to dishonor my village, which has loved and honored me so much.[23]

As always, he wanted to keep his remarks brief so as not to impose on anyone, yet he went on out of a sense of obligation: "And I would stop now, but I know—they told me—that I am expected to say a few words by way of a sermon. I don't know where to begin. They have made me preach so many times in the past few days."[24]

ARRIVING IN HIS DIOCESE

The new bishop took possession of his diocese on January 11, 1959,[25] a bleak, bitterly cold day. He had boarded a train in Belluno, and when he arrived at his destination, a greeting party consisting of clerics and municipal officials awaited him. Disembarking, Luciani looked timid as he approached them. Leaving his trainbearer empty-handed, he carried the long robes, then part of a bishop's standard ceremonial wardrobe, bunched up under his arm. He kissed the ground of his new home before heading to the Cathedral of San Tiziano, where he was to be installed as the spiritual leader of his new diocese. When he first caught a glimpse of the crowds that had gathered, he became anxious.[26]

A NEW HOME

The bishop's residence in Vittorio Veneto was a sprawling medieval castle overlooking the city. The idea of making his home there didn't appeal to Luciani, so, instead, he chose to live in a modest apartment near the city's seminary. Reluctantly, he eventually moved into the citadel because the location of his quarters caused logistical problems and diocesan personnel pleaded with him to occupy the episcopal seat of the diocese. Thus, Castle San Martino once again became the residence of a bishop, as it had since medieval times.[27]

Luciani maintained an austere existence and a grueling schedule. "He was poor. He ate poorly. He ate whatever was left. Even when he was a bishop, he ate what he found . . . Nothing was thrown away," his secretary Msgr. Francesco Taffarel recalled of his simple tastes.[28] As was true of his dedication to his previous posts, Bishop Luciani was a workhorse, typically waking at 5:30 a.m. and usually laboring until late in the evening.[29]

WINNING WIDESPREAD AFFECTION

Figure 7.1. Bishop Luciani enjoying himself at a public function.

It didn't take long for the faithful to embrace their new bishop. His unusual simplicity marked him immediately as a man of the people as well as a man of God. Unless circumstances demanded that he wear a bishop's purple-trimmed cassock and sash, he dressed in black like a parish priest. He also wasn't enamored of wearing the traditional bishop's shoes that sported a buckle, so he kept those hidden in his closet. On his public excursions Luciani enjoyed walking inconspicuously. One day, encountering a woman and her son on their way to the boy's confirmation, the mother mistook Luciani for an ordinary priest. How surprised she was, when in church, she saw that same priest enter wearing a bishop's regalia. Even on trips to the Vatican he was often mistaken for a simple priest because he dressed in a plain black cassock there as well.[30]

Because Luciani didn't have a driver's license, according to his niece, Pia, he relied on others, like his secretary, to take him to his intended destinations.[31] The automobile in which he traveled throughout the diocese was a dinosaur, which raised some eyebrows among the faithful who were unaccustomed to seeing their bishop riding in a dilapidated vehicle. If the car was unavailable, people were startled to see Luciani using an even more lowly means of transportation: "On days when there were some problems, and he did not want to miss a pastoral visit in a parish, he went by bicycle," recalled Pia.[32] Luciani eventually accepted a new car as a gift and sold the old one, donating the proceeds to the poor.[33]

The fledgling bishop was not one to hunker down in his office, spending the bulk of his time tending to administrative duties. Being among the people took priority. "He wanted to reach everyone. He wanted to be near the people. He was not closed in at home," Taffarel explained.[34]

Though shy by nature, Luciani paradoxically relished contact with individuals, often patiently listening to the problems of ordinary people. Not surprisingly, then, on June 17, 1959, he embarked on his pastoral excursions to tend to his flock.[35] During his tenure in Vittorio Veneto, he visited all 180 parishes in his diocese twice.[36]

In addition, he often called on the sick and the poor to provide them with solace and a glimmer of hope. On occasion he would trudge through snow or mud to reach them. To the poor he encountered, he would empty his own pockets of whatever cash he was carrying, and for hospital patients he frequently tucked a small amount of money under their pillows.[37] When Luciani ministered to those who were hospitalized, he did so alone, wishing his conversations with patients to be private. He was particularly effective in ameliorating fears, loneliness, and tribulation through prayer and kind words. His love for these unfortunates was obvious to them, and for those who were ordinary folks, that affection coming from a bishop was a momentous blessing. Luciani related to the sick, for his own illnesses had taught him about the lonely suffering that accompanies bad health.[38] The bishop was also famous for "visiting local parishes until 11 to 11:30 at night. Almost every night," according to Taffarel.[39]

The bishop's half sister Pia was a nun of the Sacred Heart of Mary and lived in a cloistered convent in Turin. In 1969 she passed away at age sixty-seven. Her sister, Amalia, had died thirty years before.[40] Luciani, upon learning that Pia was seriously ill, left for the distant city. The man who drove him shared the story.

> One day he left Vittorio Veneto to go to Turin, about 600 kilometers (370 miles) away, to visit his sister at 11:00 o'clock at night. She was gravely ill. He arrived at Turin at 6:00 the next morning and his sister was already dead. He celebrated Mass, and then I rested a little and around 9:30 we left. The sisters prepared 2 or 3 sandwiches, and a little water, which we ate on the highway underneath a bridge. Around 3:00 we were at the parish in Tarzo where he had a pastoral visit with adults. This meeting ended between 4:30 and 5:00 p.m. . . . he then celebrated Mass and afterwards he ate with the pastor before leaving for another appointment with the young people at a nearby church at 8:30. Around 10:00 he went home.

His companion marveled in relating the bishop's stamina.[41]

A curiosity is that Luciani remained at the convent for only a few hours. His rush to leave seems insensitive under the circumstances. No one can know his reasons for such a hasty departure, nor the depth of his grief. What is clear is that he did not allow his half sister's death to interfere with the pastoral work that occupied him for the remainder of the day.

His common touch and his respect for all were obvious in many of his actions. When Luciani learned that a certain boy who was to be confirmed was sick, he went to the boy's house. One Christmas day Luciani sent his secretary home and invited a poor parish priest to have lunch with him so that he wouldn't spend Christmas alone. He postponed until the next day his own return to Canale to celebrate with his family.[42]

Following protocol, priests and lay people would greet him with bended knee and a kiss of his ring, while Luciani himself seemed oblivious to all this, already setting his gaze on others ahead of him and eagerly heading toward his planned destination.[43] The gentleness and good cheer with which he approached everyone was expected. Nevertheless, he went beyond that: Nothing seemed to be beneath him. On one occasion, for instance, he sent the sisters of his household on a brief pilgrimage, and when they returned that evening, they were surprised that the bishop had prepared the table.

Another time he sent the Christmas meal the nuns had prepared for him to a poor family in the diocese while he contented himself with a bowl of reheated soup.[44] On one occasion he came close to having a collision with a tractor driver. The farmer later recalled the incident with amusement. "I swerved and some hay fell off the wagon I was pulling. But in an instant the bishop was down there throwing the hay back on."[45]

Despite these admirable qualities, Luciani was a man like all men in that he was imperfect. He was painfully aware of his shortcomings. Taffarel observed of the bishop, "He went to confession every week. At times he would say, 'I am sorry; perhaps I didn't treat that person well, perhaps I should have been more patient.'"[46]

PERSUASIVE PREACHER

Not only was Vittorio Veneto's new bishop unique in his dress and deportment, but he was also a captivating speaker with the capacity to connect in a meaningful way with the faithful of his new diocese. Rather than speaking formally, he continued the practice of illuminating his messages by including personal anecdotes, humorous stories, references to religious or literary works, and engaging children in brief verbal exchanges to entertain and instruct. Luciani's homilies were sprinkled with as many humble anecdotes as scriptural quotations, and they captured the rapt attention of his listeners.

His Epiphany homily delivered on January 6, 1962, is illustrative. Then, as always, he was refreshingly candid, surprising his listeners by admitting that he, too, had lingering questions about biblical passages. Regarding the circumstances surrounding the birth of Christ, he asked "Who were the magi? Princes? Astrologers? Philosophers? Very learned men? I can't say for sure."[47]

Luciani did not even shy away from employing gallows humor from historical events to illustrate his point that "Saints are happy, even when they embrace a very severe life." For example, St. Lawrence "said while roasting on a gridiron, 'I think I have been cooked enough on this side now.' So, with St. Thomas More, who asked the executioner to respect his beard while the ax was falling. 'It has done nothing wrong, poor thing.'"[48]

The bishop taught that saints, like sinners, were not free from temptation. He asserted that even saints "must reckon" with the "tyranny" of "concupiscence" and "pray to be liberated from this constant annoyance." As a lifelong celibate priest, Luciani knew that sexual abstinence was demanding, more for some than for others. For many Catholic clergymen sexual temptations threatened adherence to their vow of abstinence and even caused some to abandon the priesthood to marry.[49]

During his homily for the Feast of Corpus Christi on June 13, 1963, Luciani conceded that the miracle of what takes place at Mass, presumably the mystery of transubstantiation, "eludes our understanding." He included himself among the laity that found this event perplexing.[50] At the same time, the bishop's knowledge of sacred rituals and human nature provided him with the sagacity to reassure Catholics who harbored doubts about the Church practices they followed, including the sacraments. "Someone says to me, 'It has been such a long time that I have been going to Communion, but I seem to still be the same, with the same old faults!' I answer, 'Of course.' Because we are still poor human beings and not angels. Communion does not act miraculously, making every imperfection disappear point blank."[51]

THE SECOND VATICAN COUNCIL: REVITALIZING THE CHURCH

It was while Luciani was a bishop that the visionary Pope John convened the historic Second Vatican Council that would usher the Church into the modern world. For Luciani, this was a welcome development. The winds of change would buffet the Church for decades to come, and the bishop of Vittorio Veneto was one in spirit with the movement to reform the Church and its practices. For instance, Luciani was supportive of a more active role for the laity in the life of the Church and in the celebration of the Eucharist.

At the Council's commencement, four thousand bishops, dressed in full regalia, processed grandly as the faithful in St. Peter's Square watched the spectacle. Once inside the basilica, they crammed onto multiple platforms resembling bleachers that lined both sides of the nave. Luciani was inconspicuous in the convocation, just another face in a sea of colleagues. He would remain so for the duration of the historic assembly that would revolutionize the Church.[52]

Vatican II sessions demanded that bishops be absent from their dioceses for extended periods of time, approximately nine months altogether, over three years. Luciani was present for all four assemblies.[53] Administering a diocese from afar was a challenge, especially because the Council demanded a considerable amount of time from its participants. In effect, during the sessions, bishops were performing two full-time jobs simultaneously.

Throughout the Council sessions, Luciani immersed himself in the intricacies of the important theological texts that were generated. Like approximately 90 percent of the 2,381 attendees, he was not vocal during any of the meetings.[54] What prompted his silence is unknown; perhaps he was intimidated by the presence of more prominent colleagues and bishops of larger dioceses. Or maybe his humility held him back. Whatever the reason, his lack of vocal involvement might have been a missed opportunity for him to have made valuable contributions to the deliberations. Luciani was a man intrigued by ideas, he was enthusiastic about the possible reforms that might emanate from the Council, and he could be persuasive. With his wisdom and knowledge of the intricacies of church history, traditions, and practices, he had worthy insights to offer, but he failed to inject himself in the discussions. As a result, through his own choice, he had a negligible impact on the profound issues under consideration.

His intent, he said at the outset, was "to learn rather than to teach." Though his voice was not heard during the deliberations of any of the sessions, he did submit a document on collegiality for consideration by the assembly. His presence was not without note, however. He befriended Poland's primate, Cardinal Stefan Wyszynski, who became a guest of Luciani's on his way home from Rome. (The esteemed Polish cardinal was thrilled when Luciani was later elected pope on the Feast of Our Lady of Czestochowa, the country's foremost feast.)[55] After becoming a cardinal, Luciani reminded Polish Cardinal Karol Wojtyla that at the Council, "we were sitting fairly near each other and you never stopped writing."[56]

Fully attentive to the debates of the Second Ecumenical Council, Luciani was described by Msgr. Mario Ghizzo as being "totally absorbed" by Vatican II. "He knew the documents by heart. Further, he implemented the documents."[57] In particular, Luciani demonstrated an abiding interest in Catholic marriage and family issues, and he was sensitive to those difficulties confronting Catholic couples. That was an enlightened position for a bishop to take: learn from the wedded laity who experienced the challenges of matrimony directly, as opposed to single priests whose understanding was undermined by their remoteness from that kind of life.

Among the myriad matters discussed and debated were changing the liturgy from Latin to the vernacular, simplifying the rites of the Mass, and encouraging a more active role of the faithful in the celebration of the Eucharist. It turned out that Vatican II transformed the Church in numerous ways, all of which had Luciani's wholehearted support and which he later incorporated in his pontifical agenda. Among them were the revision of canon law; recognition of freedom of religion for all people and the expectation that the state was responsible for protecting religious liberty; an endorsement of ecumenism as a legitimate responsibility of the Church; and the correlative termination of pejorative references to other Christian denominations such as referring to Protestants as heretics; a discontinuation of the condemnation of Jews; numerous liturgical reforms; and the adaptation of the original purposes of orders of nuns, brothers, and priests to the modern world.[58]

THE DEATH OF A BELOVED POPE

On June 3, 1963, John XXIII died of cancer. Despite his advanced age, the pope's death undoubtedly caused Luciani sadness. The two had known and liked each other; a friendship had bloomed as a result, their relationship being akin to that of a father and son. Luciani paid tribute to the deceased pontiff, in the process providing insight into the late pope's faith in God, his recognition of his imperfections, and his placid acceptance of his imminent demise despite his physical pain.

The bishop related to his parishioners,

> A few days ago, when Pope John learned from his doctor that he was in grave danger, he immediately wanted the Lord. And when the priest was in front of him with the particle of the host raised, he paused first, made his profession of faith, asked forgiveness for his sins and for the offenses he might possibly have given anyone, then he received Communion. Still not content, he asked that the Blessed Sacrament be exposed in his room, and for half an hour, from his bed, he continued to contemplate and pray.[59]

(Fifteen years later Luciani would die in that same bed without the consolation of confession, or communion, or even having someone by his side.) Luciani traveled to Rome and took part in the funeral of the man who had made him a bishop.[60]

SHIFTING SOCIAL TRENDS

Luciani was a church leader during a period of sweeping political and social change that challenged conservative Catholic norms. In many ways Luciani was a traditionalist who steadfastly believed in the legitimacy of the Magisterium and the primacy of the pope. As a result, he never swerved from official Church pronouncements even when he had personal reservations about their wisdom. Obedience was an attribute formed early in his life, and it continued throughout his life.

He held conventional convictions that often clashed with the cultural changes swirling about him; however, unlike most bishops, he possessed that rare capacity to state his unequivocal views about controversial issues with firmness but also with charity. His vicar general observed, "He united strength with gentleness and paid no heed to the criticisms leveled at him." "It is enough that God is content with me," Luciani himself maintained. "What I imagine myself to be must be cut down to size. What others think of me is of no importance. What God thinks of me is important."[61] Such a view freed him to express his opinions publicly without pressure to compromise or capitulate to hostile public opinion.

The most pressing issues of concern to Luciani were the increasing popularity of communism in Italy, liberation theology, abortion, birth control, and divorce. He addressed them all boldly.

Communists were gaining a political foothold in Italy, and their prospects for increased electoral successes in the coming years encouraged their supporters. Luciani was outspoken in his opposition to any kind of support for the communists among his flock. He was adamant about this: "Marxism is incompatible with Christianity." That stark stance came as no surprise because Marxists were atheists; in addition, Luciani viewed their ideology itself as fundamentally flawed. The course of history was not predetermined, as Marx insisted, and, therefore, the demise of capitalism and the rise of utopian communism was a fantasy, raising false hope among exploited workers that a classless society was inevitable. What complicated the situation for the bishop was that some diocesan priests were sympathetic to communism because they regarded it as a promising remedy to the income inequality that capitalism had created. Luciani recognized that the wealth generated by capitalism was concentrated in the hands of a few at the expense of the working class. Although he might have sympathized with his priests' desire to promote economic equality, support for communism was unacceptable to him. If priests dissented, they were to keep their views private. The bishop would not tolerate open dissension.[62]

Also increasing in popularity was a movement known as liberation theology, which was an offspring of Marxist ideology. Clerical advocates argued that priests should become directly involved in the political struggle of the poor against the wealthy. Despite Luciani's own lamentations over the unequal distribution of wealth in his country and throughout the world and despite his frequent criticism of the excesses of capitalism that led to poverty, he condemned this approach. Said he, "It is mistaken to state that political, economic and social liberation coincides with salvation in Jesus Christ, that *ubi Lenin, ibi Jerusalem* [where Lenin is, there also is Jerusalem]."[63] He clung to the view that political activism was not consistent with the fundamental role of priests. That cleavage between the bishop and some of his priests on this issue would become problematic as time went on.

Luciani was opposed to divorce based on the teachings of Christ and the Church ("a man shall leave his father and mother and be joined to his wife, and the two shall become one flesh. So, they are no longer two, but one flesh. Therefore, what God has joined together, let no one separate").[64] The destruction of the nuclear family and the concomitant deleterious consequences for children were further compelling reasons for him to oppose divorce. Luciani, therefore, defended the "indissolubility of Christian marriage." In his typically unique fashion, however, he recognized that marriage produced strained relationships or worse from time to time and that a successful union required mutual sacrifice and frequent forgiveness by each of the partners. He also recognized the reality of spousal and child abuse in some marriages and found it loathsome and untenable. In such rare instances separation was necessary, and annulments that the Church was now granting in record numbers might be appropriate. What alarmed Luciani was the epidemic of divorce because its normalization threatened the sacrament of marriage. He quoted an insight into the institution of matrimony once observed by Michel de Montaigne, a prominent philosopher of the French Renaissance: "Marriage is like a cage. The birds that are outside do everything they can to get in. Those inside are trying to get out."[65]

Abortion was anathema to Luciani. For him, this was an irrevocable position. Only on the issue of artificial birth control did he apparently maintain a more open mind as a consultant to the papal commission studying the issue. Two situations likely contributed to his lack of rigidity on the subject. One was personal. Luciani's brother Berto and his wife, Antonietta, as good Catholics, produced a brood of ten children, which undoubtedly created financial hardships for the family. On a global scale, he recognized that large families often suffered dire privations that were detrimental to the health of children, and, especially in the Third World, led to childhood malnutrition, starvation, and other forms of severe misery including death. Even so, Luciani quickly stood behind Pope Paul when he issued his controversial 1968 encyclical *Humanae Vitae*, banning all forms of birth control except the rhythm method. Luciani supported the pope's decision despite what he had previously described as having "every doubt" about maintaining the ban.[66] Although he steadfastly defended the pope's stance, he remained sympathetic to those who, regardless of attempts to be faithful to those teachings, sometimes faltered. "How much mercy it is necessary to have" for those couples who violated the ban, Luciani preached.[67]

Artificial birth control methods, which were being used with increasing regularity as the sexual revolution gained momentum in the sixties, were a source of grave concern to the Church. The Magisterium's objection was supported by multifaceted reasons. One was that sexual acts should always be open to the transmission of life and that any attempt by man to interfere with this fundamental purpose of sexual intercourse reduced the act to pleasure alone, thereby interfering with God's procreative purpose. In addition, Pope Paul feared, and justifiably so, that easy access to contraceptives would promote rampant casual sex outside marriage. Promiscuity was regarded by the Church as sinful behavior that debased sexual relations.

Cardinal Giovanni Urbani assigned Luciani the task of conducting an inquiry into the theological and moral implications of the problem of birth control on behalf of the Episcopal Conference of Triveneto, of which he was a member.[68] Luciani's committee included physicians, theologians, and sociologists.[69] Its final report advised the pope to revoke the ban on artificial contraception. Paul VI decided to ignore the recommendation. Nevertheless, Luciani, as was his way, accepted *Humanae Vitae* as a fait accompli once the encyclical was released. He subsequently joined in a statement issued by the Italian Bishops' Conference, which echoed Paul's stance, although he simultaneously reminded Catholics that no one can act perfectly, and he demonstrated compassion for those who lapsed from adhering to this instruction if acting in good faith.[70]

SCANDAL: EMBEZZLING PRIESTS

In 1962 Luciani confronted a scandal that would test his courage and wisdom as bishop. Two of his close collaborators, the diocesan treasurer and a parish priest who was an official adviser to his administration, were implicated in a financial speculation scheme that drained the diocesan treasury of well over 100,000,000 lire, an enormous sum at the time. The scandal led to many attacks on the Church in newspapers.[71] Though far from being naive about people's propensity to sin, Luciani was still surprised by the embezzlement. A partial explanation was offered by Msgr. Taffarel: "He trusted the people; he believed that they were honest, sincere like him."[72]

The bishop demanded an honest explanation from the two clerics, who confessed to wrongdoing, and he suspended them from their official responsibilities. Although he voiced compassion for his embattled clerics, he didn't seek immunity from their legal prosecution.[73]

Determined to collect all the facts in the case before determining a final course of action, Luciani appointed a special commission to investigate the scandal. Throughout the ordeal, he was transparent with his flock. Luciani wrote an open letter to the faithful in his diocese, explaining the situation in detail and without exculpating the two offending priests.[74] In fact, in that August 9 letter, he stated unequivocally, "Two of us have done wrong."[75]

Foremost in his mind was making restitution. Justice and common decency demanded that Luciani commit himself to finding the money needed to do so, but his approach couldn't have been popular: he ordered the selling of diocesan real estate and an increase in parish contributions to the diocese.[76] He indemnified the fraud victims although the law didn't require him to do so.[77] The total income derived from those initiatives was not, however, adequate to cover the deficit that the swindle had created.[78]

On his return from a hospital visit one day, he encountered a woman at the entrance to the bishop's castle who handed him an envelope on which was written, "For your works of charity." When he entered his residence, Luciani opened it to find the exact amount he needed to pay the debt. He saw this coincidence as a sign of Divine Providence. His lingering fiscal problem was now solved.[79]

The scandal took its toll on the bishop. The stress was so intense that he could find no relief in the diocese, and for a period he would return to Canale late at night to sleep at his brother's house and leave early the next morning to resume his duties in Vittorio Veneto.[80]

THE BISHOP ASSERTS HIS AUTHORITY

Luciani's entire life was one of simplicity and modesty. Nevertheless, those who mistook his meekness for weakness did so at their own peril. There was an aspect to his character that came to the fore during his tenure as bishop and surprised those who viewed him as being malleable. When challenged, he exercised his authority with resolve. The bishop was not known for making impetuous decisions. When a conflict demanded resolution, Luciani devoted himself to prayer and reflection in solitude before acting.[81]

This became evident when another incident caused Luciani distress while displaying his firmness in resolving crises. When an elderly parish priest who had been a hero of the Resistance during the war, died in 1966 in Montaner, a small town in Luciani's diocese, the parishioners insisted that his assistant pastor replace him. Luciani was convinced that a different priest was better suited to the needs of the parish; the parishioners, however, remained adamantly opposed to his choice. Luciani invoked his power of appointment to select a pastor of his choice, once again demonstrating his refusal to capitulate to popular opinion when it conflicted with his judgment, and he ultimately resisted all attempts to undermine his authority.[82]

The bishop did not act precipitously. "He was patient with the Montaner situation . . . It seemed it was all done, but then it went on and on," Msgr. Taffarel observed. In fact, he proposed an alternative pastor as a compromise, including an interim one. He also made a pastoral visit to attempt a resolution. Neither met with the approval of the dissidents.[83]

Then some parishioners mobilized to derail the appointment of the bishop's designated successor, some going to such lengths as blocking the entrance to the church. A determined Bishop Luciani went into the church escorted by military police and removed the Holy Sacrament until such time as the parishioners capitulated. The bishop's choice as pastor mediated with the parishioners' preferred replacement, and together they prevailed upon the faithful to cooperate with the new priest. Unfortunately, the animosity generated by the conflict lingered.[84]

If anyone thought that Luciani was timid and indecisive when he was patriarch and especially as pope, they ought to have harkened back to this episode. It illustrated without a scintilla of doubt the inner strength and determination that were as much an element of his character as his humility.

PRIESTS ON RETREAT

The diocese of Vittorio Veneto had four hundred priests.[85] Luciani conducted numerous retreats for them in which he repeatedly emphasized the need to cultivate courtesy in their daily lives as a prelude to committing charitable acts. "People greatly appreciate our courtesy and kindness. This is a little thing, but sometimes the success of our work depends on just these little things: pay attention; be kind and polite with everyone, but subservient to no one," he preached.[86] Luciani knew of what he spoke, for he lived that which he preached.

SUCCESSES

Crises did not dominate Luciani's tenure as bishop. Besides his frequent visits to parishes and hospitals and his availability to those who wished to talk with him, tangible achievements were directly attributable to his leadership. They included completing a seminary, updating the House of Retreats, streamlining the diocesan archives, constructing new churches, and maintaining an active interest in the missions.[87]

In addition to earning the loyalty and affection of the people of his diocese (with some exceptions, of course), his intense prayer life also engendered admiration and emulation. He was often observed reciting the rosary, a daily practice for him and one that he deemed potent in the sometimes challenging attempts to lead a consistently Christian life. Luciani served as a fitting role model to the people of his diocese. It could very well have been his greatest legacy as bishop.[88]

LEAVE-TAKING

On December 15, 1969, with the unexpected death of Cardinal Urbani, Pope Paul VI announced his appointment of Bishop Luciani as patriarch of Venice.[89] The surprising news saddened the faithful of Vittorio Veneto. Their beloved bishop would be gone forevermore, and no successor could possibly measure up to him.

As he prepared to leave for his new assignment, Luciani turned over to the diocesan vicar general his total personal savings. A sizable crowd wishing to see him off assembled on the day of his departure. They presented him with a substantial sum of money they had raised in small contributions, including donations from priests. Luciani was moved beyond words, offered his thanks to the people for their generosity, but refused to accept their largesse. Give it to the poor, he instructed. "I came to you owning nothing, and I want to leave you owning nothing."[90]

NOTES

1. Raymond and Lauretta Seabeck, *The Smiling Pope: The Life and Teaching of John Paul I* (Huntington, IN: Our Sunday Visitor, 2004), 28.
2. Peter Hebblethwaite, *Pope John XXIII: Shepherd of the Modern World* (New York: Doubleday, 1985), 182.
3. Seabeck, *Smiling Pope*, 27.
4. Seabeck, *Smiling Pope*, 27.
5. Msgr. Francesco Taffarel (personal secretary to Bishop Albino Luciani, diocese of Vittorio Veneto, Italy), in discussion with the author, Tarzo, Italy, July 11, 2011.
6. Paul Spackman, *God's Candidate: The Life and Times of John Paul I* (Herefordshire: Gracewing, 2008), 36–39.
7. Spackman, *God's Candidate*, 38.
8. Taffarel, discussion.
9. "Pope John Paul I, Albino Luciani," Catholic Hierarchy.org.
10. Loris Serafini (director, Foundation Papa Luciani and Museum Albino Luciani of Canale d'Agordo), in discussion with the author, Gloucester, Rhode Island, October 10, 2012.
11. Albino Luciani photograph 687.JPG, Museo Papa Luciani Collection.
12. Seabeck, *Smiling Pope*, 27.
13. Seabeck, *Smiling Pope*, 27.
14. Seabeck, *Smiling Pope*, 29.
15. Serafini, discussion.

16. Death certificate of Bortola Tancon, parish archive, St. John the Baptist of Canale d'Agordo, Death Register n. 17, c. 179r, reference number 9.
17. Serafini, discussion.
18. Death certificate of Giovanni Luciani, parish archive, St. John the Baptist of Canale d'Agordo, Death Register n. 17, c. 195r, reference number 1.
19. Loris Serafini, email message to author, September 15, 2015.
20. Serafini, discussion.
21. Seabeck, *Smiling Pope*, 89.
22. Seabeck, *Smiling Pope*, 90.
23. Seabeck, *Smiling Pope*, 88.
24. Seabeck, *Smiling Pope*, 88.
25. "Albino Luciani Chronology," *Humilitas*, August 2001, 3.
26. Seabeck, *Smiling Pope*, 28.
27. Serafini, discussion.
28. Taffarel, discussion.
29. Taffarel, discussion.
30. Serafini, discussion.
31. Pia Luciani, letter to author, November 3, 2012.
32. Luciani letter.
33. Seabeck, *Smiling Pope*, 29.
34. Taffarel, discussion.
35. "Highlights of the Life of His Holiness John Paul I," March 2, 2010, http://www.vatican.va/holy_father/john_paul_i/biography/documents/hf_jp-1_jp-i_bio_01021997.
36. Spackman, *God's Candidate*, 43.
37. Seabeck, *Smiling Pope*, 31.
38. Seabeck, *Smiling Pope*, 32.
39. Taffarel, discussion.
40. Spackman, *God's Candidate*, 3.
41. Taffarel, discussion.
42. Serafini, discussion.
43. "The First Years of Albino Luciani, Part II" (The Bishop). Video. https://www.albinoluciani .com /index .php ?id =274 &L =3.
44. Serafini, discussion.
45. Spackman, *God's Candidate*, 44.
46. Taffarel, discussion.
47. Seabeck, *Smiling Pope*, 132.
48. Seabeck, *Smiling Pope*, 136.
49. Seabeck, *Smiling Pope*, 137.
50. Seabeck, *Smiling Pope*, 138.
51. Seabeck, *Smiling Pope*, 139.
52. "First Years."
53. "Highlights," March 2, 2010.
54. Spackman, *God's Candidate*, 46–47.
55. Seabeck, *Smiling Pope*, 33–34.

56. Jonathan Kivitny, *Man of the Century: The Life and Times of John Paul II* (New York: Henry Holt, 1997), 187.
57. Spackman, *God's Candidate*, 55.
58. "What Changed at Vatican II," *Catholic Register*, October 8, 2012, https://www.catholicregister.org/features/item/15194-what-changed-at-vatican-ii.
59. Seabeck, *Smiling Pope*, 141.
60. Serafini, discussion.
61. Seabeck, *Smiling Pope*, 34.
62. "A Swift, Stunning Choice," *Time*, September 4, 1978, 65.
63. "The September Pope," *Time*, October 9, 1978, 71.
64. Matthew 19:4–5, *New Revised Standard Version with Apocrypha* (New York: Oxford University Press, 1989), 21.
65. Kenneth L. Woodward, "The 34 Days of John Paul I," *Newsweek*, October 9, 1978, 73.
66. "Stunning Choice," 65.
67. Seabeck, *Smiling Pope*, 36.
68. Spackman, *God's Candidate*, 58.
69. Serafini, discussion.
70. Francis X. Murphy, *The Papacy Today* (London: Weidenfeld and Nicholson, 1981), 172.
71. Spackman, *God's Candidate*, 44–45.
72. Taffarel, discussion.
73. Spackman, *God's Candidate*, 45.
74. Serafini, discussion.
75. Spackman, *God's Candidate*, 45.
76. Mo Guernon, "The Paradox of Albino Luciani," speech, Pope John Paul I Centenary Conference, Immaculate Conception Center, Brooklyn, New York, October 13, 2012.
77. Spackman, *God's Candidate*, 45.
78. Serafini, discussion.
79. Serafini, discussion.
80. Loris Serafini, email message to the author, September 15, 2015.
81. Serafini, discussion.
82. Spackman, *God's Candidate*, 64–65.
83. Spackman, *God's Candidate*, 65.
84. Spackman, *God's Candidate*, 65.
85. Spackman, *God's Candidate*, 42.
86. Seabeck, *Smiling Pope*, 24.
87. Seabeck, *Smiling Pope*, 30.
88. Seabeck, *Smiling Pope*, 36.
89. Spackman, *God's Candidate*, 68.
90. Peter Hebblethwaite, *The Year of Three Popes* (Cleveland, OH: Collins, 1979).

• 8 •

Patriarch and Cardinal

Preparation for the Papal Pallium (1970–1978)

AN INAUSPICIOUS ARRIVAL

Figure 8.1. Patriarch Luciani walking past an honor guard in Piazza San Marco on a formal occasion.

Venice was a curious destination for Albino Luciani because the city and the new patriarch were so fundamentally dissimilar. The legendary "Jewel of the Adriatic" was a place still gushing with pride over its illustrious history despite its modern descent into splendid squalor. The unique city of canals—famous for its carnivals, regattas, and film festivals—revels in spectacle, fanfare, and ostentation. Its elite, the offspring of nobility, covets its prestige and preserves the pretentiousness that is its birthright. Venice was, in short, an incongruous home for a patriarch whose personality was better suited to tranquility, solitude, and simplicity. In light of that reality, Luciani and the city's citizens were destined to have an uneasy relationship.

The incompatibility between the two became readily apparent upon Luciani's official arrival on February 9, 1970.[1] He dashed the Venetians' expectations of their new bishop, a figure the locals regarded as a prominent presence among them. Disliking their propensity for pomp, Luciani abandoned the esteemed Venetian tradition of the new patriarch officially entering with an entourage of gondolas, military parades, and elaborate decorations. Instead, he insisted on a modest ceremony.[2] Luciani's decision to dispense with grandeur irked the local notables. His refusal to wear the gem-studded ring that belonged to the office also must have stung.[3] Apparently oblivious to the discontent he was causing, Luciani, as usual, was all smiles when greeting people upon his arrival.[4]

By insisting on his personal preferences rather than making a gesture of respect to his welcoming diocese by complying with local custom, Luciani revealed a costly lapse in judgment. Unfavorable first impressions can be enduring; and, at least among the municipality's leading citizens, it was so in this instance. Luciani instigated a contentious relationship with the elite, which he would exacerbate in the future with what they would consider additional affronts. As a result, his eight-year tenure in Venice would be more tumultuous than he expected.

To make matters worse, the city fathers were dismayed by Luciani's plain style of speaking, thinking it inappropriate for such an august figure as the city's patriarch. During his first homily, the archbishop admitted that he felt inadequate to undertake the new assignment that God had entrusted to him. It was the same theme he had struck when he became bishop of Vittorio Veneto and that he would echo in his first Angelus as pope as well as when taking possession of St. John Lateran.[5] The admission didn't inspire confidence among the city's leaders.

Although some considered his style of preaching to be simplistic, and even members of the clergy thought that it was beneath the dignity of a bishop, many of the faithful who heard him speak found his homilies to be profound but comprehensible.[6] Only over time did a number of Venetians come to realize that their bishop was a man of culture and vast learning whose simple style of speaking was deliberate.[7]

PATRIARCHAL SUCCESSION

Some three months following the sudden death of Patriarch Giovanni Urbani, Pope Paul named Luciani to the vacant post on December 15.[8] The heir apparent was dismayed by the appointment. He was content as bishop of the modest diocese of Vittorio Veneto, and yet again he attempted to decline a promotion, citing precarious health and his belief that he was not qualified for the position. And again, his protestations were in vain.[9]

Despite Luciani's reticence, a popular chorus of voices from his current diocese called for his appointment as patriarch.[10] However, the enthusiasm was far from universal. He had alienated some of his flock by making controversial decisions as bishop of his previous diocese, and upon the announcement of his impending promotion some malcontents circulated a petition that they sent to Rome protesting the pope's choice. That opposition was an exercise in futility.[11]

After Luciani's selection, but prior to assuming his duties in Venice, he was traveling by car with his secretary and dressed in black like an ordinary priest. The bishop instructed his driver to stop for a couple of youths who were hitchhiking. During the conversation that ensued, the passengers mentioned the new Venetian archbishop, explaining they had never heard of this Luciani fellow and that someone else should have been named. Without revealing his identity, the bishop explained that God's ways are sometimes at odds with the ways of men. The two passengers became enamored of him, and as they left the vehicle they exclaimed, "We wish a priest like you would be made patriarch!"[12]

When word spread that Luciani was to become archbishop of Venice, his hometown of Canale went wild. His boyhood friend, Giulio Bramezza, practically trembled with jubilation. Don Rinaldo Andrich went to the bishop's castle in Vittorio Veneto to congratulate his old friend personally. Townsmen couldn't wait for their favorite son to return to Canale. The patriarch-designate arrived home on January 11, 1970, to a joyous welcome. On hand were a host of religious and civil dignitaries who had organized a festival to celebrate.[13]

A PATRIARCH AND BASILICA LIKE NO OTHER

The Byzantine architecture of the five-domed St. Mark's Basilica dominates the 135,700-square-foot Piazza San Marco. The massive church, which opened on October 8, 1094, is adjacent to the Doges Palace and the patriarchal residence. It was there that the Dukes of Venice had been consecrated. It is frequently referred to as the Gilded Church—for good reason. The interior dazzles with gold; the Pala d'Oro, a resplendent gilt screen behind the main altar, is encrusted with 1,927 precious jewels illuminating the life of Christ.[14]

The church is perhaps most famous, however, not for its ornate appearance, but for its original purpose. It was built to house the sacred relics of Saint Mark, author of the first Gospel, whose corpse (or what remains of it) rests in the crypt. In 828 two clever merchants smuggled the body from Alexandria, Egypt, by concealing it under pork; because Muslim Arabs loathe pork, the customs officials declined to inspect the barrel.[15]

The archdiocese that Luciani inherited was an ancient and distinguished one, among a handful of the most prestigious in all of Italy despite its small size. Created in 774, it consisted of slightly more than four hundred thousand Catholics in 1978.[16] In Venice two ancient religions, Islam and Christianity, met.[17] It was fitting, therefore, that just as in Constantinople, the head of the Church here held the title patriarch.[18] The bishop of Venice is one of only four patriarchs in the Catholic Church. This now honorary title dates to 1451 when Pope Nicholas V conferred it on the archbishop of that time.[19]

According to Peter Akroyd, the distinguished author, "Because the bones of Saint Mark were preserved in the heart of Venice, the city claimed an apostolic status equal to that of Rome."[20] The saint and the winged lion with which he is associated became the emblem of the city.[21] In his enchanting book, *Venice: Pure* City, Akroyd suggests that the very idea of a city built on the sea conjured up the miraculous, like Jesus walking on water.[22]

WATER AND LUMINARIES EVERYWHERE

Known for its singular beauty, the city boasted about its notable native sons such as the adventurers and writers Marco Polo and Giacomo Casanova. The immortal composer and priest Antonio Vivaldi also hailed from Venice.[23] It was here, too, that Galileo gazed through his telescope from the top of the campanile in St. Mark's Square.[24]

PATRIARCH LUCIANI TAKES OVER

It was in this historic gem of a city that the humble Albino Luciani took up residence. Upon arriving, Luciani discovered that a car was available to the patriarch. He returned the keys, insisting on using his own old automobile.[25] The day following his arrival in Venice, Luciani got to work learning about the diocese, calling diocesan officials, and making tentative plans. As always,

Figure 8.2. Wearing a hard hat, Luciani greets laborers at a factory in Mestre.

he was a man in a hurry. Time was a precious commodity, and he was eager to maximize it in preparing himself for his new responsibilities. The sequence of tasks he undertook followed a familiar pattern: becoming acquainted with the needs of the diocese, visiting the parishes, engaging the faithful in dialogue, and after developing an agenda, beginning its implementation.

The patriarch almost always dressed in a black cassock.[26] Luciani enjoyed wandering the streets of Venice, as he had in Vittorio Veneto, appearing as a simple priest.[27] On many occasions he'd encounter a talkative woman who, believing him to be a modest priest, would ask him about the virtues and shortcomings of the patriarch. Struggling to withhold a smile, Luciani would respond wittily in trying to satisfy her curiosity.[28] After one such solitary stroll, the patriarch returned home sporting a bruised and swollen cheek. When a sister asked him what had happened, he replied dispassionately, "Oh, nothing . . . I met a drunkard . . . He hit me in the face."[29]

Luciani continued his habit of routinely visiting prisons, hospitals, factories, seminaries, the elderly, and families in need.[30] During his tenure in Venice, the city was struck by a tornado, killing thirty people and injuring others. Without delay, Luciani visited the sick in hospitals and went to the morgue to comfort the loved ones of the victims.[31]

Following the teachings of Saint Francis de Sales, Luciani was the living embodiment of an individual making a difference in people's quality of life by committing little acts of kindness that inspired others to do likewise. "The occasions for heroism and great actions are very rare. On the other hand, every day within easy reach are the occasions of doing little favors,

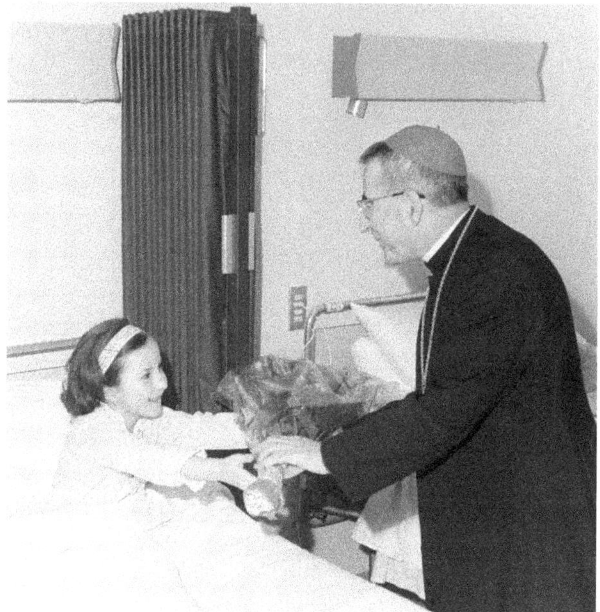

Figure 8.3. On one of his frequent hospital visits, Patriarch Luciani presents flowers to a delighted young patient.

interpreting kindly the actions of others, of being patient with those who displease us," he preached. A priest familiar with the patriarch repeatedly advised others, "If you want to understand the gospel and love the Lord more, get to know Patriarch Luciani."[32]

ELEVATION

On March 5, 1973, Pope Paul convened a consistory. Luciani was the first of thirty-nine new cardinals to receive the red hat.[33] He approached the seated pope, knelt, took both of Paul's hands in his own, bowed his head so that the pope could place the red zucchetto on his head followed by the biretta. Then he had the honor of delivering a speech of gratitude on behalf of all the newly appointed cardinals.[34] His message underscored his deep humility and dependence on his confreres. "I almost want to apologize for taking on such heavy responsibility. Be my brothers, support me, help me over my every error, save me from every weakness," he implored.[35]

Luciani was a cardinal for nearly five and a half years. Even with that status, just one level beneath the pope, he continued to hear confessions like an ordinary parish priest, a highly unusual practice among "princes of the Church."[36]

TO THINE OWN SELF BE TRUE

Msgr. Mario Senigaglia, the patriarch's first personal secretary, asserted that Luciani wanted to "demythologize" the role of bishop. That is why he typically appeared in public dressed in black. He would don the red only when ceremony demanded it and more out of respect for others. He never even bought the scarlet garments that a cardinal traditionally wears. Instead, he wore the ones that he found in the closet of the residence that his predecessor left behind.[37] As a cardinal he could have reserved seats or an entire compartment for himself on trains, but he preferred either to travel by automobile or taxi.[38] Even at the patriarch's spacious quarters in Venice, he lived as simply as he had as a country parish priest.[39]

Peter Hebblethwaite, the prolific Catholic author, related an insightful anecdote about Luciani's character. "In Luciani's case, [humility] took the form of going through the streets of Venice incognito, dressed as a simple priest, his pectoral cross and skull cap tucked into his briefcase. He once dropped in on a conference on ecology . . . and began to talk with one of the foreign participants. They still had plenty to say to each other when the time came for Luciani to go. He invited the ecologist to come and see him at home. 'Where do you live?' asked the ecologist. 'Just next door to San Marco.' 'Do you mean the patriarch's palace?' 'Yes.' 'And who do I ask for?' 'Ask for the patriarch.'"[40]

ROUTINES AND PRIORITIES

Figure 8.4. Wearing a white soutane for relief from the intense summer heat, Luciani amuses a group of children who gather around the kindly patriarch as a smiling nun looks on.

Of the multitude of invitations that Venice's secular world extended to Luciani, he responded favorably to only a few and almost exclusively those that raised money to alleviate poverty. His steadfast refusal to hobnob with the wealthy and powerful in the active social life of Venice did not endear him to that segment of society.[41]

So intense was his commitment to the poor that in 1971 he advocated that affluent Western churches donate 1 percent of their income to the poverty-stricken churches of the Third World.[42] It was a revolutionary recommendation.

Luciani's constant message to his flock was charity. He set the example himself by lavishing attention on children, the dispossessed, and the sick. He was a force for reconciliation where discord prevailed.[43] Among the many in need to whom he ministered were children who suffered mental afflictions. He was a regular visitor to the don Orione home for the mentally debilitated where he would often meet with the children in groups, say Mass, and even officiate over First Holy Communions. This aroused the ire of some priests who found the administration of the sacrament offensive because, by virtue of their mental handicaps, these children were believed to be ill-prepared to receive the Eucharist. When the home was perilously close to closing its doors because of inadequate funding, Luciani raised sufficient funds to keep it open.[44]

Not long after coming to Venice, he shocked some people by selling various treasures of the archdiocese including a pectoral cross of great value so that he could make a contribution on behalf of the Church to a sanitarium for children with handicaps. He also encouraged local parishes to sell all their precious items so that they could help the poor.[45] He thought the Church itself, as an institution, had failed in some respects in its obligations to the needy.[46]

His homilies as patriarch were little different in tone, substance, and form than those he delivered as a simple country priest in Canale. In plain terms that virtually all his listeners could readily comprehend, Luciani spoke about profundities. One of his favorite and effective techniques for reaching his audience and demonstrating the points he emphasized was to enlist the "assistance" of children to whom he would pose questions whose answers were illustrative of his message. Though it aroused scorn among some priests for being "unworthy of a bishop," Luciani didn't flinch from continuing the practice even after he became pope.[47] According to Msgr. Senigaglia, Luciani's habit of bringing children forward during the preaching originated in Belluno because he found it efficacious in gaining the attention of the congregation.[48]

Luciani cared deeply about seminarians, and it was not unusual for him to invite a few to join him for dinner. He earned the gratitude of some priests who encountered financial hardship by quietly assisting them with his own money. To those priests who were struggling about whether to honor their vows, he did not berate or condemn. Instead, he devoted considerable time counseling them and praying for them.[49]

Most especially, he gave ample time for prayer, a discipline he had developed early in his priesthood. This is how he started his mornings in the chapel; and fellow clergy were often amazed at the amount of time he spent in church, absorbed in conversation with the Lord. Whenever he faced a challenge, he would first pray.[50]

His voracious appetite for reading was not sated. Luciani subscribed to several international journals primarily devoted to spirituality and theology. He read French almost as if it were his native tongue. He had accumulated a sizable personal library in Belluno and donated it to the seminary there. When he was made bishop, he started once again to build a new collection of books as he did in Venice. At dinner he loved to talk about books and ideas.[51] Other than the personal library that he took with him to Venice, Luciani had few personal possessions. These books were his "riches."

When traveling in the city of canals, he patiently waited in line to take the vaporetto (a water taxi) with ordinary people until his turn came to board.[52] One day when he went to nearby Mestre for a pastoral visit, local leaders had restricted automotive traffic but gave the patriarch special permission to proceed. Luciani would have none of it. Instead, he traveled by bus to the hinterlands and then straddled a bicycle, his cardinal's robes billowing behind him in his urgency to arrive at the parish that expected him.[53]

Every summer from 1972 to 1977 he spent ten days at Weissenstein (Pietralba) in the province of Bolzano, a stunning Marian sanctuary where, as a child, he would go on pilgrimage afoot with his mother. There he could relax, eat with the people, play bocce, and meditate in silence. He was also able to practice his German. Luciani's love of language was evident in one of his routines: each day he would alternate his breviary readings from Latin, Italian, German, French, Spanish, and English.[54]

In April 1977 Luciani led a delegation of bishops from the Triveneto region of northern Italy in an *ad limina* visit to the pope. At the end of the audience, Paul VI was unable to locate the button that rang the bell to summon his secretary. Luciani inconspicuously guided Paul's hand to the button on the armchair. The pope turned to Luciani and whispered something foretelling, "So you have already learned where the buzzer is."[55]

SECRETARIES

In his six years as personal secretary, Mario Senigaglia developed a close friendship with Luciani. They were together almost all day every day. Often Senigaglia sought his counsel about solving problems he faced.[56] When Luciani agreed to assign Senigaglia to a parish as he had requested since that was his first love, the search for a replacement began. Diego Lorenzi, a Don Orione priest, was selected for the post shortly after returning to Venice following the completion of his studies in England.[57] Lorenzi served in Venice from the summer of 1976 until August of 1978.

KNOCK, AND THE DOOR WILL OPEN

One of the unusual but commendable practices of Luciani's years in Venice was his nearly constant availability, particularly to those in need. In his first days as patriarch, he ordered that the doors to the palace were to remain open to people at all hours, and as a direct result, he was swamped by petitioners daily. Personal audiences became available to the "least of these" whenever his schedule allowed it.[58] Authority figures, beggars, the curious, the needy, students—everyone was admitted who sought entrance. Often the patriarch himself answered the doorbell and the jingling phone. It often happened that important secular and religious personages would have to wait in the corridors of the patriarchal palace while Luciani listened to an indigent individual or an elderly woman who had stopped by to give him her regards.[59]

In 1983, Senigaglia recalled an incident that illustrates how Luciani, as patriarch of Venice, served the needy:

> Within a few days of his arrival in Venice, leaving the study, Luciani noticed the great tide of people . . . that had filled the waiting rooms. He asked me, "Who are they?" "They are the poor." He wanted to go and greet them . . . about sixty or seventy in number. For each he had a smile and a word. Then he said, "Remember, the Patriarch's door is always open. Ask don Mario, and what I can do for you, I will always do it with pleasure." "Excellence—I mumbled—you will ruin me: they will not leave me in peace." He smiled, saying, "Somebody will help us." The poor . . . drunkards, released prisoners, women who walked the streets, clients of the nocturnal asylums, and beggars . . . were his friends. For many of them we found houses and work.[60]

One day a mentally challenged boy accompanied by his mother desperately wanted his picture taken with the patriarch. Luciani promptly agreed, but the boy insisted that he wear his red ceremonial garments instead of the black cassock in which he was dressed. Without hesitation, Luciani left to change and returned to have the photo taken with the excited youngster. Several days later, the patriarch asked a sister to deliver the picture to the boy's mother, who was deeply touched by the magnanimous gesture of her archbishop.[61]

When Senigaglia first became his personal secretary, Luciani informed him that priests could see him without an appointment just as they had previously in his tiny diocese of Vittorio Veneto. It became quite common for priests facing difficulties in their ministry that perplexed them to seek the cardinal's counsel and often would be invited for lunch or dinner.[62]

DISTINGUISHED GUESTS

Figure 8.5. Pope Paul VI places the papal stole on Luciani's shoulders, Piazza San Marco, Venice.

Patriarch Luciani also hosted high-ranking prelates in Venice. As with tourists, Venice held appeal as a destination for foreign cardinals, some of whom became Luciani's guests.[63]

Joseph Ratzinger, the new archbishop of Munich, took his initial vacation as a cardinal in the summer of 1977; his destination was Luciani's archdiocese. As a young member of "the club of cardinals," Ratzinger was grateful for the courtesy that Luciani extended to him. As the future Pope Benedict XVI recalled,

> I felt impressed by the spontaneous cordiality and the great human goodness towards me that came from him. I still see him seated in front of me, dressed in his simple black cassock and the shoes rather worn out, to talk about his youth . . .When a year later, I saw him again in the Conclave, the thought came spontaneously to me that a man who had such talents of heart and a mind illuminated by the heart, should be, of necessity, a good Pope, and I was glad that many others thought like me.[64]

Only three years into his tenure in Venice, on September 16, 1972, the patriarch received Paul VI, his most illustrious guest.[65] When the pope arrived, he was accompanied by Luciani, who sat opposite him in the gondola.[66] The papal visit was a public affair of consequence, attended by an enthusiastic crowd of twenty thousand at St. Mark's Square. Wearing a flowing red cape, the pope led the way on a raised walkway leading to a stage, with Luciani following closely behind, virtually ignored by the faithful whose attention was riveted on the pontiff. Paul's presence was a public show of support for the patriarch following a bitter controversy that had erupted with a cadre of liberal Venetian priests.[67]

At one point the pope placed his left arm around Luciani's shoulder and presented him to the applauding crowd. Then, toward the end of the ceremony, the pontiff demonstrated his esteem for the patriarch in a surprisingly poignant manner. As the Holy Father was walking along a footbridge, he stopped, removed his stole, and placed it on Luciani's shoulders. That gesture embarrassed Luciani deeply.[68] Some observers later interpreted this deed as a prophetic sign that Paul was signaling the choice of his own successor. The patriarch's brother Berto, who witnessed the episode, later told his sister that he had a premonition that this meant his brother would become pope.[69] Coincidentally, that very morning, Paul had completed his last will and testament, an indication that his death was on his mind.[70]

On a subsequent occasion Msgr. Senigaglia suggested it would be suitable to make use of the stole that the pope had given to Luciani for confirmations and parish visits. When the secretary was about to pack it in Luciani's suitcase in preparation for one excursion, Luciani suddenly became very serious and indicated it should be left in his dresser because it caused him inexplicable anxiety.[71]

COLLABORATION

Luciani's priority of promoting constructive dialogue among Protestants and other faiths in the hope of someday achieving at least a degree of unity among them was evident in his outreach to these groups. He sponsored five ecumenical conferences during his nine-year tenure in Venice.[72] Two were between Catholics and members of the World Council of Churches; one with Pentecostal Christians; another with Anglicans; and one with Jews.[73]

Within the Catholic Church, the patriarch was especially active. He participated in the Second General Assembly of the Synod of Bishops in Rome, which was devoted to "The Ministerial Priesthood and Justice in the World." Then during the Italian Bishops Conference in 1972, he was elected vice president, a position he held until June 2, 1975. Luciani resumed his involvement with the Synod of Bishops in Rome, in 1974, where the discussion focused on "Evangelization in the Modern World."[74] Finally, in 1977 he took part in the fourth Ordinary General Assembly of the Synod, also convened in Rome, that discussed the issue of "Catechetics in Our Time."[75]

A SEA OF TROUBLES

The Venetian archdiocese that Luciani inherited was fraught with seemingly intractable problems. Among them were severe labor disputes, a divisive quarrel about abortion, renegade clergy, the rising tide of communism nationwide, secularization of what had once been a flourishing spiritual center, an exodus from Mass attendance, as well as intensifying criticism of Church authority.[76]

Labor-management conflicts were common, and the patriarch made valiant attempts to settle feuds between the two sides. Even during periods of political turmoil, Luciani maintained a good relationship with politicians and trade unionists,[77] though he sometimes was attacked by both sides for his pleas to negotiate.[78] To him the plight of laborers was personal, a fundamental matter of equity. He visited factories, sometimes wearing a hard hat, to meet with workers and offer encouragement. At Port Marghera he listened to their worries and difficulties.

Luciani also sought to enlist the faithful of his diocese in the cause of social justice: to settle strikes and to protect the fundamental rights of laborers. He once preached that workers faced additional hardships when Catholics didn't recognize the inherent problems with capitalism or accused workers who fought for their legitimate rights as being communists. The usually soft-spoken Luciani didn't mince words on this subject.[79]

Luciani was deeply committed to justice but maintained a rigid view of priests' role in promoting it. He always urged his clergymen to be faithful to their prayer life, charity, and the poor. But when a group of young progressive clerics calling themselves "worker priests" aligned themselves with the workers' movement in Port Marghera, the patriarch saw this as a threat to the unity of the Church. Though Luciani himself was staunchly supportive of workers' rights, these priests had taken the unprecedented move of aligning themselves with the liberation theology movement that was centered in Latin America, an intolerable development to the patriarch. He was adamant that priests should not directly involve themselves in politics regardless of the nobility of their motives.[80]

The patriarch didn't react kindly to the insurrection of such militant diocesan priests. Luciani reminded them of their obligation to be obedient to both the pope and the patriarch.[81] Their belief in political activism to redress injustices must have been so genuine that they wouldn't abide by their bishop's injunction to obey the Church's policy. Luciani's directive prohibiting their political activities prompted a group of them to write a petition to the Vatican seeking Luciani's removal, an extraordinarily extreme act. The pope ignored the request, which precipitated Paul's public appearance in Venice in support of Luciani.[82]

Luciani's most severe crisis in Venice was over the issue of divorce, which was exacerbated again by diocesan priests who openly supported a 1974 Italian referendum favoring civil dissolution of marriages, a position at odds with official Church teaching. An increasing divorce rate and remarriage outside the church led to millions of Catholics losing their good standing within the church, resulting in their being denied the sacraments.[83]

Just prior to the 1974 divorce plebiscite, a Catholic students' movement issued a public statement supporting it. Luciani responded swiftly. The Catholic University Association of Italy, known as FUCI, the acronym for the *Federazione Universitaria Cattolica Italiana* (Italian Catholic University Federation) published a booklet addressed to the bishops in which it outlined its support of divorce. Before that development Patriarch Luciani had been tolerant of the group's experimentation with the liturgy as well as with biblical scholarship. Perhaps his patience then had emboldened them to take more extreme positions.[84] This time, however, in Luciani's view they had become radical.

His gentleness was deceiving. Because of it, his strength of character and decisiveness were frequently dismissed by those who erroneously believed him to be weak. A prime example of his capacity for bold decision-making was when he removed the priest who advised the FUCI group in Venice and sternly warned twenty of his priests who backed the divorce measure that if they continued to attend pro-divorce rallies, he would suspend their right to say Mass. News of the startling development spread throughout Italy.[85]

Luciani admonished them and all the faithful to adhere to the position that the Italian bishops had taken or, at the very least, not to speak publicly about their personal dissenting views.[86]

Luciani's decisive action in this regard could be interpreted as intemperate, perhaps even rash. Could Luciani have privately engaged in discussions with those priests and attempted to persuade them that their actions were ill-advised, that they violated the vow of obedience that they had taken at their consecrations, that they were putting their bishop in an untenable position? Beyond that, was a less drastic measure available that he could have taken to chasten them?

This issue must have been painful for the patriarch because he confronted a conflict of conscience. On the one hand, he was deeply sympathetic to those trapped in marriages that were unhealthy. At the same time, the dissolution of marriages in the West was becoming increasingly commonplace and often triggered by far less serious issues—many, if not most of which, could have been resolved by less drastic means than dissolving the sacred union.[87]

Marriage was a sacrament that Christ Himself had instituted. As a priest, Luciani could not in good conscience be selective about which credos of Christ he would accept as legitimate or worthy of defending. Further complicating his decision was the virtual impossibility of a bishop tolerating priests disobeying the dictums of the Magisterium. In his considered view, widespread noncompliance with the decrees of the Church would lead to chaos, the ruination of papal authority, and possibly the ultimate dissolution of the Church itself.

Despite the patriarch's enduring affection for his diocesan priests, the ongoing tribulations that a number of them caused him fundamentally conflicted with his devotion to tradition, as was evident in an appeal to the clergy of Venice: "I exhort you about the love for the tradition. Don't be as the ones who are dazzled and want to change everything."[88]

The impasse between the patriarch and his priests caused Luciani great tribulation. During this period the anger of some priests was so intense that again they took the extraordinary move of appealing to the Vatican for Luciani's dismissal. In a blistering letter they accused Luciani of not visiting his parishes often enough and not knowing how to be patriarch. In a message directly addressed to the pope, Luciani responded in a disarming way. He rebutted the first accusation by insisting that he paid regular visits to parishes but admitted with a touch of irony, "It's true that I don't know how to be patriarch."[89]

THE TOLL OF LEADERSHIP

Once Luciani's secretary arrived with a letter to the patriarch, pointing out a message full of insults about the epistles Luciani had written in his book *Illustrissimi*. The writer accused him of debasing his position as patriarch with such drivel that he wrote about matters that shouldn't concern a bishop.[90] It was only one example of the ire he aroused among some in his diocese.

His years in Venice were years of trial and occasional regret. Luciani did not shy away from any of the controversial issues of his time and place. For example, he inveighed against what he perceived to be the immorality of the Venetian film festival. He staunchly supported the country's strict law against divorce when efforts to repeal it gained momentum. He was also vocal in his opposition to the Italian Communist Party, a group that was becoming increasingly popular.[91] Luciani often felt isolated and misunderstood, but he would hint only occasionally at his troubles. Years later, don Diego Lorenzi, the secretary who replaced Senigaglia, revealed that Luciani found the role of patriarch trying at times, which caused him "pain and fatigue."[92]

HOME IS WHERE HIS HEART IS

Luciani sought opportunities to escape Venice. "He was always in Belluno it seemed," according to Rev. Silvio De Nard[93] and returned to Canale in the summertime. He occasionally went home on other occasions, too.[94] In the winter of 1978, while he was back in his beloved hometown, the archpriest of Canale, don Rinaldo Andrich, invited the cardinal to preach a Lenten sermon. He gladly complied with the request.[95] While there, an incident took place that reinforced Luciani's concerns that his status as cardinal distanced him from people, even those who had been close to him. When the faithful were leaving the church at the conclusion of an evening Mass, a cousin of Luciani's, Giovanni Tancon, wanted to sneak out without being noticed. But Luciani spotted him and inquired why he ignored him simply because he was now a cardinal. The cousin replied that he felt uneasy in the presence of a man of such stature.[96]

The patriarch returned to Canale for the last time in June 1978.[97] It was a private affair to launch the restoration of the church that had been damaged two years earlier in an earthquake. The renovation was made possible by a donation to the parish of one million lire that he had received from a generous anonymous donor. Luciani himself was unable to contribute because his bank account was nearly depleted. And no wonder; he gave his own money freely to everyone who sought his assistance.[98] During his last homily in his beloved church, Luciani recalled that he was constantly lacking money, yet his recollections of those years were precious.[99]

FINAL DESTINATION

When Luciani became aware of Pope Paul's death, he returned to Venice to say Mass for the deceased pontiff and to prepare for his departure to the Vatican. The coming days there would be demanding: During the interregnum he would participate in the papal funeral, have informal sessions with fellow cardinals who had been summoned to Rome from around the globe, attend daily meetings with them to make decisions about the Church in the absence of a supreme ruler, and then retire to the Sistine Chapel to vote in the conclave that would elect the next pope.[100]

Venice was splashed with sunshine the morning of August 10 as the patriarch and his secretary embarked on the journey to Rome by car. As usual, Luciani preferred to leave without fanfare. A few priests who somehow got wind of the patriarch's departure time, however, appeared to see him off. Also bidding him farewell was his faithful housekeeper and friend, Sister Vincenza, who became visibly emotional as they parted. "Eminence, I hope you return," she worried. Luciani tried reassuring her that all would be well. "My dear sister, of course I will. Don't worry."[101]

NOTES

1. Raymond and Lauretta Seabeck, *The Smiling Pope: The Life and Teaching of John Paul I* (Huntington, IN: Our Sunday Visitor, 2004), 250.

2. Paul Spackman, *God's Candidate: The Life and Times of Pope John Paul I* (Herefordshire: Gracewing, 2008), 69.

3. Seabeck, *Smiling Pope*, 39.

4. "The First Years of Albino Luciani, Part III" (The Cardinal), https://www.albino-luciani.com/index.php?id=272&L=3.

5. Loris Serafini (director, Foundation Papa Luciani and Museum Albino Luciani of Canale d'Agordo), in discussion with the author, Canale d'Agordo, Italy, September 7, 2022.

6. Seabeck, *Smiling Pope*, 42.

7. Serafini, discussion.

8. "Biography of His Holiness John Paul I," https://www.vatican.va/content/john-paul-i/en/biography/documents/hf_jp-i_bio_01021997_biography.html.

9. Seabeck, *Smiling Pope*, 37.

10. J. N. D. Kelly, *The Oxford Dictionary of Popes* (Oxford: Oxford University Press, 1986), 325.
11. "The First Years of Albino Luciani, Part III."
12. Seabeck, *Smiling Pope*, 37.
13. Serafini, discussion.
14. www.St-marks-basilica.com.
15. www.St-marks-basilica.com.
16. Seabeck, *Smiling Pope*, 59.
17. Peter Ackroyd, *Venice: Pure City* (New York: Nan A. Talese/Doubleday, 2009), 45.
18. Ackroyd, *Pure City*, 353.
19. "Compassionate Shepherd," *Time*, August 21, 1978, 62.
20. Ackroyd, *Pure City*, 299.
21. Ackroyd, *Pure City*, 38.
22. Ackroyd, *Pure City*, 14.
23. Ackroyd, *Pure City*, 374.
24. Ackroyd, *Pure City*, 217.
25. "The First Years, Part III."
26. "The First Years, Part III."
27. Peter Hebblethwaite, *The Year of Three Popes* (Cleveland, OH: Collins, 1979), 104.
28. Serafini, discussion.
29. Mo Guernon, "The Forgotten Pope," *America: The National Catholic Weekly*, October 24, 2011, 19.
30. "The First Years, Part III."
31. "The First Years, Part III."
32. Seabeck, *Smiling Pope*, 41.
33. Spackman, *God's Candidate*, 82.
34. "The Patriarch of Venice," *Humilitas* 9, December 1998, 11.
35. Merrill Sheils, "A Man of the People," *Newsweek*, September 4, 1978, 42.
36. "Compassionate Shepherd," *Time*, August 21, 1978, 62.
37. David Yallop, *In God's Name: An Investigation into the Murder of Pope John Paul I* (New York: Penguin, 1984), 41.
38. Serafini, discussion.
39. Paul Fusco, "Interview with Msgr. Mario Senigaglia," http://www.amicipapaluciani.it/ma.
40. Hebblethwaite, *Three Popes*, 104.
41. Seabeck, *Smiling Pope*, 39.
42. Kelly, *Oxford Dictionary of Popes*, 325.
43. Seabeck, *Smiling Pope*, 40.
44. Seabeck, *Smiling Pope*, 41–42.
45. Yallop, *In God's Name*, 47.
46. Francis X. Murphy, *The Papacy Today* (London: Weidenfeld and Nicolson, 1982), 166.
47. Seabeck, *Smiling Pope*, 42.

48. Fusco, Senigaglia interview.
49. Seabeck, *Smiling Pope*, 45.
50. Seabeck, *Smiling Pope*, 48.
51. "Highlights of the Life of His Holiness John Paul I," March 2, 2010, http://www.vatican.va/holy_father/john_paul_i/biography/documents/hf_jp-i_jp-i_bio_01021997, March 2, 2010.
52. Albino Luciani, *A Passionate Adventure: Living the Catholic Faith Today*, ed. and trans. Lori Pieper (New York: Tau Cross Books, 2013), 19.
53. Serafini, discussion.
54. Serafini, discussion.
55. Seabeck, *Smiling Pope*, 44.
56. Fusco, Senigaglia interview.
57. Spackman, *God's Candidate*, 104.
58. Seabeck, *Smiling Pope*, 39–40.
59. Serafini, discussion.
60. Mo Guernon, "All Those Years Ago," *Orange County Catholic*, https://www.occatholic.com/all-those-years-ago/, August 11, 2018.
61. Serafini, discussion.
62. Fusco, Senigaglia interview.
63. Serafini, discussion.
64. George Weigel, *God's Choice: Pope Benedict XI and the Future of the Catholic Church* (New York: HarperCollins, 2009), 178.
65. Spackman, *God's Candidate*, 81.
66. "The First Years of Albino Luciani, Part V" (The Election), https://www.albino-luciani.com/index.php?id=274&L=2/.
67. "First Years, Part V."
68. Spackman, *God's Candidate*, 81.
69. Serafini, discussion.
70. Serafini, discussion.
71. Serafini, discussion.
72. Kelly, *Oxford Dictionary of Popes*, 325.
73. Murphy, *Papacy Today*, 167.
74. "Highlights," 3.
75. "Highlights," 4.
76. Serafini, discussion.
77. Fusco, Senigaglia interview.
78. Spackman, *God's Candidate*, 76.
79. Serafini, discussion.
80. *Tulare Advance Register* 96, no. 243, September 29, 1978, https://cdnc.ucr.edu/?a=d&d=TULAR19780929.1.3&e=-------en--20--1--txt-txIN--------.
81. Spackman, *God's Candidate*, 83.
82. Serafini, discussion.
83. Yallop, *In God's Name*, 42–43.
84. Spackman, *God's Candidate*, 85–86.
85. Spackman, *God's Candidate*, 85–86.

86. Serafini, discussion.
87. Matthew 19:6, *New American Bible, Revised—Catholic Edition.*
88. "The First Years of Albino Luciani, Part III."
89. Serafini, discussion.
90. Serafini, discussion.
91. *Encyclopedia of World Biography*, 287.
92. John L. Allen Jr., "Interview with Don Diego Lorenzi," *Crux*, May 10, 2016.
93. Rev. Silvio De Nard (pastor of Sacred Heart Church, Providence, Rhode Island, who grew up in Belluno), in discussion with the author, May 14, 2011.
94. Serafini, discussion.
95. Serafini, discussion.
96. Serafini, discussion.
97. Serafini, discussion.
98. Serafini, discussion.
99. Serafini, discussion.
100. Serafini, discussion.
101. Seabeck, *Smiling Pope*, 50.

• 9 •

Pilgrimages and Prophecies

Extraordinary Encounters (1964–1977)

Do not despise the words of prophets. —1 Thessalonians 5:20 (NRSVCE)

The summons came unexpectedly. How could it be that a cloistered nun knew that the patriarch of Venice was nearby? Or that she was even aware of who he was, for that matter? Luciani, on the other hand, knew all about her. She had achieved fame sixty years before. Now, to his astonishment, he would meet privately with a seventy-year-old seer of world renown. What could she possibly want to discuss with him? He was but a stranger.

THE MYSTERY OF FATIMA

For three days beginning on July 9, 1977, Cardinal Luciani led a pilgrimage of thirty-five or so Venetians to a revered memorial featuring a statue of Christ's mother and the Chapel of the Apparitions in Portugal.[1]

The Marian shrine in the tiny village of Fatima is a popular destination for Catholics. It was there that on May 13, 1917, Lucia de Jesus dos Santos, age ten, and two of her cousins witnessed the first of six apparitions by the Virgin Mary. Word spread quickly throughout the tiny town. Skepticism and ridicule ensued at first, but eventually curious hordes of people gathered at the site while the apparitions continued, and many ultimately became convinced of their validity.[2]

On October 13, five months after the first apparition, a crowd of as many as seventy thousand assembled where the Blessed Mother again revealed herself before the children and spoke to them as they knelt silently.

The crowd, however, could not see or hear her, but whatever incredulity they might have felt about the authenticity of the phenomenon was dispelled by an inexplicable incident. The massive gathering was dumbfounded by a vision of the sun that defied the physical laws of nature: the startled witnesses claimed they saw the celestial ball of fire leaping and twirling about in the heavens. Most disconcerting of all, it then seemed to plummet toward the crowd before it abruptly retreated.[3]

The Virgin had extraordinary messages for the children that they kept secret for years. With the publication of Lucia's memoirs in the 1930s the first two prophecies became public. The earliest was a reaffirmation of the existence of hell; the children claimed to have witnessed a vivid vision of what the souls of the damned experience there. The second predicted the end of World War I and the onset of another great war. (World War II began just twenty-one years after the conclusion of the first global military conflict.) Lucia wrote down the third secret, which eventually found its way to the Vatican in a sealed envelope. It was not made public until 2000. This prediction told of a violent attack on "a bishop dressed in white." On May 13, 1981, the very feast day of Fatima, Pope John Paul II was shot and seriously wounded while circulating among the tourists in St. Peter's Square. The pope attributed his survival to Mary's intercession.[4]

There were disconcerting personal predictions as well. As foretold by the Virgin Mary, Lucia's companions died young, Francesco Marto at age ten and Jacinta Marto at nine. Lucia, on the other hand, lived until age ninety-seven. In 1948 she entered the Carmelite convent in Coimbra, Portugal, and subsequently chose Sister Maria of the Immaculate Heart of Mary as her religious name.[5] She claimed the apparitions continued in her adulthood and became the repository of additional secrets about the future revealed by the Blessed Mother.[6]

Luciani's meeting with Lucia (some have noted the coincidental similarity of their names) almost immediately afterward became the subject of endless speculation. Exactly what transpired between them remains a tantalizing matter of conjecture because various versions emerged. The only certifiable fact is that the two spoke in person.

Prophecy or Fantasy?

The encounter took place on July 11, in the Carmelite convent in Coimbra on the last day of the patriarch's visit.[7] According to one widely circulated account whose source remains unknown, the informal session between the two religious figures was shocking, even eerie. The poised visionary greeted him as "Holy Father." Luciani was unnerved by this puzzling salutation. Was Sr. Lucia hallucinating? Was it a case of mistaken identity? Both were highly unlikely. According to one account, Luciani later told a Venetian theologian that the sister had predicted that he would become pope.[8] There has been no known corroboration of this claim.

The prospect of being elected pope seemed preposterous to Luciani, yet the nun's assertion couldn't be dismissed easily. She was, after all, an exceptional woman, one who had crossed the threshold to the spiritual world and had been entrusted with secret prognostications by the Virgin Mary herself.

One pilgrim in the group claimed Luciani revealed something that supports at least a portion of the story. The assembly accompanying the patriarch waited eagerly to hear what he would say upon leaving the meeting with Lucia. "This sister was tiny, but great at talking. She kept on calling me 'Holiness,' and the more that I said I was a simple cardinal she continued to address me with great respect, and bowing to me. She kept saying 'Holiness!'"[9] No other reported conversations with Luciani about this meeting, nor Luciani's later writing about it, made reference to his being called "Holiness," a moniker reserved exclusively for the pope.

Nonbelievers would find this pilgrim's report incredulous, but to the faithful who trusted in mysticism, it was entirely plausible. Moreover, Luciani's own brother lent credibility to the account. "Every time when this meeting was mentioned in conversations with us, his face would go white. It was as if some dark thought disturbed him in his innermost self . . . on that day, the seer of Fatima told him something which concerned not only the Church but also his own life: the destiny that God had prepared for him," the pope's brother Edoardo insisted. He recounted an incident that took place in his home in Canale during the winter of 1977–1978, which seems to add further legitimacy to his astonishing account. The cardinal was a houseguest for a few days. One evening, perceiving him to be anxious, Edoardo asked his brother what was troubling him, and he answered, "I cannot stop thinking of what Sister Lucia has told me."[10] On another occasion when the topic of his meeting with Lucia surfaced at the dinner table, the cardinal immediately grew silent, excused himself without explanation, and retired to his bedroom. Edoardo and his wife, Antonietta, looked at each other perplexed and concerned.[11] Lina Petri, however, said that her uncle never mentioned his meeting with Sr. Lucia in any of their conversations.[12]

Luciani published an article titled "My Meeting with Lucia" in which no reference was made to anything unusual having transpired between the two. He described their meeting as lengthy and praised the nun's "joviality" and "spiritual youthfulness." She spoke to him about priests and other church matters, but their conversation never touched on the apparitions. Luciani, though, curious about the so-called dance of the sun of October 13, 1917, inquired about it. Lucia responded that she did not see it; she and her companions witnessed the apparition of the Holy Family and the Virgin Mary only. He claimed the spectacle was witnessed even by "nonbelievers and anticlericals." The phenomenon, reportedly of ten minutes' duration, included the sun spinning on three occasions and changing colors numerous times. Luciani made no mention whatsoever of any premonitions by Lucia about a future papacy.[13]

Curiously, though, after Luciani was elected pope the following year, he repeatedly indicated that he expected his pontificate to be fleeting. Whether this belief resulted from a prophecy he was told at Coimbra or was attributable to intimations of mortality caused by illness are subject to speculation.

THE DOUBTERS

Msgr. Taffarel, Luciani's personal secretary in Vittorio Veneto, was dubious about the account but didn't rule out the possibility of its veracity. "Regarding the discourse with Lucia, I don't know. I don't know. I think that's exaggerated. I don't believe that Lucia greeted him as 'your Holiness.' It could be, but I wouldn't give it too much importance. It may be a fantasy; it could also be true, but I do not know."[14]

Others were more certain about what took place—or didn't.

Several individuals who spoke both to the patriarch and to the seer about the meeting provided some evidence that the version described above was fictitious. Luciani's own account of the visit is included in *The Last Secret of Fatima*, but here Sister Lucia is supposed to have said of the patriarch merely, "If he were elected pope, I think he would make a good one."[15] Determining what transpired during that meeting at Fatima would demand the specialized skills of a sleuth. And even then, the truth would likely be elusive.

Staying Close to Home

Luciani's voyages fit a discernible pattern: visits to Italian immigrant communities and shrines. According to don Diego Lorenzi, Luciani didn't like to travel, and evidence substantiates that claim. In the nearly sixty-six years of his life, he left Italy only ten times; eight of those trips were to nearby European countries, and they were brief. All were to fulfill pastoral obligations.[16] He took no tourist trips and no vacations abroad. Of his foreign excursions, six took place while he was patriarch.[17]

FRANCE

A devotee of the Blessed Mother, Luciani placed importance on the Marian shrines around the world; he believed in their capacity to have a transformative impact on the lives of those who visited. He described them as "living centers of piety." To Luciani the visions associated with these shrines were not so significant for having revealed dogma; rather, they provided practical guidance by reminding the faithful of the necessity of prayer and penance that he knew led to a greater tenderness toward others.[18]

In 1964 Bishop Luciani went on a weeklong pilgrim's journey to Lourdes with sick Italian priests.[19] Like Fatima, this was a shrine dedicated to Mary and one that had long been famous for miraculous healings. Here was a spring where those with physical afflictions could bathe in hopes of being cured of their illnesses—whatever they might be. And many testified that they had been healed in this holy place. Although more than seven thousand healings have been attributed to Lourdes, as of 2018 only seventy have been confirmed by the Church as miracles.[20] That hasn't discouraged pilgrims from journeying there.

The Blessed Virgin Mary allegedly appeared eighteen times to a fourteen -year-old girl named Bernadette Soubirous between February 11 and July 16, 1858, in that small town of southern France. Mary directed Bernadette to unearth the soil near the grotto where the apparitions took place, and it became the source of the healing spring. A basilica was consecrated in 1876, and the site became a destination for multitudes of believers. Bernadette, like Lucia in Portugal, became a nun, joining the Sisters of Notre Dame at Nevers in 1866. Thirteen years later she died at age thirty-five. On December 8, 1933, the Feast of the Immaculate Conception, she was canonized.[21] Luciani returned to Lourdes on June 29, 1971, with a group of Venetians on pilgrimage.[22] At one point during this pilgrimage, he disappeared. After a while, someone located him among a group of French pilgrims. Wearing his plain black clothing, he had blended in with the priests.[23]

In January 1971 the patriarch returned to France, this time visiting Paris for three days. Accompanied by a Venetian delegation, he attended a benefit for Venice's preservation. While in Paris, he took advantage of the opportunity to call on Cardinal Gabriel Marty, the city's archbishop.[24]

NEIGHBORING COUNTRIES

Switzerland

From June 12 to 14, 1971, Luciani visited Switzerland on another pastoral mission.[25] His destinations were Basel and Muttenz, where he met with more Italian immigrants, a group about which he cared. On his return trip, he indulged in a personal priority, a stop at Annecy (Savoy) in southeastern France to pray at the tomb of his beloved saint, Francis de Sales, at the Basilica of the Visitation. Perhaps no other saint had had a more profound influence on his thinking than de Sales, and biographically the two men had much in common.[26]

Austria

Austria was a virtual neighbor to Luciani as he grew up in Canale d'Agordo. As a "mountain man," he undoubtedly savored his trip there as well as the one he had made to Switzerland. In November of 1974 while at Innsbruck, Austria, Luciani visited the Hofkirche, a former Franciscan church dating from the Renaissance, where he paused at the tomb of Andreas Hofer, a Tyrolese patriot who had been the victim of a firing squad ordered by Napoleon in 1810.[27]

On the Austrian border, Luciani made an annual trek to the Shrine of Pietralba, another Marian sanctuary nestled in the Dolomite Mountains in Italy. There he joined the Servite Fathers, where he found tranquility in the confines of the abbey. This site beckoned for another reason: While in residence, he eagerly climbed Corno Bianca for the spectacular view it afforded, and he enjoyed taking leisurely, placid walks in the nearby woods.[28]

Germany

On May 18, 1975, Luciani went on a pastoral visit to Germany, where he spent time in many Italian immigrant communities.[29] Three years later he returned to Germany to visit his friend, Cardinal Hermann Volk.[30]

Yugoslavia

From September 10 to 13, 1977, Luciani was in Communist Yugoslavia as the official representative of the Italian Episcopal Conference. There he participated in the commemoration of the millennial anniversary of the first Croatian Marian sanctuary.

TO SOUTH AMERICA: BRAZIL

In 1975 Luciani embarked on a fifteen-day trip to Brazil, from November 6 to 21.[31] The invitation came from his friend, Ivo Lorscheiter, the bishop of the archdiocese of Santa Maria, who hoped the patriarch would join in the centenary celebrations of a large-scale Italian immigration to that South American country.[32] There was something of personal significance about this for Luciani; many who had left Italy to settle in South America, Brazil in particular, were from his Veneto region. Even his father at one time had entertained the possibility of moving his family there, and one of his mother's cousins had done so.[33]

The trip was multifaceted. In addition to visiting several Italian immigrant communities, he met with the Brazilian Episcopal Conference as vice president of the Italian Episcopal Conference and received an honorary doctorate from the State University of Saint Mary.[34] His itinerary included visits to Italian parishes, where he learned about plans for the re-Christianization of Latin America, frequent interactions with poor Italian immigrants in the country, stops at various institutions, churches, religious orders, and the original community settled by the Italian emigrants.[35] In his typical understated way, the patriarch wore a Roman collar and a plain black suit during his stay.[36]

Luciani concelebrated a Mass with some Brazilian bishops before a congregation of two hundred thousand people and delivered a homily at the Cathedral of Santa Maria Rio Grande do Sul.[37] At the celebration for the Feast of the Madonna, Luciani gave a beautiful homily in Portuguese. A mere month prior to leaving for Brazil, Luciani had taken Portuguese lessons. Describing himself as being "more or less proficient," he sermonized in that language to a delighted assembly on November 9. His homily focused on the Italian migration, devotion to Mother Mary, and the redemption of sinners. Observing so many Italian immigrants present, Luciani said that he felt as if he were still in Italy, a statement that endeared him to his listeners.[38]

Luciani began by identifying Abraham of the Old Testament as "the most famous emigrant." He then segued into the topic of Italian migration. "The situation of the Italians, who one hundred years ago, left Italy to come to Brazil, resembles somewhat the emigration of Abraham . . . Their journey, unlike Abraham's, did not have a religious aim; but when they left a great many of them brought the religion of their fathers with them."

Then came a personal remembrance. "When I was a boy, my parish priest read in Church a letter sent him from Brazil which I still remember. Four or five families of my parish had arrived in the State of St. Caterina in Brazil. They found a warm welcome. With little money they had bought a great deal of land and cattle. They rejoiced in their real well-being in comparison with the hunger suffered at home."

He went on to quantify the number of Italians who made the transition over the course of nearly seven decades, in the process demonstrating his keen interest in the subject and broad knowledge of it. "From 1875 to 1932 there were 329,431 Italians who were counted as emigrants to Brazil. Of these, about one-fifth were from Veneto."

"Here we are at the very heart of Christianity," he said as he went on to speak of devotion to the mother of Christ and her role as a mediator between sinners and her son, the Savior. "Our Lady behaves as her Son Jesus Who loathes sin but was called 'friend of sinners.'" Luciani concluded with an appeal to the faithful to continue praying to Our Lady: "Let us continue to invoke her and try to imitate her!"[39]

It was during this trip that Luciani developed a relationship of mutual admiration with Cardinal Aloisio Lorscheiter.[40] Lorscheiter later reminisced that during this visit he and many others speculated that the patriarch could one day become pope. In turn, Luciani was so impressed by Lorscheiter that he quickly considered *him* a prospective pope. "He is a man of faith and culture, and he has a good knowledge of Italy and of Italian. The time has come to choose a pope from the Third World," he confided to a friend upon returning home. When it came time to select a successor to Pope Paul in the August 1978 conclave, Lorscheiter was Luciani's candidate.[41] (Rumor had it that at the conclave on the fourth ballot when Luciani was elected, Lorscheiter received a single vote; it was undoubtedly Luciani's.)[42]

On the morning of his return from Brazil, the patriarch delivered a homily on the Feast of the Madonna *della Salute* (health). His topic was faith and conversion. "A faithful copy of this painting of the *Madonna della Salute* which we are venerating here . . . was requested by the descendants of Venetian immigrants who live down there (Rio Grande do Sul, Brazil) in great numbers. They also requested that the Patriarch personally bring it onto Brazilian soil. At the urging of the Pope, I had to consent!" he began jovially.[43]

He had seen a banner that read, "When you return to Italy, tell the Venetians that we have remained faithful to our devotion to our Lady!" He also described a monument erected to the Italian emigrants that had impressed him. "It rose majestically in bronze, halfway up a hill," Luciani recalled. It depicted a married couple, the husband carrying a hoe and the mother with an infant in her arms "with a rosary peeking out of her apron pocket."[44]

Following his tribute to the Venetians who moved to Brazil in search of a better life, he transitioned to their faith, which he described as a "decisive act," and that "achieving human glory is not an absolute." Conversion is the realization that we need God's assistance to do good in the world, he told them.[45]

In synchronization with the theme of the journeys of Venetians to a distant land, he preached regarding conversion, "There must be a break with the past . . . Let's decide to be citizens not only of this little transitory world, but of the great world that never ends!"[46] Luciani described the "truths of faith" as an "incandescent fire . . . bursting with energy that compels us to take eager and passionate action."[47]

He took away from Brazil a lesson that he would put into practice at home with a renewed sense of dedication: "I have been told that as a bishop I must sell the honey of the faith, of the love of God."[48] He had traveled to the largest country of South America to commemorate and commend, as well as to preach, to open minds, and to evangelize. On multiple levels, the trip had been a success. The Brazilians loved him. It was a feeling he reciprocated.

TO (THE DARK CONTINENT) BURUNDI

In 1966 Bishop Luciani made a thirty-five-hundred-mile journey to Burundi, an impoverished east central African country, on an extended visit, staying from August 16 to September 2.[49] There he visited priests from Vittorio Veneto who were serving in a diocesan mission.[50] He had yoked his diocese with that of Naozi and wanted to observe firsthand the work of his diocesan priests.[51] More than half the country's population was Catholic.[52]

He arrived on August 18 accompanied by Dr. Italo Fantin, chief of staff of a Vittorio Veneto hospital. Fantin would provide the bishop with detailed explanations of the rampant diseases that afflicted the Burundi population. He and his priests visited "branch churches" in the sprawling parish in which they served.[53] True to his reputation for being unpretentious, he accompanied one of the missionaries, riding in a jeep.[54] When the vehicle sank in mud on one occasion, Luciani jumped out and helped push it out of the quagmire.[55]

Bishop Andrew Makarakiza of Ngozi joined Luciani on his travels throughout the country. To deflect the intense heat, Luciani wore a white cassock. It wouldn't stay pristine very long. The Italian bishop was a hit wherever he went, enjoying the hospitality of the locals. According to one of his priests, Luciani was greeted with wild enthusiasm following the celebration of Mass at one stop. "[E]veryone pressed around him and he shook hands with all of them effusively . . . his white cassock changed color, with the prints of so many hands, and the babies' dirty noses!"[56]

A new church in Kitega had been constructed with financial assistance from the churchgoers in Vittorio Veneto, so Bishop Makarakiza thought it appropriate for Luciani to preside over its official opening ceremony. Luciani politely demurred. "Not for the world! You are the bishop here; we are only here to give you a helping hand," he explained to Makarakiza.[57]

But the joy Luciani experienced was ephemeral. The rampant poverty tore at his heart. He toured a leper colony with Dr. Fantin and wrote about the experience: "In this place a European has difficulty in holding back tears: one sees hands and feet eaten up . . . faces covered with enormous spots and nodules." In the countryside, the lack of bare necessities was almost inconceivable. "[N]o one had sandals or shoes, a number of children were completely naked," he lamented. He described their dwellings: huts of straw and dried mud. It got worse. The combination of inadequate diet and lack of modern medicine led to epidemics of dysentery, malaria, tuberculosis, worms, and other life-threatening afflictions. The single major cause of death among Burundi's young was gastroenteritis, attributable to inadequate nourishment. The infant mortality rate was astounding because of a simple lack of hygiene.[58]

It was then that the bishop and the doctor determined they would find a way to build a maternity hospital and a medical clinic in Kitega. Through their persistent efforts, enough financial resources were raised through government and private contributions that those facilities were eventually erected.[59] The people apparently never forgot Luciani; a few years following his visit, a center dedicated to him was opened.[60]

Luciani had gone to Burundi primarily to ascertain the level of success in evangelizing the population. He returned with the understanding that suffering, poverty, disease, and the needless deaths of innocents could not be alleviated by spiritual fervor alone. The destitution that was prevalent there vastly superseded what he had experienced as a child. The faithful there filled the churches, unlike in Italy and the West in general. One logical explanation for this phenomenon was that people prayed that God would alleviate their deprivation. God offered hope where it was to be found nowhere else.

Following a lengthy discourse back home on what he had witnessed on his extensive travels, Luciani concluded, "More than a month has passed since my trip. But a little of my heart has remained down there with those good people."[61]

NOTES

1. Udo Padoan, "On Pilgrimage with Patriarch Luciani: The Memories of a Pilgrim," *Humilitas* 17, no. 1 (2006): 10.
2. https://www.ewtn.com/catholicism/saints/our-lady-of-fatima-423.
3. www.ewtn.com.
4. "What Are the Three Secrets of Fatima?" Our Pilgrimage travel blog, https://joewalshtours.ie/what-are-the-three-secrets-of-fatima/.
5. "Heart of Mary, Our Lady of Fatima, Sr. Maria Lucia of Jesus and of the Immaculate Heart, Visionary of Fatima," 1907–2005 © Recompiled by SCTJM, https://www.piercedhearts.org/hearts_jesus_mary/apparitions/fatima/fatima_lucia_biography.html.
6. "Heart of Mary—Our Lady of Fatima," https://www.ewtn.com/catholicism/saints/our-lady-of-fatima-423.
7. "Albino Luciani, Pope John Paul I Chronology," *Humilitas* 12, no. 3 (August 2001): 4.
8. Paul Spackman, *God's Candidate: The Life and Times of Pope John Paul I* (Herefordshire: Gracewing, 2008), 107.
9. Padoan, "On Pilgrimage with Patriarch Luciani," 10.

10. Andrea Tornielli, "Luciani Spoke to Sr. Lucia of Apostasy and the Problems of the Church," *La Stampa*, May 12, 2017, https://www.lastamp.it/vatican-insider/en/2017/05/12/news/luciani-spoke-to-sr-lucia-of-apostasy-and-the-problems-of-the-church-1.34599250/.

11. Loris Serafini (director, Foundation Papa Luciani and Museum Albino Luciani of Canale d'Agordo), in discussion with the author, Canale d'Agordo, Italy, July15, 2011.

12. Lina Petri (niece of Pope John Paul I), in discussion with the author, Rome, July 11, 2011.

13. "Chronology," 4.

14. Msgr. Francesco Taffarel (personal secretary to Bishop Albino Luciani, diocese of Vittorio Veneto, Italy), in discussion with the author, Tarzo, Italy, July 11, 2011.

15. James Day, "The Bridge Builder: Rediscovering Pope John Paul I," *Catholic Exchange*, November 17, 2017, http://catholicexchange.com/bridge-builder-pope-john-paul-i.

16. John L. Allen Jr., "Fr. Diego Lorenzi, John Paul I's Closest Collaborator," *National Catholic Reporter*, August 29, 2003, http://nationalcatholicreporter.org/word/pfw082903.htm.

17. "Chronology," 4.

18. Brother Nicholas Schneider, OP, "Pilgrimages to Our Lady's Shrines," *Humilitas*, May 2015, 9.

19. Raymond and Lauretta Seabeck, *The Smiling Pope: The Life and Teaching of John Paul I* (Huntington, IN: Our Sunday Visitor, 2004), 250.

20. https://www.catholicnewsagency.com/news/37743/the-70th-miracle-lourdes-healing-officially-declared-supernatural.

21. Rev. Matthew R. Mauriello, "Our Lady of Lourdes," University of Dayton, https://udayton.edu/imri/mary/o/our-lady-of-lourdes.php.

22. "Chronology," 4.

23. Seabeck, *Smiling Pope*, 48–49.

24. Seabeck, *Smiling Pope*, 250.

25. "Chronology," 4.

26. Seabeck, *Smiling Pope*, 250.

27. Spackman, *God's Candidate*, 92.

28. Seabeck, *Smiling Pope*, 49.

29. "Chronology," 4.

30. Francis X. Murphy, *The Papacy Today* (London: Weidenfeld and Nicolson, 1982), 167.

31. "Chronology," 4.

32. Spackman, *God's Candidate*, 94.

33. Serafini, discussion.

34. Seabeck, *Smiling Pope*, 251.

35. Spackman, *God's Candidate*, 94.

36. "The First Years of Albino Luciani, Part III," https://www.albino-luciani.com/index.php?id=272&L=3.

37. *Opera Omnia*, vol. 7, trans. Lori Pieper, 193–97.
38. Spackman, *God's Candidate*, 95.
39. *Opera Omnia*, vol. 7, 193–97.
40. Murphy, *Papacy Today*, 167.
41. Spackman, *God's Candidate*, 95.
42. Spackman, *God's Candidate*, 133.
43. Albino Luciani, *A Passionate Adventure: Living the Catholic Faith Today*, ed. and trans. Lori Pieper (New York: Tau Cross Books, 2013), 84.
44. Luciani, *Passionate Adventure*, 84.
45. Luciani, *Passionate Adventure*, 85.
46. Luciani, *Passionate Adventure*, 86.
47. Luciani, *Passionate Adventure*, 87.
48. Luciani, *Passionate Adventure*, 88.
49. "Chronology," 3.
50. Lori Pieper, "We Are All Guests at the Same Table," *Humilitas*, December 1990, 14–15.
51. Spackman, *God's Candidate*, 55.
52. Spackman, *God's Candidate*, 56.
53. "We Are All Guests at the Same Table," 15.
54. Seabeck, *Smiling Pope*, 30.
55. Spackman, *God's Candidate*, 57.
56. "We Are All Guests at the Same Table," 15.
57. Spackman, *God's Candidate*, 57.
58. "We Are All Guests at the Same Table," 15.
59. "We Are All Guests at the Same Table," 14–15.
60. Albino Luciani, "Fifteen Days in Africa," *Humilitas*, December 2013, 4.
61. Luciani, "Fifteen Days in Africa," 8.

Part III

ALLURE

• 10 •

Pontiff—Week III/Hope

God's Promise (September 14–20, 1978)

[H]ope does not disappoint us. —Romans 5:5 (NRSVCE)

Let us hold unswervingly to the confession of our hope without wavering, for he who has promised is faithful. —Hebrews 10:23 (NRSVCE)

No one could have guessed it, but John Paul's days were dwindling rapidly.

Already, he was beyond the halfway point of his pontificate. He had been an immediate sensation, and his personal popularity, without regard to religious denomination, was intensifying and expanding far beyond the boundaries of Italy and the Western world. The international press corps that covered the papacy was beguiled by him. The cardinals who had elected him continued to be effusive about their choice. Seemingly all who met with him were touched by his meekness, impressed with his wisdom, delighted with the prospects of a revitalized church under his leadership. Cardinal Carlo Confalonieri provided proof of the public's esteem of John Paul: "St. Peter's square was jammed to the brim for the noon blessing the past two Sundays—something that had occurred only very seldom previously."[1]

But there were detractors, too, mostly among career Vatican officials who harbored doubts about the new pope, particularly his administrative abilities, or, to put it more bluntly, his very competence to govern the Church. No amount of public popularity could provide him with the skills to do that. How many among the curial elite thought themselves superior leaders? How many of them regarded John Paul as a pathetic, insecure, and unsophisticated little man who was so intimidated by the demands of the papacy as to be rendered impotent as its leader? How many of these accomplished administrators ridiculed the pope, made him the victim of cruel jokes that they circulated with smug satisfaction among themselves?

Having a blundering pope, of course, gave them potential advantages: consolidating power for themselves at his expense, providing opportunities to circumvent his directives, and/or institutionalizing their own priorities. However, this brought danger, too: Left to his own ineptitude, how much damage could this pope inflict on Holy Mother Church? And perhaps most perilous of all, John Paul was widely perceived as unpredictable.[2] Would he make major personnel changes in scandal-tinged departments, reverse Pope Paul's encyclical banning artificial birth control, divest the Church of its treasures, or modify an array of traditional Church teachings and policies?

John Paul seemed oblivious to all this complaining and went about exercising the duties of his office to the best of his ability.

Loris Serafini, a distinguished Luciani scholar, contends that John Paul's intention was to shake the Church's very foundation by reforming its power structure and altogether eliminating the power and privileges that its leaders coveted. And of course, John Paul had already begun with the papacy itself. Banished were the regal flourishes, the imperious language, the staid formality that had characterized it as an outworn relic of a bygone time. This unassuming pastor, this champion of the poor, this servant of servants, this human font of joy and charity was rejuvenating the Church, making it relevant and appealing to a world gone astray.[3]

NOTEWORTHY EPISODES

There was no denying that he was an unconventional pope.

According to John Magee, one Sunday morning John Paul made an unusual request of his senior secretary. The Holy Father approached Magee for a "favor." Not expecting anything beyond the ordinary, Magee agreed immediately. Then the pope softly asked that Magee celebrate Mass while John Paul acted as his altar server. Flummoxed, Magee stammered that he could do no such thing, all the while pondering why the pope would make such a bizarre request. John Paul explained that acting in this subservient capacity was an essential reminder of his "smallness" before God and the continued cultivation of humility. Despite his intense discomfort, Magee ultimately acquiesced to John Paul's wish. When the moment arrived, the Holy Father insisted that the Mass be said in English. It was done; and at the conclusion of the sacrament, the pope thanked Magee. On two other occasions, John Paul acted as Magee's altar server in his private chapel. The third and final time occurred two days before the pope's death.[4]

His niece Pia provided insight into the pope's humility. It was a virtue that didn't come naturally, one that the power of his superior intellect threatened to annihilate without warning. "His humility was a choice, because he was always conscious of his intelligence," she explained.[5]

His papacy also had lighter moments, albeit sometimes at the pope's expense. On one occasion, John Paul was walking on the rooftop while reading a sheaf of documents from the Secretariat of State. Absorbed by the reports, the pope apparently was oblivious to the blustery conditions at that altitude. A sudden gust scattered the pages in all directions, some landing on walkways and rooftops while others fluttered to the ground. The panicked pope summoned Magee to rescue him from what he perceived to be a potential disaster. His secretary expeditiously assembled a cadre of employees to conduct a thorough search of the surrounding areas to retrieve the lost papers. Somehow, to the pope's relief, all were found, collated, and returned to an embarrassed John Paul. "He could have canonized me for that!" Magee teased decades later.[6]

Such occasions, dramatic and droll, were exceptions to the daily grind of the pontiff's schedule.

PRESSING ON

John Paul was relentless in adhering to a routine that would have taxed the energy of a much younger man; his workload was weighty, his schedule crammed, his days long, and his commitment to implementing the program outlined on the first full day of his papacy, unwavering. In fact, as was his wont, he was proceeding at a galloping pace to further the goals of his apostolic agenda. His secretary, don Diego Lorenzi, characterized John Paul as a man in a hurry, even during his days in Venice.[7] He never had time to waste. (That was poignantly true as the fateful date of September 28 rapidly approached.) He planned to bestow unprecedented influence on the conference of bishops; he preferred collaborating with these church leaders rather than dictating to them, though reserving for himself final decisions.[8] Beyond that, John Paul thought that his role as bishop of Rome should be a priority. What that would have entailed is unknown, but that it was at the forefront of his mind was evident by his talk to the Roman clergy early in his papacy.

But the Holy Father's time was not consumed exclusively with work. As always, he devoted a substantial portion of each day to prayer: celebrating Mass each morning, reading his breviary, meditating in silence, and privately reciting the rosary. His routine continued to consist of eating meals with his two secretaries, scanning the newspapers, taking a brief afternoon nap, engaging in phone conversations, entertaining sporadic guests for lunch or dinner, watching the evening news on TV, and retiring to his room around 9 p.m., where he would continue to work in bed until slumber overtook him.[9]

DAY 19/SEPTEMBER 14

On this morning John Paul met with Bishop Albert Tshomba Yungu of Tshumbe, Congo, and Cardinal Eduardo Pironio, the prefect of the Congregation for Religious.[10] The African and the Argentinian, the diocesan "pastor" and the curial leader, both demanded the pope's time and attention.

Family Insights

Much to his delight, John Paul was joined for lunch by his niece Pia Luciani.[11] The two were very close. In fact, Pia considered him a second father. She loved him, and like his other niece, Lina Petri, admired him. He loomed large in the eyes of both. To this day, Lina Petri can't remember how tall he was. Her explanation reveals her level of esteem for him. "After our interview [with this author], many times I wondered about it and concluded that maybe I remembered him being taller than he actually was. Probably, in my girlish eyes, physical stature was idealized in relation to his moral stature!" she revealed.[12]

"He had a wonderful sense of humor," Pia recalls. "It was very, very interesting to speak with him." Though he sometimes talked about problems, he was an optimist and always injected humor in conversation, she explained. When she was single, she spent Easters with him and remembers watching Charlie Chaplin movies on television together, films that elicited robust laughter from him. "He liked music very much; the opera, too." When he was patriarch, he took her to see a Goldoni performance in Venice.[13]

Most impressive to her, though, was his selflessness. "He always put aside his own problems to help others in need," she recalled long after his passing. Indelibly etched in her memory was his soothing presence and gentle encouragement that eased her mind when she left home as a nervous young girl to attend a distant school. Her uncle, then a bishop, volunteered to accompany her when her father fell ill.[14]

DAY 20/SEPTEMBER 15

The pope's official schedule for this day listed only two appointments. One was with Gabrielle Garrone, the prefect of the Congregation of Catholic

Education, and Archbishop Antonio Javierre, secretary of the Congregation for Catholic Education (for Institutes of Study); and the other with Dominic Kodwo Andoh, the bishop of Accra, Ghana.[15] Sadly, detailed accounts of these and his other private meetings are unavailable. Neither of his secretaries were present to take notes, and when interpreters were in the room, they subsequently maintained silence about what had transpired. Only partial recollections from the participants would sometimes become available; and most of those became public following John Paul's death and lacked details of the substance of the discussions.

DAY 21/SEPTEMBER 16

Unlike the previous day, this one consisted of private sessions with a variety of visitors. One conference was with a political leader, General Mohamed Siad Barre, president of Somalia,[16] who had come to power through a military coup.[17] The session between the pope and a tyrant who was credibly accused of human rights violations was controversial because it risked conveying the impression that John Paul was lending legitimacy to Barre's presidency. Still, meetings with such notorious leaders could be beneficial. It's reasonable to assume that the Holy Father attempted to persuade him to pursue humanitarian policies that would respect the God-given rights of the Somalian people. Nothing constructive would be achieved by ignoring or publicly denouncing him. Engaging him in dialogue was an opportunity to influence the dictator to soften the harshness of his rule.[18]

The pope then had an audience with Alfonso Lopez Trujillo, a Colombian bishop, followed by audiences with the apostolic nuncios of Cuba and Canada.[19]

DAY 22/SEPTEMBER 17

Lessons for Life

This was a Sunday, the day designated for the pope to deliver his noontime Angelus. His talk, specifically addressed to students, centered on school and society.[20] Not surprisingly, his message was another deviation from the norm. The typical Angelus address delivered by Pope Paul during his fifteen-year pontificate was subdued and formal in tone and concentrated on issues of deep religious importance. Nothing about that was objectionable; Paul was a profound thinker, well versed in doctrine, and his messages were substantive.

However, they tended to be leaden and cerebral. John Paul's lighthearted informality and simplicity connected with his audience on an emotional level.

His remarks following the recitation of the Angelus each week were meant to teach but also to address timely events that directly affected ordinary people's lives. Embedded in them were moral teachings, but they were delivered nonchalantly, often with humor, and inescapably with amusing, illustrative anecdotes.

Delivered from his study window on the top floor of the apostolic palace, his remarks on this day were less religious than secular in emphasis. It was the start of a new school year, and the pope, a longtime teacher, specifically addressed twelve million Italian children including those in elementary school who were about to begin a new academic year.

He offered them encouragement, urged them to study, and wished them success. He cited Napoleon and Wellington as historical figures from whom they could learn important life lessons, and he sprinkled his advice with gentle humor.

"The season draws our attention to the resumption of school activity and awakens our interest in that great human and social phenomenon which is school," he began.

"I would like to remind elementary school students of their friend Pinocchio: not the one who skipped school one day to go and see the puppets; but that other one, Pinocchio who took a liking to school, so much so that during the entire school year, every day in class, he was the first to enter and the last to leave," he explained.

Referring to his own experience as a student, he noted good-naturedly, "No one came to tell me: 'You will become Pope.' Oh! If they had told me! If they had told me, I would have studied more; I would have prepared. But now I'm old; there's no time."

"But you, dear young people . . . you have the time, you have youth, health, memory, ingenuity: try to exploit all these things."

The pope singled out Catholic schools and their special mission. "[W]e want our Catholic schools, an expression of civil freedom, of pedagogical intensity, of a Christian conception of life, to know how much they are appreciated by the Church of God, and how much they are still encouraged and blessed by us."

The pope included a more sophisticated message to secondary school students. He advised them to prepare for important professions in adulthood and cautioned them about the tribulations of life they would inevitably confront: "[Y]ou will have battles in life at 30, 40, 50 years old, but if you want to win them, now you have to start, now prepare, now be assiduous in study and school."

John Paul closed with a prayer for divine assistance to teachers, students, and their families. And then he disappeared from the window to return to the narrow confines of his world in the papal apartment.[21]

A Time to Talk

In the afternoon John Paul and Secretary of State Villot strolled together in the Vatican Gardens.[22] Official photographers recorded the event. Side by side, they ambled down the walkways, casually conversing. Their pace was leisurely as they talked in private amid towering trees, blooming flowers, lush grass—a virtual paradise. From time to time they paused briefly, perhaps one emphasizing a particular point to the other. They were an odd-looking couple, Villot in his black cassock with red buttons and sash nearly a head taller than the pope in his pristine white attire. John Paul's hands were clasped at his waist; Villot's, hidden behind his back. The two men looked ahead mostly, only glancing at each other occasionally. The pope appeared pensive as he listened to Villot. The likelihood was that they conversed in French, Villot's native language. What confidential information they shared forever remained their secret.[23]

The pope also sent a letter to the archbishop of Freiburg, Germany, on the occasion of "Catholic Day," which was to be attended by Mother Teresa and Cardinal Joseph Ratzinger, archbishop of Munich. He wished the participants a successful gathering, writing, "We can sometimes have the impression that Christian hope has lost its stimulating force in our world." John Paul saw the assembly as one that could help promote the Church as a "sign of hope for the world."[24]

DAY 23/SEPTEMBER 18

The pope conducted two individual meetings, one religious and the other secular in nature. The first was with Cardinal Laurean Rugumbwa, archbishop of Dar es Salaam, Tanzania. The second was with Msgr. Giovanni Cheli, the Vatican's permanent observer to the United Nations.[25]

He also wired a telegram to the apostolic nuncio to Iran expressing his grief and prayers over a massive earthquake that had rumbled through the land, leaving behind death and devastation.[26] More than fifteen thousand people lost their lives as the natural disaster struck at 7:38 in the evening, destroying forty villages.[27]

DAY 24/SEPTEMBER 19

Private audiences continued on this day as the pope became increasingly familiar with the religious and political realities in a number of countries, most of them suffering from widespread poverty. He met with Bishop Ivo Lorscheiter of Santa Maria, Brazil, who was secretary of the Bishops' Conference in his country. The two were familiar with each other and had spent time together during Luciani's trip to Brazil. He also had an audience with the apostolic nuncio to Yugoslavia, a communist country at the time but one that maintained a certain independence from the Soviet Union. In his ongoing pursuit of achieving unity with eastern rites, John Paul also conferred with a delegation from the Syrian Orthodox Church.[28]

DAY 25/SEPTEMBER 20

Intervening for Peace

In his quest for peace, the pope wrote a letter to the Episcopal Conferences of Argentina and Chile about the so-called Beagle Conflict, a border dispute that nearly erupted in war.[29] His message was bold, clear, and uncompromising in its condemnation of violence and the moral imperative to insure peace.

He wrote,

> [T]he present circumstances, with their tensions and threats, request our attention and move our purpose to raise awareness among all our children and all people of good will, so that open differences do not exacerbate the spirits and may lead to unforeseeable consequences . . . we want to urge you, with all the moral strength at your disposal, to do the work of pacification, encouraging everyone, rulers and governed, towards goals of mutual understanding and generous understanding for those who, due to national barriers, are brothers in humanity.
>
> It is necessary to create a general climate in which, once any bellicose or animosity attitude is removed, the reasons for concord prevail over the forces of hatred or division, which only leave destructive traces behind.[30]

Another General Audience

Figure 10.1. The pope waving to the audience with Magee to his left looking on.

John Paul held his third general audience on this day; his topic this time was hope. He relished these weekly opportunities to bond with thousands of people. The pope taught that it was necessary for Christians to maintain hope even though "the bad are often fortunate and the good oppressed."

The pope related a poignant, personal story from the confessional in which both mercy and hope prevailed. He referred to a woman whose identity he didn't know. He had heard her confession years before, and this was his recollection: "She was discouraged by life because, she said, 'I have a very stormy moral life behind me.' 'May I ask,' I said, 'how old you are?'" She answered thirty-five. "But you can live forty more, fifty more years, you can do a lot of good still," he advised her. "Let go of the past, repentant as you are, project yourself to the future, change with God's help your life. You will see, everything will be changed."

"And I explained, 'God detests shortcomings . . . However, in another respect, God loves failures because they are opportunities for Him to show His mercy and . . . for us to . . . to be humble, to understand and pity the failings of others.'"[31]

He went on to allude to his "favorite author," Saint Francis de Sales. "God loves our faults because they are opportunities . . . for us to remain lowly, to be humble, and understand and sympathize with the failings of others."[32]

John Paul often used illustrative examples from secular life. On this occasion, he spoke of Andrew Carnegie who, "was born in misery" yet never forgot how precious his poor upbringing was long after becoming a millionaire. "When I was a boy, I read the life of a Scotsman, who moved to the United States with his parents; he became the richest man in the world. He [Carnegie] says, 'I was born in poverty, nevertheless I would not exchange the memories of my boyhood for those of the rich, the children of millionaires. What do these know of the joys of the family, of the mother, who combines together the duties of nanny, laundress, cook, teacher, angel and saint?'"[33]

The pope seemed even more passionate than he had been in his two previous audiences, the cadence of his voice emphasizing his teaching, his hands gesturing enthusiastically and synchronized with his inspiring words. The faces in the audience seem transfixed.[34]

Hope, proclaimed the pope, is an "obligatory virtue" for all Christians.[35]

He then quoted from Dante, Nietzsche, and Saint Augustine.[36] His frequent allusions to renowned writers didn't mar the simplicity of his messages, nor did they make him sound like an intellectual, though much of his audience was unfamiliar with some of the notables' names. He talked as if he were explaining concepts to a child but without condescension.

John Paul admitted that "in this world often the scoundrels are the most fortunate, and the poor are the most oppressed." Nevertheless, "hope . . . carries us forward in life."

This pope was intimately familiar with history, biography, and transcultural episodes of significance. Like Abraham Lincoln, he had the memory and the sense of occasion to relate these to his listeners, not only to amuse but to convey practical wisdom—wisdom to guide one's life in the path of righteousness.

In talking of the importance of cheerfulness, he shared with the audience a story he once told his students, and he brought down the house in doing so. A mason, he said, plunged from a second story scaffolding and broke both legs. When arriving at the hospital, the attending nun said, "You poor man! You hurt yourself when you fell." "No, Mother," the injured man responded, "when I hit the ground, that's when I hurt myself."[37]

The pope commended the man for making others smile while he was personally in pain. The implication was that we should always try to maintain hope and even good cheer in the midst of difficulties.

The Holy Father, as always, was almost apologetic for having spoken too long: "To finish, and I have almost finished," he reassured the audience.[38] He stressed that we all have a sacred mission on earth—to embrace and spread the social gospel by the examples of our own lives, lives inspired by hope.

An Overnight Visitor

Berto delighted his brother the pope with a surprise visit to the Vatican, where they dined together.[39] He stayed overnight, sleeping in a guest room in the attic. He was supposed to join the pope for Mass at seven the next morning, but, sleepless, he slipped away to the pope's private chapel at 6 a.m. There he found his brother already in prayer, and he stayed to meditate with him. After Mass they chatted "like good brothers" before Berto prepared to leave.

It had been a brief visit and though happy to see his brother, he was concerned because the pope seemed exhausted. As John Paul accompanied his younger brother to the elevator, he paused and embraced him before bidding him farewell. Berto, though emotionally moved, found it to be a curious gesture; his brother did not usually demonstrate his affection in such an intimately physical way. He wondered what moved his sibling to linger as they said their good-byes. It was their final parting.[40]

NOTES

1. Edward Magri, *Sarasota Herald-Tribune*, September 30, 1978, 5-A.
2. Peter Hebblethwaite, *The Year of Three Popes* (Cleveland, OH: Collins, 1979), 84.
3. Loris Serafini (director, Foundation Papa Luciani and Museum Albino Luciani of Canale d'Agordo), in discussion with the author, Canale d'Agordo, Italy, July 11, 2011.
4. John Magee (bishop emeritus, diocese of Cloyne, Ireland), in discussion with the author, Cobh, Ireland, February 17, 2010.
5. Pia Luciani (niece of Pope John Paul I), in discussion with the author, Canale d'Agordo, Italy, July 12, 2011.
6. Magee, discussion.
7. "His Light, Only for a Moment," *Humilitas* 13, December 2002, 9.
8. Serafini, discussion.
9. Paul Spackman, *God's Candidate: The Life and Times of Pope John Paul I* (Herefordshire: Gracewing, 2008), 153–55.
10. Stefania Falasca, *The September Pope: The Final Days of John Paul I*, © 2017, PIEMME; 2020, Libreria Editrice Vaticana. English translation published by *Our Sunday Visitor*, 2021,160.
11. Falasca, *September Pope*, 160.

12. Lina Petri, email to author, February 23, 2024.
13. Luciani, discussion.
14. Luciani discussion.
15. "L'attivita della Santa Sede 1978," Tipografica Pompei SPA—Pompei (Napoli), 1979.
16. Falasca, *September Pope*, 160.
17. "Mohamed Siad Barre," *Encyclopedia Britannica*, April 8, 2024.
18. Fr. Victor Feltes, "Is the Pope a Friend of Caesar?" The Pope John Paul I Papacy—Day by Day, August 6, 2014, https://johnpauli.wordpress.com/2014/09/16/is-the-pope-a-friend-of-caesar-day-22/.
19. Falasca, *September Pope*, 160.
20. Falasca, *September Pope*, 160.
21. Discourse before the Sunday Angelus, September 17, 1978. Collection of recordings of the original speeches and statements of Blessed Pope John Paul I of the archives of the Foundation Papa Luciani of Canale d'Agordo (Belluno-Italy).
22. Falasca, *September Pope*, 160.
23. Albino Luciani photograph 323.JPG, John Paul I Museum Collection.
24. Fr. Victor Feltes, "Lessons for Life," The Pope John Paul I Papacy—Day by Day, August 6, 2014, https://johnpauli.wordpress.com/2014/09/17/lessons-for-life-day-23/.
25. Falasca, *September Pope*, 160.
26. Falasca, *September Pope*, 160.
27. "Massive Earthquake Devastates Iran, Killing 15,000 and Destroying Towns," *Harvard Crimson*, September 19, 1978, https://www.thecrimson.com/article/1978/9/19/massive-earthquake-devastates-iran-killing-15000/.
28. Falasca, *September Pope*, 160–61.
29. "Beagle Channel Dispute," Encyclopedia.com.
30. John Paul I, letter on the occasion of the Argentine and Chilean Bishops' Conference, https://www.vatican.va/content/john-paul-i/en/letters.index.html.
31. "General Audience: Hope," September 20, 1978. Collection of recordings of the original speeches and statements of Blessed Pope John Paul I of the archives of the Foundation Papa Luciani of Canale d'Agordo (Belluno-Italy).
32. "General Audience: Hope."
33. "General Audience: Hope."
34. "The First Years of Albino Luciani, Part V" (The Election), https://www.albino-luciani.com/index.php?id=274&L=3.
35. Raymond and Lauretta Seabeck, *The Smiling Pope: The Life and Teaching of John Paul I* (Huntington, IN: Our Sunday Visitor, 2004), 104.
36. Seabeck, *Smiling Pope*, 104–5.
37. Seabeck, *Smiling Pope*, 107.
38. Seabeck, *Smiling Pope*, 108.
39. Falasca, *September Pope*, 161.
40. Seabeck, *Smiling Pope*, 64.

• *11* •

Interregnum

Out of Danger (August 6–25, 1978)

> [D]o not worry about tomorrow: for tomorrow will bring worries of its own. Today's trouble is enough for today. —Matthew 6:34 (NRSVCE)
>
> For everything there is a season, and a time for every matter under heaven. —Ecclesiastes 3:1 (NRSVCE)

Shortly before dusk on August 9, a black Mercedes hearse with large rectangular side windows that provided an unobstructed view of the coffin within wended its way from the Alban Hills, destined for Rome. It was preceded and flanked by an official escort of police-mounted motorcycles. A cortege of dark automobiles occupied by family members of the deceased and Church dignitaries followed closely in an undulating line. The motorcade was conveying the body of Pope Paul VI on the fourteen-mile route from the papal summer palace at Castel Gandolfo to the Vatican, where it would lie in state at St. Peter's Basilica.[1]

RITUALS, BURIAL, AND PREPARATIONS

With Paul's death on August 6, an interregnum began. The term refers to the interval of time between the death of one pope and the election of another. Paul's body already had been placed on a catafalque at Castel Gandolfo, the papal summer retreat where he had died, and the doors there were opened to mourners. An estimated five thousand people, including high Italian government officials such as Prime Minister Giulio Andreotti and former president Amintore Fanfani, paid their respects.[2] The same ritual was repeated thereafter at St. Peter's.[3] In total, approximately a quarter of a million people viewed Paul's body.[4]

That impressive turnout came as somewhat of a surprise because Paul had not been a universally beloved figure, partly due to his leaving behind a Church riven by discord, partly because of a taciturn personality. According to tourists interviewed in an ABC news report from Rome, the pope's death was received by the public with very little emotion; cameras didn't detect large crowds assembled in St. Peter's Square.[5] The pope's advanced age also contributed to the subdued reaction.

Following tradition, Cardinal Jean Villot, the Vatican's secretary of state, who was now to serve as the "papal chamberlain" (camerlengo) until a new pope was elected, notified all the cardinals and publicly issued the official announcement of Paul's death on August 7.[6]

The first General Congregation of Cardinals—a daily assembly—took place in the Apostolic Palace; the initial order of business was finalizing arrangements for Paul's funeral, a process that was simplified by the late pope, who had drafted a detailed will. In it he specified his personal wishes regarding both his funeral and burial. Utmost minimalism was to mark the memorial service, and his grave would be located "in the real earth, with a simple covering indicating the place . . . No monument for me."[7] (His will included instructions that his personal papers be burned, reducing to ashes whatever private thoughts he had recorded during his reign.)[8]

On Saturday, August 12, when the public viewing of the late pope's body concluded, Cardinal Villot covered the pope's face with a purple veil and then spread an ermine-colored blanket over the body. The *sediari* then fastened the lid of the coffin with sixteen solid-gold screws before carrying it into the piazza for the funeral Mass.[9]

Cardinal Carlo Confalonieri was the principal celebrant of the Mass.[10] The modest rite would be replicated in just a matter of weeks, a certainty that no one could have imagined.

Then it was down into the grottoes where the earthen grave awaited its occupant. Adhering to protocol, the *sediari* placed the cypress coffin in a lead one that sat inside an oak casket. After sealing the coffins to make them airtight, laborers lowered them directly in the ground.[11]

SADNESS IN VENICE

Albino Luciani thought highly of Paul VI, referring to him often as "*un papa grande*," a great pope, according to his niece Pia Luciani.[12] The patriarch of Venice had admired Paul's courage and steadfastness throughout the storms of controversy that had buffeted his pontificate. And although the two had had some disagreements about significant Church issues, they always maintained a relationship of mutual respect, each honoring the other's intellectual and doctrinal integrity.

That Luciani was saddened by Paul's death there could be no doubt, but like everyone else who had witnessed his flagging energy and physical misery, the patriarch was not surprised by his passing, which tempered his bereavement. On August 9, the cardinal, dressed in purple vestments and wearing a white miter, celebrated a commemorative Mass for Paul in Venice's Basilica of San Marco.[13] He appeared somber throughout the celebration of the Eucharist. However, in a subsequent public statement, in which he paid tribute to the late pontiff, he seemed hopeful about the status of the Church despite its difficulties, as he talked extemporaneously about the upcoming conclave and its significance for the future of his beloved institution.[14]

A LEADERLESS CHURCH

When the Church is without a pope, it enters an interlude officially known as *sede vacante*, Latin for "vacant seat." Not only is the papacy itself unoccupied, but even Church officials at the Vatican no longer retain their offices. The camerlengo is the sole exception because he must perform an essential role during the interregnum and the subsequent conclave. The cardinal holding this position oversees the Vatican treasury and is also responsible for managing the regular affairs of the Vatican during the period when the governing departments are not functioning. He is not empowered, however, to make any major decisions; he is solely an interim administrator charged with carrying out explicitly prescribed functions. It is the camerlengo, for example, who officially confirms a pope's death, even performing a strange ancient ritual of gently tapping the pontiff's head three times with a small silver hammer while calling out his name. He then seals the pontifical residence, which remains unoccupied until a new pope unfastens the red ribbons fastened to the doors. Following tradition, the camerlengo also destroys the Fisherman's ring worn by the pope with a special hammer. The ritual signifies the conclusion of his reign.[15]

On this occasion French Cardinal Villot, the Vatican secretary of state, also served as camerlengo. Historically, the man holding this position is the first official to be informed of a pope's death. There was no need for any notification this time because Villot was present when Paul passed and had administered the Last Rites to the pontiff.[16] Besides performing such formalities, he also presided over the General Congregation of Cardinals and, most significantly, took charge of the forthcoming conclave.[17]

Cardinals Descend on the Vatican

Cardinal Villot had swiftly summoned the cardinals from around the world to the Vatican after sharing the news of the pope's death. Arriving in staggered fashion, they gathered in Rome to oversee routine Church affairs as well as to establish a calendar for the opening of the gathering of cardinal electors, known as a conclave, that would select a new pope. During the daily gatherings, they were prohibited from soliciting votes for the papacy, though they were permitted to discuss the election process itself. However, "campaigning" was conducted subtly at receptions, dinners, and other social events at which many of the cardinals gathered. No overt solicitation of votes was allowed.[18]

Scores of cardinals were conspicuous in St. Peter's Square, walking singly or in pairs to and from the General Congregations, some of the more prominent among them—prospective popes—gesturing exuberantly to the omnipresent television cameras. The mass media were obsessed with attempting to determine which of the cardinals was most likely to succeed Paul. Many of the potential pontiffs were not only willing but eager to grant interviews, particularly for television media, which had its largest presence ever at this conclave. Cardinal Sebastiano Baggio, considered in the top tier of candidates, was especially effusive on TV.[19]

BROTHER CARDINALS GETTING ACQUAINTED

The two and a half weeks between Paul's death and the beginning of the conclave afforded the cardinals multiple opportunities to get to know each other better, to exchange views about the state of the Church, to discuss the kind of leadership it needed, and to develop a consensus about the qualities the new pope should possess. Well over one hundred princes of the Church, as cardinals are known colloquially, congregated in Rome. Eligible to vote in the conclave were 115 under the age of eighty, but one of those had died, and three others did not participate because they were too ill.[20] The sheer numbers dictated that many of the cardinals were strangers. Observed Italian Cardinal Silvio Oddi years later, "Cardinals didn't travel as much [then] as now. They didn't know each other as they do now."[21] Consequently, informal gatherings acquired importance, for it was at those functions that cardinals from far flung countries of the world became acquainted.

The status of the Church's health varied depending on geography. In the West, the institution faced challenges that threatened its wellbeing; they included a drastic decline in attendance at Sunday Mass and reception of the sacraments by self-identified Catholics, along with a similar decline in vocations. Then there were the cleavages in ideology between reformers and traditionalists regarding practices that seemed at odds with modernity, conflicts that appeared unyielding.

Not so in Africa, though, where the faith was expanding. But an entirely different set of difficulties beset those sons and daughters of the Church. Their populations tended to live in far-flung villages, making it difficult for priests to minister to the spiritual and corporal needs of their parishioners. This increased the role and responsibilities of deacons. The poor were hardly able to support the Church financially on which it, like any other organization—secular or religious—was ultimately dependent for survival.

Fundamental differences and needs seemed endless. Who among the Sacred College of Cardinals possessed the extraordinary personal characteristics and talents to successfully navigate the disputes, unite the factions, and begin to solve the problems that would lead to a healthy Catholicism everywhere? That dilemma was of staggering proportions. There could be no doubt that the decision facing the cardinals in conclave was of vital importance and that it would be, as Luciani had asserted, "difficult to find the person able to face so many problems, which are very heavy crosses."[22] Ultimately, the electors would have to combine their knowledge of the issues and personal qualities of their colleagues to make the right selection. But that alone was inadequate. They had to depend on the Holy Spirit's guidance.

The Next Pope Arrives at the Vatican

Luciani departed Venice for Rome four days after Pope Paul's death and the day after his body had been returned to the Vatican.[23] He had hoped to escape his diocese stealthily.[24] Msgr. Renato Volo, chancellor of the Venice archdiocese, saw Luciani for the last time when he escorted him to the boat dock as he prepared for the drive to Rome. Volo, an admirer of the patriarch, was impressed by his capacity to listen patiently and with empathy to people's struggles and to solve problems in a deliberate, practical manner. He also was charmed by Luciani's delight in life's simple things. He recalled that on the day Luciani left for Rome he wore the plain clothes typical of ordinary clergymen. Despite his title, Luciani always seemed to consider himself, first and foremost, a priest.[25]

Despite his ever-present smile, all was not sunshine in Luciani's life. Shortly before leaving for the conclave, he suffered from a chronic condition of swollen feet, which, when intense, caused him considerable discomfort and required rest. The need to relieve the inflammation was a troublesome omen but one unknown to his fellow cardinals.[26]

According to an associate of Luciani's, he was accompanied only by his driver, don Diego Lorenzi. The two engaged in virtually no conversation. The patriarch spent nearly the entire five-hour trek in prayerful silence. When the two men arrived at their destination, Luciani's modest five-year-old Lancia developed mechanical problems. The cardinal instructed Lorenzi to have it repaired as soon as possible; he hoped that his stay in Rome would be brief.[27]

Prior to the conclave, Luciani occupied modest accommodations as a guest of the Augustinian Fathers. St. Monica's International College was conveniently located a short distance from St. Peter's. The superior of the order had opportunities to observe the patriarch during his stay and later wrote that "his holiness radiated from his smiling face. His fatherly love encouraged everyone to feel he was his closest friend." His presence there was unobtrusive, just as he wished it to be. He enjoyed taking isolated afternoon walks in the garden while reading his breviary. Afterward, he would sit on a bench and pray the rosary. In addition to prayer, the cardinal had time to engage in one of his favorite pastimes: reading. Work, though, intruded on this pleasure. Planning a retreat for his priests back in Veneto on his return home, he devoted part of his time to developing talks he planned to deliver.[28]

Feeling comfortable among his Augustinian acquaintances, Luciani easily slipped into the community's routine, joining the friars in their dining hall for meals.[29] Living among members of the order, however, was an effusive ninety-year-old lay brother named Franceschino with whom Luciani often conversed. Though the self-effacing patriarch wanted to be as inconspicuous as possible among his hosts, and most definitely did not wish any preferential treatment, Franceschino insisted that a man of Luciani's stature should be honored. As a gesture of respect, he took it upon himself to buy a red placemat for the cardinal to use at the dinner table. To Luciani's discomfiture, it contrasted conspicuously with the white ones that the Augustinians used, a reminder to the priests that their guest was a high-ranking prelate.[30]

One afternoon Franceschino accompanied the cardinal to St. Peter's. As they approached the bronze doors, a Swiss Guard on duty who knew Franceschino inquired about the identity of the priest who accompanied him. He replied with pride, "the cardinal patriarch of Venice," at which point the guard promptly saluted. Franceschino reveled in the moment though the incident caused Luciani momentary embarrassment.[31]

Like the rest of his colleagues, Luciani took part in the morning meetings of cardinals. Whether he was a vocal participant in the proceedings is unknown. It was not unusual, though, to spot him in St. Peter's Square dressed in a simple black cassock sans zucchetto and carrying a briefcase while often absorbed in lively conversation with a colleague or two.[32]

Figure 11.1. Cardinal Luciani engages in convivial conversation with a fellow cardinal.

SUCCESSOR SCUTTLEBUTT

Pope Paul left behind a deeply divided church.[33] A struggle over succession was expected to be a battle between conservatives and liberals, a contest that many expected to be protracted and perhaps even discordant.[34] Some cardinals were so obstinate in their opinions, they were unwilling to free themselves even a smidgeon from their ideological prisons. That had profound implications for the election of a new pope. If enough of them were supporting *papabili* of opposing viewpoints, the result could be a deadlocked conclave, which could undermine confidence in the new pontiff's efficacy among the faithful. Because of the tensions between traditionalists and reformers resulting from Vatican II and the ban on artificial means of birth control in the encyclical *Humanae Vitae*, it was widely believed that the next pope should be someone with the capacity to unify the Sacred College of Cardinals along with the faithful, a task of Herculean proportions under the circumstances.[35]

THE GUESSING GAME

Papabile is the term referring to a cardinal who is considered a likely pope. Although many to whom the moniker is ascribed are flattered, it can be a jinx. History teems with accounts of cardinals thought to have a lock on the papacy who didn't triumph. Thus, the old Vatican adage, "He who enters the conclave a pope, emerges a cardinal."[36] That reality didn't dampen the excitement that rampant speculation generated about which cardinals were viable candidates. Besides the international media, the guessing game involved Vatican pundits and the cardinals themselves. With the record-setting number of cardinals taking part in the conclave, roughly twice the number who had participated in the 1965 gathering, the number of *papabili* expanded as well. According to some sources, as many as a score of names was included in the list.[37]

Though it might be unseemly, speculation about who would emerge victorious in the forthcoming conclave had started even before Paul's burial.[38] *Newsweek* reported that no heir apparent was readily identifiable. Conjecture was even that the first non-Italian in nearly five centuries might be elected.[39] *Time* had been compiling files on possible papal successors to Paul VI three years prior to his death. During the interregnum the magazine whittled its list of likely contenders by interviewing cardinals as they left their daily meetings. Foreign cardinals, when arriving in Rome, also were interviewed for their views.[40]

Upon the death of Paul VI, *Time*'s cover featured a photograph of the papal crown atop regal pontifical vestments conspicuously but oddly draped over an absent human figure. Flanking both sides of this symbol of the empty seat were photographs of five cardinals thought by the "experts" in Vatican politics to be the most likely successors to Paul. Three were powerful members of the Curia: 65-year-old Sebastiano Baggio, 70-year-old Paolo Bertoli, and 68-year-old Sergio Pignedoli. The other two were diocesan cardinals, 68-year-old Johannes Willebrands of the Netherlands and 57-year-old Eduardo Pironio of Argentina. Between the Pignedoli and Pironio images was a bold question mark superimposed on a yellow background. It signified that despite the speculation about Paul's likely successor, successfully determining the identity of the next pope was essentially conjecture.[41]

Time described the list of credible contenders as "unusually large."[42] Of the sixteen most likely candidates identified in the magazine's cover story, Luciani received not a single mention, though the publication speculated that an Italian moderate might prevail.[43]

The Ostensible Contenders

Although most informed members of the international press agreed that there didn't seem to be a clear frontrunner, several prominent cardinals headed by Italians topped their lists of contestants. Besides those identified by *Time*, widespread speculation focused on Giuseppe Siri, Pericle Felici,

Corrado Ursi, and Salvatore Pappalardo. Long-shot non-Italians most frequently mentioned were Jean Villot of France and Basil Hume of England.[44]

During the interregnum, journalists from around the world handicapped the race. Predictions were made, and biographies of cardinals were prepared and disseminated. Even London's Ladbroke bookmakers posted odds: Pignedoli, a 5–2 favorite; Baggio and Poletti, 7–2; Giovanni Benelli, 4–1; Willebrands, 8–1; Pironio, 12–1; Franz Koenig, 16–1; Hume, 25–1; Joseph Cordeiro, Aloisio Lorscheiter, and Leo Suenens, 33–1.[45]

Most of the public guesswork did not consider Luciani to be a viable contender. That was fine with him.[46] He did not want to be pope; in fact, he did not consider himself qualified. Luciani's name had been circulated widely as a *papabile* only in northern Italy—his home territory, where some people even boldly predicted that he would be the next pope. Few outside the area took the prognostication seriously, however.[47]

One American TV network, after identifying Pignedoli as *papabile*, also mentioned Luciani, but almost as an afterthought. Its videotape showed Pignedoli once catching up with Luciani during a stroll in the piazza and grabbing his elbow. A correspondent described the patriarch of Venice as "soft spoken." It might have been the sole fact he knew about him.[48] Only a small handful of news media included Luciani's name among the contenders—the *Daily American* (an English language Roman paper), the *Irish Press*, and the *Sunday Times*.[49]

Almost as an afterthought, an NBC news reporter contacted Luciani to request biographical information in the event of his election. Luciani replied dismissively, "There is a Class A list of candidates, a Class B list of candidates, and a Class C list of candidates. I am surely on the Class C list."[50] Casually dismissing his chances and using self-deprecating humor, Luciani asserted, "You can't make gnocchi out of this dough!"[51]

MEDIA OBSESSION

Additional television crews from around the world descended on the Vatican as the cardinals began arriving. Many, including Cardinals Terence Cooke of New York and Humberto Medeiros of Boston, granted interviews to the hungry press. It was almost universally believed that no American had any chance of becoming pope because it would be politically unwise to elect a cardinal from a superpower such as the United States.[52]

Cardinals couldn't walk anywhere in public, either individually or in small groups, without being approached by television, magazine, and newspaper reporters.[53] Television had its largest presence ever for a conclave.[54]

Despite Luciani's improbable prospects for election, some members of the media stalked him, though without eliciting much pertinent information. Whenever reporters and their omnipresent television cameras approached cardinals for interviews, Luciani would deliberately fade into the background.[55] Always uncomfortable in the media glare, Luciani did his best to be inconspicuous at all times. On those rare occasions when the press successfully cornered him to inquire about his chances for election, he deftly deflected their questions.

Once, when he thought he had escaped the media frenzy, enterprising reporters tracked him down in a corridor and found him reciting the rosary. Besieged with questions about the conclave, Luciani maintained his silence until, becoming exasperated, he admonished the group, "Journalists should learn to write less, talk less, and pray more. I am thinking only of praying that the Lord will enlighten me in such a way that I may vote for the right person."[56] It was an unusually sharp rebuke from the man known for his mild temperament.

Another time, reporters were lying in wait at his Augustinian lodgings to question the dark horse candidate. As he and a fellow cardinal left the car, Luciani's discomfort at seeing them was readily apparent. He waved shyly to the journalists, smiled, but ignoring their questions, headed swiftly for the entrance. Then, attempting a quick escape, he frantically rang the doorbell repeatedly while unsuccessfully searching his pockets for a key, all the while good-naturedly pointing to his colleague as the one deserving the media's attention. Smiling self-consciously, he tried the door again, but it wouldn't yield. Almost in a panic, he pressed the doorbell button with force once more. Finally, deliverance: The door swung open, and he quickly entered the sanctuary with palpable relief while shyly gesturing good-bye to the journalists. He had escaped, but not for long.[57]

CLANDESTINE CONSENSUS-BUILDING

Away from the public glare, there was intrigue among some electors. One of the more politically astute cardinals feared leaving the outcome of the conclave to chance. The stakes for the Church were too high if the wrong cardinal won the papacy. A deliberate effort was considered essential to secure enough cardinals to coalesce around an acceptable candidate who could ultimately gain adequate support to emerge victorious. Cardinal Confalonieri had first broached Luciani's name.[58] But it was the wily bishop of Florence, the former effective Vatican political infighter, Cardinal Giovanni Benelli, who was orchestrating the effort on Luciani's behalf. He had once been the closest adviser to Pope Paul, and for a decade he was a powerhouse in the Secretariat of State. Though he had made many enemies within the Vatican bureaucracy, he was still influential.[59]

Benelli knew Luciani from his work with the bishops of northern Italy, and he recognized his friendliness, intellectual abilities, and communications skills.[60] Albino Luciani was a man with virtually no enemies among the College of Cardinals. In fact, those who knew him loved and admired him, and those who had only passing acquaintance with him were taken with his humility, intellect, and sense of humor, which was often self-deprecating.[61] A cardinal with those qualities, reasoned Benelli, would be a formidable candidate for the papacy. Not only was he likable, but Luciani also defied easy categorization as a liberal or conservative. His views on central issues facing the Church were nuanced, making it difficult to brand him as an ideologue on either end of the spectrum. For example, he was a fervent supporter of the reforms stemming from the Second Vatican Council, but he also was a traditionalist regarding the magisterium and in his opposition to divorce, married priests, consecration of women to the priesthood, and a host of other progressive ideas that were anathema to the conservatives. As a result, he could be a nearly ideal consensus candidate acceptable to the staunchest of liberals and conservatives as well as to the so-called moderates. No polarizing figure was he.[62]

Even from Florence, Benelli had phoned friends among the non-Italian cardinals to lobby for Luciani. Later, in Rome, he feverishly manned the phones on Luciani's behalf. His pitch to conservatives was to reassure them that Luciani was in solidarity with them in opposing communism, divorce, liberation theology, and a host of other imminent threats to the traditional church. To moderates, he trumpeted the patriarch's admirable personal virtues. In all instances his advocacy of Luciani was conducted with the utmost caution.[63]

Later, a widespread rumor in Rome had it that Benelli had orchestrated Luciani's election covertly from his favorite table at L'Eau Vive restaurant, where he held an informal meeting of cardinal electors prior to the start of the conclave.[64] Benelli unofficially became known as the "Grand Elector" for his successful promotion of Luciani. His courting of non-Italian cardinals was a strategically wise decision, given Luciani's well-known affinity for the Third World and the fact that this would be the most international conclave in history. Also, the most notable *papabili* were Italians, likely leading to the fracturing of the twenty-six members of their delegation and thereby diluting their influence in the eventual outcome of the balloting. Benelli was encouraged by the response to the idea of a Luciani candidacy. He, therefore, intensified his campaign to bring other cardinals into the fold. Eventually, he was successful in building a sizable block of pro-Luciani supporters who would, even on the very first ballot of the conclave, provide a surprisingly substantial number of votes for the patriarch that Benelli hoped would generate momentum in subsequent scrutinies, the official term used in referring to rounds of balloting.

Luciani himself was blissfully unaware of Benelli's intensive "draft" efforts.

Brazil's Cardinal Lorscheiter told the media before entering the conclave, "The pope should be, above all, a good shepherd . . . to encourage collegiality among bishops." In retrospect, it sounded like an endorsement of Luciani. Between the two there was mutual admiration. Benelli, without betraying his advocacy of Luciani, told the press that the next pope must be "pious, discreet, a shepherd of souls, and moderately conservative." Little did reporters realize it was an accurate description of Luciani.[65]

The night before the conclave was to begin, Luciani engaged in conversation with a member of the papal guard named Camillo Cibin, a man he knew, when another guard named Giusto Antoniazzi, also familiar to Luciani, arrived. A lively dialogue ensued. Cibin greeted Luciani with, "Let me wish you every success, your Eminence!"

"What are you saying? You are wishing me misfortune!" replied the cardinal half in jest.

Cibin retorted, "I did not wish you success because the papacy is too heavy a cross." Luciani meekly replied, "I know, I know, but there is nothing to be worried about; it's not for me."

Antoniazzi interjected, "They say John XXIII once said that someone has to accept that cross."

Resignedly, the cardinal conceded, "Yes, that's true. Well, if I were sure it would carry me to heaven, I'd have no difficulty in accepting it."[66]

DISMISSING PREMONITIONS

After Luciani's election, Mario Senigaglia revealed a conversation he had had with the patriarch some time before the conclave was imminent: "One day we were alone at table, and I talked about the possibility of his becoming pope. And he told me, 'No. You know this is the time for a foreigner, and you know who I'm going to vote for—Lorscheiter, whom I met in Brazil.' And I kept on telling him, 'Yes, but what you're saying it's just to hide; you are afraid to become pope and not to come back.' He kept silent."[67]

Senigaglia had gone so far as to predict that his former boss would be elected because he was the holiest of the cardinals. Luciani summarily dismissed the notion. The man pressed him, asking how Luciani would respond if, in fact, he was elected. He said with an air of certainty that he would refuse. He simply didn't want to be pope.[68]

In mid-August, don Giovanni Lucchetta, a priest from Luciani's hometown, predicted to a pastor that Luciani would be elected—fully fifteen days before the event took place. He wrote in a letter his prediction that in a few ballots Luciani would be chosen, and the locals had to prepare for a celebration. The letter is extant.[69] Even the archbishop of Dakar, Hyracinthe Thiandoum, who had met Luciani in Venice in 1977, had confided to his secretary that one day Luciani would become pope.[70]

But Luciani, shortly before entering the conclave, wrote confidently to his niece Pia, "Luckily, I'm out of danger. Even so, it is a very grave responsibility to vote in these circumstances." In that same letter he wrote that he had been assigned to cell #60, "a parlor made into a bedroom . . . It is like the seminary in Feltre in 1923, iron bed, mattress, a basin for washing."[71] Pia had long since suspected that his "out of danger" assertion was wishful thinking. Her view was that her uncle was trying to reassure himself that he would not become pope.[72] He asked Pia to convey his greetings to her parents, explaining that he was pressed for time.[73]

On the afternoon of August 25, as the cardinals made their way to the apostolic palace, Luciani walked to the foyer carrying his luggage and said to a friar, "Let us hope it will be over quickly. My suitcase is . . . packed to go back to Venice."[74]

NOTES

1. William Claiborne, *Washington Post*, August 10, 1978, https://www.washingtonpost.com/archive/politics/1978/08/10/paul-vi-returns-to-rome/7eaae0f0-a7ba-4ebd-9bd2-5f6fe65bfac1/.
2. Sari Gilbert, "Pope Dies after Heart Attack," *Washington Post*, August 7, 1978.
3. Kenneth L. Woodward, "Choosing a New Pope," *Newsweek*, August 21, 1978, 48.
4. Gordon Thomas and Max Morgan-Witts, *Pontiff* (Garden City: Doubleday, 1984), 126.
5. ABC News Report, August 6, 1978, https://www.youtube.com/watch?v=K5hXO0NGV3Q.
6. Paul Spackman, *God's Candidate: The Life and Times of Pope John Paul I* (Herefordshire: Gracewing, 2008), 121.
7. Richard Ostling, "In Search of a Pope," *Time*, August 21, 1978, 62.
8. Ostling, "In Search of a Pope," 63.
9. Thomas and Morgan-Witts, *Pontiff*, 128.
10. Spackman, *God's Candidate*, 122.

11. "Papal Interregnum," Viewer@EWTN.com, https://www.ewtn.com/catholicism/holy see/interregnum.

12. Pia Luciani, interview with Mo Guernon, July 12, 2011.

13. Raymond and Lauretta Seabeck, *The Smiling Pope: The Life and Teaching of John Paul I* (Huntington, IN: Our Sunday Visitor, 2004), 251.

14. "The First Years of Albino Luciani, Part III" (The Cardinal), https://www.albino-luciani.com/index.php?id=272&L=3.

15. "Pope Names New 'Camerlengo' to Run Vatican in Papal Transition Period," February 14, 2019, https://www.reuters.com/article/us-vatican-camerlengo/pope-names-new-camerlengo-to-run-vatican-in-papal-transition-period-idUSKCN1Q31ZG.

16. "The Papal Transition: An Overview," interview with Rev. Thomas Reese, NPR, April 2, 2005.

17. Peter Hebblethwaite, *The Year of Three Popes* (Cleveland, OH: Collins, 1979), 44.

18. Woodward, "Choosing a New Pope," 48.

19. "The First Years of Albino Luciani, Part IV" (The Conclave), https://www.albino-luciani.com/index.php?id=273&L=3.

20. Spackman, *God's Candidate*, 123.

21. Jonathan Kivitny, *Man of the Century: The Life and Times of John Paul II* (New York: Henry Holt, 1997), 282.

22. Seabeck, *Smiling Pope*, 53.

23. Loris Serafini (director, Foundation Papa Luciani and Museum Albino Luciani of Canale d'Agordo), in discussion with the author, Canale d'Agordo, Italy, July 15, 2011.

24. Seabeck, *Smiling Pope*, 50.

25. John L. Allen Jr., "From Palace to Garbage Dump: A Hint of What Might Have Been," *National Catholic Reporter*, January 24, 2003.

26. John Cornwell, *A Thief in the Night: Life and Death in the Vatican* (New York: Penguin, 1989), 57.

27. Anonymous interview by the author.

28. Seabeck, *Smiling Pope*, 50–51.

29. "A Look Back at the Conclave That Elected Albino Luciani Pope," August 25, 2015, https://www.lastampa.it/vatican-insider/en/2015/08/25/news/a-look-back-at-the-conclave-that-elected-albino-luciani-pope-1.35235480/.

30. Seabeck, *Smiling Pope*, 51.

31. Seabeck, *Smiling Pope*, 51.

32. "The First Years of Albino Luciani, Part IV" (The Conclave), https://www.albino-luciani.com/index.php?id=273&L=3.

33. Woodward, "Choosing a New Pope," 49.

34. "Pope Paul VI Dies after Heart Attack: Death of 'Pilgrim Pope' Comes while Resting Up from Illness," *Lodi News-Sentinel*, August 7, 1978, 1, lodinews.com/site/about.html.

35. Woodward, "Choosing a New Pope," 48.

36. Harry F. Waters, "Cardinal Candidates," *Newsweek*, August 23, 1978, 50.

37. Mayo Mohs, "After Paul: The Leading Contenders," *Time*, August 21, 1978, 66.
38. "The Church after Pope Paul VI," *Newsweek*, August 21, 1978, 3.
39. Woodward, "Choosing a New Pope," 48.
40. Ostling, "In Search of a Pope," 2.
41. Ostling, "In Search of a Pope," cover photo.
42. Ostling, "In Search of a Pope," 62.
43. Ostling, "In Search of a Pope," 65.
44. "The September Pope," *Time*, October 9, 1978, 81.
45. Leighton Vaughan Williams, "Three Strikes of the Clock: Betting on the Man to Be Pope since 1503," April 18, 2017, https://leightonvw.com/2017/04/18/three-strikes-of-the-clock-betting-on-the-man-to-be-pope-since-1503/.
46. Serafini, discussion.
47. Seabeck, *Smiling Pope*, 53.
48. "The First Years, Part IV" (The Conclave).
49. Spackman, *God's Candidate*, 124.
50. Spackman, *God's Candidate*, 124–25.
51. David Yallop, *In God's Name: An Investigation into the Murder of Pope John Paul I* (New York: Penguin, 1984), 69.
52. "The First Years, Part IV" (The Conclave).
53. Seabeck, *Smiling Pope*, 52.
54. "The First Years, Part IV" (The Conclave).
55. Seabeck, *Smiling Pope*, 52.
56. Seabeck, *Smiling Pope*, 52.
57. "Per questo, ho detto, mi chiamero Giovanni Paolo," Fondazione Vaticana Giovanni Paolo i, 5:27, June 8, 2022, https://www.youtube.com/watch?v=TpWQLJGnfCk.
58. "A Swift, Stunning Choice," *Time*, September 4, 1978, 66.
59. "Giovanni Cardinal Benelli Dead; Was Called Candidate for Papacy," *New York Times*, October 27, 1982, D 25, https://www.nytimes.com/1982/10/27/obituaries/giovanni-cardinal-benelli-dead-was-called-candidate-for-papacy.html.
60. Peter Hebblethwaite, *The Next Pope: A Behind-the-Scenes Look at the Forces That Will Choose the Successor to John Paul II and Decide the Future of the Catholic Church* (New York: HarperCollins, 2000), 77.
61. "John Paul I: The Pope of Unity," *Newsweek*, September 4, 1978, 3.
62. Andrew Greeley, *The Making of the Popes 1978: The Politics of Intrigue in the Vatican* (Kansas City: Andrews and McMeel, 1979), 138.
63. Greeley, *Making of the Popes*, 140.
64. George Weigel, *God's Choice: Pope Benedict XVI and the Future of the Catholic Church* (New York: HarperCollins e-books, 2009), 121.
65. "The First Years, Part IV" (The Conclave).
66. Seabeck, *Smiling Pope*, 52.
67. "The First Years of Albino Luciani, Part V" (The Election), https://www.albino-luciani.com/index.php?id=274&L=3.
68. Anonymous interview with the author.

69. Serafini, discussion.
70. Serafini, discussion.
71. Seabeck, *Smiling Pope*, 53.
72. Pia Luciani (niece of Pope John Paul I), in discussion with the author, Canale d'Agordo, Italy, July 12, 2011.
73. Seabeck, *Smiling Pope*, 53.
74. "A Look Back at the Conclave That Elected Albino Luciani Pope," 25, https://www.lastampa.it/vatican-insider/en/2015/08/25/news/a-look-back-at-the-conclave-that-elected-albino-luciani-pope-1.35235480/Agosto 2015 alle 19:07.

• 12 •

Destiny

Vicar of Christ (August 25–26, 1978)

> [T]hus says the Lord God: I myself will search for my sheep, and will seek them out. —Ezekiel 34:11 (NRSVCE)
>
> A bright light will shine to all the ends of the earth. —Tobit 13:11 (NRSVCE)

This was Albino Luciani's first conclave, and he was nervous. As his note to his niece, written on the morning of August 25, made clear, he understood the gravity of the decision the cardinal electors were about to make.[1] The magnitude of tribulations that awaited the next pope was staggering. At various intervals in its two-thousand-year history, the Church had been battered by internal and external threats but somehow had managed to survive. Now the ancient institution's relevance to the modern world was at stake; only the next vicar of Christ, guided by the Almighty, could rescue the institution from its existential peril. There was no paucity of cardinals with impressive credentials to be pope, but Luciani's personal enthusiasm for Cardinal Aloisio Lorscheiter notwithstanding, he was worried. It would take an extraordinary man—a skillful administrator who was also holy, wise, vigorous, and charismatic—to navigate the Church through the tsunami of troubles it confronted. And so Luciani prayed.[2] The conclave could not make a mistake in its chosen one. Not this time.

THE EMERGENCE OF CONCLAVES

The word "conclave" means "with key" in Latin.[3] It's an appropriate term because cardinals, when gathering to elect a pope in conclave, deliberate behind locked doors. In modern times this practice seems anachronistic, but historically it was desirable if not altogether necessary.

Popes were not always elected in secret gatherings inaccessible to outsiders. During the Church's early history, they were often chosen by clergy, sometimes joined by faithful laymen.[4] The precursors of modern conclaves originated in 1139, primarily to prevent external interference with the selection of popes; concurrently, voting became a responsibility reserved exclusively for cardinals who needed to be free of political pressure in making their choices.[5] On occasion, secular rulers such as Roman emperors, Italian monarchs, and other sovereigns had influenced the elections.[6] Keeping the cardinals beyond reach by locking them in was helpful in holding powerful political leaders at bay.

There was another incentive for sequestering cardinal electors; it discouraged them from prolonging the papal selection process. Unlike modern times when the election of popes has taken only days, prior conclaves often dragged on for weeks, even months, as ambitious men connived to become a successor to Saint Peter.[7] Incarcerating the electors didn't guarantee a swift conclusion to the electoral machinations, though. The best evidence of this is the conclave that convened in 1268; spanning two years and eight months, it was the longest conclave ever. To break the deadlock, drastic measures were taken. Frustrated villagers removed the roof of the Palazzo dei Papi di Viterbo in northern Italy where the cardinals were gathered to expose them to inclement weather. As an added inducement for them to conclude the conclave, the locals reduced their rations and ultimately served the cardinals a daily diet consisting exclusively of bread and water. Even so, the conclave dragged on until a compromise was finally reached, and Pope Gregory X was elected in 1271.[8]

EXTRAVAGANT CARDINALS AND UNSCRUPULOUS PONTIFFS

Unfortunately, entrusting the election of popes to cardinals didn't guarantee that the holiest men would occupy the chair of St. Peter, particularly because some of these Church dignitaries themselves had assumed their exalted positions through spurious means, including nepotism. Luxury-loving Pope Leo X, for example, elevated two cousins and three nephews to the Sacred College in addition to selling red hats to numerous other men.[9] Being designated "Princes of the Church" was apt because they lived like royalty in sumptuous palaces.

REGRETTABLE CHOICES

The power and prestige of the papacy, along with the temporal influence the office once wielded, enticed some ambitious men who were more attracted to wealth, authority, and prestige than committed to following the Savior's example of embracing a virtuous life.

Blatantly corrupt and ruthless men occasionally became the Vicar of Christ. Notable examples include Alexander VI, who, prior to his pontificate, fathered eight children born of three different mothers.[10] He gained fame for excommunicating Florence's notorious Dominican friar, Savonarola, and calling for his arrest and execution. Presumably, the pope's antipathy toward the outspoken priest had something to do with the monk's contemptuous, though candid, attack on the papacy of his day: "Popes and prelates speak against worldly pride and ambition and are plunged in it up to their ears. They preach chastity and keep mistresses . . . They think only of the world and worldly things; for souls they care nothing . . . They have made the Church a house of ill fame."[11] Julius II, who repeatedly commanded armies,[12] was himself far from being chaste; he long suffered from syphilis, which conceivably contributed to his death.[13] Under Leo's pontificate, the sale of indulgences that allegedly sprang souls from purgatory flourished and ultimately led to the schism in Christianity known as the Protestant Reformation.[14]

ITALIAN DOMINATION OF THE PAPACY

Historically, electing Italians was sensible because the pope is also the bishop of Rome. Only 50 of the 263 popes prior to Polish Cardinal Karol Wojtyla's election as John Paul II on October 16, 1978, were non-Italians, the last being Adrian VI from Holland, whose brief twenty-month reign ended in 1523.[15] With the ever-increasing internationalization of the College of Cardinals, the likelihood of another Italian winning the papacy has diminished considerably. John Paul I holds the distinction of being the last Italian pope, and the likelihood is that the era of Italian control of the papacy died with him.

An International Gathering

The conclave of August 1978 was the largest and most diverse of any held until that time. Cardinals from all six continents participated.[16] Europe, with its fifty-six electors, was the dominant delegation, comprising just over half of the assembly. Italy still boasted the most cardinals of any single country with twenty-six. The next largest deputation, consisting of eight, was from the United States.[17]

Thus, the possibility of electing a non-Italian pope was real. In 1963 the Italians represented one-third of the cardinal electors; in 1978 that had been reduced to 22 percent. Although they were still the single largest delegation, their power had waned with Paul's expansion of the college.[18] Besides, it was preordained that they would not vote as a unit, especially given the number of Italian *papabili*. The discord between curial and diocesan cardinals would further fracture the Italians' influence. For the first time in a conclave, diocesan cardinals outnumbered those in Vatican administration, a fact that partially explains why the electors eventually chose a pastoral cardinal as pope.[19]

One hundred of the electors had been appointed by Paul VI.[20] Only eleven cardinals had previously participated in a conclave. For the remaining hundred, this was an unfamiliar experience.[21] Their average age was almost sixty-nine.[22] The youngest was Jaime Sin, the archbishop of Manila, at fifty; Cardinal Trin-nhu-Khuê of Hanoi, Vietnam, was the oldest at seventy-nine.[23] Under Paul's new rules, cardinals aged eighty and over were banned from the conclave. Even Carlo Confalonieri, the dean of the Sacred College of Cardinals, at age eighty-five was excluded. The irony was that octogenarians were still eligible to become pope.[24]

CONCLAVE PREPARATIONS

Arrangements for the conclave were extensive. Over a period of ten days, some one hundred Vatican architects, bricklayers, carpenters, and plumbers, among other specialists, converted a portion of the Apostolic Palace into small temporary units to accommodate cardinal electors and essential personnel. Unofficial estimated costs for the modifications amounted to between $2 and $3 million.[25]

On August 23, representatives of the international media along with ambassadors to the Holy See toured the soon-to-be restricted area in which the cardinals would live and select the new pope in secrecy.[26]

ACCOMMODATIONS FIT FOR PAUPERS

The electors' quarters were appropriately referred to as cells, a term conjuring the vision of jails.[27] Because they would be incarcerated, the designation was appropriate. Though cardinals form an exclusive group, second in prestige and influence only to the pope, they didn't enjoy opulent quarters—not by any means. Their rooms were cubicles, only marginally better than those occupied by prisoners. They were hastily constructed within the apostolic palace with direct access to the Sistine Chapel but nowhere else.[28]

The cardinal electors were not alone in their temporary quarters. Some eighty aides including doctors, nurses, fire personnel, priests, pharmacists, nuns, barbers, workmen, and technicians were housed with them. Meals were served in the dining room of the Borgia apartments.[29]

All these makeshift quarters were austere, some larger than others, but all containing similar simple furnishings: a single metal bed frame, a *prix dieu* (a kneeling bench for praying), a small reading lamp, a crucifix, a towel-draped nightstand, along with a wash basin, a bar of soap, and a fresh roll of toilet paper. Some cardinals even shared bathrooms.[30]

Further, the cells allotted to the electors were stifling in Rome's searing August heat.[31] The cardinals were not only denied air conditioning but were not even afforded the luxury of fans or a fresh breeze because the windows were fastened shut.[32] The confined cardinals, particularly the more elderly among them, suffered mightily from the oppressiveness of their quarters.[33]

"My cell was a kind of sauna," complained Cardinal Leo Suenens of Belgium. "It is difficult to describe what it is like to sleep in an oven. It was enough to make somebody ill. There was only one window, but it was sealed hermetically. The next day, using all my strength, I managed to break the seal: Finally, oxygen and a bit of fresh air."[34]

The temperature was so unbearable that one North American cardinal who had access to the luxury of a shower used it to cool off three times in a single night, the sound of the spraying water disrupting the sleep of nearby colleagues. Additional complaints came from the oldest cardinals: The beds were uncomfortable; the food, unpalatable.[35]

SECRECY AT ALL COSTS

In 1975, Paul had prescribed a new set of rules for the conclave that would follow his death, some designed to preserve the secrecy of the proceedings.[36] His detailed directives were strict and arguably excessive. An inspection team painstakingly scrutinized the premises for hidden cameras or recording devices prior to the beginning of the assembly.[37] All who were privy to the proceedings swore an oath not to reveal anything that transpired during the conclave. A harsh penalty awaited any who violated the oath: excommunication.[38] The participants had restricted access to the outside world, the only exceptions being death and critical illness.[39] Even personal secretaries of the cardinals were barred from the conclave.[40] The extreme precautions included blocking corridors and staircases, and sealing doors.[41] Basements, courtyards, halls, and staircases surrounding the Sistine Chapel were rendered inaccessible.[42] A couple of revolving trapdoors were used to serve food and transmit official correspondence.[43] Paul's rules also prohibited keeping cardinals' notes taken during the conclave, allowing only Papal Chamberlain Cardinal Villot's record of the proceedings to be preserved.[44]

Ironically, all these precautionary measures would prove ineffective.

DURATION EXPECTATIONS

Because no dominant candidate was apparent, a common expectation was that this conclave was likely to be lengthy. *Time*, in its cover story of August 21, predicted a "complex, difficult and possibly protracted" conclave. One anonymous *papabile* jokingly told the magazine that he was bringing with him into the conclave "enough personal linen to last two months."[45]

One experienced cardinal knew better. Days before the assembly's commencement, Genoa's Giuseppe Siri told a reporter, "The Conclave will not last more than three days, four at most. After three days these conditions are simply unbearable."[46]

"One does not feel very comfortable in a conclave. In a certain sense, one is buried alive. This is why I think those who believe we will have a long conclave are not well informed." He was right. It would take slightly more than eight hours to conduct this election,[47] one of the shortest in all Church history.[48]

WHAT KIND OF POPE?

Though it was not publicly known, an overwhelming number of cardinals believed that the church needed a pastor rather than a bureaucrat at its helm.[49] According to the Italian news agency ANSA, foreign cardinals ultimately agreed to another Italian pope on the condition that he was not a member of the Curia or the diplomatic corps.[50]

Much of the speculation prior to the onset of the conclave centered on the personal qualities and professional experience the new pope should possess. There was no shortage of opinions. "The next pope will need to catch the flagging attention of a world caught up with Mammon," asserted conservative Catholic columnist William F. Buckley.[51] According to Theologian F. X. Murphy, Paul's successor needed to have two preeminent qualities: "*pazienza e presenza*," patience and presence.[52] Rev. Andrew Greeley, an American priest, sociologist, and novelist who had been a keen analyst of the interregnum activities, urged that Paul's successor be a "hopeful, holy man, who can smile, delegate responsibility, and trust other human beings." In Greeley's view such a pope would transcend the liberal-conservative divide. Without knowing it, he was describing Albino Luciani.[53]

The patriarch of Venice shared Greeley's vision of the new pope and had already discovered the requisite qualities in a cardinal he had decided to vote for long before entering the conclave. Luciani was ahead of his time in favoring a foreigner, especially a non-European, but he was not alone in thinking that way. Extensive speculation in the media was that the first non-Italian in nearly five centuries might be elected.

SUPPORT FOR LUCIANI

An anonymous observer explained to a *Time* magazine writer following the election, "The foreigners, the eighty-five non-Italians, did not want a bureaucrat from the Curia but a man who, like John XXIII, had the warmth of a good pastor. In addition, almost all the cardinals seemed to want a man who emblemized faith as well as hope and . . . Luciani fitted both bills."[54] (The irony was that Luciani had never been a pastor, though he had the demeanor of one.)

Corriere della Sera, an Italian daily newspaper, reported that foreign cardinals widely viewed Luciani as "a man of God, poor, humble but intelligent . . . intransigent on matters of doctrine and discipline but also ready to listen and enter into dialogue."[55]

In truth, Luciani could not have won without substantial support from the progressives of Latin America. They viewed him as a force for reconciliation among factions in the Church, a man who could, through the sway of his captivating personality combined with his wisdom, bring unity to a divided church while inspiring the faithful with his holiness.[56] Besides, they recognized him as one of their own; he was Italian, but his heart was with the suffering people of Third World countries whose plight would be a priority of his papacy.

Despite the growing number of electors covertly coalescing in support of Luciani, he was not everyone's favorite. An unfamiliar figure to many, he seemed insecure to some, and others worried that he had limited (perhaps inadequate) administrative experience, having been a bishop solely of small dioceses. Luciani certainly was not the preferred candidate of members of the Curia. One anonymous church official observed of the patriarch, "He was one of those cardinals who always kept his distance from Rome, and he is virtually an unknown quantity in the Curia."[57]

THE SISTINE CHAPEL: ELECTION DESTINATION

Until the sixteenth century, the election of popes took place in diverse locations. It wasn't until 1513 that the first conclave was held in the Sistine Chapel. From that time until 1775, it was the site of papal elections on thirteen other occasions, and since 1878 all conclaves have taken place within its confines.[58] The world's most famous chapel, built in 1477, is an idyllic setting for a conclave. It is the repository of the master Italian Renaissance sculptor Michelangelo's greatest religious paintings.[59] He began the improbable four-year venture in 1508 painting the 5,800-square-foot vaulted ceiling with more than three hundred figures.[60] Then he devoted seven years to creating another tour de force, the 48 by 44 feet *The Last Judgment* located on the wall behind the chapel's high altar.[61]

It was to this splendid edifice that Villot would lead fifty-five pairs of cardinals. At 9:30 a.m. on August 25, the camerlengo celebrated a Mass of the Holy Spirit at St. Peter's and delivered the homily.[62] In the afternoon Master of Ceremonies Msgr. Virgilio Noe spoke to the electors when they first gathered in the Pauline Chapel. From there the electors entered the Sala Regia, which leads directly to the Sistine Chapel.[63] While the cardinals prepared to depart from the Pauline Chapel, the Sistine Choir sang "Veni Creator Spiritus" (Come Holy Spirit).[64] They formed a slowly looping line of crimson, each cardinal outfitted in a red biretta, cape, and cassock augmented by a white garment with lace trim known as a rochet. The splendid formality conveyed the solemnity of the occasion.[65]

As the procession commenced, immediately following the cross bearer in the lead was Cardinal Villot. Cardinals Baggio and Siri followed closely behind.[66] The cardinals walked slowly, all looking somber, an indication of the burden each carried in anticipation of voting for a new pope. Some sang while others were close mouthed. The pairs walked in clusters. First in the second group was Albino Luciani, his biretta slightly tilted to the left. One camera caught a subdued-looking Luciani now clutching the biretta in his hands, unlike the others. During the broadcast, cameras focused on him more than on most of his colleagues, perhaps because of his position at the head of the second group. Although the commentators named several of the well-known cardinals, no one identified him, no doubt because they didn't know who he was. He entered the conclave with reverence for the process and a keen recognition of his responsibility. He saw himself as a minor player in the drama that was to begin soon, just as he had been at Vatican II. He would vote his conscience and hope that he and his fellow cardinals discerned the will of the Holy Spirit in their deliberations.[67]

There were temporary halts as those in the middle and back of the line waited for those entering the Sistine Chapel to be seated at their assigned places—the ones they would occupy throughout the electoral proceedings. All stood at their tables while the remainder of the cardinals entered. During the procession, wearing the biretta was part of the ceremony, but the cardinals removed the square, three-peaked hats as they entered the chapel. Two brightly dressed Swiss Guards stood at rigid attention on either side of the chapel's entrance.[68]

The cardinals passed by the conspicuous hundred-foot scaffolding that held aloft the chimney from which the smoke from the burning ballots would signal the election of the new pope. It was located to the rear of the chapel. The squat reconditioned round stove with the tiny opening stood in front of the makeshift chimney. Next to it was a chemical container divided in half, the portion on the left labeled "nero," black, and on the right, "bianco," white.[69]

This was the first time that the procession of the cardinals into the Sistine Chapel was televised. However, television cameras were not allowed behind the marble screen that separates the chapel from the entrance.[70]

The conclave was scheduled to begin at 5:30.[71]

As the singing ceased, with the cardinals at their assigned seats, Villot, facing the altar, chanted the opening prayer in Latin. At its conclusion, Msgr. Noe, the master of ceremonies, walked down the central aisle of the chapel heading toward the doors the cardinals had just entered. When he announced "*Ex Omnes*" (all out), the nonessential personnel immediately exited the chapel. The massive ornate wooden doors were then closed, locked, and sealed. The Sacred College of Cardinals was locked in its own private little world.[72]

It was now late afternoon, too late for voting to begin. Instead, the cardinals swore their oaths of secrecy, and Villot lectured about the weighty task awaiting the electors. With that the first official ceremonies of the conclave were over. Its real business would commence the next morning.[73]

RULES, RITUALS, AND TRADITIONS

The next morning, the cardinals prepared for the first vote. First, they celebrated Mass followed by a light breakfast. At 9:30 they entered the chapel for the first round of balloting.[74] Two rows of twelve long tables draped in garnet fabric faced each other, and the electors went to their places identified by name cards. One deviation from previous conclaves was the absence of "thrones," each covered by a canopy. In the past when a pope was chosen, only his canopy remained in place.[75] Because of the unprecedented size of this gathering, the canopied velvet thrones were replaced by straight-backed chairs upholstered in red velvet.[76]

A Latin homily was delivered at the outset, but unlike political conventions, no speeches were delivered, and no debates were conducted.[77] Latin was used for official business because that was the only language that all participants from around the world had in common.

The procedures observed in conclaves are highly ritualized and meticulously planned. Such was the case now. The voting process was elaborate and time-consuming. Two scrutinies were conducted in the morning and another two in the afternoon. To ensure accurate tabulation of votes, prescribed procedures were faithfully obeyed. Selected by lot, three cardinals, known as scrutineers, were responsible for counting the ballots; another three were accountable for checking the accuracy of their totals.[78]

Each cardinal received rectangular ballots with the words "I elect as supreme pontiff" (written in Latin) printed at the top beneath which he wrote the name of his choice. Cardinals were expected to disguise their penmanship to maintain their anonymity. They then folded their ballots in half before individually approaching the altar where they knelt and recited the Latin prayer, "I call as my witness Christ the Lord, who will be my judge, that my vote is given to the one before God I think should be elected." They then placed their ballots on a patten, a circular plate. Tipping the patten, they slid the ballot into a large chalice.[79]

After all votes were delivered in this manner, the painstaking process of counting began. The first scrutineer vigorously shook the chalice before handing it to the third scrutineer who counted each ballot to assure that the number matched the exact number of electors. Only then did the actual tabulation of votes begin. The first scrutineer opened the ballots and copied the names before passing them to the second scrutineer who repeated the act. Then the third scrutineer divulged the name on each ballot aloud to the entire assembly; most electors at their seats kept their own tabulations. When the counting concluded, ballots were strung together with needle and thread for burning. Following the conclusion of the second ballot, both piles were consigned to the stove's fire.[80] In this conclave, seventy-five votes were required for election.

Though overt politicking was condemned, a more subtle brand of campaigning took place both before and during the conclave. "Candidates" refrained from openly proclaiming their ambition, and they were circumspect regarding overtures to their fellow electors. They, like all the cardinals in conclave, however, were free to converse with their fellows before, between, and after balloting. Presumably, discussions relating to the election, issues of major concern to the Church, and the future of the institution were topics of conversation as the cardinals ate meals together and visited each other in their cells. The electors were not forbidden to inquire about the views, experience, reputations, and characters or personalities of prospective popes with whom they were not familiar.[81]

Figure 12.1. The College of Cardinals in conclave in the Sistine Chapel.

VOTING BEGINS

The Astonishing Morning Balloting

Prior to conducting the initial round of balloting, the assembled cardinals called upon the Holy Spirit to descend on their proceedings by reciting the *Veni Creator Spiritus*:[82] "Come, Holy Spirit, and from heaven direct on man the rays of your light."[83]

At least four sources with varying degrees of reliability provided vote tallies for each ballot as relayed by cardinals or others privy to the proceedings. Relying only on memory, these individuals, not surprisingly, reported dissimilar results, although some of the tallies were strikingly similar. John Allen, the veteran Vatican reporter, in his book *Conclave* provided an account that likely most accurately reflected the actual results.[84]

According to Allen, an array of cardinals received votes on the first ballot, as was expected. What was surprising to many was the cardinal who received the second most votes: Albino Luciani. Siri led with twenty-five, but Luciani nearly tied him with twenty-three. The remaining sixty-three votes were scattered.[85] Luciani was stunned at the results.[86] That the patriarch of Venice was such a strong contender from the very start caused many cardinals to consider him seriously for the first time. "After the first votes, the name came out immediately. 'Luciani, why not?' so many electors thought. A good, intelligent, and pious person. And the consensus spread rapidly," Cardinal Silvio Oddi reported.[87]

On the second ballot, immediately following the first, a dramatic shift in the results fundamentally altered the course of the election. Luciani's vote total more than doubled to fifty-three while Siri lost a vote.[88] Now ahead by a better than 2–1 lead, Luciani was already the only viable choice after Siri had stalled and no one else commanded more than a handful of votes. Barring an implausible turn of events in the afternoon balloting, the patriarch of Venice would become pope in a few hours.

At this juncture the cardinals around Luciani observed that he looked like a man who sensed danger but could find no escape.[89] The patriarch later admitted that the conclave had reached a point when "things began to look dangerous for me."[90] He was rattled. His colleagues, many of whom shared his surprise at the scope of his support, had a contrary reaction. The ensuing enthusiasm among them was intense. Luciani, though, simply couldn't comprehend how or why this was happening.[91]

The overwhelming majority of electors had experienced an epiphany, and the silence that had pervaded the chapel gave way to animated conversations that continued during the lunch break now at hand.[92]

A mishap occurred while burning the ballots after the morning votes: black smoke drifted into the chapel from the malfunctioning stove. One mischievous cardinal responded to the incident tongue in cheek: "The smoke of Satan was trying to enter the Conclave."[93]

Lunch Break: Luciani Encounters

As the electors exited the chapel to gather for lunch, Cardinal Lazlo Lekai, archbishop of Esztergom, Hungary, observed, "I remember that . . . we met Patriarch Luciani in the elevator. Then we told him: 'The votes are increasing.' He shielded himself saying: 'This is only a summer shower.'"[94] At one point Cardinal Jaime Sin asked Luciani the location of a toilet. When the patriarch responded that he didn't know, Sin teased, "But you will know soon because you are going to be the owner of this house." "Are you a prophet?" Luciani replied nervously.[95] The frontrunner was either in denial or trying to convince himself that the tide in his favor would recede somehow during the afternoon balloting. It was wishful thinking. Luciani was "in danger" after all.

During the reprieve from voting, more foreign cardinals began to inquire about the frontrunner.[96] Consensus quickly emerged at lunch in favor of Luciani.[97]

THE COALITION

Benelli, the wily "Grand Elector," had already approached several groups of cardinals to gain support for the patriarch of Venice. They included about twenty Third World cardinals with whom he stressed that Luciani was a man of the poor.[98] The archbishop of Sao Paulo, Brazil, Cardinal Paulo Evaristo Arns, was friends with Luciani. Together they had had detailed discussions about poverty and the Church of the Third World. Arns was disposed to support Luciani and likely revealed the patriarch's commitment to the needy to other electors from poor countries.[99] With the conservatives, Benelli stressed Luciani's loyalty to doctrine and church discipline.[100] It was a crafty and efficacious strategy.

THE CONCLUSIVE AFTERNOON BALLOTING

Anticipation was mounting rapidly now. The third ballot was held around 4:30 in the afternoon. Luciani's total leapt to seventy, only five votes shy of the two-thirds needed to win. That made him invincible. He was enough of a realist to recognize at this moment that he was about to become pope.[101] Luciani admitted, "After the third scrutiny, I'd have wanted to disappear without attracting attention."[102] Cardinal Felici conveyed a message to Luciani addressing it "to the new Pope." "Thank you," the patriarch replied, "but it is not yet final."[103]

The fourth and final ballot got underway almost immediately following the conclusion of the third. When the ballots were opened and the names read aloud, only one was repeated in uninterrupted succession: Luciani.[104] As his vote total swelled, Luciani grew deeply distressed. "I saw him put his head in his hands several times," Cardinal John Cody of Chicago remembered.[105] The final verdict was nearly unanimous, according to one source: 101 for Luciani out of 111 votes.[106] The few protest ballots were blank, except for one vote for Cardinal Lorscheiter—cast by Luciani.[107] "It was the greatest day of my life," said the new pope's friend Cardinal Thiandoum. "The Holy Spirit helped us," said Cardinal Koenig of Austria. And from Benelli, the mastermind of Luciani's election, "A striking manifestation of the unity of the church supported by the presence of the Holy Spirit."[108] Cardinal Joseph Hoffner of Cologne, Germany, confirmed, "There was no need to count the names because the only name read out by the scrutineers was that of Luciani."[109] Harmony had prevailed. Benelli's gambit on behalf of the patriarch had exceeded his expectations.

POPE-ELECT LUCIANI

"We stood up to applaud, but we did not see him. He was curled up on his chair; he had become little, little. He wanted to hide. It's a pity we cannot tell what we have lived through, because it has been much more beautiful than you can imagine," marveled Cardinal Vicente Tarancon.[110]

As Luciani prayed fervently, a colleague whispered, "He has exalted the humble."[111] The new pope sat silently in prayer with his eyes shut.[112]

"Then the tension gave place to a kind of resignation or better, to a great serenity," Detroit's Cardinal John Deardon explained.[113] And so on the fourth ballot of the first day of voting, the little-known Albino Luciani became pope. The cardinals were thrilled both with their choice and the speed of the election.[114]

Luciani followed Pius X and John XXIII as the third patriarch of Venice in the twentieth century to assume the papacy.[115] He was also the first pope since Pius X, elected seventy-three years before, to lack diplomatic experience.[116]

ACCEPTANCE AND CHOICE OF NAME

With the election finalized, Villot approached Luciani to pose the essential question, "Do you, Most Reverend Lord Cardinal, accept your election as Supreme Pontiff, which has been canonically carried out?" The answer was supposed to be a formality, but at this moment there was a degree of uncertainty about the response. Some in the chapel wondered for a second or two whether the obviously distraught Luciani might refuse. After a suspenseful pause, Luciani almost inaudibly uttered, "May God forgive you for what you have done in my regard." It was a startling statement and taken by some cardinals as a criticism. Then the patriarch smiled and quietly spoke the word "*acceto*" (I accept).[117] It was an act of selfless obedience. At the very moment he consented, he became pope. According to one elector, Luciani then said under his breath, "How unsearchable the designs of God and how inscrutable His ways."[118] A mere month later a multitude would utter the same words in response to an unforeseen tragedy.

The electors were unaware that Luciani previously had told Senigaglia that in the unlikely event he was elected, he would refuse. But following through on that resolution was problematic in the extreme. A rejection would be a snub of his colleagues who had placed their faith in him. It would also require the conclave to begin the election process anew, creating uncertainty about the outcome because no other candidate had commanded an abundance of votes. A substitute pope would live with the disconcerting knowledge that he was not the electors' first choice. More troubling for Luciani personally, declining would have been a contemptible act of hubris; convinced that the Cardinals were motivated by the Holy Spirit, the humble Luciani could not abide contradicting the will of God. And so, however reluctantly, despite his grave misgivings, he assented.[119]

When Villot asked what name Luciani wished to adopt, he broke the deep silence by announcing in a muted voice, "*Joannes Paulus Primus*," Latin for John Paul the First.[120]

Adding the number one after his name was unusual. Always, it had been used only after a second pope had selected that same name. The double name itself was precedent-shattering; it was the first double name in papal history since the first pope, Simon Peter.[121] It was also the first new name in a thousand years.[122] American Cardinal Lawrence Shehan of Baltimore speculated when the name became public, "Perhaps we can take it as a sign of his independence."[123] "The name is of great importance," noted Protestant theologian José Miguez Bonin of Argentina. "It shows that the new Pontiff is ready to continue with the program of reforms launched by the [Second] Vatican Council."[124] Responding to the name, a Latin American priest in St. Peter's Square told a *Newsweek* reporter that Luciani's reign would not be revolutionary in character: "He is telling us that he represents neither retrogression nor revolution. What our new Pope represents is continuity."[125]

Time would tell. Or would it?

The new pope himself would soon explain that his name was a tribute to his two immediate predecessors and an unmistakable signal that he embraced the modernization of the Church that was the legacy of the Second Vatican Council.[126] Beyond that, it also provided an element of ambiguity about the nature of John Paul's forthcoming pontificate. John XXIII, who had convened the Council, had been an unexpectedly bold leader who had dragged a sometimes-reluctant Church into the contemporary world. Luciani had been personally fond of John and loyally supported the Council's reforms. Paul VI, a more cautious pope, had nevertheless implemented Vatican II's changes. Many wondered whether the new pontiff would be more like John or Paul.

CHANGING CLOTHES AND ACCEPTING CONGRATULATIONS

Joined by the papal master of ceremonies, the new pontiff headed to the Room of Tears, a small, unadorned chamber off the Sistine Chapel. Its name derives from the supposed tendency of some newly elected popes to become so overwhelmed by emotion that they shed tears in this room where they were shielded from the gaze of the cardinals.[127] There the papal tailor, a member of the Gammarelli family that had fashioned garments worn by popes since 1798, awaited him.[128] He had prepared three different sizes of white soutanes (cassocks). John Paul slipped on the small one, which was ill fitting and had to be hemmed because it was too long. He then donned a mozzetta and stepped into the conventional papal red shoes.[129]

After the fitting, he returned to the chapel in his papal garments looking serene, even luminous.[130] The swift change in his demeanor was striking. John Paul assumed the throne that had been placed in front of the altar while he was being fitted.[131] One by one, the cardinals approached him to offer their congratulations. The Holy Father greeted each with an embrace. He spoke briefly to all and requested prayers. When Cardinal Suenens expressed his gratitude for Luciani's acceptance, the pope wistfully responded, "Maybe I should have said no."[132] As Jaime Sin of Manila who had earlier in the day told Luciani, "I am sure you will be the new Pope" approached, Luciani said to him, "You were a prophet, your Eminence! But my pontificate will be short." Sin himself recalled this cryptic remark following Luciani's death. It was an arresting exchange between one "prophet" and another.[133]

PRE-CONCLAVE PREDICTIONS COME TRUE

Diego Lorenzi was not surprised by the outcome. In fact, he had expected it and told Luciani so. Late in the morning the day before the conclave commenced, Lorenzi had said to Luciani, "By this time tomorrow, you will have a nice pile of votes." When Luciani asked him on what basis he made such a prediction, Lorenzi answered, "They cannot fail to elect the holiest man."[134]

Lorenzi was not alone in thinking his superior would be elected. Both John Paul's sister, Nina, and niece Pia believed Luciani himself had had a premonition that he would succeed Pope Paul. It was a presentiment that some of his family had shared. Berto recalled the scene in Venice six years before when Paul VI had placed his papal stole on Luciani's shoulders, as if signaling to the world his preferred successor.[135]

The predictions and premonitions had come to pass, along with the fulfillment of the fears of the pope's siblings. And the former patriarch's own.

POST-CONCLAVE REVELATIONS

After the election, so many of the cardinals, notwithstanding their vow of secrecy, felt a need to share details with their secretaries and other intimates who, in turn, compared their versions with those of others, leading to credible reconstructions of what took place with regard to the balloting.[136] Beyond that, the cardinals themselves, overcome with awe and delight, shared information directly with the press. Some divulged details on condition of anonymity while others spoke openly.[137] Ecstatic, they revealed numerous incidents in addition to voicing their conviction that the Holy Spirit had inspired their choice. What other explanation could there be for the speedy election of a virtually unknown cardinal? "I hope not to have broken any secret of the conclave," Belgian Cardinal Suenens worried out loud.[138]

Several of the cardinals revealed that at the onset of voting not a single individual was viewed as the universal heir apparent, but after the first couple of ballots Luciani quickly became the frontrunner.[139] Exclaimed Cardinal Paolo Bertoli, "A magnificent stroke . . . it's a sin that we are not able to tell you what went on."[140] Cardinal Silvio Oddi asserted, "I'd say it was definitely an inspiration. So many electors, from so many parts of the world; and voila, all over in a few minutes." When asked how the new pope reacted, he responded, "Moved, greatly moved. But . . . I did not see him cry."[141] Cardinal Basil Hume described Luciani as "God's candidate." He elaborated, "Once it had happened, it seemed totally and entirely right. The feeling that he was just what we wanted was so general . . . we felt as if our hands were being guided as we wrote his name on the paper!"[142] "We have been witness to a real moral miracle," Argentinian Cardinal Antonio Pironio said of the electoral outcome.[143] Cardinal Karol Wojtyla of Kraków, who would soon succeed Luciani, commented, "God chose Cardinal Luciani. At first He kept him . . . in the shade, and he himself, the predestined one, sought to be hidden. Then all of a sudden the Lord revealed the face and the name of him whom He had chosen."[144]

The editor of the journal *Theological Studies*, Rev. Walter Burghardt, observed about the new pope, "He looks like someone who has the ability to get close to people. We need someone . . . who is a leader, someone who can move the minds and hearts of people."[145]

Following the election, Cardinal Confalonieri told a television audience about Luciani's selection: "It was certainly not a surprise for me . . . The name of Patriarch Luciani was one that had attracted the attention of the cardinal electors in the last days of the pre-conclave period . . . I have to admit that, at the start, a number of cardinals did not know him well, but this could no longer be said after the various daily meetings."[146]

The entire conclave was over in just twenty-five hours. Immediately after accepting the felicitations of his former colleagues, Pope John Paul I walked the short distance to St. Peter's central balcony to be introduced to the world.

NOTES

1. Raymond and Lauretta Seabeck, *The Smiling Pope: The Life and Teaching of John Paul I* (Huntington, IN: Our Sunday Visitor, 2004), 53.
2. Seabeck, *Smiling Pope*, 48.
3. "Selection Heavy on Tradition," *Beaver County Times*, August 7, 1978, A9.
4. "Papal Elections," *New Advent*, newadvent.org/cathen/11456a.htm.
5. "Papal Elections."
6. "Papal Elections."
7. "A Swift, Stunning Choice," *Time*, September 4, 1978, 65.
8. George Ryan, "Why the Papal Conclave of 1271 Was the Longest in History," *uCatholic*, March 29, 2023, https://ucatholic.com/blog/why-the-papal-conclave-of-1271-was-the-longest-in-history/.
9. John Julius Norwich, *Absolute Monarchs: A History of the Papacy* (New York: Random House, 2011), 291–92.
10. Norwich, *Absolute Monarchs*, 264.
11. Norwich, *Absolute Monarchs*, 269–70.
12. Norwich, *Absolute Monarchs*, 277.
13. Norwich, *Absolute Monarchs*, 287.
14. Norwich, *Absolute Monarchs*, 292–93.
15. Richard Ostling, "In Search of a Pope," *Time*, August 21, 1978, 64.
16. Richard W. Daw, "Nights of Sorrow, Days of Joy," *National Catholic News Service*, 1978, 71.
17. Daw, "Nights of Sorrow, Days of Joy," 71.
18. Kenneth L. Woodward, "Choosing a New Pope," *Newsweek*, August 21, 1978, 54.
19. Jonathan Kivitny, *Man of the Century: The Life and Times of John Paul II* (New York: Henry Holt, 1997), 285.
20. Fr. Victor Feltes, "The Conclave Begins," Pope John Paul Papacy—Day by Day, https://johnpauli.wordpress.com.

21. Kivitny, *Man of the Century*, 282.
22. "Conclave—August 1978," *Catholic Hierarchy*, catholichierarchy.org/event/c1978.html.
23. Andrew Greeley, *The Making of the Popes 1978* (Kansas City: Andrews and McMeel, 1979), 136.
24. Dennis Montgomery, "111 Cardinals Gather to Select New Pope," *Victoria Advocate*, August 25, 1978, 2D.
25. Paul Hoffmann, "Papal Conclave Setting Resembles a Monastery," *The Times-News*, August 24, 1979, 12.
26. Fr. Victor Feltes, "Conclave Accommodations," Pope John Paul Papacy—Day by Day, https://johnpauli.wordpress.com.
27. Feltes, "Conclave Accommodations."
28. Feltes, "Conclave Accommodations."
29. Hoffmann, "Papal Conclave Setting Resembles a Monastery," 12.
30. "The First Years of Albino Luciani, Part IV" (The Conclave), https://www.albino-luciani.com/index.php?id=273&L=3.
31. David Yallop, *In God's Name: An Investigation into the Murder of Pope John Paul I* (New York: Penguin, 1984), 64.
32. Daw, "Nights of Sorrow, Days of Joy," 72.
33. Yallop, *In God's Name*, 64.
34. Cardinal Leo Suenens, "The Conclave (August 25th–26th, 1978): Memories from the Conclave," Gloria C. Molinari, 2001, www.papaluciani.com.
35. Don Jesus Infiesta, "The Conclave (August 25th–26th, 1978): Memories from the Conclave," Gloria C. Molinari, 2001, www.papaluciani.com.
36. Woodward, "Choosing a New Pope," 48.
37. Russell Watson, Loren Jenkins, and Elaine Sciolino, "We Have a Pope," *Newsweek*, September 4, 1978, 41.
38. Woodward, "Choosing a New Pope," 53.
39. "The First Televised Papal Conclave," ABC News, August 25, 1978, Pope John Paul Papacy—Day by Day, https://johnpauli.wordpress.com.
40. Daw, "Nights of Sorrow, Days of Joy," 71.
41. "Selection," *Beaver*, A9.
42. Hoffmann, "Papal Conclave Setting Resembles a Monastery," 12.
43. Feltes, "Conclave Accommodations."
44. Woodward, "Choosing a New Pope," 53.
45. Ostling, "In Search of a Pope," 63.
46. Cardinal Giuseppe Siri, "The Conclave (August 25th–26th, 1978): Memories from the Conclave," Gloria C. Molinari, 2001, www.papaluciani.com.
47. "A Swift, Stunning Choice," *Time*, 65.
48. "Conclave," *Hierarchy*, 1.
49. "A Swift, Stunning Choice," *Time*, 61.
50. "Non-Italians Played Key Role in Election of John Paul I," *Daily News*, August 29, 1978, 14.

51. William F. Buckley, "The Pope I Want: A Consumer Speaks Out," *New Republic*, September 2, 1978, https://newrepublic.com/article/76324/the-pope-i-want.
52. Mayo Mohs, "After Paul: The Leading Contenders," *Time*, August 21, 1978, 66.
53. Mohs, "After Paul," 66.
54. "A Swift, Stunning Choice," *Time*, 61.
55. "Non-Italians Played Key Role in Election of John Paul I," *Daily News*, 14.
56. Kenneth L. Woodward, "The 34 Days of John Paul I," *Newsweek*, October 9, 1978, 73.
57. "A Swift, Stunning Choice," *Time*, 66.
58. "Sistine Chapel," The Holy See, vatican.va/content/Vatican/en/ra/cappella-sistina.html.
59. Fr. Michael Collins, *The Vatican: Secrets and Treasures of the Holy City* (New York: Dorling Kindersley, 2008), 138.
60. Collins, *The Vatican*, 138.
61. Robert Coughlan, *The World of Michelangelo* (New York: Time, 1966), 127.
62. Montgomery, "111 Cardinals Gather to Select New Pope," 2D.
63. Peter Jennings and Frank Reynolds, "The First Televised Papal Conclave," ABC News, August 25, 1978.
64. Seabeck, *Smiling Pope*, 52.
65. Gordon Thomas and Max Morgan-Witts, *Pontiff* (Garden City: Doubleday, 1984), 165.
66. Jennings and Reynolds, "First Televised," August 25, 1978.
67. Jennings and Reynolds, "First Televised," August 25, 1978.
68. Jennings and Reynolds, "First Televised," August 25, 1978.
69. Jennings and Reynolds, "First Televised," August 25, 1978.
70. Jennings and Reynolds, "First Televised," August 25, 1978.
71. Hoffmann, "Papal Conclave Setting Resembles a Monastery," 12.
72. Jennings and Reynolds, "First Televised," August 25, 1978.
73. John L. Allen Jr., *Conclave: The Politics, Personalities, and Process of the Next Papal Election* (New York: Doubleday, 2004), 132.
74. Allen, *Conclave*, 132.
75. Hoffman, "Papal Conclave Setting Resembles a Monastery," 12.
76. "A Swift, Stunning Choice," *Time*, 65.
77. Woodward, "Choosing a New Pope," 53.
78. Allen, *Conclave*, 113–14.
79. Allen, *Conclave*, 114.
80. Allen, *Conclave*, 115–16.
81. Woodward, "Choosing a New Pope," 53.
82. Watson, Jenkins, and Sciolino, "We Have a Pope," 41.
83. EWTN (Eternal Word Television Network), https://www.ewtn.com/catholicism/library/veni-creator-spiritus-come-holy-spirit-creator-blest-11897.
84. Allen, *Conclave*, 132.
85. Allen, *Conclave*, 132.

86. Paul Spackman, *God's Candidate: The Life and Times of Pope John Paul I* (Herefordshire: Gracewing, 2008), 131.
87. Cardinal Silvio Oddi, "The Conclave: August 25–26, 1978," www.papaluciani.com.
88. Allen, *Conclave*, 132.
89. Thomas and Morgan-Witts, *Pontiff*, 226.
90. Peter Hebblethwaite, *The Year of Three Popes* (Cleveland, OH: Collins, 1979), 76.
91. Thomas and Morgan-Witts, *Pontiff*, 227.
92. Thomas and Morgan-Witts, *Pontiff*, 227–28.
93. Don Jose Maria Javierre, "The Conclave: August 25–26, 1978," www.papaluciani.com.
94. Spackman, *God's Candidate*, 132–33.
95. Cardinal Jaime Sin, "The Conclave: August 25–26, 1978," www.papaluciani.com.
96. Kivitny, *Man of the Century*, 286.
97. Spackman, *God's Candidate*, 133.
98. Greeley, *The Making of the Popes 1978*, 139–40.
99. Hebblethwaite, *Three Popes*, 81.
100. Greeley, *The Making of the Popes 1978*, 139.
101. Allen, *Conclave*, 132.
102. "More Stories from the Conclave," papaluciani.com/eng/conclave.htm.
103. Seabeck, *Smiling Pope*, 54.
104. Seabeck, *Smiling Pope*, 54.
105. Seabeck, *Smiling Pope*, 54.
106. Allen, *Conclave*, 132.
107. Greeley, *The Making of the Popes 1978*, 153.
108. Greeley, *The Making of the Popes 1978*, 159.
109. Allen, *Conclave*, 132.
110. "More Stories," papaluciani.com/eng/conclave.htm.
111. Seabeck, *Smiling Pope*, 54.
112. Seabeck, *Smiling Pope*, 54.
113. Seabeck, *Smiling Pope*, 54.
114. Spackman, *God's Candidate*, 143.
115. John W. O'Malley, SJ, *A History of the Popes* (Lanham, MD: Rowman & Littlefield, 2010), 313.
116. "John Paul I," *Encyclopedia Britannica*, updated September 24, 2020, https://www.britannica.com/.
117. Spackman, *God's Candidate*, 134–35.
118. Seabeck, *Smiling Pope*, 54.
119. Spackman, *God's Candidate*, 134.
120. Seabeck, *Smiling Pope*, 54.
121. Seabeck, *Smiling Pope*, 54–55.
122. "A Swift, Stunning Choice," *Time*, 60.
123. "A Swift, Stunning Choice," *Time*, 66.

124. "A Swift, Stunning Choice," *Time*, 66.
125. "We Have a Pope," *Newsweek*, September 4, 1978, 40.
126. Seabeck, *Smiling Pope*, 58.
127. Anna Mitchell, "The Room of Tears," "Son Rise Morning Show," EWTN Global Catholic Radio Network, March 23, 2013, https://integratedcatholiclife.org/2013/03/mitchell-the-room-of-tears/.
128. Gammarelli DAL 1798, https://www.gammarelli.com/.
129. "We Have a Pope," *Newsweek*, 47.
130. Seabeck, *Smiling Pope*, 55.
131. Francis X. Murphy, *The Papacy Today* (London: Weidenfeld and Nicolson, 1982), 162.
132. Seabeck, *Smiling Pope*, 55.
133. Seabeck, *Smiling Pope*, 55.
134. Allen, *Conclave*, 177.
135. Loris Serafini (director, Foundation Papa Luciani and Museum Albino Luciani of Canale d'Agordo), in discussion with the author, Canale, d'Agordo, Italy, September 6, 2022.
136. Thomas and Morgan-Witts, *Pontiff*, 217.
137. Spackman, *God's Candidate*, 143–47.
138. Leo Suenens, "The Conclave: August 25th–26th, 1978," 2001, www.papaluciani.com.
139. Seabeck, *Smiling Pope*, 53–54.
140. Spackman, *God's Candidate*, 143.
141. Spackman, *God's Candidate*, 143.
142. Spackman, *God's Candidate*, 144.
143. Eduardo F. Pironio, "The Conclave: August 25th–26th, 1978," 2001, www.papaluciani.com.
144. Seabeck, *Smiling Pope*, 55.
145. Marjorie Hyer, "See Hope of Solving Problems: Pope Impresses U.S. Catholics," *Los Angeles Times*, September 1, 1978.
146. Spackman, *God's Candidate*, 146.

Part IV

FINALE

• *13* •

Pontiff—Week IV/Love

The Journey Nears Its End (September 21–27, 1978)

This I command you: love one another. —John 15:17 (NABRE)

DAY 26/THURSDAY, SEPTEMBER 21

This day's meetings were devoted exclusively to Church matters. The pope had an audience with a group of bishops from the United States in their *ad limina* visit.[1] John Paul was delighted to welcome them. "It is a real pleasure . . . to meet, for the first time, a group of American bishops . . . I want you to feel at home," he said in greeting. He referred to himself as "just a beginner" pope but wanted, he said, to speak of topics that were vitally relevant to their ministry. His message was brief and focused on marriage and the family. John Paul viewed the Christian family in grand terms, as "basic in transforming the world." He expressed a genuine and profound respect for conjugal love, which he insisted "mirrors the divine love." He reiterated the Church's stance in opposition to divorce while acknowledging that "the indissolubility of Christian marriage" was "a difficult part of our message." The pope advised the bishops that they must be sensitive to the difficulties that married couples experience. "They [spouses] must always know that we love them." This was despite the Church's thorny opposition to divorce, a stance that a host of troubled married couples considered intransigent and irresponsible.[2]

Later, he conducted an audience with the secretary of the Congregation for the Doctrine of the Faith.[3]

DAY 27/FRIDAY, SEPTEMBER 22

John Paul met individually with two important Church figures: the prefect for the Congregation for the Causes of the Saints and the apostolic nuncio to Indonesia. For dinner that night, he was joined by his old friend Maffeo Ducoli, the bishop of Belluno-Feltre.[4] Such infrequent occasions when he could enjoy the company of esteemed former associates were precious to the pope, for he often felt lonely in the Vatican, describing himself as a prisoner in a gilded cage. He even confided to a Guatemalan cardinal that he had no friends there. This was true in Rome but not beyond its borders, where companions were plentiful.[5] Ducoli was one of them; he happened to be in Rome and called don Diego Lorenzi to request a meeting with John Paul. The papal secretary told him to wait a minute. When he returned to the phone, Lorenzi extended an invitation: "The Pope wants to know if you can come to dinner with us this evening." The bishop readily accepted. "It was a meeting characterized with great affection," he remembered years later. He described the meal as "frugal" but revealed that he and the pope "talked about delightful past events." It was to be their last reunion.[6]

DAY 28/SATURDAY, SEPTEMBER 23

This was an exceptionally busy day consisting of several appointments and an excursion of some consequence. The pope met with Cardinal Baggio, prefect of the Congregation for Bishops and then with the director of *l'Osservatore Romano* (The Roman Observer), a daily newspaper published in Vatican City, and, in effect, the voice of the Holy See in print. It was then, and continues to be, one of the most influential papers in Italy. John Paul also had audiences with the apostolic nuncios of Madagascar and Switzerland.[7]

Dr. Da Ros paid yet another visit, this time reaching an agreement with Dr. Renato Buzzonetti of the Vatican Health Service about their respective roles as John Paul's physicians.[8] According to author David Yallop, Da Ros conducted his third physical exam of the pope at the Vatican on this occasion. After Da Ross and Buzzonetti "discussed Luciani's medical history," they concurred that Buzzonetti, who was far more readily accessible to their patient, would provide medical services to the pope; Da Ros would continue serving as his primary physician though he lived more than 350 kilometers away.[9] This arrangement seems awkward. The implication is that Buzzonetti would be on call if the pope needed medical attention without delay, while Da Ros would conduct periodic monitoring of the pontiff's health by traveling a time-consuming distance from home to the Vatican.

Escape from the Gilded Cage

Figure 13.1. John Paul's only escape from Vatican City on his way to take possession of his cathedral, St. John Lateran.

For the first and only time during his pontificate, the Holy Father left the confines of Vatican City, if only for a few hours. His ultimate destination was the Basilica of St. John Lateran, the seat of the Bishop of Rome. On his way there he made a scheduled stop at the capitol to meet briefly with the communist mayor of Rome, Giulio Carlo Argan, and the city council.[10]

The pope, riding in the back of a black Mercedes convertible limousine with the top down, was accompanied by Cardinal Villot and two other Vatican clerics. Two small white and yellow papal flags fastened to the hood of the car fluttered as the vehicle proceeded to its destination. A crew of uniformed police astride motorcycles escorted the pontiff: three in front, four on each side of the car, with another squad immediately behind. The motorcade consisted of two advance cars and another eight following the pope's vehicle.

Temporary wooden barricades erected along the route prevented enthusiastic spectators, who waved to the pope excitedly and shouted out his name to gain his attention, from spilling into the street. The sober-looking public dignitaries awaiting the pontiff's arrival stood motionless on a stage. The papal procession crawled before coming to a halt parallel to a red carpet spread over the cobblestone street. A bugler wearing a white and black military uniform performed as the pope arrived. Argan approached to greet John Paul even before the pope had completely disembarked from the automobile. The pope clasped the mayor's hands in both of his. John Paul was attired in a red mozetta and an ornate red stole; they were the same habiliments that he had worn when making his first public appearance as the newly elected pope. Argan was dressed in a dark suit augmented by the ceremonial tricolor sash of green, white, and red, the colors of the Italian flag.

Figure 13.2. Greeting the mayor of Rome before exchanging formal statements.

Then the two men stepped up to microphones and addressed brief statements to each other some distance apart, fittingly symbolic of the gap between Church tenets and Marxist ideology. Throughout the perfunctory ceremony church bells tolled. The cordial meeting conveyed the desire of the two leaders to promote courteous coexistence between the religious and civil leaders of Rome whose dissonant beliefs could be an obstacle to cooperative relations. The mayor spoke first with the pope listening attentively and smiling slightly.[11]

John Paul's comments on this occasion, although gracious, gently but unambiguously reminded the atheist mayor of the Church's vital role in Rome and the responsibility of the city's municipal government to dedicate itself to the well-being of all the city's citizens. Said the pope, "I . . . express the wish that the Administration, adopting a view of the common good which includes all true human values, will give open and cordial attention also to the requirements raised by the religious dimension of the City, which, owing to the incomparable Christian values which characterize its features, is a center of attraction for pilgrims from all over the world.

"With these sentiments, I invoke God's blessing on this City, which I now feel mine, and I wish to you, Mr. Mayor, to your Collaborators, and to the whole large family of the Roman people, serene prosperity and civil progress in hardworking concord, mutual respect and sincere aspiring to a peaceful, harmonious and just society," John Paul concluded.[12] The pope had diplomatically but emphatically communicated to the city's secular leaders their fundamental responsibility to the city's citizens and the Church's own prominent role in their lives while hoping for concord between the two.

At the conclusion of the pope's remarks, the mayor approached him again and cordially held both his hands while the two exchanged private words that, judging by their facial expressions, must have been constructive. The pope then returned to his car and waved upon leaving while the bugler played again.[13]

Taking Possession

The primary reason for the pope's temporary absence from the Vatican was the traditional visit to the Archbasilica of St. John Lateran where he concelebrated Mass. Like his predecessors, he took possession of the cathedral in his role as Bishop of Rome. Of the city's four major basilicas, it is the oldest and serves as the cathedral church of Rome, and, therefore, the official seat of the pope. The original basilica, razed after having been severely damaged by two fires in the distant past, had been dedicated initially in 324 as the Church of the Most Holy Savior. Nearby communities of monks lent it the name of Saint John. The current structure was completed in 1735. Its bronze doors, however, are ancient, having in antiquity graced the entrance to the Senate in the Roman Forum.[14]

The crowds, patiently waiting to catch a glimpse of John Paul upon his arrival, were massive and enthusiastic, as always. The faithful got a clear view of the pope because once again he was carried in the *sedia gestatoria*. He was resplendent in his white vestments and white miter decorated with red roses. Making his way to the basilica's entrance, he bore an enduring smile as he cheerfully greeted the euphoric faithful. He carried his simple metal crozier in his left hand.[15]

The occasion, though, caused some close observers to become concerned about his health. Certain bishops reported that his exhaustion was readily apparent and that he seemed to have lost weight. However, film of the event did not capture anything other than jubilance on the pope's face. Others questioned why he didn't stand in his car to greet the crowds enroute to the cathedral. Speculation was that his legs were so swollen that he could not stand painlessly, though standing in a moving convertible with no handhold would be a feat of extraordinary balance for anyone.[16]

The pope's homily was about forming a true Christian community in Rome. The theme evolved from his explications of the three readings of the liturgy, two from the Old Testament and one from the New Testament. As was typical of his talks, the pope spoke forthrightly, informally, and humbly.

Appropriately, he spoke about the pope in his role as bishop of Rome. "[T]the Pope acquires authority over the whole Church inasmuch as he is the bishop of Rome, that is, the successor of Peter in this city." He referenced the meeting he had just conducted with the mayor as he recollected "one of the prayers that I used to recite with my mother when I was a child. It went like this: 'The sins that cry out for vengeance in the sight of God are . . . to oppress the poor, and to defraud the workers of their just wages.'" Rome, he explained, would become "a true Christian community" if it loved the poor, whom he described as "the real treasures of the Church."

The second reading focused on obedience, which John Paul amusingly characterized as putting him in "a rather embarrassing position" because "the rights of the person are in confrontation with the rights of authority and the law!" He candidly admitted,

"Harmonizing . . . liberty and authority has become a social problem. And a problem for the Church as well."

Finally, the pope addressed the difficulty of his job, self-effacingly admitting, "Although I have already been a bishop for twenty years . . . I confess that I have not yet really 'learned my trade.'" In Rome he would try to follow the advice of St. Gregory the Great, who had written, "Let the pastor be close to each of his subjects with compassion, forgetting his rank, let him consider himself the equal of his good subjects." In that vein, he concluded, "I desire only to be at your service and to put at your disposal all of my poor strength, the little that I have and that I am." He had made a similar pledge when becoming bishop of Vittorio Veneto.[17]

DAY 29/SUNDAY, SEPTEMBER 24

The pope delivered his final Angelus on this day from the window of his study.[18] He spoke with passion to the masses assembled in the square. He cited with poignancy the incident of the homicide involving a Roman student that had taken place a few days before, and talked about how only love can conquer violence. He also lamented the kidnapping of Luca Locci, a seven-year-old who had been held hostage for three months. The very next day, the young victim was released to the relieved parents, who publicly thanked John

Paul for having secured the boy's freedom.[19] Luca's mother declared, "It's a happy coincidence and I'm infinitely grateful to the Holy Father for having remembered my child, for having invited to pray the crowd present at St. Peter's and all persons sensitive to such a bitter drama."[20]

DAY 30/MONDAY, SEPTEMBER 25

Two audiences were held on this day, the first with Angelo Rossi, prefect of the Congregation for the Evangelization of Peoples, and the other with Cardinal Jose Humberto Quintero of Caracas, Venezuela.[21]

Focus on the Third World

It would be reasonable to expect John Paul to have made the Third World a priority of his pontificate. Early in his tenure he had received numerous invitations from abroad, and he was inclined to make his first excursions to Africa and Asia, where the ranks of Catholics were growing. Besides, it was necessary to bring to the world's attention the plight of impoverished nations and the dispossessed, the neglected, the hopeless who inhabited them. Only with international recognition of the widespread suffering would ample assistance be forthcoming.[22] He had always been their champion; now, in his commanding role on the global stage, he could provide succor to millions by appealing to the collective conscience of people of goodwill in affluent nations.

Priority: The Poor

From the moment of his birth, the pope's life had been one of poverty. As a young man and throughout his adulthood, he had led an existence of self-denial and envisioned the Church created by Christ as a sacred institution of and for the poor. These were his people. He had spent a lifetime visiting them, encouraging them, blessing them, supporting them. It's no wonder that the masses were drawn to him, referring to him as "the good pope," and in Italy as "Gianpaolo," a familiar designation of friendship. In four weeks, he continued to win the admiration and affection of peoples the world over. To Christians and non-Christians alike, he had become a venerated personage. All who met him were beguiled by his warmth. The people who worked at lowly jobs at the Vatican were especially taken with him. It was as if one of their own was the Vicar of Christ.[23]

DAY 31/TUESDAY, SEPTEMBER 26

Just because only one appointment appeared on the pope's official agenda, doesn't mean that he was free for the rest of the day. Certain meetings might not have been listed on his official schedule (including contact with curial officials as well as daily meetings with Villot). Making personal and business phone calls, writing communications, preparing public talks, plowing through mounds of paperwork, and reaching decisions about ongoing problems that only the pope could make filled his typical days.

DAY 32/WEDNESDAY, SEPTEMBER 27

He had an audience with Maximos V Hakim, patriarch of Antioch of the Melkite Greeks, another indication of his commitment to ecumenism.[24]

The Closing Discourse

John Paul's final general audience was held on this day.[25] To accommodate the overflowing crowds, the pope delivered his remarks to two different assemblies. In this final public appearance, his fourth general audience, the pope's smile was as radiant as always, and he appeared vigorous.[26]

As was his habit, he waved somewhat self-consciously to the people seated on both sides of the central aisle. Occupying the *sedia gestatoria* that he so disliked, at one point he turned to his right as if he had inadvertently missed someone craving his attention. The blinking bulbs of cameras filled the hall as the merry crowd applauded and held aloft white handkerchiefs in greeting.[27]

His talk on this day was about *caritas*, the Latin word for love. He would speak about the duty of Christians to love all humanity, which reflected God's love for His entire creation. What more fitting topic for his final public address; he was a pope who at all times conveyed love for all. It might well have been the most touching and the most poetic of his four Wednesday speeches. Love, after all, had characterized his entire life and was to be his legacy. As much as the pope sprinkled his remarks with allusions to notable intellectuals, this message was highly personal, coming directly from the heart. As he said in English, "I love you all very much."[28]

First, he greeted the bishops in attendance and confessed that it is "difficult to be a bishop"—something he knew from personal experience. Then he began his message on a personal note, traveling back through time to his boyhood and sharing fond recollections of his mother, who had taught him a prayer he never forgot. "My mama taught it to me, but I still recite it several times a day," he revealed.[29] He shared the brief prayer, which focused on love of God, love of neighbor, and forgiveness. Luciani himself had said that his mother was his first catechism teacher.[30]

Disarmingly, he told his audience, "I will try to explain," as if he wasn't certain of his ability to do so after all these years of teaching and preaching. He parsed the prayer before asking his audience, "Do you understand?" He was still the professor, checking for comprehension.

The pope's remarks included recollections from his school days, personal reminiscences that humanized him further, helping him to connect more intimately to his listeners. He recalled his love of literature and the adventures he experienced vicariously through books, particularly the voyages in the novels of Jules Verne. None of them, he emphasized, compared to "the journey towards God."

He first addressed love of God, the prerequisite to love of neighbor. "God is too great . . . for us to throw to him, every now and then, only the crumbs of . . . our hearts." People must reciprocate God's love for them by returning it abundantly. Love of neighbor, John Paul acknowledged, was sometimes difficult. "[C]ertain people have hurt me, or they annoy me. But I must love them all the same," he insisted. "I will succeed," he emphasized, "only if I extend to them the great love that I already have for God." He admitted that though it is essential, forgiveness "is perhaps the most difficult thing."

The Holy Father put the gratifications of the world that most people seek in perspective: "Money, pleasure, all the careers in this world are only fragments of good, only fleeting moments of happiness. It is not wise to give so much of ourselves to these things, and on the other hand to give God little of ourselves."

He spoke cogently without relying on a text, notes, or even a crude outline; and the complexity of thought, the profusion of ideas flowed smoothly, coherently, and with unity much like the harmony of a symphony. His normally weak voice was unusually strong, and the delivery of his speech was ablaze with fervor. The gesticulations of his hands synchronized with his words. His countenance glowed; his eyes danced.

There couldn't have been a starker contrast to the formal, stilted discourses of his immediate predecessor. Yet, as he had on previous occasions, John Paul quoted "the great Pope Paul VI" and adopted some of his views as his own, quoting him: "Private property is not an inalienable and absolute right. No one has the right to be able to make use of his goods exclusively for his own benefit, when others are dying because they have nothing."

It was at this point that a man in the audience, an admirer, interrupted the pope. "May you enjoy a long life," he shouted. The audience burst into applause. Appearing slightly embarrassed, the pope smiled briefly, said, "OK," and waved his right hand in a gesture meant to stifle the approbation, as if to signal, "Enough of this." Then, while the acclamation continued, he looked down, pressing his fingers, his smile suddenly vanishing into a grave expression. It lasted a mere moment before he resumed his talk, but something was strangely somber about his reaction.[31]

The next day he would be dead.

BRAVO

Figure 13.3. Danielle Bravo engages the pope in a spirited dialogue before an enchanted crowd at John Paul's last general audience on September 27,1978. The pope died the next day.

Having made his central point in dramatic fashion, the pope returned to his favorite ploy of calling forward a youngster to "assist" him in enlightening his congregation. It was a teaching moment that almost always amused the communicants. A class of elementary students from an Italian Catholic school was in attendance, and John Paul saw them. "Can one of the children come up to help the pope?" he asked. Apparently, there was a rush toward the stage, for the pope waved a finger, and smiling, said, "Uno solo"—one only!

That one was Danielle Bravo, who flew up several steps to stand at the pope's side. The audience applauded. Unlike the painfully shy, self-conscious altar boy who had barely whispered a response to the Holy Father's questions at a previous audience, this youngster was unphased by his moment in the spotlight with a grand personage. Such unscripted, unrehearsed appearances always had the potential to derail the pope's message, but that did not deter him. He relished the challenge, confident that he could improvise and readily redirect the dialogue to convey his point.[32]

John Paul took the boy's hand in his and turned the microphone toward the youngster. (After learning of the pope's death, Danielle would remember, "His hands were so warm.")[33] This time the dialogue did not go quite as the pope had planned. John Paul asked the young student a series of questions to illustrate man's unyielding yearning to make progress. The following conversation ensued to the delight of all, including the pontiff.

"What grade are you in?"

"Fifth grade."

"Good. Now, listen carefully. Do you want to stay in the fifth grade again, or do you want to go to another grade next year?"

"It's all the same to me, but . . . I would like to stay in the fifth grade because otherwise, when I go to the sixth, I will lose my teacher."

Surprised, the pope's eyebrows shot up and he beamed in sheer glee. It was a moment of levity, no one enjoying his predicament more than the pope himself. Laughing along with the audience, the pope responded, "Oh! Well, this boy is different from the pope because when I was in fourth grade, I used to say, 'Oh, if only I were in fifth!' and when I was in fifth grade, I would say, "Who knows if I'll go to sixth, if they promote me!"

And then came the lesson.

The pontiff understood children, and he concluded his brief exchange by encouraging the boy—and, by extension, the entire audience. "You see, Danielle, the Lord has put inside us a strong desire to make progress, to go forward . . . Everyone wants to advance." And he recited a litany of man's progress over the centuries. Still holding the boy's hand in his, the pope drove home his message: We must always move forward, striving to make progress, especially in love. "Make progress . . . in loving God. All right?" the Holy Father advised Danielle. "There, I'll let you go now." He patted the boy's cheek gently and let escape a slight giggle. Then to the audience, "Did you see how he helped me?" And applause concluded the formal talk in Italian.[34]

But the pope was not quite done yet. "We have some sick people present. Let's hope they recover. But let's really urge those in their families . . . to take very good care of them." He let them know how he suffered with them, confiding that he had been hospitalized eight times and had undergone four surgeries. And he urged caregivers to aid the ill "with great love and kindness."

John Paul then greeted some newly married couples, giving him yet another chance to speak about a different manifestation of love—conjugal love. "Let's hope that the love of these married couples will always be preserved intact, as it is now." The sentiment aroused enthusiastic approval from the crowd.

Finally, he directly addressed a contingent of English-speaking visitors.

Figure 13.4. The pope sitting and smiling with his hands clasped at a general audience.

Much to the surprise of many, he summarized his talk in their language. The pope's pronunciation was flawed, making it difficult to understand his entire message. Nevertheless, he gamely proceeded, urging his listeners to love all their neighbors because "we have still not fulfilled the command of Jesus, to love our neighbors as ourselves." "To love God," he continued, "is a wonderful journey! But sometimes it involves sacrifice. We cannot embrace Christ on the cross without being hurt by a thorn . . . Because love is a journey, we must not stop . . . God wants us to make progress in love."[35]

Those were his last and lasting public words. They revealed not only what he believed but who he was, an emissary of divine love. It encapsulated the arc of his life . . . always striving to become more selfless, more charitable, and, above all, more loving.

It's what made the world love him so.

NOTES

1. Raymond and Lauretta Seabeck, *The Smiling Pope: The Life and Teaching of John Paul I* (Huntington, IN: Our Sunday Visitor, 2004), 66.
2. Address to American bishops making *ad limina* visit. Collection of recordings of the original speeches and statements of Blessed Pope John Paul I of the archives of the Foundation Papa Luciani of Canale d'Agordo (Belluno-Italy).
3. Stefania Falasca, *The September Pope: The Final Days of John Paul I* © 2017, PIEMME; 2020, Libreria Editrice Vaticana. English translation published by *Our Sunday Visitor*, 2021, 161.
4. Falasca, *September Pope*, 161.
5. Loris Serafini (director, Papa Luciani Pope John Paul I Museum and Archives), in discussion with the author, Gloucester, Rhode Island, October 11, 2012.
6. John Norton, "Pope John Paul I's Hometown Diocese Begins Work on His Canonization Cause," *Humilitas* 13, December 2002, 8–9.
7. Falasca, *September Pope*, 161.
8. Falasca, *September Pope*, 161.
9. David Yallop, *In God's Name: An Investigation into the Murder of Pope John Paul I* (New York: Penguin, 1984), 234.
10. Falasca, *September Pope*, 161.
11. "Pope John Paul Meets Mayor Argan," September 25, 1978, youtube.com/watch?v=Wnrws5HgcSA.
12. Response to the greeting address of the mayor of Rome, September 23, 1978. Collection of recordings of the original speeches and statements of Blessed Pope John Paul I of the archives of the Foundation Papa Luciani of Canale d'Agordo (Belluno-Italy).
13. "John Paul Meets Mayor Argan."
14. "Basilica of St. John Lateran Rome," *Britannica*, https://www.britannica.com/place/Basilica-of-St-John-Lantern.
15. "The Papal Liturgy and Pope John Paul I," *Caeremoniale Romanum*, https://www.youtube.com/watch?v=ZHWfgcIJvIQ.
16. Seabeck, *Smiling Pope*, 67.
17. Homily at Mass in Basilica of St. John Lateran, September 23, 1978. Collection of recordings of the original speeches and statements of Blessed Pope John Paul I of the archives of the Foundation Papa Luciani of Canale d'Agordo (Belluno-Italy).
18. Falasca, *September Pope*, 161.
19. Paul Spackman, *God's Candidate: The Life and Times of Pope John Paul I* (Herefordshire: Gracewing, 2008), 202.
20. "Pope Helps Free Kidnapped Boy," *The Voice*, September 29, 1978, 12.
21. Falasca, *September Pope*, 161.
22. Serafini, discussion.
23. Serafini, discussion.
24. Falasca, *September Pope*, 161.
25. Falasca, *September Pope*, 161.

26. Spackman, *God's Candidate*, 203–4.
27. "John Paul I on Love, Part I," Tau Cross Media, August 26, 2009, https://www.youtube.com/watch?v=f-XAWEfvMEk.
28. "John Paul I on Love, Part I," Tau Cross Media, 2009, https://www.youtube.com/results?search_query=john+paul+I+speaking+about+love+in+english.
29. "General Audience: Love," September 27, 1978. Collection of recordings of the original speeches and statements of Blessed Pope John Paul I of the archives of the Foundation Papa Luciani of Canale d'Agordo (Belluno-Italy).
30. Serafini, discussion.
31. "John Paul I on Love, Part I," https://www.youtube.com/watch?v=f-XAWEfvMEk.
32. "John Paul I on Love, Part II," Tau Cross Media, 2010.https://www.youtube.com/watch?v=KkO08g6JKGg.
33. Danielle Bravo (fifth grader who appeared with John Paul at his last general audience), interview with Dino Cimagalli, October 14, 1978.
34. "John Paul I on Love, Part II," https://www.youtube.com/watch?v=KkO08g6JKGg.
35. "John Paul I on Love, Part II."

• 14 •

The Last Supper

"See You Tomorrow, God Willing" (September 28, 1978)

> [Y]ou are a mist that appears for a little while and then vanishes. — James 4:14 (NRSVCE)

DAY 33/THURSDAY, SEPTEMBER 28

Something was amiss in the papal household.

The day started unremarkably enough, much like the previous thirty-two, but events went awry beginning in the early afternoon, and nothing was normal after that. Nor the next day. Nor those that followed.

JUST ANOTHER MORNING

A habitually early riser, John Paul awoke at 4:30 a.m. and adhered to his daily routine: having coffee and completing his morning ablutions before leaving the privacy of his room. He allocated the dawn hours to personal prayer in his private chapel just a short distance from his bedroom, and at seven o'clock he celebrated Mass attended by the household staff.[1] Joined by his personal secretaries, Fr. John Magee and don Diego Lorenzi, he then ate a light breakfast consisting of coffee and croissants in his dining room while scanning the newspapers.[2]

BUSINESS AS USUAL

Today, like all days since becoming pope, John Paul prepared for a demanding schedule that included three hours usually dedicated to afternoon paperwork. Mornings were typically devoted to meetings and private audiences, and this one was no different.

The pontiff's first audience was with Cardinal Julio Rosales and ten Philippine bishops who were at the Vatican for their *ad limina* visit.[3] The pope spoke with them in English about the importance of preaching the Gospel assiduously in the Far East. His passion for evangelization blazed, and he encouraged the bishops to make it a priority in their country. "More than ever before, we must help people to realize just how much they need Jesus Christ . . . the key to their destiny," he told them.

John Paul also emphasized to the bishops that "the Church is irrevocably committed to contributing to the relief of physical misery and need." Moreover, he reiterated the necessity of augmenting the dissemination of the Gospel teachings with good works to "fulfill the requirements of justice and Christian love." Then the pope went beyond that, citing the centrality of responsibility to be borne by these bishops because "the Philippines has a great vocation in being the light of Christ in the Far East." With his recognition of the mass media's importance as essential instruments for spreading Church teachings, he cited Radio *Veritas*, a noncommercial broadcasting station in Asia, as a "great means" for accomplishing the goals he outlined.[4]

The Vatican photographer arrived toward the session's conclusion and captured the group in pictures, one with the pope and the cardinal shaking hands. These were the final photos taken of John Paul alive.[5]

As the Holy Father was departing from the session, he apologized to his American translator, Msgr. Justin Rigali, for having disrupted his work to attend the meeting. Rigali responded by explaining to the pope that it was an honor to facilitate the conversation. In response, John Paul told him with a smile, "Thank you, thank you, disturbed Monsignor."[6] Rigali acted as interpreter because, although the pope spoke English, his syntax was obviously tortured, and he preferred to converse in Italian.

The pontiff subsequently met with the apostolic nuncios to Brazil and Holland, and then with the editor of *Il Gazzettino*, a popular newspaper in northeast Italy.[7] The journal held special significance to John Paul because for years he had been a frequent contributing writer.

The ensuing conferences of the morning focused exclusively on Church affairs. The pope met with influential Cardinal Bernardin Gantin of Benin, president of the Pontifical Commission for Justice and Peace, as well as the Pontifical Council *Cor Unum* ("One Heart"), along with two of his assistants.[8] John Paul held Gantin in high esteem and valued his views. This was to be the last audience granted to the head of a dicastery (a department of the curia). The trio briefed the pope about some of the most troublesome issues regarding poverty in Third World countries and promoting evangelization. Recalling the meeting shortly after the pope's passing, Gantin noted that John Paul had rearranged the chairs so that his visitors could be by his side. One of the cardinal's assistants said of the pope, "I found that he was the hearty, happy man everyone was talking about. We left the room filled with joy."[9] The implication of these observations, of course, was that John Paul neither looked nor acted like a sick man. The pope's subsequent visitors that day also gave no indication that the pontiff seemed ill or uneasy; he was his usual jubilant self.

Next, he met with Cardinal Sebastiano Baggio, prefect of the Sacred Congregation of Bishops, to "discuss pressing business."[10] Rev. Andrew Greeley reported that the consultation was about "appointments and replacements." According to Greeley, John Paul and Baggio discussed the removal of controversial Cardinal John Cody as archbishop of Chicago. There is no evidence that the pope had decided irrevocably to take that action. Greeley maintained that Baggio had asked the cardinal to step aside, but Cody refused. It is reasonable to deduce that Greeley's reporting was substantive. Cody's reputation had long been sullied by widespread criticism among diocesan clergy, much of which spilled into the public realm and eventually came to Baggio's attention. Among the charges leveled against the cardinal were fiscal irresponsibility, incompetent and authoritarian administration, widespread unpopularity with the faithful, and a personal penchant for secrecy and vindictiveness. Cody, in short, was an embarrassment to the Church, but previous popes had been shackled by a stubborn reluctance to discipline errant cardinals.[11] The American certainly did not conform to the profile of what John Paul believed a cardinal should be, and the pope was devoted to preserving the integrity of the Church, wishing it to be as pristine as a human institution could be. Had he removed Cody, it would have been a decision of unusual courage and a declaration of independence from past practice. But this pope had never flinched from making difficult decisions, however unpleasant or controversial they might be, during his tenure as bishop of Venice and Vittorio Veneto.

Cody wasn't the only high-ranking cleric whose behavior demanded immediate attention. Rev. Pedro Arrupe, the superior general of the Society of Jesus, had run afoul of the pope's beliefs regarding the proper role of priests in civil society. John Paul was scheduled to meet with him and members of the order on Saturday to express his dissatisfaction with some aspects of Arrupe's leadership and the consequent necessity of taking corrective action. The content of the undelivered speech, which was released posthumously, was stern but couched in soothing language. (On November 18, 1978, a copy was sent to Arrupe along with notification that John Paul II shared the views that his predecessor had expressed in the speech.) John Paul's directives were explicit: Adhere to the teachings of the Magisterium of the Church, inculcate "solid" doctrine in the formation of young Jesuits, practice religious discipline, shun secularizing tendencies, avoid becoming assimilated into the world, observe religious vows in full, and adhere faithfully to the rules of the order. Before explaining the reforms that he expected to be executed, the pope commended the admirable works of the Jesuits: "you are justly concerned with the great economic and social problems which afflict humanity today and which are so much related to the Christian life." But Jesuits, he insisted, must distinguish their role in solving problems from those "which are proper to the laity." And the pope invoked his authority over the Society of Jesus. "It is the Vicar of Christ who speaks to you, it is the new pope who expects and hopes so much from the Society."[12] John Paul was not making a request; he was conveying an expectation, one that he hinted without subtlety he would enforce.

The pope's next meeting was with Msgr. Giuseppe Bosa, the vicar general of Venice, with whom he conducted a lively conversation during which John Paul joked about the unending piles of daily reports he had to scrutinize. "They have machines for writing—why don't they invent one for reading?" he asked with a smile.[13] Though he said this in jest, he sometimes felt overwhelmed by these demands on his time.[14]

Despite the ongoing gossip among some Vatican administrators that John Paul was not up to the job of the papacy, one Roman church official made an observation at odds with the criticism. "It was almost as though his first month had given him a feel for the Vatican. He suddenly seemed to be enjoying it."[15] The good humor that John Paul exhibited with Bosa suggests that his opinion bore an element of truth. Magee validated the assessment. "He was gradually fitting into and getting to know . . . what was expected of him." Referring to the pope's death, Magee asserted, "[T]hings were looking up when that happened."[16]

BACK TO THE RESIDENCE

His audiences concluded, the pope had a light lunch with Magee and Lorenzi at 12:30 before taking his brief afternoon siesta.[17] Typically, he ate little. In fact, it was not unusual for him to satisfy his hunger with a mere handful of nuts. Accompanying the meal was his usual dose of pills for what a Vatican insider referred to as "aged ailments."[18]

The pope remained in the residence for the duration of the afternoon in virtual solitude. He received no visitors. Nor did he go to the rooftop garden for his walk, an activity that had become routine. The terrace features an assortment of bushes and plants in containers, in addition to arched walkways. The place was a sanctuary of sorts for him. There he could work and pray without distractions. (On a couple of occasions, he had walked in the magnificent Vatican gardens, but he had stopped because his presence interfered with the ability of sightseers to tour them.) "[I]t was a very windy day so he [John Paul] decided he wouldn't go outside, so he walked inside in one of the halls," Magee explained.[19] "Every day he would go in that garden roof, and he would bring with him papers that Cardinal Villot would send up to him . . . The only day that he didn't go on that garden roof was the day of his death," according to Magee.[20]

WORKING WHILE WALKING

The pope spent almost the entire afternoon pacing in the apartment, reading documents and scribbling notes. He also composed a document intended for some unidentified bishops. When he saw young Sr. Margherita Marin ironing, he said to her, "I make you work so hard . . . you don't need to iron that shirt so well because it's hot . . . Just iron the collar and the cuffs—you can't see the rest, you know."[21] "I could hear him walking round and round and round," Magee recalled.[22]

WITH VILLOT JUST ONE MORE TIME

At 6:30 p.m. John Paul met with Secretary of State Villot for about half an hour in his study.[23] The two spoke about foreign affairs and the status of the church.[24] At no time did Villot even hint that the pope showed the slightest sign of malaise.[25]

FINAL PRAYERS

As usual, the pope went to the chapel in the early evening to recite compline, the seventh and final part of the canonical hours. Among the prayers was a quotation from St. Paul's letter to the Thessalonians: "May the God of peace make you perfect in holiness. May He preserve you whole and entire, spirit, soul and body, irreproachable at the coming of the Lord Jesus Christ."[26]

THE LAST SUPPER AND ONE FINAL CALL

At 7:50 p.m., the pope and his two secretaries arrived in the dining room. The meal consisted of veal, salad, soup, and beans. The pope drank water while the secretaries savored red wine.[27] Magee observed that the pontiff had a healthy appetite that evening.[28]

It was John Paul's last supper.

After eating, the Holy Father spoke by phone with Milan's Cardinal Giovanni Colombo. The pope was eager to have a conversation with his old friend. The topic of the half hour call was to determine the pope's replacement as patriarch of Venice.[29] Of the tenor of their exchange, Colombo said afterward, "He spoke to me . . . in a voice that was very normal; it conveyed no evident weariness nor was it possible to infer any physical illness from it." He further described the pontiff as "full of serenity and hope."[30]

Later that evening John Paul learned of a tragedy in Rome. Two boys were shot by neo-fascist youths, one of whom died, and the other was wounded.[31] The disconcerted pope responded, "They kill each other—even the young people."[32] He shook his head in disbelief.[33]

That is about the extent of what is known with certainty about the pope's final day. The rest is a jumble of alternate realities replete with disturbingly contradictory details combined with a jumbled chronology of disputed incidents.

Three individuals residing in the pope's private apartments are the central sources of relevant information because they were witnesses or participants in the day's events.

THE GOSPEL TRUTH ACCORDING TO FATHER MAGEE

In the aftermath of September 28, 1978, John Magee, by nature a loquacious man, suddenly seemed to have taken a vow of silence as if he had developed a case of amnesia. Only with the distance of time did he gradually reveal detailed versions of what had transpired in the papal living quarters on the day of John Paul's death and the one that followed. When he decided to talk, the floodgates opened. He granted interviews to authors (including this one) who pressed him about some of the most delicate and confounding developments to which he was witness. Most importantly, he testified before a commission that was meticulous in collecting information about John Paul I for the canonization process. An examination of both Fr. Magee and don Diego Lorenzi's accounts of what happened on the last day of the Pope's life are sometimes frustratingly contradictory.[34]

A Pope in Pain?

In the afternoon Magee heard the pope calling him in an agitated voice. In response, he dashed off to find the pope standing by a table, holding his hand to his chest. Complaining of intense, localized pain, John Paul asked Magee to fetch Sr. Vincenza who, he informed his secretary, had medicine that would alleviate his acute discomfort. The Irishman dutifully summoned her. When Magee informed Sr. Vincenza of the pope's ailment, she reacted without alarm. "Oh, yes, this has happened before," he quoted her as saying almost nonchalantly. The nun brought the medication to the pope.[35] The papal secretary described the pills as "the kind you put under your tongue."[36] (Magee did not identify the drug that was administered, but nitroglycerin is used in that manner to relieve angina, chest pain resulting from coronary artery disease.)

When junior secretary Lorenzi, who had been out that afternoon, returned to the apartment, Magee informed him of the pope's health scare, telling him that he intended to call the doctor. Lorenzi agreed with him, although neither one summoned a physician.[37] The pope subsequently called Magee to assure him that he was feeling fine and was "ready to receive Cardinal Villot" at the appointed hour.[38]

That neither secretary summoned the Vatican physician is peculiar, especially because Magee claimed to be aware that the pope had what he described as a circulatory problem that manifested itself in swollen ankles, sometimes a symptom of heart disease. Supposedly, for that reason John Paul had long before embarked on a daily walking regimen.

Magee related a slight variation of this account in 1987, claiming the pope confided to him that he was feeling ill after taking his nap but still declined Magee's offer to alert his new physician, Dr. Renato Buzzonetti, the Vatican doctor.[39]

Around 6:30 p.m., after accompanying Villot to the door following the secretary of state's conference with John Paul, Magee asked the pope directly how he felt. The pope replied that he was well, thanks to the efficacy of Sister Vincenza's medication.[40]

At this time the daily routine called for evening prayers, and John Paul felt well enough to walk to the chapel. "I always accompanied the pope into the chapel, where we would have compline—evening prayers," claimed Magee.[41] The two men did so at this time.

An Upsetting Dinner Conversation

Magee inquired about the pope's health again at supper. He recalled, "I said, 'Holy Father, how are you now?' 'I'm great! Those are great tablets!' he responded."[42] At table Magee also asked if the pope had selected the individual to preach the Lenten retreat for the curia. The pope responded, "[T]he retreat I would like to have now would be for a good death." Shortly thereafter he recited a prayer that his mother had taught him, "God, give me the grace to accept the death with which you will strike me."[43] According to Magee, death was a subject that John Paul raised repeatedly. "He was constantly talking of death, constantly reminding us that his pontificate was to be of short duration . . . All of this was a great enigma to us then. I said to him, 'Oh, Holy Father, not again! Coming again to that morbid subject!'"[44]

Ironically, on this last day of his life, the pope addressed the joy of reaching heaven in a letter he wrote to the Church of St. Severus in Germany, which was celebrating its seven hundredth anniversary: "[T]his church instills into one's mind the desire for that heavenly home, where one may enjoy for all eternity the gifts which the eye cannot see, about which the ear cannot hear, nor can they be adequately represented by any thought . . . This certainly gives true meaning and real importance to this short and often arduous life on earth. In times of adversity, let us long for that blessed life which will never fail."[45]

Toward the end of the meal, the Holy Father instructed Lorenzi to call Cardinal Colombo. Don Diego did so, and shortly afterward he informed the pope that the cardinal was on the line. Once John Paul heard that Colombo was waiting to speak with him, he rushed to the phone, according to Magee. He "took off down the corridor at such a speed I was worried he would slip and fall on the marble floor."[46]

Escorting the Pope to Bed?

When the pope retired to his bedroom at approximately 9:30 p.m., Magee accompanied him, adding that the Holy Father took one of his homilies with him. "I followed the pope into his bedroom because I wanted to bring to his attention the presence of the two alarm buttons on either side of the bed which had been fixed up only that morning. You may consider that to be a remarkable coincidence. But it is the truth," he insisted.[47]

Leaving John Paul in his bedchamber, Magee visited the nuns and talked to them for about thirty minutes. He claimed that they asked him how the pope felt, and the secretary indicated that he was concerned about his condition. But Sr. Vincenza reassured him, "No, no, don't worry!"[48]

Fascination with Death and Brief Papacies

"Then I said a most extraordinary thing in the light of subsequent events . . . Believe it or not, this is the gospel truth! I said to Sister Vincenza, 'It would be terrible to lose a pope now after losing Paul VI. How many days is it now? Thirty-three?'" He then picked up a copy of the *Annuario Pontificio*, a book that includes a list of popes along with the years of their pontificates. "And I said to the sisters," recalled Magee, "'I wonder how many popes lived less than thirty-three days.' And we sat down there in the kitchen, and we went right through the list of the popes that very night."[49]

Upon returning to his bedroom with his mind still occupied with papal deaths, Magee looked through photos of Paul VI's funeral and became so absorbed that he lost track of time. When he finally checked the clock, he noticed that it was 11:05, a late night for him. Needing to be up at five the next morning, he climbed into bed and apparently slept soundly.[50]

Magee reported that Lorenzi didn't return to the papal apartment until after midnight.[51] According to the doctor who examined the pope's body the next morning, John Paul was already dead by then.

LORENZI'S VERSION(S) OF EVENTS

For whatever reasons, Lorenzi had been reluctant to discuss any aspects of the pope's life for some time after his death. Nevertheless, he ultimately did so on several occasions. In his deposition, interviews with authors and reporters, television appearances, and published articles, Lorenzi shared his accounts of what had transpired on the day the pope died.

A Troubling Supper

"At about 8 p.m. the pope, Msgr. Magee, and I had dinner. Rather suddenly, while seated at the table, the pope put his hands to his chest complaining, 'I am having some pains, but they are passing.'"[52] Both secretaries reacted by recommending that they call the doctor, but the pope declined. "It [the pain] is passing; there is no need," John Paul insisted.[53] (Lorenzi disclosed that information for the first time in October 1987, on a live television broadcast.)[54] Neither Dr. Buzzonetti nor any other medical professional was alerted. Sister Vincenza was not informed, and no medication was administered. Lorenzi justified his failure to alert the doctor because secretaries simply did not contravene the pope's wishes—evidently even if there might be dire consequences from a possible medical condition that manifested itself in a sharp but fleeting chest pain.[55]

Regarding the pope's distress at dinner, Lorenzi claimed, "My inexperience . . . regarding the premonitory symptoms of heart problems linked to those pains played a notable part in our continuing with dinner."[56] That would seem to suggest that he had no knowledge of any similar occurrences during his two years with Luciani in Venice, though Sr. Vincenza supposedly told Magee that such instances had taken place before.

Lorenzi insisted that he had remained in the apartment that night to prepare sermons to be delivered in Veneto the next day.[57] He claimed that he later joined Magee in accompanying the pope to the entrance to his bedroom and asserted that Magee alerted John Paul to a device on the bed's headboard, explaining that if the pain struck him again to call them.[58] But then in an article he wrote for *Il Gazzettino* in September of 1979, Lorenzi remembered that "the pope appeared at the door of our study wishing us a 'good night,' as he did every evening."[59]

AN ALTERNATIVE ACCOUNT

Sr. Margherita Marin's recollections seem precise and credible, despite coming three decades after the events took place. The youngest nun in the papal household at the time remembered that the pope spent the entire time pacing "with papers in his hand that he was reading. Every now and then he would stop to make a few notes."[60] Apparently, he was preparing a document for the upcoming Latin American Bishops' Conference.[61] John Paul remained in the private apartment all afternoon and received no visitors other than Villot in the early evening.[62]

Regarding his secretaries' claims that the pope complained of chest pains during the afternoon, Sr. Vincenza Taffarel, who provided daily care for the pope's health, spoke with the pope's niece Dr. Lina Petri on the morning that the pontiff's body was found. Dr. Petri recalled the nun telling her, through her tears, that she "simply couldn't believe it because he had been so well, much better in Rome than in Venice." She remembered the nun adding that "he'd felt really well the evening before."[63] Sister Margherita was confident that the pope did not experience any pain, and she did not witness "any particular activity either by Sr. Vincenza, or by the secretaries, that would make me suspect otherwise."[64]

After his meeting with Villot, John Paul recited compline with Magee and Lorenzi.[65] It was at approximately nine o'clock that he had the phone conversation with Cardinal Colombo.[66] Sr. Margherita also recalled that "after passing the telephone . . . to the Pope, don Diego Lorenzi left the papal apartments."[67] Before turning in for the night, John Paul thanked the sisters for dinner and bid them a good evening.[68] Observing the pope take his leave, Sister Margherita recalled, "He went alone to his room as usual . . . after he said good night to us, the Holy Father stood at the door of his study, turned around again and waved goodnight to us, smiling . . . I can still see him there at the door. It is the last image I have of him."[69]

Additional Relevant Information

Dr. Antonio Da Ros, the pope's physician since 1959, testified that he made a phone call to the papal residence around 7:30 that night and spoke with Sr. Vincenza, who reported that the pope's health was good, and she had no incidents of illness to report.[70] The doctor wrote this information in his diary contemporaneously.

THE ELUSIVE TRUTH

The troubling mélange of explanations that the pope's aides provided raises serious questions. Was there a lack of shared information about the pope's health? Was the pope well served by those closest to him, or was there a degree of indifference toward him and his needs? Were there dysfunctional relationships among members of the household? Were people keeping secrets concerning their whereabouts on this day? Were there self-serving reasons for some residents to dissemble about their actions on that day?

The sisters had clearly delineated domestic chores that they seem to have carried out diligently and in a spirit of joyful cooperation. Their affection for the pope was beyond question. He frequently visited the kitchen for brief chats or simple requests, and he repeatedly expressed his appreciation to them for their loyal service. He concluded each day by wishing them a good evening and the hope of seeing them the next morning. Mutual warmth existed in this quarter of the household at least.

Sr. Vincenza was not only a long-serving employee but an individual with whom the pope had forged a bond of friendship. Their familiarity is perhaps best illustrated by a widely circulated account that was considered apocryphal by some: Vincenza in private conversation addressed John Paul as "don [Father] Albino"; he, in turn, referred to her as "my little Vincenza."[71] These terms of endearment suggest that a degree of affection developed over the course of decades. If anyone in the household knew of any ailments from which the pope suffered or who felt a responsibility for ministering to his health needs, it was she.

An indication of her devotion to Luciani was her apprehension upon his departure from Venice to Rome that he might not return. Following his election, she agreed to move to the Vatican despite deep personal reservations; if the demands on her at the Vatican were more arduous than those in Venice, she must have worried about the possible adverse effects on her own health because she had already suffered a heart attack.[72] Yet she acquiesced to the pope's request that she come, and she did so out of a sense of responsibility to look after him.

Unlike the cooperation among the nuns in the household, the relationship between the pope's personal secretaries seems to have been impersonal at best. Magee and Lorenzi spent the most private time with the pope every day. They were the two individuals in the household on whom he was most dependent, yet they did not appear to consistently act in harmony on the pope's behalf. There appeared to be a blurry division of labor between them, a lack of coordination, and perhaps even a dearth of consultation. Their distant relationship was best symbolized by the remote location of their bedrooms: they slept on different floors of the palace. Their personalities didn't seem to mesh either. Magee was unfailingly polite and gracious whereas Lorenzi tended to be gruff and taciturn.[73] Jealousy and insecurity might have contributed to the dysfunction between them. Lorenzi, as "junior" secretary, was, in effect, overshadowed by Magee, the experienced Vatican hand. As a result, it is not unlikely that don Diego would have felt resentful, even irrelevant.

The young Don Orione priest seemed out of his element and felt forlorn. His discontent was publicly on display at a general audience when, seated to the pope's right on stage, he fidgeted like a bored schoolboy.[74] However, when he became suspicious that he was about to be dismissed from his position, he was understandably upset.[75]

John Paul, who first met Magee in the apartment quite by accident, seemed to have asked him spontaneously to stay on as papal secretary. But he had sound reasons for doing so. Anxious about his own lack of knowledge of the Vatican and its personnel, the pope assumed that Magee, who had been one of Pope Paul's secretaries for four years, was intimately familiar with the operation of the papal household, the demands on the pope's time, the functioning of the Vatican bureaucracy, and the major figures who exerted the most influence at the highest levels of the centralized Church organization. He could serve as a personal "tutor" to John Paul about such things, guiding him through the maze of the establishment, coaching him on how to maximize his time, easing him more quickly and effectively into his new role. The extent to which Magee fulfilled those expectations is not fully known, but judging by the pope's struggles with the bureaucracy in the first few weeks, it would seem to have been minimal—something that is difficult to explain, especially because the two men had considerable daily contact throughout the thirty-three days of John Paul's papacy.[76]

If Magee was inadequate as a counselor to the pope, he nevertheless became the pope's shadow. He never left the confines of the apartment during John Paul's pontificate. Not once.[77] He was always on call. Magee concelebrated Mass with the Holy Father each morning, joined him for meals three times each day, recited compline with him each evening, and accompanied him to general audiences on alternate weeks. Beyond that, he claimed to have developed a personal relationship with John Paul. His recollection was that the two spent time together engaging in casual conversation. Accurately or not, Magee believed the two had the closest of friendships, "in a sense I was all he had. I was his family there . . . he spoke to me as if he was speaking to his own brother."[78] Magee admired the pope; indeed, he loved him. "He was always so gracious and so thankful for the slightest thing that you would do for him. He was such a beautiful, beautiful person."[79]

John Paul's schedule was so intrusive on his time that he had few opportunities to relax or to enjoy the company of friends. Besides prayer, meals, perusing newspapers, and watching a smidgen of television news, the pope's days consisted exclusively of work. That could not have been a boon to his health. "Possibly he didn't do enough to relax. He needed to relax," Magee confided in an interview with this author.[80]

The heads of Vatican departments seemed to have little, if any, concern for John Paul's well-being. Villot, for example, buried the pope in paperwork each day and demanded that he make a multitude of decisions, some of which presumably could have been reached by subordinates, including Villot himself.

The one escape from his burdens and the source of his greatest joy was sharing meals with his family and friends. Magee observed, "It was he (John Paul I) who introduced to his morning Mass and to his breakfast table his family . . . He liked to have people with him at table. And he enjoyed people so much, young people and his nephews and nieces. All of them came to visit with him." Magee amplified his thoughts: "He was as normal a person as you could expect anyone to be, especially when he was with his family. He was like a father figure to them. They absolutely loved him."[81] But the frequency of such occasions was insufficient to provide the pope with the degree of respite he required.

NAGGING QUESTIONS

The discrepancies regarding what took place and when they took place appear irreconcilable. How to account for them then? Only three possibilities seem reasonable: one or more of the individuals who were knowledgeable of the events had faulty recollections, or they blurred the truth, or they lied outright.

Did the pope sustain chest pains and, if so, when and where? Magee said the pope's complaint occurred while he was walking in the early afternoon. Later, he claimed that the event took place following the pope's nap. Lorenzi maintained that the incident happened at the dinner table. Sisters Margherita and Vincenza insisted that it never transpired at all.

Magee reported that Sr. Vincenza administered medication to the pope. Lorenzi, who was present in the dining room, said the pope complained of passing pain during dinner and that it subsided on its own. Sister Margherita, who worked closely with Sister Vincenza, denied that the elder nun ever intervened in any incident involving the pope's health.

If John Paul had suffered acute chest pain, why did he refuse to see a doctor? Had such an event occurred on prior occasions and was treated with medication so that it caused him no consternation? Did he somehow minimize the seriousness of the "attack"? Was it that he didn't want to trouble Dr. Buzzonetti, or did he lack faith in this physician, who had neither treated him before nor had detailed knowledge of the pope's medical history? More darkly, was it an indication that he was prepared to die? If his secretaries' assertions that the Holy Father was preoccupied with his death are correct, that unpleasant possibility is plausible.

Mystery has masked the main events of John Paul's final eleven hours of life. And the fact that mystery lingers is, in a sense, itself a mystery. Logic suggests that re-creating the day's major incidents would be uncomplicated; after all, only a few people in the papal residence on the afternoon and evening of the pope's death interacted with him or witnessed or heard what took place: his two secretaries and two of the four nuns. Why would their accounts differ so dramatically?

Before John Paul died, both Magee and Lorenzi admitted to having become curious about the briefest pontificates, a strange coincidence. In addition, Lorenzi admitted that he had the unspoken thought during dinner on that last night that the pope's days might be numbered.[82] If these musings resulted from the pope's chest pain, both secretaries must have suspected that whatever ailed him could be life threatening, yet they still failed to summon medical help. Their inaction is baffling.

At least subconsciously, Magee and Lorenzi were aware of the possibility that the pope's chest pain could have been a harbinger of a potentially serious, if not fatal, condition. And still they did nothing, something that prudent people could conclude amounted to negligence.

That night before entering his bedroom for the final time, John Paul uttered his last words; they were addressed to the nuns who cared for him selflessly. "*A domani se Dio vuole*" (See you tomorrow, God willing),[83] he said with a soft smile. He then climbed into bed with papers in his hand—still more work to be done. Shortly thereafter he slipped into eternal sleep. Alone. Utterly alone.

For him, there would be no tomorrow.

NOTES

1. David Yallop, *In God's Name: An Investigation into the Murder of Pope John Paul I* (Penguin, 1984), 167.
2. Yallop, *In God's Name*, 168, 190.
3. Stefania Falasca, *The September Pope: The Final Days of John Paul I* © 2017, PIEMME; 2020, Libreria Editrice Vaticana. English translation published by *Our Sunday Visitor*, 2021, 161.
4. Speech delivered to Philippine bishops on their *ad limina* visit, September 28, 1978. Collection of recordings of the original speeches and statements of Blessed Pope John Paul I of the Archives of the Foundation Papa Luciani of Canale d'Agordo (Belluno-Italy).
5. Paul Spackman, *God's Candidate: The Life and Times of Pope John Paul I* (Herefordshire: Gracewing, 2008), 213.
6. Fr. Victor Feltes, "Parting Words," September 29, 2014, The Pope John Paul I Papacy—Day by Day, www.johnpauli.wordpress.com.
7. Falasca, *September Pope*, 161–62.
8. Falasca, *September Pope*, 162.
9. Spackman, *God's Candidate*, 210.
10. "The September Pope," *Time*, October 9, 1978, 68.
11. Andrew Greeley, *The Making of the Popes 1978* (Kansas City: Andrews and McMeel, 1979), 89–92, 172.
12. Message the pontiff intended to address to the procurators of the Society of Jesus in audience, September 30, 1978, published posthumously. Collection of recordings of the original speeches and statements of Blessed Pope John Paul I of the Archives of the Foundation Papa Luciani of Canale d'Agordo (Belluno-Italy).
13. Raymond and Lauretta Seabeck, *The Smiling Pope: The Life and Teaching of John Paul I* (Huntington, IN: Our Sunday Visitor, 2004), 68.
14. "A Death in Rome," *Newsweek*, October 9, 1978, 74.
15. "A Death in Rome," *Newsweek*, 74.
16. John Magee (bishop emeritus, diocese of Cloyne, Ireland), in discussion with the author, Cobh, Ireland, February 17, 2010.
17. Spackman, *God's Candidate*, 214.
18. "A Death in Rome," *Newsweek*, 74.
19. Magee, discussion.
20. Magee, discussion.
21. Falasca, *September Pope*, 60–61.

22. John Cornwell, *A Thief in the Night: Life and Death in the Vatican* (New York: Penguin, 1989), 239.
23. Cornwell, *A Thief in the Night*, 241.
24. "A Death in Rome," *Newsweek*, 74.
25. Spackman, *God's Candidate*, 224.
26. Seabeck, *Smiling Pope*, 69.
27. Yallop, *In God's Name,* 200.
28. Spackman, *God's Candidate*, 219.
29. Cornwell, *A Thief in the Night*, 105–6.
30. Falasca, *September Pope*, 68–69.
31. "Parting," Day by Day, www.johnpauli.wordpress.com.
32. Hebblethwaite, *Three Popes*, 128.
33. Greeley, *The Making of the Popes 1978*, 172.
34. Cornwell, *A Thief in the Night*, 324–25.
35. Cornwell, *A Thief in the Night*, 241.
36. Falasca, *September Pope*, 63.
37. Spackman, *God's Candidate*, 218.
38. Falasca, *September Pope*, 63.
39. Cornwell, *A Thief in the Night*, 238.
40. Cornwell, *A Thief in the Night*, 242.
41. Magee, discussion.
42. Magee, discussion.
43. Falasca, *September Pope*, 67.
44. Spackman, *God's Candidate*, 219–20.
45. Letter of His Holiness John Paul I to Monsignor Hugo Aufderbeck on the Seventh Centenary of the Church of Saint Severus. Copyright © Dicastero per la Comunicazione—Libreria Editrice Vaticana. https://www.vatican.va/content/john-paul-i/en/letters/documents/hf_jp-i_let_28091978_mons-aufderbeck.html.
46. Spackman, *God's Candidate*, 220.
47. Cornwell, *A Thief in the Night*, 243–44.
48. Cornwell, *A Thief in the Night*, 244.
49. Cornwell, *A Thief in the Night*, 244–45.
50. Cornwell, *A Thief in the Night*, 245.
51. Cornwell, *A Thief in the Night*, 244.
52. Falasca, *September Pope*, 63.
53. Falasca, *September Pope*, 64.
54. Cornwell, *A Thief in the Night*, 104.
55. Cornwell, *A Thief in the Night*, 104.
56. Falasca, *September Pope*, 67.
57. Cornwell, *A Thief in the Night*, 266.
58. Cesare Vazza, "His Light, Only for a Moment," trans. Lori Pieper, *Humilitas*13, December 2002.
59. Falasca, *September Pope*, 71.
60. Falasca, *September Pope*, 61.
61. Spackman, *God's Candidate*, 215.

62. Falasca, *September Pope*, 162.
63. Cornwell, *A Thief in the Night*, 302.
64. Falasca, *September Pope*, 64.
65. Yallop, *In God's Name*, 200.
66. Spackman, *God's Candidate*, 221.
67. Falasca, *September Pope*, 69.
68. Gordon Thomas and Max Morgan-Witts, *Pontiff* (Garden City: Doubleday, 1984), 311.
69. Falasca, *September Pope*, 71–72.
70. Spackman, *God's Candidate*, 225.
71. Spackman, *God's Candidate*, 150.
72. Cornwell, *A Thief in the Night*, 102.
73. Cornwell, *A Thief in the Night*, 328–29.
74. Cornwell, *A Thief in the Night*, 95.
75. Cornwell, *A Thief in the Night*, 239–40.
76. Magee, discussion.
77. Magee, discussion.
78. Magee, discussion.
79. Magee, discussion.
80. Magee, discussion.
81. Magee, discussion.
82. Yallop, *In God's Name*, 200.
83. Spackman, *God's Candidate*, 221.

• 15 •

Shock

The Pope Is Dead (September 29, 1978)

Surely everyone stands as a mere breath.

Surely everyone goes about like a shadow. —Psalm 39, 5:6 (NRSVCE)

On this blackest evening of the year, a solitary light glowed dimly through a window hovering high above St. Peter's Square, although the embodiment of luminosity within the room had already been extinguished.

The apostolic palace, a massive building rising above the lofty columns of Bernini's colonnade, was cast in deep shadow while the piazza itself was spectacularly illuminated, the waters of its fountains dancing with life. Around midnight a security officer patrolling the square noticed that one third-floor window still shone.[1] He expected that in another hour or so the pope's bedchamber would be darkened like all the others in the complex. He, like the taxi drivers in the vicinity, assumed that John Paul was working late.[2] But the night lapsed into dawn, and the room remained unexpectedly illumined, puzzling the guards in the square who speculated that the pope must have fallen asleep with the lights on.[3]

MORNING: UNTOUCHED COFFEE

The small table outside the pope's bedchamber stood in silence. Laid out neatly on top was a cup of coffee. That tableau was a familiar one, re-created every morning in every residence that Albino Luciani had inhabited since Sr. Vincenza Taffarel had first begun her service to him nineteen years before while he was bishop of Vittorio Veneto. Following her daily routine, the nun had brought the tray of coffee for the pope at approximately 4:30 a.m. and returned to the kitchen to join the other nuns in preparing breakfast. About a half hour later, she was back in the outer area of the pope's room to retrieve the tray but found the coffee untouched. She was baffled. In the nearly two decades she had been in Albino Luciani's employ, he had never overslept. Not once.[4]

A GHASTLY DISCOVERY

Unsure about what to do, she approached the door and listened closely. Silence greeted her. The pope was not moving about. She knocked gently but received no response. She rapped on the door again, more vigorously this time. Still nothing. Confused and growing increasingly concerned, Sister Vincenza reluctantly opened the door just enough to glimpse inside.[5]

She observed the pope sitting in bed as stiff as a statue. His eyes were open, and he was wearing his eyeglasses but made no acknowledgment of her presence.[6] Unnerved, she beckoned Sr. Margherita, who later described the scene in detail: "the reading light over the headboard was on. He had two pillows under his back that propped him up a bit . . . his arms were on top of the bedsheets, he was wearing pajamas, and . . . he was clutching some typewritten pages . . . I touched his hands; they were cold, I noticed, and was struck by his fingernails, which were a little dark."[7]

In a frenzy, Vincenza hurried to inform Magee, who slept upstairs, while Margherita ran to Lorenzi's room, located on the same floor as the pope's. Both nuns conveyed the identical message: the pope appeared to be dead. Startled but skeptical, Magee slipped on a cassock over his nightwear and promptly arrived in the pope's bedroom. The door was ajar as Vincenza had left it. Instructing the nun to wait outside, Magee entered alone. "At first he seemed to be still reading, but it soon became obvious that he had been dead for some hours," said Magee.[8]

The scene he described was consistent with the details that Sr. Margherita had provided. "I knelt beside the bed. I prayed. I cried," he revealed.[9] Then at 5:42 Magee informed Cardinal Villot and Dr. Buzzonetti of the pontiff's death. The two men arrived around six.[10] Lorenzi also appeared. Buzzonetti confirmed Magee's impression that death had claimed the pope hours before: "The pontiff is dead. He has been dead for some time."[11]

Cardinal Carlo Confalonieri, who viewed the body in bed somewhat later, reported, "I prayed, kissed his hand, then went to the papal chapel to say Mass." He added, "We are all with our eyes turned upward wondering about the inscrutable designs of God."[12]

NOTIFYING THE FAMILY

After the doctor confirmed John Paul's death, Lorenzi made a series of phone calls to inform members of the pope's family and his longtime personal physician, Dr. Antonio Da Ros, of the startling news. Pia Luciani, the Holy Father's niece, was the first among the relatives to be notified. "[A]t the beginning I could hardly believe my ears," Pia said.[13]

According to her, Lorenzi was terse and tactless in sharing the devastating information. "You must be brave. Your uncle is dead," he began. He offered no condolences, conveyed no compassion whatsoever. Lorenzi's tone and message were cold and businesslike. The pope's secretary wasted no time in raising the inappropriate matter of inheritance, as if that would be of any concern to the pope's eldest niece. He did so in a tactless manner: "I am going to warn you right now that there is no money. You know very well that he had given everything away."[14] The painful memory of that abrasive call still rankled as she recounted it thirty years later.[15]

Lina Petri, another niece, was a medical student, living a short distance from the Vatican. Without delay, she departed for the Apostolic Palace. Upon arrival, she navigated her way to the pope's bedroom, the only family member to view the pope's body while it still lay in bed. By then the body was already clothed in a white cassock, and she noticed a tear in the fabric. Grief-stricken and dazed, she gazed upon the remains, eventually taking a chair at the foot of the bed. The door to the adjacent study was open, and conversation taking place there drifted into the bedroom. For some twenty minutes she sat and looked at him, occasionally scanning the room. She noticed that the top of the pope's desk was bare except for a crucifix and a picture of his parents.[16]

The pope's brother Berto was in Australia on business when he learned of his older sibling's death.[17] Pia Luciani broke the news to her fellow villagers by interrupting a Mass attended by some thirty worshippers in Canale d'Agordo.[18]

MEDICAL OBSERVATIONS AND QUICK CONCLUSIONS

After he was summoned by Magee, Dr. Buzzonetti examined the body briefly. The pope's corpse, as described by the doctor in a then confidential document certifying the death, was propped up in a semi-sitting position. His head was turned a little to the right, and his glasses were still on. Printed sheets of paper, the contents of which were not inspected, were in his hands.[19] "His eyelids and mouth were partly open," the physician noted. Rigor mortis—"intense cadaverous rigidity," as he referred to it, had set in. There were "hypostatic spots" (pooling of blood) in the pope's backside, causing reddish discoloration of the skin.[20] Based on his examination, Buzzonetti concluded that the pope had died at about eleven the previous night.[21]

The doctor also noted that the expression on the pope's face was "composed and calm."[22] John Paul had died peacefully of a sudden, massive heart attack—acute myocardial infarction—the medical jargon cited in the death certificate that Dr. Buzzonetti signed.[23] The attack struck so suddenly and so forcefully that he was unable to seek assistance and likely suffered little, if at all.[24] That Buzzonetti, who had never examined or treated the pope and whose knowledge of John Paul's health history was sketchy at best, should have determined the cause of death by conducting only a cursory examination of the body is curious. However, his conclusion was not necessarily erroneous.

From afar, Dr. Pier Luigi Prati, a heart specialist, observed, "Pope John Paul died the death of modern executives, a heart attack. But it also could have been a cerebral hemorrhage . . . In order to ascertain this, an autopsy would be necessary." No autopsy was performed, however.[25]

Though the pope's family confirmed that the pope had had a recent physical exam by Dr. Da Ros, they were unaware whether an electrocardiogram had been administered at the time to detect any heart abnormalities.[26]

THE STRUGGLE TO CLOTHE THE BODY

With Buzzonetti present, Magee and Lorenzi removed the pope's pajamas and dressed the deceased in a white cassock. The rigidity of the limbs, particularly the hands, in a fixed position made the unpleasant task difficult.[27] The tear in the fabric that Lina Petri noticed had probably resulted from the awkward undertaking. Buzzonetti explained the intensity of the body's inflexibility. "[I]t was necessary to exert a certain amount of tractive force to pull the sheets out from between the fingers," he reported officially.[28] (Despite an extensive search, those papers were never located.)

Villot, for the second time in only a few weeks, then performed the ritual to which he was already too familiar. Wielding a silver hammer, he lightly touched the corpse on the forehead while intoning, "Albino, Albino, Albino, are you dead?"[29]

THE COVER-UP BEGINS

At this point Villot started spinning a fictitious tale of what had transpired that morning. According to Magee, the secretary of state insisted that the senior papal secretary be identified publicly as the person who discovered the pope's body to prevent what Villot referred to as "unfortunate misunderstandings."[30] The camerlengo feared that if the truth were made public, a scandal would erupt—a nun had been in the pope's bedroom! And so, the Vatican reported a falsehood in the guise of news. Everything possible had to be done immediately to suppress the truth. That meant making everyone in the papal household complicit in the cover-up, willingly or not. Magee and Lorenzi swore the nuns to secrecy about the facts of the body's discovery, and they grudgingly complied. They had no choice.[31]

Sr. Vincenza, herself, did not conceal the truth very long. On the evening of September 30, she was visiting with the pope's niece Lina, and his sister, Nina, when she said, "The truth is that I found him myself that morning." The news was of some consolation to them all.[32] Dr. Petri expressed her gratitude that "my deceased uncle was found by someone who loved him very much and had been familiar to him for years."[33] In 2011 she amplified the nature of the relationship between the pope and Sister Vincenza. "She was a nurse, cook . . . She was the person who helped him the most and was very close to him. She was like a sister [sibling]."[34]

The official public announcement of John Paul's death came at 7:30, some two hours after the nun had made her horrific finding. That's when the world first learned the shocking but deceptive news. As had been arranged, the Vatican Press Office erroneously identified Magee as the person who discovered the body. At 7:42 a program director interrupted the news anchor at RAI (an Italian broadcasting company) to announce the death. The Vatican Radio news director compounded the impact of the initial lie by later announcing the falsehood that the pope had been reading the *Imitation of Christ* when he died. Vatican Radio later made a retraction on air, but the fabrication had already spread.[35] Public pandemonium ensued. Reporters went into a frenzy trying to ascertain additional information; any further news coming from the Vatican became suspect by some, dismissed as blatantly unreliable by others; and the public rumors of foul play began swirling like an ever-expanding cyclone.

Newsweek, *Time*, and other reputable publications faithfully reported the official Vatican version of events: John Magee had entered the room to find the pope dead in bed. The *Imitation of Christ* lay open next to the body. The final and seemingly most outrageous claim was that John Paul had died with a smile on his face—an implausible expression for a victim of a stroke or heart attack and one that Dr. Buzzonetti contradicted.

L'Osservatore Romano, the newspaper of the Holy See, printed the dry official notice in its entirety: "This morning, 29 September 1978, about 5.30, the private Secretary of the Pope, contrary to custom not having found the Holy Father in the chapel of his private apartment, looked for him in his room and found him dead in bed with the light on, like one who was intent on reading. The physician, Dr. Renato Buzzonetti, who hastened at once, verified the death as having presumably taken place around eleven o'clock yesterday evening through an acute coronary thrombosis."[36] Pope Paul VI had once contemptuously commented about the newspaper that it published what should have happened rather than what, in fact, did happen.[37] So it was with its initial report about John Paul's death.

The staggering news flash of the Holy Father's sudden death sent the entire world reeling. *Time* publisher John A. Meyers wrote that the event "left the world stunned." He was echoing what everyone felt.[38] Albino Luciani's death was even more surprising than his election had been. And the sorrow it engendered was as intense as the elation that his election had caused. "It's impossible," groaned Giovanni Benetti, a Venetian laborer, who had witnessed the pope's installation. "It seems like only yesterday that we saw his smiling face radiating from the balcony of St. Peter's. God is sometimes cruel," he lamented.[39]

STUPEFIED CARDINALS

Reports of the pontiff's passing reached cardinals with the speed of a wildfire. All were badly shaken by the news. Cardinal Karol Wojtyla, who would succeed John Paul and take his name, was home in Kraków, Poland. Msgr. Stanislaw Dziwisz, his secretary, told him about the death a couple hours after Luciani's body was discovered. Though he responded to the report with surprising silence, the cardinal walked to his chapel and prostrated himself. Despite the shock, he maintained a normal schedule that day, but he seemed preoccupied throughout. Said Bishop Bronislaw Fidelus, "Everyone noticed he was much absorbed. It's hard to explain, but it was on his face."[40]

Cardinal Johannes Willebrands of the Netherlands bluntly reflected the thoughts of many: "It's a disaster," he said. "I cannot put into words how happy we were on that August day when we had chosen John Paul. We had such high hopes." And Denver's Archbishop James Casey understated the frustration that so many others felt: "When we woke up this morning, we were a little disappointed and annoyed with God."[41]

At least two cardinals—Franz König and Leo Suenens—speculated that the burdens of the office that Luciani himself admitted were on his "fragile shoulders" might have contributed to his premature death.[42] "The amount of work and the excitement may have been too much. It should serve as a warning against the physical and mental stress to which the Pope is exposed," Suenens asserted. He advocated greater delegation of authority to mitigate against the deleterious effects of papal burdens.[43]

Msgr. Mario Senigaglia, who had served devotedly for seven years as Luciani's personal secretary in Venice, supposedly echoed that sentiment. He allegedly speculated that the pope "broke down under a burden too great for his frail shoulders and from the weight of his immense loneliness."[44] Similarly, a cartoon appearing in *Le Monde*, a French publication, depicted John Paul I as crushed beneath the weight of St. Peter's dome.[45]

A few days prior to his death, the pope's personal doctor, Antonio Da Ros, had met with the pontiff at the Vatican and described his health as good. Nevertheless, the doctor expressed a note of concern: "But the stress of his new post was great. He perhaps was not prepared, accustomed to that responsibility. I told him he could not continue at that pace, and he replied he could not do anything about it."[46]

Washington's Cardinal William Baum asserted, "His death is a message from the Lord quite out of the ordinary . . . This was an intervention from the Lord to teach us something." What that "something" referred to was left unsaid.[47]

MOVING OUT

In the papal apartment, arrangements were being made for the remainder of the day.

Between eight and nine, the body was dressed anew by his secretaries and Msgr. Noe, the papal master of ceremonies, this time in the traditional papal vestments for lying in state. Dr. Buzzonetti was present as well.[48] The pope's few personal possessions were retrieved from the room. Magee handed Sr. Vincenza his eyeglasses and bed slippers. The nun later gave the glasses to Msgr. Francesco Taffarel, the pope's former secretary in Vittorio Veneto. (They are now on exhibit in the Luciani museum in Canale d'Agordo.)[49] His wallet, containing only a photo of his mother and one of his beloved role models, Leopoldo Mandic, was returned to the family. Once, Luciani had spoken simply to Lorenzi of his last will and testament: "I do not have anything; the books I leave to the seminary, my good example to the relatives."[50] Regarding the pope's will, the only information available at the time came from Lorenzi: "Certainly it exists. However, I don't know how long it is or what it says. But I remember the pope referred to it over lunch some fifteen days before he died."[51]

Later, a childlike prayer was found in his breviary; it implored God to take him gently from this earth. Further, he asked the Lord to be by his side as he slid into his final rest, adding that he would like Him to hold his hand like a mother does to her child when he is seriously ill.[52]

Then the time arrived for the deceased pope to be removed from the apartment that had been his home for just over a month, and all who were present departed so that, again in conformance with past practice, the residence could be sealed as ordered by Cardinal Villot, the camerlengo. It was stripped of Luciani's personal belongings and would remain vacant and inaccessible to anyone until a new pope was elected and ready to occupy it. Magee, Lorenzi, Sr. Vincenza, and the other nuns left to take up residence nearby.[53] Vatican flags were lowered to half-staff.[54]

PUBLIC MOURNING

Figure 15.1. Only hours after the pope was found dead, his body lies in state in Clementine Hall.

Only a few hours after the pope was found dead, his body was transferred to Clementine Hall to lie in state. The body lay on an inclined catafalque draped in silver velvet; a tall crucifix stood directly behind it. It was attired in an embroidered white ankle-length robe covered by a red chasuble. Around John Paul's neck was the shepherd's pallium that he had insisted replace the crown at his papal investiture. His head, adorned with a white bishop's miter, rested on two silver pillows, and a silver crozier lay parallel to the body on his left side. A rosary was entwined in the pontiff's clasped hands. Swiss guards in full regalia stood ramrod straight on either side of the bier, as rigid and motionless as the corpse in whose honor they remained on duty. On one flank was a *prix dieu* (a piece of furniture designed for kneeling), where visiting dignitaries, clerics, family, friends, and Vatican staff could pause and pray.

John Paul looked natural, as if he were sleeping peacefully, but seemingly not so deeply that he couldn't awake at the slightest murmur. His face had not the pallor of death, instead appearing perfectly natural like that of a robustly healthy man. His lips were slightly parted; death had robbed him and the world of his singular smile. Otherwise, he looked much the way he had appeared in life—with two exceptions: his striking eyes were closed; and without his ever-present glasses, his large, aquiline nose eclipsed his more flattering features.[55]

Shortly after John Paul's body was transferred to Clementine Hall, the doors were opened for the first visitors to pay their respects. People from the mighty to the ordinary began gathering to pay homage to the pope. The outpouring of grief from the public was astounding: a line of pilgrims stretched for a mile and a half waiting to view the body. A wooden barrier separating the mourners from the bier was breached by two disconsolate nuns, who kissed the pope's hands. Ushers in white tie approached them, pleading, "*Per favore, suore*!" (Please, sisters!)[56] Thousands filed by the body, many weeping openly.[57]

People of all ages and all walks of life, some dressed formally, others more casually, stood shoulder to shoulder, some mothers carrying babies. Mixed in among the laity were men of the cloth. Respectful silence filled the room. Men in black suits and ties kept the seemingly endless line moving. At one point, Lorenzi, in simple black cassock and white surplice, stood by the side of the bier.

In St. Peter's Square, queues of mourners proceeded along barricades in the drenched square, umbrellas protecting them against the rain. Some knelt in prayer.[58] At noon the bells of Rome's churches tolled in mourning, a stark reminder of the same bells that had rung joyously in unison at the announcement of John Paul's election just thirty-four days earlier. The giant bronze bells of St. Mark's tower in Venice also rang out at the announcement of the former patriarch's death.[59]

Around 7 p.m. the hall was closed to visitors so that the body could be embalmed.

The temporary preservation of the remains was deemed necessary because it would be on display for four days in Rome's autumn heat prior to the funeral Mass and interment. Dr. Mario Fontana summoned a four-member team of forensic doctors along with the embalmer, one of the two Signoracci brothers, who had performed the procedure for two previous popes. The process began just after 7 p.m. and lasted more than eight hours, an unusually long time.[60] Why the process was so time-consuming is a mystery because a typical embalming takes approximately two hours to complete.[61]

Besides retarding decay, an important purpose of embalming is to restore a lifelike appearance to the body. Regrettably, that was not accomplished successfully with the pope's remains. In fact, in this instance the temporary preservation resulted in a startlingly unpleasant transformation of the late pope's appearance. His entire face was bloated like that of a boxer who's endured endless pummeling. His features were distorted, and his complexion was discolored. His eyebrows were arched abnormally, seemingly pushed upward by bulging eyelids. The lips were tightly stitched together, his chin compressed and puffy. John Paul's appearance now bordered on the grotesque.

ACCOLADES

A period of national mourning was announced by the Italian government as a flood of condolences arrived at the Vatican from around the world.[62] The United Nations General Assembly observed a minute of silence, and the UN flag was lowered to half-staff. Diplomats, even including those from godless communist countries, issued statements of praise. Spain's King Carlos admitted, "On learning the news, I turned to stone." The primate of Ireland, Archbishop Tomas O'Fiaich, said of John Paul that he quite possibly could have been "one of the great popes of this century," a sentiment that Cardinal Sin shared.[63]

An airport employee strike was curtailed out of respect for the beloved pope, and the Latin American bishops' conference to be held in Mexico on October 12 was postponed.[64] It was as if the world, immobilized by grief, was shutting down. The mourners gathered in the Cortile (courtyard) of San Damaso crying together and lamented that they had lost a father figure, not just the leader of their church.[65] Bishop Maffeo Ducoli, the late pope's dear friend, reported, "People are crying in the streets and the shops as if someone in their family had died."[66]

A grim-faced Cardinal Baggio met with reporters in St. Peter's Square to express his astonishment and grief at the pope's passing. "I never saw such eagerness in people as in the persons who listened to him," he remarked in wonder.[67]

IN CANALE: SHOCK AND SORROW

In Canale d'Agordo, the pope's home village, the priest interrupted the morning Mass as soon as he received the news. "The pope's niece rushed into the church and told me she had just learned the sad news," announced Rev. Rinaldo Aldrich. The thirty people in attendance immediately wept in response.

The priest, tolling the church bells, caught the attention of the villagers among whom the news of the death quickly spread. Don Aldrich observed, "Many were shocked. They knew Albino Luciani, the pope, very well. Many were his friends." As the news traveled to surrounding villages, an increasing number of Catholics flocked to their churches. One of John Paul's cousins, Amalia Luciani, responded, "The great joy of his election has been suddenly faded by the unexpected death."[68]

ANOTHER FUNERAL AND ANOTHER CONCLAVE

All too soon, cardinals from around the globe once again descended on the Vatican for a pope's funeral and yet another conclave scheduled to begin on October 14.[69] This time they arrived to mourn the unexpected passing of a pope they had just elected and believed to be God's candidate. Incredulous, the cardinals paused at the body to pay their respects and to wonder why this had been God's will.[70] They couldn't imagine facing another funeral and another election so soon.[71] Nevertheless, the Congregation of Cardinals met on September 30 to plan the pope's funeral and prepare for the selection of a successor.[72] Newspapers even now were speculating on a possible replacement. Headlines such as "5 Are Mentioned for Papacy" and "With Pastoral Backgrounds Top Prospects for New Pope" appeared in the *Sarasota Herald-Tribune* and countless other periodicals.[73]

A HOARY PROPHECY AND RECENT FORESHADOWINGS

For those who put stock in such things, a twelfth-century monk named St. Malachy supposedly wrote a book known as *Prophecies on the Popes* in which he made pithy divinations about the subsequent 111 popes. Among them was John Paul I. His sobriquet for Luciani's pontificate was *De medietate Lunæ* (of the half of the moon); elected pope on August 26, John Paul's reign lasted about a month, from half a moon to the next half.[74] His reign of thirty-three days was the eleventh shortest in papal history.[75]

Whether John Paul knew that illness would soon claim him is not known with certainty. What is sure, however, is that the pope made repeated comments to various people about his own mortality and the swiftness of his pontificate. Lorenzi recalled that one evening at dinner back in Venice,

Luciani confided, "Sometimes I ask the Lord to take me with him."[76] Why? How ironic that the man with the smile, good cheer, and sweet and gentle disposition would have a death wish.

John Paul himself had a premonition that can't readily be dismissed because he shared it with Fr. John Magee, who remembered that the pope had told him he would be succeeded by "a foreigner" who had been seated right across from him during the conclave. Years later, while Magee was rummaging through a closet in the apostolic palace where he served John Paul's successor, he came across a seating chart of the conclave that elected Luciani. Seated across from him was Poland's Karol Wojtyla.[77]

NOTES

1. Gordon Thomas and Max Morgan-Witts, *Pontiff* (New York: New American Library, 1984), 311.
2. "The September Pope," *Time*, October 9, 1978, 58.
3. Thomas and Morgan-Witts, *Pontiff*, 311.
4. Thomas and Morgan-Witts, *Pontiff*, 311.
5. Thomas and Morgan-Witts, *Pontiff*, 311.
6. Paul Spackman, *God's Candidate: The Life and Times of Pope John Paul I* (Herefordshire: Gracewing, 2008), 223.
7. Stephania Falasca, *The September Pope: The Final Days of John Paul I* © 2017, PIEMME; 2020, Libreria Editrice Vaticana. English translation published by *Our Sunday Visitor*, 2021, 74.
8. "A Death in Rome," *Newsweek*, October 9, 1978, 7
9. Falasca, *September Pope*, 75.
10. Spackman, *God's Candidate*, 225.
11. "A Death in Rome," *Newsweek*, 74.
12. Fr. Victor Feltes, "Epilogue," The Pope John Paul I Papacy—Day by Day, August 6, 2014, https://johnpauli.wordpress.com/.
13. "Tears Flow in the Church of the Pope's Hometown," *Montreal Gazette*, September 30, 1978, 9.
14. Falasca, *September Pope*, 80.
15. Pia Luciani (niece of Pope John Paul I), in discussion with the author, Canale d'Agordo, Italy, July 12, 2011.
16. John Cornwell, *A Thief in the Night: Life and Death in the Vatican* (New York: Penguin, 1989), 302.
17. Peter Hebblethwaite, *The Year of Three Popes* (Cleveland, OH: Collins, 1979), 129.
18. Spackman, *God's Candidate*, 225.
19. Cornwell, *A Thief in the Night*, 220.
20. Falasca, *September Pope*, 78.

21. Spackman, *God's Candidate*, 225.
22. Cornwell, *A Thief in the Night*, 220.
23. Cornwell, *A Thief in the Night*, 346.
24. "A Death in Rome," *Newsweek*, 74.
25. "Vatican Medical Care Questioned," *Ottawa Citizen*, October 2, 1978, 12.
26. "Could Popes Have Lived Longer? Papal Health Care Debated," *Eugene Register-Guard*, October 1, 1978, 5A.
27. Cornwell, *A Thief in the Night*, 111, 220.
28. Falasca, *September Pope*, 81.
29. "A Death in Rome," *Newsweek*, 74.
30. Thomas and Morgan-Witts, *Pontiff*, 316.
31. Thomas and Morgan-Witts, *Pontiff*, 316.
32. Cornwell, *A Thief in the Night*, 203.
33. Falasca, *September Pope*, 84.
34. Dr. Lina Petri (niece of Pope John Paul I), in discussion with the author, Rome, July 6, 2011.
35. Spackman, *God's Candidate*, 227.
36. "The Death of Pope John Paul I," *L'Osservatore Romano*, October 5, 1978, 1.
37. Peter Hebblethwaite, *In the Vatican* (London: Sidgwick & Jackson, 1986), 183.
38. John A. Meyers, "A Letter from the Publisher," *Time*, October 9, 1978, 3.
39. "A Death in Rome," *Newsweek*, 74.
40. Jonathan Kivitny, *Man of the Century: The Life and Times of John Paul II* (New York: Henry Holt, 1997), 290.
41. "The September Pope," *Time*, October 9, 1978, 68.
42. "The September Pope," *Time*, 79.
43. "A Death in Rome," *Newsweek*, 74.
44. Carl Bernstein and Marco Politi, *His Holiness: John Paul II and the History of Our Time* (New York: Doubleday, 1996), 225.
45. Bernstein and Politi, *His Holiness*, 227.
46. "Catholics Bid Fond Farewell to Pope John Paul," *Lewiston Evening Journal*, October 4, 1978, 1.
47. David Yallop, *The Power and the Glory: Inside the Dark Heart of John Paul II's Vatican* (New York: Carroll & Graf, 2007).
48. Spackman, *God's Candidate*, 228.
49. Loris Serafini (director, Foundation Papa Luciani and Museum Albino Luciani of Canale d'Agordo), in discussion with the author, Canale d'Agordo, Italy, July 11, 2022.
50. Don Diego Lorenzi (personal secretary to Pope John Paul I), interview with Sandro Vigani, http://www.albino-luciani.com/index.php?id=65&1=4.
51. "Catholics Bid Fond Farewell to Pope John Paul."
52. Serafini, discussion.
53. Spackman, *God's Candidate*, 230.
54. David Yallop, *In God's Name: An Investigation into the Murder of Pope John Paul I* (New York: Penguin, 1984), 209.

55. Albino Luciani photograph, 84.JPG. Foundation Papa Luciani of Canale d'Agordo (Belluno-Italy).
56. "The September Pope," *Time*, 71.
57. "Mourning: Thousands View Pope's Body as Vatican Prepares Funeral," *Evening Independent*, September 20, 1978, 3A.
58. Feltes, Video: The Death and Funeral of Pope John Paul I, "Epilogue," The Pope John Paul I Papacy—Day by Day, September 29, 1978, https://johnpauli.wordpress.com/.
59. Feltes, "Epilogue," https://johnpauli.wordpress.com/.
60. Spackman, *God's Candidate*, 230–31.
61. "Frequently Asked Questions," Williams Funeral Homes, https://www.williamsfh.com/faqs-about-embalming).
62. Feltes, "Epilogue," https://johnpauli.wordpress.com/.
63. "World Shocked, Grieved at Death," *Deseret News*, September 29, 1978, 1.
64. "The September Pope," *Time*, 71.
65. Serafini, discussion.
66. "The September Pope," *Time*, 71.
67. "The Death and Funeral of Pope John Paul I," The Pope John Paul I Papacy—Day by Day, video, 7:59, https://johnpauli.wordpress.com/.
68. "Tears Flow in the Church of the Pope's Hometown," *Montreal Gazette*, September 30, 1978, 9.
69. "The September Pope," *Time*, 71.
70. "The September Pope," *Time*, 68.
71. "The September Pope," *Time*, 80.
72. Spackman, *God's Candidate*, 231.
73. "World Shocked, Grieved at Death," *Deseret News*, 1.
74. "The Prophecy of St. Malachy," *Our Catholic Faith*, https://ourcatholicfaith.org/prophecy-of-st-malachy/.
75. "The Shortest Papacies of all Time? Pope John Paul I Barely Makes the List," Catholic News Agency, https://www.catholicnewsagency.com/news/252309/the-shortest-papacies-of-all-time-pope-john-paul-i-barely-makes-the-list.
76. Anonymous discussion with the author.
77. John Magee (bishop emeritus, diocese of Cloyne, Ireland), in discussion with the author, Cobh, Ireland, February 17, 2010.

• *16* •

Murder Hysteria

Poison (September 29, 1978–Present)

"Who has done this to you?" shrieked distraught mourners who passed by the bier on which John Paul's body lay.[1] "Who has murdered you?"[2]

Suspicion was stirring about the official cause of the beloved pope's death. Virulent rumors that he had been assassinated spread within hours of the Vatican's public announcement of the pontiff's passing. Before long, skepticism swept the rest of the world.[3]

Vatican Secretary of State Cardinal Jean Villot's fabrication about the discovery of John Paul's body was largely to blame. As soon as fragments of facts emerged, the Church's credibility was seriously compromised. The hierarchy's lack of transparency created a perception that dark secrets lurked within the confines of Vatican City, and its ensuing silence enhanced the plausibility of unsubstantiated tales of homicide that, in turn, generated mass hysteria and bitterness toward the Vatican.

UNDERSTANDABLE INCREDULITY

Even if the Vatican had been honest about the events surrounding John Paul's death, the likelihood is that disbelief would have prevailed—at least temporarily. The popular pope's passing was too sudden and too traumatizing to be comprehensible. John Paul was only sixty-five years old. In his public appearance just the day before his death he had exuded vitality. He had been animated and joyful. He had laughed good-naturedly while delivering a stirring talk. He had looked and sounded like a healthy, cheerful man. Further, there had been no public disclosure or discussion about any preexisting physical ailment prior to or after his election. And now he was dead of a massive heart attack? The very notion that natural causes had snuffed out his life seemed preposterous. There had to be a more plausible explanation.

Compounding the credibility dilemma was the depth and breadth of the public's grief. John Paul was widely perceived as a man of almost mystical righteousness who radiated divine love. He provided a weary world with joy and hope, and his pontificate had held unlimited promise for the future. No act of God could possibly be responsible for terminating such a saintly life so soon, the widespread thinking went.

DELIRIUM

So other explanations seized the public imagination. Initially, conjecture—flimsy but uncomplicated—prevailed. But as time elapsed, ever more elaborate conspiracy hypotheses emerged, taking on lives of their own; and, eventually, in the minds of millions, the outrageous became credible. Ironically, all nefarious accounts of John Paul's demise were grounded in lapsed logic, reckless assumptions, and/or labyrinthine justifications virtually impossible to comprehend. Spinning increasingly complex narratives of assassination plots in the ensuing years became an obsession of the unenlightened and learned alike, often proving lucrative for writers publishing book-length fantasies appealing to the gullible masses.

This wave of irrationality had precedents.

In days of old, intrigue in the Vatican sometimes led to violence. Romans were susceptible to foul speculation about sudden deaths of popes, particularly those who had known or suspected enemies. "If this were the time of the Borgias, there'd be talk that John Paul was poisoned," a young Roman teacher asserted shortly following John Paul's death. That's exactly what ensued following the gentle pope's passing. The decade of the seventies was atypical of the era of the Borgia popes of the fifteenth and sixteenth centuries, but the climate was just as ripe for believing nonsense.[4]

ANTECEDENTS

Segments of the public have long been fascinated with stories focused on popes and poison. Chronicles of foul play accounting for the deaths of previous popes are plentiful (though often dubious). According to some, at least thirteen pontiffs were murdered between 258 and 1516, nine of whom were purportedly the victims of poisoning.[5] But those accounts have been disputed and some debunked. Two of the supposed victims of poisoning might have been murdered in other ways: Benedict VI by strangulation and John XIV by starvation. It is nearly certain that Celestine V, far from being the victim of murder, lived to become the first pope to abdicate.[6] Credible evidence indicates that John VIII was poisoned and, when that wasn't immediately efficacious, he was bludgeoned to death in 882.[7] However absorbing, the historical evidence supporting these assassinations, with few exceptions, is scanty and contradictory. But intrigue pleases the imagination, regardless of the times, and there are always those who choose to believe in events that are merely apocryphal. Such is the case with the death of John Paul I.

VATICAN SECURITY

The supposed murder of John Paul took place in a private residence that was difficult, if not impossible, to penetrate. The private apartment of the pope is located on the third floor of the fourteen-hundred-room Apostolic Palace, which was well protected.[8] According to don Diego Lorenzi, the private apartment has few points of entry, and they are guarded around the clock.[9] Hans Rogen, a sergeant of the Swiss Guards, corroborated Lorenzi's report that no one could gain access to the papal apartment because of the seamless security at the door.[10] Pia Luciani, who visited her uncle at the Vatican, wrote, "the papal apartment is very difficult to get access to, completely isolated from the large salons on the lower floors; even the elevator only functioned with a special key that very few people possessed!"[11]

"Security is an ongoing concern of Vatican authorities," according to Fr. Michael Collins, an authority of the Vatican.[12] "Those who visit the Vatican on official business are subject to stringent security measures."[13]

Apparently, the Swiss Guards and the Vatican's 130-member Central Security Corps provide multilayered protection at the entrances.[14] The Swiss Guards, best known for their distinctive regalia, perform more than ceremonial duties. They also assist in protecting the pope. Members are required to serve in military school and undergo rigorous physical as well as combat training.[15] The guards are, therefore, competent to defend the pope in any circumstances; they secure entrances to Vatican City as well as all those of the Apostolic Palace.[16] In addition, they patrol the building's corridors, scrutinize lists of those authorized to enter the palace, and alert the guard at the next station by phone of anyone about to arrive at his station.[17]

Augmenting those legendary soldiers are members of a civilian police force, the Security Corps, informally known as the gendarme corps.[18] They, too, are trained to protect the pontiff's life. Responsible for all aspects of internal Vatican security, these armed officers also protect all entrances.[19]

Because there was no evidence of forced entry, and no guard was killed or injured the night of September 28 in a supposed breach of the premises, the pope's murder by an outsider would have necessitated the complicity of at least one of the security employees who permitted the assassin access to the apartment. Not a shred of evidence supports such a notion.

The papal apartment was occupied by only six people other than the pope. The four nuns and two priests who lived in those quarters had no credible motive to kill the pope. If the culprit was an intruder, at least one of the inhabitants almost inevitably would have become aware of his presence, and the pope likely would have sounded an alarm when confronted with an invader in his room. Assuming that the pope died around eleven that night, the assassin would have had to enter the premises in advance, a time when all in the apartment were still awake and about. Not one of these people saw or heard such a prowler, and not a scintilla of evidence exists that one had somehow breached the confines of the papal residence.

A CAUSE OF SUSPICION: MISINFORMATION

Besides the lie that Magee had discovered the body, other fabrications were disseminated. Vatican radio announced that the pope had been reading the *Imitation of Christ* when death struck, a falsehood that was later amended by reporting that he had been perusing some of his old sermons instead. The most detrimental disclosure to the Vatican's credibility, however, was the admission that Sr. Vincenza, not Magee, had discovered the body.

The independent media also inadvertently disseminated incorrect information, the sources of which are difficult, if not impossible, to trace. ANSA, the leading news service in Italy, reported an inaccurate time line in reconstructing the chronology of events related to the death. It announced that the body had been discovered at 4:30 a.m., an hour earlier than it occurred. Without adequate substantiation, it also disclosed that at the time the pope died, he was holding a list of personnel changes that he intended to make.[20] The morticians, Ernesto and Renato Signoracci, allegedly were summoned to the Vatican at 5 a.m.—before the actual discovery of the body. Oddly, the Vatican did not repudiate these erroneous details.[21] Later, in 1983, the morticians reportedly estimated the time of death as 4 a.m. on the 29th rather than 11 p.m. on the 28th as established by the physician who examined the body.[22]

ANOTHER CAUSE OF SUSPICION: GOSSIP

If those reports didn't create enough confusion, word-of-mouth rumors of unknown origin spread like an epidemic. Examples are abundant and easily refutable:

It was alleged that John Paul's personal belongings, including his eyeglasses, slippers, and will went missing. In fact, all the personal items in the pope's room (and there were only a few) were given to the family.[23]

The morticians did not follow the usual procedures of draining blood.[24] The embalmers were experienced professionals who had prepared the bodies of Popes Pius XII, John XXIII, and Paul VI for viewing.[25]

Contrary to the assertion that the death certificate was withheld from the public,[26] in reality it was completed, signed, filed, and subsequently made public.[27]

There was more:

Allegedly, Villot had ordered a swift sweep of the papal bedroom including the removal of Luciani's last reading material. True enough, the pope's personal belongings were removed fairly quickly, but this was in keeping with the standard procedure of vacating the premises and sealing the apartment without delay. All those who were present at the time, including the individuals who lived in the apartment, were ushered out with dispatch as was customary.[28] Magee stated that "when a pope dies, the secretary dies with him." He explained that he is unceremoniously evacuated from the papal apartment and left to find new housing on his own.[29]

Some claimed that the pope had suffered no health problems. However, as his medical records and the testimony of his closest relatives make clear, the pope did suffer from maladies. His swollen legs and ankles were indisputable evidence.[30] John Cornwell, an author who was commissioned by the Vatican to investigate the circumstances of John Paul's death, corroborated this particular ailment in an interview: "He had an apparent circulation problem in his ankles."[31] His evening dash to answer the phone could have caused death by heart failure if the pope was afflicted by pulmonary edema, one of the symptoms of which is the swelling of legs and feet.[32]

THE POSTMORTEM ERROR

Performing an autopsy on John Paul's remains could have curbed, if not altogether silenced, the deafening buzz of murder stories. No postmortem had been permitted, though failure to do so caused consternation even among some cardinals.[33] The failure to perform a postmortem was a blunder of disastrous dimensions. *Corriere della Sera*, a respected Italian newspaper, questioned why no autopsy was permitted; "we cannot understand why an autopsy was not performed, especially since the Vatican constitution does not explicitly forbid this."[34] A comprehensive autopsy, especially one conducted prior to embalming, would have validated beyond any reasonable doubt the cause of death and halted, or at least minimized, the epidemic of conspiracy theories. Even after chemically preserving a body, it is still possible to detect poisoning, though arguments could have been made that the results would not be conclusive.[35]

The lack of a postmortem, however, in itself does not lend legitimacy to the allegation that one was avoided deliberately to cover up murder by poisoning or any other means. Autopsies on popes are generally frowned upon by Vatican authorities. Dissection of a pope's body, necessarily entailing the removal and segmentation of internal organs, is viewed as undignified. Given the Vatican's predilection for not breaking with tradition, that a postmortem was not conducted in this case, while ill-advised, should not have been surprising.

COMMON CONSPIRACY CHARACTERISTICS

All the murder "theories" had three fundamental characteristics in common: they weren't built on foundations of firm facts, poisoning was the consensus murder method, and the culprit was someone within the Vatican bureaucracy.

Misinformation, outright lies, half-truths, suppositions, and incongruities all combined to create an inclination to believe the unbelievable. And for those who became convinced that John Paul had been slain, three fundamental questions demanded answers. Who was the culprit? What was the motivation for the murder? How had the evil deed been carried out? No shortage of answers swirled about, though not one was credible.

An Inside Job

Murder advocates believe that the killer was either someone within the Vatican who opposed or feared what John Paul might do to the institution or its key personnel or an insider acting on behalf of a rogue organization.

Prime Suspects: Magee

The first individual suspected of killing the pope was Fr. John Magee. By virtue of his ready access to the Holy Father, the reasoning went, he could have poisoned John Paul's drink or substituted a lethal pill in place of the pope's prescribed medication. And because he was the person who found the body, it was evident that he had private access to the papal bedchamber. Left unanswered is what motive Magee could have had for wanting the pope dead. The pressure he felt as a result turned to outright panic, causing him to execute a decision that only made his "guilt" seem more credible.

"I had to leave after the funeral of Pope John Paul I. I had to leave because Italian television, one particular person in Vatican service, pointed me out as the assassin of John Paul I," Magee explained. "Archbishop Marcinkus, who was a most wonderful person . . . helped me enormously, and he got me to the airport, and I flew out from Italy and I went to stay with my sister in England. The following morning when my sister came in with a cup of tea for me in my bedroom, she had the *Liverpool Echo*, and the headlines, 'Investigation of the Death of John Paul I. The Private Secretary Is Missing.' And there was a photograph of me in the paper, and they said Interpol (the international criminal police organization) are now searching."[36]

Escaping the Vatican in haste to an undisclosed destination where Magee remained incommunicado was a rash decision that only intensified belief in his culpability. His "friend" Archbishop Marcinkus had not helped but compounded Magee's problems. Ironically, the banker himself subsequently became a suspect. Quite contrary to Magee's characterization of him, Marcinkus was hardly "a most wonderful person." If anything, associating with the widely reviled Vatican boss could have intensified suspicions about the papal secretary.

Prime Suspect: Marcinkus

Paul Marcinkus became a marked man for a couple of reasons. First, he was a powerful figure as head of the Vatican Bank, formally known as the Institute for Religious Works, and his close connection with unsavory characters was no secret. A haughty, autocratic administrator, Marcinkus was a man not to cross. Known in some Vatican circles as "the gorilla," presumably not only because of his imposing six-foot-four muscular physique and intimidating disposition, he wielded power with a cudgel.[37] His business associates included such villainous characters as Roberto Calvi, who was at the center of scandals at Banco (bank) Ambrosiano and later suspiciously found hanging from a London bridge. Another "acquaintance" was Michele Sindona, also an Italian banker, swindler, and convicted felon.[38]

Further, rumor had it that in a meeting with patriarch Luciani years earlier, he had treated the cardinal disrespectfully, and now he feared that the pope was about to fire him because of the scandal-ridden institution he headed.[39]

Marcinkus was indicted in Italy in 1982 as an accessory in the $3.5 billion collapse of Banco Ambrosiano, an Italian financial institution that had dealings with the Vatican Bank and allegedly laundered money for the Mafia. Marcinkus escaped arrest because of an Italian court decision that exempted Vatican personnel from prosecution. Nevertheless, the Vatican confessed to "moral involvement" in the fiasco and remunerated Ambrosiano's creditors a total of $241 million while denying any culpability in the bank's failure. In addition, the U.S. Department of State issued a statement that alleged the Vatican Bank was complicit in the money-laundering scheme. American investigators were stymied in their pursuit of justice because Marcinkus, though a native of Chicago, enjoyed diplomatic immunity as an official of the Vatican City State.[40]

More Potential Assassins

Over time additional suspects emerged. They included the U.S. Central Intelligence Agency, the Mafia, and a shadowy group known as the Freemasons,[41] among others. Some conservative publications charged that certain elite Vatican leaders were covertly Freemasons, supposedly including Cardinal Baggio, Archbishop Marcinkus, and Cardinal Villot.[42] But no credible evidence appeared of a connection between any of these figures and that group.

Motives

In the muddled collective consciousness, no paucity of reasons existed for wanting John Paul's life extinguished. For those who were inclined to believe in a Vatican cabal, there was a treasure trove of motives. The old guard in the Vatican, an institution where traditions are inviolable, feared that this pope was about to make drastic changes in personnel and policy. Those plans included not only firing Marcinkus, but also Secretary of State Villot (whom the pope had just reappointed); reversing Pope Paul's encyclical banning artificial contraception; eliminating priestly celibacy; allowing ordination of women; pursuing ecumenism without restraints; divesting the church of its wealth; and opening Vatican operations to public scrutiny. Such intolerable plans justified taking drastic action, including murder, to protect Holy Mother Church, some suspected.

And that wasn't all. It was commonly thought in the inner sanctums of the Vatican that John Paul was unfit to be pope. Some in the curia believed that he was an embarrassment to the Church with his foolish references to Pinocchio, his homely anecdotes at general audiences, his reference to God being more of a mother than a father. They perceived him as a weak man incapable of administering the Church, an incompetent executive, ignorant of the Vatican's governing bodies, unable to cope with the pressures of the office, and incapable of making decisions. He had in moments of unguarded self-evaluation admitted that he was not qualified for the job. An Australian reporter described him as "an extremely anxious, nervous little man."[43]

Murder Methods

The author of a popular novel who claimed that all the facts in his story were true made an outrageous assertion in an interview appended to the book: He had personally spoken with the pope's murderer, who explained how he had committed the evil deed: suffocation with a pillow. Armed with this knowledge and capable of bringing the killer to justice, the novelist neither revealed the murderer's identity nor, presumably, did he report his implied ironclad incriminating information to the police.[44]

Smothering the pope was not the most popular explanation for how he was killed though. Poison was, as previously noted. According to subscribers of this fantasy, the killing could have been carried out effortlessly by someone within the household or well-known Vatican officials whose presence in the papal apartment would not have aroused suspicion. Dinner guests could have slipped lethal substances into the pope's coffee. Besides, the popular notion was that the papal quarters were porous, easily accessible to anyone who knew the layout. What could be easier?

Film, Theater, Television, and Music

Newspaper and magazine articles trumpeting the case for conspiracy surely impacted public opinion. But other forms of media also sensationalized the pope's death. In the film *The Godfather Part III*, which premiered in 1990, a cardinal named Lamberto who hears the confession of Mafia boss Michael Corleone becomes Pope John Paul I and reigns briefly before dying in bed after drinking tea poisoned by members of the Vatican administration. Author Brian Meltzer conducted a television "investigation" of the pope's death in 2011 as part of a series on the History channel known as *Decoded*. He and his investigators tantalized their viewers by delving into the major conspiracy theories without solving the mystery of the pope's death but implying that foul play could very well have accounted for the fatality. The theater in London had its opportunity to showcase a play that focused on John Paul's death and Vatican scheming. Roger Crane's *The Last Confession*, starring English actor Sir David Suchet and billed as a conspiracy thriller by Bondo Wyszpolski of the *Orange County Register*, enjoyed positive reviews and a decent run in 2014. It was later performed in Australia. Even the British post-Punk band known as The Fall performed a song titled "Hey, Luciani" in 1986 that blamed the Curia for the pope's murder.[45]

Books

Full-scale, detailed descriptions of assassination schemes in books proliferated. Some were authored by reputable writers; others by well-intentioned amateurs determined to discover, through their own slapdash research, what took place. Still others were self-published sensationalists who spun tall tales in clumsy prose with fundamental premises that were utterly absurd. Nonetheless, some of these volumes became popular.

To date, at least thirteen conspiracy books have been written in English, the latest one published in 2024. That, of course, is exclusive of those printed in a host of other languages. The world continues to be saturated with conspiracy theories about John Paul's death nearly half a century later.

The "Plausible" Plot: David Yallop

The most famous and popular of all the murder conspiracy books, *In God's Name: An Investigation into the Murder of Pope John Paul I*, sold more than six million copies. It was written by David Yallop, a noted British author.[46] Years later, he published another volume, *The Power and the Glory: Inside the Dark Heart of John Paul II's Vatican*, in which he elaborated on the alleged murder of the first John Paul. In compiling his "evidence" for his initial book, Yallop used a researcher to do much of the investigative work. The author refused to reveal the identities of the individuals who provided him with information because he claimed that doing so would put them in danger. While reassuring the reader that all the book's details had been substantiated, his sources remained anonymous. Beyond that, the book contains no footnotes and no bibliography. Further, the pope's niece Dr. Lina Petri, a woman of impeccable integrity, insisted that her remarks had been distorted in the book.[47] Hans Roggen, a Swiss Guard, told a writer that he also had been misquoted.[48] In light of this, skepticism about the reliability of the information contained in the volume, particularly in reference to the murder theory, is justifiable. Some of the biographical information about the pope, however, is accurate, having been confirmed by independent researchers.

Yallop subscribed to poisoning as the most likely means of murder, citing digitalis, a drug to treat heart conditions, as a toxin that could have caused the pope's death.[49] In a videotaped interview, Yallop reiterated his belief that the pope was murdered but was tentative in his assertion and provided no hard evidence. "I believe the pope was poisoned. He was taking only one medication at that time for low blood pressure. I believe the medicine was tampered with. Probably, and *this is a hypothesis* [author's emphasis], that is sustainable and circumstantial evidence by Digitalis."[50]

He also claimed that some cardinals suspected a cover-up of a crime, though no irrefutable evidence supports it. The author implausibly interpreted comments that the cardinals made in response to the pope's unexpected death as reactions to a murder plot. Thus, a remark by Cardinal Gantin following the death, "We are groping in the dark." And Cardinal Benelli, who said, "We are left frightened."[51] These quotes, taken out of context, are hardly indicators of foul play.

According to Yallop's second book, Luciani, at his own instigation, received a report detailing the results of an investigation into Vatican finances. This information was damning and precipitated his decision to undertake substantial bureaucratic reforms. Late on the afternoon of September 28, John Paul informed Secretary of State Jean Villot of his plans. Villot and others who stood to lose power, therefore, had the motive and the means to be the slayers.[52] To eliminate incriminating evidence, Villot supposedly removed John Paul's medicine and the notes that he was holding that detailed the personnel changes he was about to implement.

Other details seem as fictitious as plots in a Dan Brown novel. One was that Luciani had in his possession a list containing the names of 121 alleged Freemasons who had been banned from the Vatican, many of whom were currently in Vatican service. On September 28, John Paul shared with Villot his intention to rectify this situation as well as to make wholesale changes in the scandal-plagued Vatican Bank. Among these restructurings was exiling Marcinkus and dismissing his criminal associates who were senior executives at the bank.[53]

In evaluating the legitimacy of any conspiracy theories, it is imperative to adopt the most stringent test of validity, the preponderance of evidence standard. Vincent Bugliosi, the famed prosecutor and author of *Reclaiming History*, the book that destroyed the credibility of all JFK assassination conspiracy theories, employed that test. Because the "theories" of the pope's assassination do not meet that standard, they should be dismissed as little more than speculation.

The Vatican Responds at Long Last

Its credibility endlessly undermined by conspiracy theories, the Vatican belatedly determined that the proliferating rumors must be discredited. But the institution that is famous for proceeding with the swiftness of a snail didn't take bold action to dispel the allegations until 1987, nearly ten years after John Paul was laid to rest. Long before then, various conspiracy allegations had firmly taken hold.

The means of extinguishing the falsehoods, a high-ranking Vatican prelate decided, was to commission an award-winning journalist who had written extensively about Catholicism to investigate the plethora of conspiracy theories in a book that would explain factually and rationally what had transpired. The author's name was John Cornwell, a respected writer who had studied for the priesthood. American Archbishop John Foley, president of the Vatican's Commission for Social Communications, convinced him to undertake the project.[54] In a genuine attempt to exculpate the Church by revealing the truth, Foley imposed no restrictions on Cornwell's research, though the author encountered considerable stonewalling on the part of Church officials. Through sheer persistence he succeeded in interviewing key figures associated with the drama of John Paul's death. Ultimately, he published a book on his findings titled *A Thief in the Night: Life and Death in the Vatican*. It did not lead to the conclusion that Foley had hoped for.

Cornwell Contradicts Murder Fantasies

Cornwell's book is indispensable to understanding the circumstances surrounding John Paul's death. Not only did he uncover information that contradicted popular notions about John Paul's demise, but he also revealed portions of interviews with Vatican authorities that provide an insider's vantage point into how the institution functions. His depiction is not flattering. Cornwell encountered resistance from formidable figures who refused to discuss aspects of the pope's death with which they were familiar. He found this deeply disturbing. Among the Vatican figures that Cornwell questioned in depth were Dr. Buzzonetti; Fr. Francesco Farusi of Vatican Radio; Lorenzi; Magee; Marcinkus; the director of the Vatican Press Office, Dr. Joaquin Navarro-Valls; and Hans Roggen. In addition, he interviewed Dr. Lina Petri, the Signoracci brothers, and the most celebrated conspiracy theorist of all, David Yallop.

Marcinkus told Cornwell that he had had a cordial relationship with the pope, despite rampant rumors to the contrary. "I went to see John Paul a few days before he died, and he was very kind, very fatherly; he thanked me for all the work I'd been doing and said he hoped I would stay on."[55] Fr. Farusi claimed otherwise, telling Cornwell that, as patriarch, Luciani had met with Marcinkus in Rome over the planned takeover of the Catholic Bank of the Veneto by the Banco Ambrosiano. He had wanted to stop it but was rebuked by Marcinkus, who told Luciani "quite crudely that the patriarch of Venice should be concerned with his people and not with banking." Despite Marcinkus's denial of the incident, Farusi claimed that everybody at the Vatican was saying that after Luciani's election, "Marcinkus changed completely. He was depressed and desperate."[56]

Marcinkus's own criticism of John Paul was couched in sly sympathy. "This poor man . . . all of a sudden, he's thrown into a place, and he doesn't even know where the offices are. He doesn't know what the secretary of state does." Then came the clincher, "They called him the 'smiling Pope.' But let me tell you something . . . that was a very nervous smile."[57] Marcinkus alluded to the pope's ill health and denied any truth to the widespread rumors that John Paul was about to fire him. He was not alone in belittling the pope. An unnamed monsignor with inside information about the operations of the Vatican was cruel in his assessment of John Paul. "[H]e was out of his depth. Everybody here knew it . . . Hopeless . . . he was at his wit's end . . . He just couldn't cope." As if that weren't enough, the monsignor added a personal denigration. "He was ungainly. He used to waddle along, flat-footed, like a duck."[58] Before disparaging the pope, the anonymous monsignor might have considered the possibility that any man with swollen ankles with his feet crammed into red slippers without heels would have been hard-pressed to walk more gracefully.

Cornwell maintained, as did others, that Luciani didn't function well as pope because of ill health, lack of experience, and an overwrought disposition. The author claimed that the pope was overwhelmed by the amount of work required of him and the endless decisions he had to make. To make matters worse, he had little assistance. Don Diego Lorenzi was absent much of the time. Cornwell suspected that Lorenzi and Magee were at odds. Of greatest concern, Cornwell insinuated that the secretaries neglected the pope's health—mental, emotional, and physical. "John Paul was suffering from blinding headaches, loneliness, and claustrophobia," he contended.[59]

The author suspected that the cause of death was a coronary embolism. John Paul "required rest and monitored medication . . . The warnings of a mortal illness were clear for all to see; the signs were ignored."[60] He never even had the benefit of having been examined by a Vatican doctor.[61]

Cornwell's conclusion made irrelevant the claims of murder but indicted the Vatican: "The whisperings, the rumors, the theories—far-fetched, sensational, fantastic—all serve a purpose: they deflect attention from the most obvious and shameful fact of all: that John Paul I died scorned and neglected by the institution that existed to sustain him."[62]

The reluctance of some Vatican personnel to talk candidly to Cornwell was not an isolated incident. Even Diego Lorenzi lived in a virtual "cone of silence" regarding his service with the pope.[63] "When his memory was still fresh, I have talked and written a few things about Pope John Paul I. Then I closed in silence: a silence not rude; I just said enough. I preferred to live again in my memory the time spent at his side, trying to put into practice the example of his life," Lorenzi rationalized.[64]

CONCLUSIVE MEDICAL SCIENCE

Health History

It wasn't until the 2017 publication of a book by Stefania Falasca that murder conspiracy fantasies were finally refuted with comprehensive medical evidence. Falasca, a prolific journalist who serves as vice postulator of the pope's cause for canonization as well as vice president of the John Paul I Vatican Foundation, was in a position to know the relevant facts. Her book provides a detailed record of the pope's medical history going back to his childhood and includes a fully documented account of his state of health as pope that confirms a death by natural causes. In addition, it reproduces medical documents written and signed by physicians.

Serious and Related?

Following Albino Luciani's trip to Brazil in 1975, he was hospitalized in Mestre for a retinal thrombosis, a blood clot in the eye that affected his vision and indicated circulation and coagulation issues.[65] The incident likely resulted from his flight when he was confined to his seat for nearly the entire duration of the fifteen-hour trip. Luciani recovered, but he was cognizant of the gravity of his affliction. In a letter he sent to his sister Nina, he divulged that "the doctor told me that if this thing I had in my eye had ever reached my heart, I could have died."[66] He suffered from extreme swelling of his legs and feet, making it painful to wear shoes. "This is a sign of venous stasis, that the blood isn't circulating in the veins, and it's probable that clots have formed in the arteries," explained Dr. Lina Petri, the pope's niece. Dr. Petri also shared that her uncle had been treated with anticoagulant medication.[67] She added that he also ingested "mild cardiotonics and multivitamins."[68] (Cardiotonics lead to improved blood flow through an improvement of the heart muscle's contractions.)[69]

CAUSE OF DEATH

Dr. Buzzonetti's professional assessment that the pope died of a massive heart attack was corroborated by Dr. Giovanni Rama, who had treated the pope's retinal thrombosis.[70] He observed, "Pope Luciani tended to be hypotensive . . . thrombotic events ran in his family. The most likely scenario is that he had a cardiac thrombosis or a cerebral thrombosis . . . He died from the same circulatory disorder that affected the retina of his eye . . . This time it was his heart or his brain that was affected."[71] Additional validation was provided by Rev. Silvio De Nard's father, who had been told by the pope's brother Berto that in a two-year period, five cousins had died of the identical cause.[72] Berto elaborated on this in a taped interview. Dismissing foul play in his brother's death, he asserted, "For me all these rumors are false. It is the journalists who are trying to make themselves interesting, creating a controversy. Especially all the fuss about that English writer." (He was referring to David Yallop, the most prominent advocate of an assassination scenario.) Then he divulged the Luciani clan's susceptibility to sudden fatal heart attacks. "It runs in the family. There have been several sudden deaths. The idea of our family being predisposed to this is the most solid one [explanation] to me."[73]

Dr. Mario Dina, who chaired the department of pathological anatomy at Catholic University, wrote that the pope's abrupt death "was typical of cases where an embolus completely occludes the pulmonary artery . . . the pope had swollen feet and legs in the days before his death (perhaps due to a phlebothrombosis in the lower limbs) from which the embolus that would have obstructed the pulmonary artery could have started."[74] This conclusion is supported by Dr. Petri, who said in an interview, "The manner of his death is more consistent with an embolism . . . One is not aware of death with a pulmonary embolism; it's a question of a fraction of a second."[75]

The late Dr. Sherwin B. Nuland, a distinguished surgeon and professor at Yale Medical School, wrote about heart disease and its manifestations in his book *How We Die.* Some of his general observations support Dr. Buzzonetti's conclusion regarding the pope's cause of death. Some 80–90 percent of sudden deaths are attributable to heart disease, he reported.[76] The onset of an attack "can happen so rapidly that only minutes pass before the moment of death."[77] "Often there is no warning of the imminence of death from this cause."[78] He estimated that in about 20 percent of victims of myocardial infarction, the patient feels no pain.[79]

Further, members of the Luciani family—without exception—did not dispute the official cause of death and gave no credence to the possibility of murder. Proclaimed Pia Luciani, "it is our conviction, my family's and mine, in fact, for us it has always been clear, that it was a natural death."[80] Dr. Da Ros, who was surprised to learn of John Paul's death, agreed with Dr. Buzzonetti's conclusion when he viewed the body at the Vatican on September 29.[81]

Autopsy

Only an autopsy could have identified the cause of death with virtual certainty. But even to a layperson, the medical evidence, in condensed form, is corroboration that natural causes claimed the pope's life. For any reasonable and objective person, the preponderance of medical evidence leads to the conclusion that John Paul I died of either a heart attack or an embolism. But reason does not always prevail. It has not in this case, and that is not unusual. In many high-profile cases, especially when the deaths are of beloved and admired public figures, no amount of evidence can eradicate public doubt about the truth. The most striking example in modern times is the 1963 assassination of President John Kennedy. As of 2023, a full sixty years following that dreadful event, 65 percent of Americans remained convinced that his death was the result of a conspiracy.[82]

Pope John Paul I has long been laid to rest, but the falsehoods about his death live on. The tragedy is that these deceptions about his death have for far too many eclipsed the legacy of his life.

NOTES

1. Paul Spackman, *God's Candidate: The Life and Times of Pope John Paul I* (Herefordshire: Gracewing, 2008), 235.
2. David Yallop, *In God's Name: An Investigation into the Murder of Pope John Paul I* (New York: Penguin, 1984), 211.
3. John Cornwell, *A Thief in the Night: Life and Death in the Vatican* (New York: Penguin, 1989), 16.
4. "The September Pope," *Time*, October 9, 1978, 79.
5. Cornwell, *A Thief in the Night*, 47.
6. Jon M. Sweeney, *The Pope Who Quit: A True Medieval Tale of Mystery, Death, and Salvation* (New York: Image Books, 2012), 209.
7. Christopher Klein, "10 Grisly Papal Deaths," May 5, 2023, https://www.history.com/news/10-grisly-papal-deaths.
8. "Apostolic Palace Vatican City: Where Does the Pope Live?" https://visitvatican.info/apostolic-palace.
9. Cornwell, *A Thief in the Night*, 107.
10. Cornwell, *A Thief in the Night*, 261.
11. Pia Luciani, "And It Is Our Conviction It Was a Natural Death," *Humilitas* 24, March 2013, 18.
12. Fr. Michael Collins, *The Vatican: Secrets and Treasures of the Holy City* (New York: Dorling Kindersley, 2008), 258.
13. Collins, *The Vatican*, 172.
14. Collins, *The Vatican*, 173.
15. Collins, *The Vatican*, 256.
16. Collins, *The Vatican*, 173.
17. Collins, *The Vatican*, 258–59.
18. Collins, *The Vatican*, 173.

19. "Car Rushes Vatican Gate, Is Fired on by Gendarmes; Driver Apprehended after Reaching Courtyard," May 18, 2023, https://apnews.com/article/vatican-gendarmes-swiss-guard-gate-ef111c2f461fa7d9094dbf4b5ca63077.
20. Cornwell, *A Thief in the Night*, 18.
21. Cornwell, *A Thief in the Night*, 19.
22. Cornwell, *A Thief in the Night*, 22.
23. Cornwell, *A Thief in the Night*, 190.
24. Yallop, *In God's Name*, 214.
25. Marta Falconi, "Body of Pope John Paul II Not Embalmed," April 6, 2005, https://www.starnewsonline.com/story/news/2005/04/06/body-of-pope-john-paul-ii-not-embalmed/30778158007/.
26. Cornwell, *A Thief in the Night*, 23.
27. Cornwell, *A Thief in the Night*, 346.
28. Spackman, *God's Candidate*, 230.
29. John Magee (personal secretary to John Paul I), in discussion with the author, Cobh, Ireland, February 17, 2010.
30. "Pulmonary Edema," Mayo Clinic, https://www.mayoclinic.org/diseases-conditions/pulmonary-edema/symptoms-causes/syc-20377009.
31. "The Last Day of John Paul I," youtube.com/watch?v=oWf5wOedS7w. 13.20 minutes. September 19, 2024.
32. Piergiuseppe Agostoni, MD, PhD, Gaia Cattadori, MD, Michele Bianchi, MD, and Karlman Wasserman, MD, PhD, "Exercise-Induced Pulmonary Edema in Heart Failure," https://www.ahajournals.org/doi/10.1161/01.CIR.0000097115.61309.59.
33. Yallop, *In God's Name*, 216.
34. Gordon Thomas and Max Morgan Witts, *Pontiff* (New York: New American Library, 1984), 340.
35. How Embalming Fluid Can Impact an Autopsy, Direct Cremate, © 2024 Direct Cremate—No Nonsense Cremation™, https://www.directcremate.com/how-embalming-fluid-can-impact-an autopsy/#:~:text=Poisons%20Are%20Harder%20to%20Detect,some%20types%20of%20poisoning%20difficult.
36. Magee, discussion.
37. Cornwell, *A Thief in the Night*, 84.
38. Wolfgang Saxon, "Michele Sindona, Jailed Italian Financier, Dies of Cyanide Poisoning at 65; At the Center of Scandals," *New York Times*, March 23, 1986, 44.
39. Spackman, *God's Candidate*, 79.
40. "Obituary: Archbishop Paul Marcinkus," February 21, 2006, http://news.bbc.co.uk/2/hi/europe/4737372.stm.
41. Michelle La Rosa, "Was Pope John Paul I Murdered?" *The Pillar*, October 15, 2021, https://www.pillarcatholic.com/p/was-pope-john-paul-i-murdered.
42. Cornwell, *A Thief in the Night*, 17.
43. Sandra Miesel, "A Quiet Death in Rome: Was Pope John Paul I Murdered?" *Crisis Magazine*, April 1, 2009, 3.
44. Luis Miguel Rocha, *The Last Pope* (New York: Penguin, 2006), 416.
45. "The Annotated Fall," http://annotatedfall.doomby.com/pages/the-annotated-lyrics/hey-luciani.html.

46. Yallop, *In God's Name*, xiii.
47. Lina Petri (niece of Pope John Paul I), in discussion with the author.
48. Miesel, "A Quiet Death in Rome," 6.
49. Yallop, *In God's Name*, 203–4.
50. "The Last Day of John Paul I."
51. David Yallop, *The Power and the Glory: Inside the Dark Heart of John Paul II's Vatican* (New York: Carroll & Graf, 2007), 4.
52. Yallop, *The Power*, 3.
53. Yallop, *The Power*, 54.
54. Yallop, *The Power*, 33.
55. Cornwell, *A Thief in the Night*, 23.
56. Cornwell, *A Thief in the Night*, 74.
57. Cornwell, *A Thief in the Night*, 208.
58. Cornwell, *A Thief in the Night*, 95.
59. Cornwell, *A Thief in the Night*, 330.
60. Cornwell, *A Thief in the Night*, 331.
61. Cornwell, *A Thief in the Night*, 332.
62. Cornwell, *A Thief in the Night*, 336.
63. Sandro Vigani, "Interview with Don Diego Lorenzi," http://www.albino-luciani.com/index.php?id=65&1=4.
64. Vigani, "Interview with Don Diego Lorenzi," 6.
65. Cornwell, *A Thief in the Night*, 304.
66. Falasca, *September Pope*, 225.
67. Cornwell, *A Thief in the Night*, 304–5.
68. Falasca, *September Pope*, 96.
69. "Cardiotonic Agent," ScienceDirect, https://www.sciencedirect.com/topics/chemistry/cardiotonic-agent.
70. Cornwell, *A Thief in the Night*, 306.
71. Falasca, *September Pope*, 106.
72. Silvio De Nard (pastor, Sacred Heart Church, East Providence, Rhode Island), in discussion with the author, East Providence, May 14, 2011.
73. "The Last Day of John Paul I."
74. Falasca, *September Pope*, 106.
75. Cornwell, *A Thief in the Night*, 305.
76. Sherwin B. Nuland, *How We Die: Reflections on Life's Final Chapter* (New York: Vintage, 1995), 19.
77. Nuland, *How We Die*, 34.
78. Nuland, *How We Die*, 41.
79. Nuland, *How We Die*, 41.
80. Luciani, "Our Conviction," 18.
81. Cornwell, *A Thief in the Night*, 224.
82. Megan Brenan, "Decades Later, Most Americans Doubt Lone Gunman Killed JFK," November 13, 2023, https://news.gallup.com/poll/514310/decades-later-americans-doubt-lone-gunman-killed-jfk.aspx.

• 17 •

Into Eternity

A Meteor That Lit Up the Heavens (September 30–October 4, 1978)

There are better things ahead than we leave behind. —C. S. Lewis[1]

It was a ghastly spectacle.

John Paul surely would have found it undignified, verging on the indecent. The man who had prized his privacy would have none on this day. Instead, he became the object of vulgar curiosity. He had died without expressing his wishes for his funeral;[2] thus, the Vatican predictably resorted to customary practices, however unsavory they might be. Tradition dictated that a deceased pope's body should lie in state in St. Peter's Basilica, where mourners could pay their respects. But the transfer of the remains from the Apostolic Palace on October 1 would not take place privately, nor under the cloak of darkness, but in the glaring light of day. What's worse, St. Peter's Square was transformed into a virtual theater occupied with an audience eager to behold the show that would soon begin.

A formal procession, carefully choreographed and rich with ritual, was enacted in full view of the curious onlookers and broadcast on television. The embalmers, who had plied their craft hours before, made the public display possible by infusing the corpse with preservative chemicals. Because of that, there was no reason to worry now that the heat would accelerate the decomposition of the body in the next four days that would have rendered it utterly unfit for viewing.

THE PUBLIC TRANSFER

By the time the ceremony began, St. Peter's Square was teeming with people who had gathered to gaze at the late pope's body. It would be transported from the Apostolic Palace to St. Peter's, where it would rest until the funeral Mass and entombment. The RAI television network broadcast the ritual live.

As the somber observance commenced, a choir chanted a cappella a Latin refrain of the "Magnificat," a hymn of praise to Mary, a melody that resonated throughout the expansive square. It continued seemingly forever in a monotonous refrain. Meanwhile, conversations taking place in small groups among the restless throng reached a crescendo that competed with the echo of the chorus. As the onlookers, all standing, waited impatiently for the appearance of the procession, some, including nuns, made their way to the top of the curving balcony that encompasses the piazza to get a birds'-eye view of the pageant about to begin. Others sought a better vantage point along the route of the procession that would feature the departed pope's remains. Their options were limited by the wooden barricades that kept them from trickling into the pathways of the marchers.

A contingent of Swiss Guards stood at attention, as still as wooden toy soldiers, in an orderly line leading to the basilica, their dangling swords parallel to their stiff bodies. Their dazzling multicolored uniforms of blue, orange, red, and yellow stripes, complemented by ancient looking metal helmets, pointed at the front and back and ornamented with fluffy red feathers, alone broke through the dreariness of the immediate surroundings. Though clouds blotted out the sun, subdued rays of light intermittently bathed the colonnade and surrounding structures in a spray of light. Otherwise, everything was shades of gray, reflecting the mood in the square. In fact, John Paul's death alone had bleached the color of life far beyond the confines of Vatican City.[3]

At 6 p.m. twenty-four cardinals and one hundred bishops, among other clergymen, walked through the famous bronze door to enter the piazza.[4] Hours after the first curious spectators had arrived, the appearance of a retinue of clergymen in black cassocks and white surplices appeared, one carrying a cross above his head, signaling the onset of the procession. Two rows of similarly clad clerics followed closely behind. Still, unseemly conversations among the observers continued. Suddenly, the pace of the marchers accelerated as did the lengthy convoy behind the leading figures. From the start they marched in a measured cadence. Far behind, the remains of the pope, lying on a solid stretcher, entered the square feet first. It was the moment the mourners had gathered for. When the body came into sight, with bishops trailing it, polite applause erupted. Then the pallbearers paused briefly before resuming the march. The crowds watched attentively though the chatter persisted. All those who were marching stared straight ahead, their faces as immobile as stone, oblivious to the onlookers who flanked them.

John Paul's body was held aloft on the broad shoulders of his pallbearers. Some in the audience took pictures as the body passed by them as morbid mementos of the occasion. The pope's masklike face was as white as a ghost's, drained of all color. It bore no trace of a smile. As the men carrying the body walked forward in lock step, the body swayed slightly from side to side like the movement of a cradle. The omnipresent Virgilio Noe, the papal master of ceremonies, strode immediately ahead, singing from a hymnal.

The distinguished looking pallbearers were attired in formalwear: black suits with vests, white shirts with white bowties and white gloves. At no time did they exhibit a hint of fatigue from the heavy burden they carried—both physically and emotionally. Cardinals who already had arrived in Rome emerged into the square next, forming another segment of the line, their royal red robes striking a sharp contrast to the predominantly black attire of those preceding them. As the pope's body approached the basilica, a burst of applause sounded again. Ostensibly inappropriate given the melancholy mood, it was a sign of respect for the dead pontiff, a gesture that would be repeated at his funeral.

The leaders of the convoy turned to the right, past the mourners and onto a path that had been cleared to provide easy access to the cathedral. The body passed by the Swiss Guards as the eight *sediari* painstakingly ascended the steps leading to the basilica's entrance.

Some eleven minutes after the procession began, Pope John Paul I entered St. Peter's for the last time.[5] He had held general audiences there but, oddly enough, had never celebrated Mass in the celebrated church.[6] He just hadn't had enough time.

The largest church in the world, exceeding 227,000 square feet[7] and with the capacity to accommodate sixty thousand people,[8] was filled with mourners on this occasion. In contrast to those gathered outdoors, this group was reverently silent. However, subdued applause greeted the arrival of the pope's body; the civilized volume was in stark contrast to the boisterous, sustained ovations that John Paul had received in all his public appearances. Sporadic clapping echoed spontaneously as the body made its way to the main altar. Flashbulbs popped randomly. In the procession priests held flickering candles that added yet another dimension of sadness to the overall melancholy mood.

Upon arriving a short distance before the altar, the pallbearers made a tight right turn so that the body now faced the gathering. Those in procession moved to the aisles as the body approached the red draped inclined bier on which it would rest. The catafalque awaited the deceased pontiff in front of what is known as the *Confessio*, the semicircular open space that provides a view of the grotto below where rest the bones of Saint Peter. Behind it is the main altar beneath Gian Lorenzi Bernini's baldachin, an ornate canopy. Gently, the formally clad attendants lowered the stretcher onto its surface. The pallbearers genuflected in unison before the remains and departed immediately.

All the cardinals, holding candles, stood in a line some distance away. The choir inside St. Peter's continued chanting. Then a brief ceremony began with incense released before the body, its fragrant scent drifting toward the mourners. Prayers, including the Our Father, were sung in Latin. As the choir intoned a final hymn, the cardinals and all others exited the basilica, leaving the solitary lifeless pope in sustained stillness. Shortly thereafter, the doors opened again to allow the public to pay their respects. The basilica would remain open until the October 4 funeral.[9]

A STEADY STREAM OF MOURNERS

The previous day, September 30, and earlier in the morning thousands of people, many weeping, walked by the bier, made the sign of the cross, or recited a silent prayer as they paused momentarily by the body in the Apostolic Palace's Clementine Hall.[10] The morticians' handiwork that had disfigured the pope's appearance shocked not a few observers; to their horror, John Paul was hardly recognizable in death.[11]

Those who now waited to view the pope's body included Romans, members of the clergy, students, tourists, and people of all walks of life, including the poor for whom John Paul had demonstrated a special affection. The queue that formed outside was about half a mile long.[12] Among them were a vast number of grief-stricken young people, who insisted on paying their respects. That should not have been surprising. John Paul had delighted in young people, had publicly talked about them in glowing terms as the promise of the future. He had expressed faith in them and their potential and had even provided them guidance in facing the inevitable tribulations their futures would bring. His wisdom, his personality, and his holiness had stirred them.

The outpouring of love for John Paul inspired awe. Braving steady, heavy rain, hordes of shocked and sodden people waited for hours without complaint for their turn to say a final good-bye.[13] Even on October 4, the day of the funeral, viewing was permitted beginning at seven in the morning.[14] The endless lines were still forming until just before the body was placed in the coffin to be carried outdoors for the funeral ceremony.[15] The *Catholic Herald* estimated that as many as 850,000 people paid their respects before the viewing concluded.[16]

ANOTHER INTERREGNUM

Meanwhile, the Church was in limbo. It was *sede vacante* all over again, a repeat of the period following Paul VI's death in August, when the pope's chair was vacant, and the bureaucratic machinery of the Vatican practically stopped functioning. Cardinal Secretary of State and Camerlengo Jean Villot again filled the leadership vacuum in the interim. The strain on him was almost unendurable both because of his physical frailty and the dissatisfaction over his lack of leadership by detractors in the Vatican hierarchy. It wasn't easy being a Frenchman in the Italian-dominated Vatican. The chain-smoking seventy-three-year-old was seriously ill; in five months he would join John Paul in death.[17]

The mood among the cardinals was altogether depressing. Mostly elderly men, they were taxed to the limit emotionally and physically by the shocking death, long flights to Rome, extended time away from home, and the prospects of again occupying the intolerable conclave cells. An additional burden weighed heavily on them: finding a suitable successor to John Paul. Who among them could possibly compare to him? Who among them could win the affection and devotion of a bereaved global flock whose adulation was for a dead pope? Who among them had the charisma to win the broken hearts of the faithful? Who? Did such a man even exist? As if that were not enough of a challenge, a new complicating component was of paramount importance in determining the next pope: robust health and stamina.

In Albino Luciani they had chosen a relatively young pope, a man just shy of sixty-six. It was reasonable for the cardinals to expect that he would have ten years, perhaps more, ahead of him. But they were not aware of the precarious state of Luciani's health. This time would have to be different. They had no guarantees, of course, no matter how physically fit their next choice might be, but they had to play the odds that a man in his fifties or early sixties who exuded strength and vitality would enjoy longevity.

Again, the camerlengo would oversee the implementation of decisions made in general congregation sessions. The cardinals who arrived in Rome from around the world in staggered fashion had three major responsibilities to fulfill: participate in daily meetings with their brethren, join in the funeral Mass of the dead pope, and meet in conclave to elect a successor. Each day an increasing number of them participated in the daily morning meetings to plan another funeral and prepare for another conclave. It was an unwelcome replay of the previous interregnum of August.

At the initial meeting held on September 30, 29 (mostly Italians) of the world's 127 cardinals (112 would be eligible to vote in conclave this time) took part planning the funeral, which was set for Wednesday, October 4. The group also decided that the conclave would begin on October 14.[18]

THE FUNERAL MASS

Figure 17.1. John Paul's plain wooden coffin lies before the altar outside St. Peter's Basilica during his funeral mass, October 4, 1978. Fittingly, the rain came down in torrents as if the very heavens were weeping.

Although John Paul had left no instructions for a funeral, all the cardinals knew from planning his initiation ceremony that he would have insisted on something simple. Nevertheless, that entailed complicated, time-consuming preparations by numerous workers. The planners decided, therefore, to replicate the unassuming ceremony held for Pope Paul. Like Paul's funeral, this one would be held outdoors to accommodate the massive crowds that were anticipated. Even inclement weather could not force the ceremonies indoors. In an unsettling recurrence of the preparations for John Paul's installation Mass held just four weeks before, Vatican workers set out thousands of chairs in the piazza that would be occupied by the masses attending his funeral.[19] October 4 marked the fifth straight day of intermittent rain in Rome.[20] Despite the precipitation, Luciani's funeral Mass was conducted in St. Peter's Square beginning at four in the afternoon.[21]

The inhospitable weather did not deter people from attending; in total, one hundred thousand were present for the funeral Mass, a larger crowd than had attended the funeral of any previous pope. Ninety-five cardinals participated in the service.[22] Security was tight; about five thousand police officers carrying firearms patrolled the area to protect the dignitaries in attendance. The rite was broadcast worldwide because of the universal affection for the departed pope.[23]

With the basilica emptied of mourners, the body was placed in a wooden coffin and the lid fastened. Carved on the cover was an unadorned cross.[24] John Paul's coffin was plain and simple, like the man himself. The dozen papal gentlemen exited the basilica and shouldered their burden steadily down the steps, then walked past the altar as the pontifical choir filled the square with the sounds of Gregorian chant. They positioned the coffin on a multicolored Persian rug in front of the sizable altar before the mourners. The wider portion of the cypress box faced the altar. An open red bound copy of the Gospels lay on the coffin. At its head, positioned slightly to the side, stood a tall flaming white paschal candle, a representation of the resurrection. The altar dominated the area at the top of the steps to the basilica. Its front was ornate, featuring gold symbols imposed on a deep red background. The top was covered by a plain white cloth that fully draped its sides.[25]

Following the coffin were the red clad cardinals, who initially took seats lined parallel to the facade of the basilica. The rains started shortly after the service began.[26] Sporadic precipitation drenched the gathering during the ninety-minute ceremony. The heavens opened as if nature itself wept for the departed pope. The dark clouds and pouring rain captured the mood of the occasion. The slick, wet cobblestones of the piazza gleamed, and the soaked pages of the New Testament open on the coffin barely fluttered despite the brisk breeze. As the attendees were pelted with rain, thousands upon thousands of black umbrellas unfurled; the huddled masses seeking shelter beneath them could barely be discerned. Regardless of the recurrent downpours, the crowd remained.[27]

The distraught Luciani family sat to one side of the altar. Nina's husband, in an ill-fitting gray suit, had a cane in hand. Nina, visibly crestfallen, wore a simple gray coat and a black shawl. Berto, dressed in a dark suit with a white shirt and tie, sat next to his wife, Antonietta, who was in a black dress. In the row behind them gathered the pope's nieces and other relatives, anguish frozen on their faces.[28]

These humble folk joined some of the most notable people in the world: heads of state, ambassadors, monarchs, and diplomats. Also in attendance were delegations from other Christian churches and an assortment of organizations along with some 117 states and international mission groups. People in thirty-one countries viewed the ceremony on live television.[29] Some of John Paul's fellow villagers crowded together, standing shoulder to shoulder holding signs imprinted with the words, "Canale d'Agordo."[30]

The other side of the altar was reserved for bishops, who lifted their zucchetti in unison as the coffin passed by. Clerics from the Orthodox Church in their distinctive garb were given seats of prominence near the cardinals. At one point in the Mass, the cardinals lined either side of the coffin in rows of three, reciting prayers.[31]

Eighty-five-year-old Cardinal Carlo Confalonieri was the principal celebrant at this pontifical funeral Mass conducted in Latin. It was the second time he had had to perform that unwelcome mission in just a matter of weeks. At one point eight men held aloft a large white canopy to shield the aged celebrant from the elements.[32]

A Tender Tribute

If any modicum of solace could be derived on this day, it came from the stirring words spoken by Confalonieri in his homily as he beautifully captured the wonder of John Paul.

"We ask ourselves, why so quickly?" he began in Italian, posing the unfathomable question about the brevity of John Paul's pontificate that haunted the collective mind.

"We have scarcely had the time to see the new pope. Yet one month was enough for him to have conquered hearts—and for us it was a month in which we loved him intensely. It is not length which characterizes a life in the pontificate, but rather the spirit that fills it. He passed as a meteor which unexpectedly lights up the heavens and then disappears, leaving us amazed and astonished. Already the Book of Wisdom [4:13] spoke of this when telling of the just man 'coming to perfection in so short a time that he achieved long life.

"[I]n the brief contact with him we were quickly struck and fascinated by his instinctive goodness, by his innate modesty, by his sincere simplicity in deed and word.

"Was it the need for spirituality, now more deeply felt because of the general neglect of spiritual values, that pushed the multitudes towards the Pope? How else can we explain the very crowded audiences of Wednesday? Visitors came from everywhere! How else can we explain the crowds, which literally filled St. Peter's Square at midday each Sunday?

"Who has not been moved—and deeply moved—by seeing in these recent days the endless, spectacular lines of the faithful, of Rome, of the whole world?

"He called for peace . . . He had a thirst for justice for all—for the oppressed, the suffering, the poor, the needy . . . he preached charity. And always with a smile on his lips, that smile which never left him . . . This is his will and testament."[33]

Confalonieri, in a few words, had said all we needed to know and to remember about John Paul I, though tributes would flow for decades to come.

Following the consecration of the bread and wine, 150 priests spread out among the crowd to administer Holy Communion to Catholics who wished to receive the host.[34] Not long afterward, the Sistine Chapel choir sang as Confalonieri encircled the coffin with incense in the final commendation.[35]

DESCENT INTO THE GROTTOES

Figure 17.2. The pope's coffin is carried into St. Peter's Basilica and then into the grottoes below to be entombed in a sarcophagus.

The service that had started at 4 ended at 5:50. At the conclusion of the Mass, in the gathering darkness, the pallbearers carried the coffin into St. Peter's for interment in the grottoes as everyone sang, "May the Angels Lead You into Paradise."[36]

As it disappeared, the attendees in the square paid their final tribute to John Paul I by clapping four times, a Roman gesture of gratitude[37] and as a final farewell to a pope who had won their hearts in a whirlwind courtship.[38] The bells of St. Peter's tolled their sonorous sound, and despite the continuing presence of the multitude, the feeling in the piazza was one of emptiness.

The entombment was private. Only the immediate family, the pope's secretaries, and other top Vatican dignitaries descended into the vast crypt for the final rites and entombment. John Paul's remains were encased in three separate coffins: the first made of cypress was placed inside an 880-pound lead liner inside one made of oak.[39]

The thirty-three-day pope was laid to rest in a sarcophagus whose panels were assembled around the triple-layered coffin. Located under an unadorned arch, the tomb is embellished by bas relief angels, their arms crossed, and their heads turned to view the simple Latin engraving of the pope's name, *Ioannes Paulus PP.I*, with the chi-rho monogram beneath it.[40] Though the two letters look like P and X in the English alphabet, they are *chi* and *rho* from the Greek alphabet. They are the first two letters of "Christ" in Greek (*Christos*).[41] Subsequent to John Paul's beatification on September 4, 2022, the last step to sainthood, the Latin word "*Beatus*," meaning blessed, was carved above his name replacing *Venerabilis*, Latin for the title "venerable."

John Paul became the most recent of 147 popes laid to rest in this hallowed ground beneath the basilica.[42] Among them are the mortal remains of the man who is considered the first pope, the apostle Peter. Interestingly, John Paul's tomb is across from the sepulcher of Pope Marcellus II, whose own pontificate lasted only twenty-two days.[43] Buried nearby is his predecessor, Pope Paul VI.[44]

POSTSCRIPT

Figure 17.3. Pope John Paul II prays with Luciani family members at his predecessor's tomb in the grottoes of St. Peter's Basilica. Behind the pope, kneeling left to right, are niece Dr. Lina Petri; sister-in-law, Antonietta, next to her husband, Edoardo, the pope's younger brother; sister Nina (her face partially obscured by veil), and personal secretary don Diego Lorenzi.

The world first greeted John Paul in the glow of sunshine and bid him farewell in the gloom of darkness. Nature's elements reflected the mood of humanity on both occasions: the first, filled with hope and joy; the latter, filled with pessimism and misery. On the day of his funeral, the devastating feeling of grief engulfing St. Peter's Square was a microcosm of that enveloping the globe. Solace was elusive; the hurt was too raw and too deep. John Paul's sudden passing left a void in people's lives. They yearned to see his smiling face again, to be soothed by his encouraging words again, to witness the fulfillment of his promise. It would take weeks for the shock to recede, months for the agony to diminish, years for the memories to produce smiles rather than sorrow.

Almost immediately, people prayed to Papa Luciani for his intercession as if he were already proclaimed a saint. And a saint he was—both in life and in death—though canonization has not yet formalized his holiness. Visitors in record numbers still linger by his tomb in silent meditation nearly half a century after his passing. Around the globe his photo is proudly displayed in people's homes, as if he were a departed member of their own families. Thousands make pilgrimages to his village in the Dolomites where the Fondazione Papa Luciani Museum beside his parish church, St. John the Baptist, houses his personal memorabilia and archives.[45] Now open to the public is his birthplace, renovated and expanded by his brother who raised his family there but still preserving the rooms Albino Luciani inhabited when growing up and the place where he ate, chatted, and slept when visiting before becoming pope. His car is housed in the garage. In front of the house stands a bronze statue of the kindly John Paul greeting a young girl who holds a small bouquet of flowers that she extends to him. Commemorating the centenary of his birth is a bronze bas relief depicting him as a child and as pope, holding a bishop's staff in his left hand and wearing his miter and vestments. His right hand hovers above the child Albino's head in a gesture of blessing. The poor child from a tiny village becoming Vicar of Christ was an unlikely but exalted journey.

In a real sense, Pope Albino Luciani is still with us, albeit more distant. His words live on in his books and other writings, in sound and video clips where he comes alive again, flashing that irrepressible smile of joy and charity that continues to touch our hearts. His revolutionary transformation of the papacy is likely to last as long as the Church exists. The pope as "servant of servants" brought subsequent popes closer to the people. Like Christ and John Paul I himself, modern popes are friends of sinners and champions of those who suffer. Gone forever are the portable throne and crown that for two thousand years designated the pope as a religious monarch and the faithful as his simple subjects. Modern popes ride in the open "popemobile," where they can be in proximity to those around them. As Francis consistently demonstrates, popes now wade into crowds, making physical contact, holding and kissing babies, embracing the infirm and the disfigured. A faded memory is the practice of greeting a pope by kneeling and kissing his ring. A simple handshake now suffices. John Paul I was the progenitor of this modern papacy, and that is no small accomplishment.

His enduring legacy is that all people must grow in love, for love alone can unite humanity, bring peace to individuals, communities, countries, continents, and the entire world. Love is the fountain of joy, respect, kindness, humility, and forgiveness—all of which are essential to a fulfilling life. By example, Albino Luciani taught us how to live and how to love.

There has never been another pope quite like him.

Figure 17.4. Albino Luciani, 1912–1978; Pope John Paul I, August 26–September 28, 1978.

NOTES

1. C. S. Lewis, *Letters to an American Lady* (Grand Rapids, MI: Eerdmans, 2014).
2. "John Paul's 34 Days," *Newsweek*, October 9, 1978, 75.
3. "Rito della traslazione della salma di papa Giovanni Paolo I Albino Luciani Ottobre 1978 RARISSIMO!!!!" video, 48:52, https://www.youtube.com/watch?v=sZICPMqlnQ0&t=50s.
4. David Yallop, *In God's Name: An Investigation into the Murder of Pope John Paul I* (New York: Penguin, 1984), 217.
5. "Rito," video.
6. "A Death in Rome," *Newsweek*, October 9, 1978, 75.
7. R. A. Scotti, *Basilica, The Splendor and the Scandal: Building St. Peter's* (New York: Penguin, 2006), 273.
8. "St. Peter's Basilica," *New World Encyclopedia*, https://www.newworldencyclopedia.org/entry/St._Peter%27s_Basilica.
9. "Rito," video.
10. "John Paul's 34 Days," 74.
11. "The First Years of Albino Luciani, Part V" (The Election), video, https://www.albino-luciani.com/index.php?id=274&L=3.
12. Hilmi Toros, "Pope Funeral Set Wednesday; Conclave Soons," *Star News*, October 1, 1978, 1.
13. Raymond and Lauretta Seabeck, *The Smiling Pope: The Life and Teaching of John Paul I* (Huntington, IN: Our Sunday Visitor, 2004), 71.
14. Gordon Thomas and Max Morgan-Witts, *Pontiff* (New York: Doubleday, 1984), 343.
15. Edward Magri, "Catholics Bid Fond Farewell to Pope John Paul," *Lewiston Evening Journal*, October 4, 1978, 1.
16. Paul Spackman, *God's Candidate: The Life and Times of Pope John Paul I* (Herefordshire: Gracewing, 2008), 236.
17. Yallop, *In God's Name*, 199, 285.
18. Yallop, *In God's Name*, 216.
19. "The First Years," https://www.albino-luciani.com/index.php?id=274&L=3.
20. Spackman, *God's Candidate*, 235.
21. Seabeck, *Smiling Pope*, 71.
22. Spackman, *God's Candidate*, 236.
23. Magri, "Catholics Bid Fond Farewell to Pope John Paul," 1.
24. Seabeck, *Smiling Pope*.
25. "Death and Funeral of Pope John Paul I," *Caeremoniale Romanum: Liturgia et Mores Curiae Romanae*, video, 7:58, May 6, 2011, https://www.youtube.com/watch?v=voH-OQ7KJ0Q.
26. Magri, "Catholics Bid Fond Farewell to Pope John Paul," 1.
27. "Death and Funeral," *Caeremoniale Romanum*.

28. Albino Luciani photograph 84.JPG, Foundation Papa Luciani of Canale d'Agordo (Belluno-Italy).
29. Albino Luciani photograph 84.JPG.
30. Loris Serafini (director, Foundation Papa Luciani and Museum Albino Luciani of Canale d'Agordo), in discussion with the author, Canale d'Agordo, Italy, July 11, 2011.
31. "Death and Funeral of Pope John Paul I—Colour," British Movietone, 3:00, https://www.youtube.com/watch?v=ni_fw-eJv6E.
32. Peter Hebblethwaite, *The Year of Three Popes* (Cleveland, OH: Collins, 1979), 130.
33. Carlo Cardinal Confalonieri, "Funeral Mass for Pope John Paul I," *L'Osservatore Romano*, October 4, 1978, https://www.ewtn.com/catholicism/library/funeral-mass-for-pope-john-paul-i-1636.
34. Spackman, *God's Candidate*, 237.
35. "Death and Funeral of Pope John Paul I," https://www.youtube.com/watch?v=ni_fw-eJv6E.
36. "He Was the Perfect Teacher," *Catholic Northwest Progress*, October 4, 1978, 1.
37. Seabeck, *Smiling Pope*, 72.
38. Magri, "Catholics Bid Fond Farewell to Pope John Paul," 10.
39. "Why Are the Popes Buried in Three Coffins," January 6, 2023, https://dominicanmedia.com.ng/2023/01/06/.
40. "The Tomb of John Paul I, Vatican Grottoes," St. Peter's Basilica.info, https://www.stpetersbasilica.info/.
41. "What Is the Meaning of the Chi Rho Symbol?" Christianity.com, https://www.christianity.com/wiki/christian-terms/what-is-the-meaning-of-the-chi-rho-symbol.html.
42. Spackman, *God's Candidate*, 237.
43. "The Tomb," https://www.stpetersbasilica.info/.
44. Magri, "Catholics Bid Fond Farewell to Pope John Paul," 1.
45. Serafini, discussion.

Epilogue

What If?

One enduring question about John Paul I tantalizes the imagination: What would he have achieved if blessed with longevity?

Delving into the realm of what might have been, however, is a hazardous enterprise. At best, it is informed guesswork, and it raises at least as many questions as it seeks to answer. Nevertheless, the endeavor beckons irresistibly.

John Paul's character, deeds, and articulated beliefs and goals can provide clues as to what a pontificate of five, ten, or more years might have yielded. Yet, times change, and so do points of view. Some of John Paul's beliefs were malleable; others were inflexible. Despite the risks involved, what follows is a tentative voyage into the realm of the possible.

What is virtually certain is that any significant changes would have evolved; the pope was no revolutionary. He was, in fact, a naturally cautious man who habitually subjected major decisions to spiritual, intellectual, and practical scrutiny. When he considered an issue that might demand action, his approach was to gather and analyze all relevant facts, solicit diverse opinions from knowledgeable sources, and circle the subject from every possible vantage point to anticipate any potential adverse repercussions but knowing that any policy change inevitably leads to unintended consequences. As always, prayer guided his every decision. Prudence would have dictated any changes he would have made and the timing and means of implementing them.

He inherited a Church in turmoil, an institution beset by an array of seemingly intractable problems. The secularization of societies, especially in the West, was on the rise; and its impact on Catholicism was devastating. Aside from internal divisions within the Vatican, Catholics in numbing numbers were becoming alienated from the Church, its teachings increasingly irrelevant to their lives. Mass attendance was waning. The sacrament of Reconciliation, formerly known as Confession, was on the brink of extinction. Vocations were declining precipitously. Clergy and other religious were deserting the Church in droves, and many who remained were increasingly restive, demanding an end to celibacy and promoting the ordination of women. Increasingly, nuns and priests were becoming political and social activists. The numbers of so-called cafeteria Catholics—those who chose for themselves which Church teachings they accepted—were rapidly rising. Divorce rates were soaring. The sexual revolution was exploding. The use of birth control, particularly with the availability of the pill, was swelling, as were the number of abortions.

No pope, regardless of the length of his tenure or his personal magnetism, could have resolved all those dilemmas, if any. The tides were overpowering.

JOHN PAUL'S PROCLAIMED PROGRAM

On the first full day of John Paul's papacy, he had outlined an ambitious agenda. Much of it, however, was only tangentially related to the powerful currents of change sweeping Catholicism. It's reasonable to assume that the pope would have completed Vatican II's program regardless of expected fierce opposition within the hierarchy of the Church. That would have proven popular with the faithful at large. He would have been a fervent advocate for peace, another endeavor that would have been hailed universally. Promoting Christian unity likely would have yielded at least modest progress, and evangelization, particularly in Third World countries, would almost certainly have led to considerable conversions among peoples desperately seeking hope from a benevolent deity. Those initiatives would have been embraced by Catholics elsewhere but considered of secondary importance to other issues that directly affected their lives in the "advanced" nations.

The two additional components of his agenda involved internal Church affairs: enhanced collegiality among bishops and revisions of Canon Law, which guides the central administration of the Church. These endeavors probably would have been greeted with benign indifference by the faithful. Although the pope surely would have engaged in greater dialogue with the world's bishops, John Paul would have reserved final decisions exclusively for himself. He had always been a staunch supporter of papal primacy.

RESPONSIBILITY FOR THE POOR

One of the Holy Father's unalterable beliefs was that the Church should be of and for the poor. He never abandoned his proposal that each parish had an obligation to provide a percentage of its income to the underprivileged, and he might well have mandated such a policy in advanced countries. As a bishop himself, he had repeatedly sold precious items that his dioceses owned, the proceeds of which went to the disadvantaged. What might he have done with the vast Vatican treasures on behalf of the destitute? The possibilities tickle the imagination.

CHURCH HIERARCHY AND PAPAL PREEMINENCE

John Paul's traditional views about the structure of the Church would not have been well received by Catholics clamoring for decentralization. He was an unyielding believer in the hierarchical order of the Church. Yet, he was also a pastor at heart, one who was known to care deeply about his flock, and that knowledge might have ameliorated dissatisfaction with his defense of the status quo.

CELIBACY, WOMEN'S ORDINATION, POLITICAL ACTIVISM

Causing continued controversy would have been his consistent positions on issues regarding the clergy. Celibacy was sacrosanct to John Paul, and the concept of female priests had no foundation in Scripture. (He even frowned on nuns shedding their habits, a trend of relatively minor concern.) He likely would not have budged in reversing his lifelong stance on those issues. Doubtless, John Paul also would have continued to vociferously oppose liberation theology, communism, and direct political activism by priests in any form. He had been a staunch opponent of all these movements, and there were no indications whatsoever that he would have reversed himself.

INSTITUTIONAL OPENNESS, PRESERVING CHURCH SANCTITY, PROTECTING THE INNOCENT

Though the Vatican bureaucracy coveted secrecy, all indications were that he would have ushered in an era of public scrutiny of the Church's policies and practices that would have been welcomed by both the laity and the press. Beyond that, the pope was committed to a Church of integrity. John Paul was not one to tolerate illegal or immoral behavior on the part of church personnel, lay and clerical alike. Unscrupulous church leaders such as Paul Marcinkus, who governed the Vatican bank like a Mafia boss, undoubtedly would have been relieved of their duties in addition to facing legal consequences if they had committed criminal acts. Any rogue Church organizations would have been disbanded or reorganized to prevent future abuses.

It's inconceivable, for instance, that John Paul would have concealed the sexual abuse crimes of clergymen and bishops to protect the reputation of the Church when those felonies first became public knowledge in the 1980s. It is virtually certain that he would have removed predator priests from their ministry swiftly, demanded the resignations of bishops who had covered up the epidemic by transferring abusive priests to other parishes, insisted that the Church make reparation to the victims, alerted law enforcement of felonies that clergy perpetrated, and institutionalized rigorous procedures to prevent future transgressions. John Paul would have been appalled by such depravity. His compassion would have been for the victims of predator priests; he would have consoled them, provided them with counseling and reparations while cleansing the Church itself. Candor, decency, and justice would have prevailed, and healing would have been his priority. Such a response ultimately would have re-instilled Catholics' faith in a clergy purged of predators and the Church itself.

ABORTION

Because the Catholic Church teaches that human life is a precious gift from God, and the Church preaches that life begins at conception, it considers abortion at any stage of pregnancy a moral evil. John Paul would not have countenanced any change in that fundamental teaching. It is even unlikely that he would have approved of exceptions for victims of rape and incest. In instances where complications necessitated a choice between preserving the life of the mother or the child, one wonders whether he would have left that agonizing moral choice to the parents.

DIVORCE

Before becoming pope, John Paul had opposed a referendum on divorce in Italy. Divorce violated Christ's injunction that in marriage a man and woman become one flesh, and the sacrament of matrimony, therefore, was inherently indissoluble. The increasing prevalence of divorce was of concern to the pope. At the same time, however, he recognized that marriage posed numerous difficulties, and in some cases untenable behaviors such as spousal and child abuse or unremitting infidelity justified separation. Luciani had always demonstrated great compassion for Catholic divorcees despite his aversion to divorce itself, and he likely would have been amenable to annulments in such circumstances.

BIRTH CONTROL

The single most intriguing possibility is whether John Paul would have reversed the Church's formal opposition to the use of artificial means of birth control. The pope would have been in a bind on this issue. Before Paul VI had banned the use of contraceptives, Bishop Luciani had submitted a report on behalf of the bishops of Italy's Triveneto region that advised the pope to search for a way to permit couples to engage in responsible family planning. Luciani publicly revealed that he considered the matter to be the paramount theological question with which the church had to deal. He disclosed that he had hoped for a way to allow some form of birth control, especially in situations where couples faced dire circumstances. He sympathized with spouses confronted with economic crises that rendered them unable to provide for their large families. He had also been wounded profoundly by personally witnessing the pervasive suffering of children that resulted from uncontrolled procreation in Third World countries.

But to reverse *Humanae Vitae* in a single stroke was untenable. It would have been a repudiation of Pope Paul and a radical departure from the teaching of a decade. Thus, any change would have been incremental. He likely would have introduced a modification of Paul's encyclical in which some limited use of birth control would have been acceptable to alleviate suffering in families unable to provide for their children.

IN VITRO FERTILIZATION

In contrast to those who wanted to prevent pregnancies were married couples who wanted children but were unable to conceive. In vitro fertilization was becoming an increasingly viable option for them. When the first "test-tube baby," Louise Brown, was born just over a month before Luciani was elected pope, he had publicly offered his congratulations to the parents, and his statement about the scientific advance that made this procedure possible was so nuanced that it left open the door to his possible support, though he warned of the procedure's potential for abuse. It's difficult to ascertain whether he eventually would have given Church sanction to the practice.

Other unforeseen controversies would have demanded John Paul's attention as well. His response to them would have been as deliberate, prayerful, and compassionate as it had always been to previous problems.

HOMOSEXUALITY

Though the modern world has, in the main, accepted homosexuality, including unions, Luciani in the spirit of his times considered it unnatural and would not have allowed marriage within the Church, though, undoubtedly, he would have demonstrated and urged compassion toward gays and lesbians. Although he didn't speak at length about the topic, he did believe in the traditional view of marriage: that it was exclusively the union of a man and a woman.

LEGACY

Death spared John Paul the disaffection that unpopular decisions might have engendered. The pope was aware of the fleeting nature of public idolization. When Sr. Vincenza expressed her glee over the outpouring of affection he kindled, John Paul reminded her that public approbation tended to be fleeting, noting how Christ had been hailed before becoming reviled. He knew that the initial infatuation he enjoyed would likely fade eventually.

And yet . . .

His immediate successor, an actor before entering the priesthood, was an alluring figure on the world stage, enjoying widespread personal popularity during his twenty-five-year pontificate though he had little influence stemming the waning commitment to the faith by Catholics, especially in First World countries. It's possible, even likely, therefore, that John Paul I's stellar popularity would have been forever undiminished, for his holiness reached the supposedly unreachable.

One of the most unlikely admirers of the man was Patti Smith, the edgy punk rocker of the seventies, who was so enamored of John Paul that she wrote a stirring song in praise of him in her 1979 *Wave* album in which she described her personal bond despite having seen him only from afar.[1] In 2022 she met with Loris Serafini, director of the pope's museum, in Venice. They spoke of him wistfully, though Smith revealed that she still is not a religious person. Even so, when Serafini gave her a tiny piece of John Paul's white papal cassock as a relic, she wept.[2]

Albino Luciani's simplicity had such nobility that his meekness helped make people more compassionate. His embodiment of love, the source of his unmitigated joy, transfixed a world starving for harmony. His life was so exemplary that it ennobled a globe grown weary and cynical, yearning for the "greater gifts" and a "more excellent way."[3] Nearly half a century after his death, however, humankind seems more mired than ever in moral decay. As the late Peter Gomes, Plummer Professor of Christian Morals at Harvard Divinity School, wrote about America, "we live in a land of fractured families, poisoned personal relationships, unfulfilling work, disloyal corporations, fragile self-esteem, and social distrust. Our public life seems riven by one scandal after another."[4]

John Paul I was a rare and radiant man who showed us the way to the light. Granted a longer life, he could have ameliorated the darkness that continues to envelop us. Perhaps he would have been heard and heeded regardless of any controversial decisions he might have made. Because he was a Christlike figure, untold numbers of conversions to Catholicism might have ensued, and just maybe, the sweetness of his character and his reassurance that all repentant sinners were worthy of redemption might have motivated innumerable disaffected Catholics back to the Church. Only the very hardened of heart could not be enthralled by his self-consciousness at receiving ovations from the multitudes who gathered to see him. Such a humble pope could not help but soften people's attitudes toward the faults of others, a necessity for a kinder world. His compelling discourses on humility, faith, hope, and love provided the prescription for attaining the joy we all seek.

On September 4, 2022, John Paul's heroic virtues were recognized when he was beatified, earning him the title "blessed." Millions pray for his intercession in their lives. Whether another miracle attributed to him is ever verified, paving the way to his canonization is almost irrelevant, for he demonstrated his saintliness in his lifetime. Joining the pantheon of "official" saints, however, will make him an even more singular spiritual force to untold future generations just as he was to those of us who marveled at the sway of his brief but inspiring papacy.

Santo subito!

NOTES

1. Jim Higgins, "Listening to Patti Smith 'Wave' (1979)," *Milwaukee Journal Sentinel*, September 8, 2014, Jsonline.com.

2. Loris Serafini (director, Foundation Papa Luciani of Canale d'Agordo (Belluno-Italy) and the Museum Albino Luciani of Canale d'Agordo (Belluno-Italy), in discussion with the author, April 27, 2024.

3. Mo Guernon, "The 33-Day Papacy," *St. Anthony Messenger*, April 2016, 24.

4. Peter Gomes, *The Good Life: Truths That Last in Times of Need* (New York: HarperCollins, 2002), 3.

We have seen the best of our time.
—Shakespeare, King Lear

Bibliography

Ackroyd, Peter. *Venice: Pure City*. New York: Nan A. Talese/Doubleday, 2009.

Agostoni, Piergiuseppe, MD, PhD, Gaia Cattadori, MD, Michele Bianchi, MD, and Karlman Wasserman, MD, PhD. "Exercise-Induced Pulmonary Edema in Heart Failure." *Circulation* 108, no. 21 (November 25, 2003). https://www.ahajournals.org/doi/10.1161/01.CIR.0000097115.61309.59.

"Aides Describe Last Moments of Pope Paul." *Pittsburgh Post Gazette*, August 7, 1978.

"Albino Luciani Pope John Paul I Chronology." *Humilitas* 12, no. 3 (August 2001).

"Albino Luciani's Personal Book of Daily Mass." 1946–1951, sub anno 1948, March, Foundation Luciani Archive.

"Albino Luciani's Personal Book of Daily Mass." 1951–1956, sub anno 1952, January, Foundation Luciani Archive.

Allen, John L., Jr. *All the Pope's Men: The Inside Story of How the Vatican Really Thinks*. New York: Doubleday, 2004.

———. *Conclave: The Politics, Personalities, and Process of the Next Papal Election*. New York: Doubleday, 2004.

———. "Fr. Diego Lorenzi, John Paul I's Closest Collaborator." *National Catholic Reporter*, August 29, 2003. http://nationalcatholicreporter.org/word/pfw082903.htm.

———. "From Palace to Garbage Dump: A Hint of What Might Have Been." *National Catholic Reporter*, January 24, 2003.

———. "How a Pope Is Elected." *National Catholic Reporter*, 2005. https://www.nationalcatholicreporter.org/update/conclave/how_to.htm.

———. "Secretary to Three Popes Has Vivid Memories." *National Catholic Reporter*, 2005. www.nationalcatholicreporter.org/update/conclave/pt040505a.htm.

———. "Who Will Succeed Pope Paul VI? Papal Candidates Profiled." *Spokesman-Review*, August 20, 1978.

———. "The Word from Rome." *National Catholic Reporter*, September 5, 2003. http://www.nationalcatholicreporter.org.

"American Cousin Recalls Pope as a 'Smiling Boy.'" *Toledo Blade*, September 3, 1978.

"American Not Impossible: Italian Likely to Be Selected Pope." *Lodi News-Sentinel*, August 7, 1978.

Anderson, Jack. "Pope John Paul I Opened Communications." *Prescott Courier*, October 13, 1978.

"Apostolic Palace Vatican City: Where Does the Pope Live?" Info Visit Vatican. https://visitvatican.info/apostolic-palace.

"Area Officials, Clergy Mourn Pope Paul VI." *Pittsburgh Post-Gazette*, August 7, 1978.

Bernstein, Carl, and Marco Politi. *His Holiness: John Paul II and the Hidden History of Our Time.* New York: Doubleday, 1996.

Bertone, Tarcisio. *The Last Secret of Fatima.* New York: Doubleday, 2008.

"Biography of His Holiness John Paul I." The Holy See. Dicastero per la Comunicazione—Libreria Editrice Vaticana. https://www.vatican.va/content/john-paul-i/en/biography/documents/hf_jp-i_bio_01021997_biography.html.

"Bomb Explodes following Rites." *Spokesman-Review*, no. 113, September 4, 1978.

Bradlee, Ben. *Conversations with Kennedy.* New York: Pocket Books, 1976.

Braun, Joseph. "Tiara." *Catholic Encyclopedia*, vol. 14. New York: Appleton, 1912. http://www.newadvent.org/cathen/14714c.htm.

Brenan, Megan. "Decades Later, Most Americans Doubt Lone Gunman Killed JFK." November 13, 2023. https://news.gallup.com/poll/514310/decades-later-americans-doubt-lone-gunman-killed-jfk.aspx.

Bricker, Vivian. "What Is the Meaning of the Chi Rho Symbol?" February 15, 2023. https://www.christianity.com/wiki/christian-terms/what-is-the-meaning-of-the-chi-rho-symbol.html.

Briggs, Kenneth A. "Pope Paul VI Guided the Church through Era of Change." *New York Times*, August 7, 1978.

Buckley, William F. "The Pope I Want: A Consumer Speaks Out." *New Republic*, September 2, 1978.

Bull, George. *Inside the Vatican.* New York: St. Martin's Press, 1983.

Burke-Young, Francis A. *Passing the Keys: Modern Cardinals, Conclaves and the Election of the Next Pope.* Seattle: Madison Books, 1999.

"Car Rushes Vatican Gate, Is Fired on by Gendarmes; Driver Apprehended after Reaching Courtyard." May 18, 2023. https://apnews.com/article/vatican-gendarmes-swiss-guard-gate-ef111c2f461fa7d9094dbf4b5ca63077.

"Cardinals to Fly to Rome." *Sydney Morning Herald*, August 8, 1978.

"Carillons Peal, Lights Turn Off, as Word of the Death Spreads." *Lodi News-Sentinel*, August 7, 1978.

"Catholics Bid Fond Farewell to Pope John Paul." *Lewiston Evening Journal*, vol. 118, October 4, 1978.

Child, Jack. "Beagle Channel Dispute." Encyclopedia.com. https://www.encyclopedia.com/humanities/encyclopedias-almanacs-transcripts-and-maps/beagle-channel-dispute.

Childhood, Boyhood, Youth. November 1852. Childhood, boyhood, youth quotes. 2024. https://www.goodreads.com/work/quotes/1685249.

"Chronology." *Humilitas*, August 2001.

"The Church after Pope Paul VI." *Newsweek*, August 21, 1978.

Cimagalli, Dino. Interview with Danielle Bravo, October 14, 1978.

Collins, Michael. *The Vatican: Secrets and Treasures of the Holy City*. London: Dorling Kindersley, 2008.

Collins, Roger. *Keepers of the Keys of Heaven: A History of the Papacy*. New York: Basic Books, 2009.

"Compassionate Shepherd." *Time*, September 4, 1978. https://time.com/archive/6845867/religion-compassionate-shepherd/.

"Conclave A.D. 1978—Election of Pope John Paul I." Caeremoniale Romanum: Liturgia et Mores Curiae Romanae, video, 7:17, https://www.youtube.com/watch?v=8d1TSlDnc1c.

"Conclave—August 1978." *Catholic Hierarchy*. www.catholichierarchy.org/event/c1978.html.

"Conclave of Cardinals to Choose Next Pope Will Be a Secret Affair." *The Dispatch* 97, no. 82, August 8, 1978.

Confalonieri, Carlo Cardinal. "Funeral Mass for Pope John Paul I." *L'Osservatore Romano*, October 4, 1978. https://www.ewtn.com/catholicism/library/funeral-mass-for-pope-john-paul-i-1636.

Coppa, Frank J. *The Modern Papacy since 1789*. Oxfordshire: Routledge, 2017.

———. *Politics and the Papacy in the Modern World*. Westport: Praeger, 2008.

Cornell, George W. "Historical Accident? Why Are Popes Always Italian?" *Eugene Register-Guard*, August 13, 1978. https://news.google.com/newspapers?id=9gZFAAAAIBAJ&sjid=6uEDAAAAIBAJ&pg=6652%2C3439693.

———. "How Pope Will Handle Big Issues Not Clear." *Observer-Reporter*, August 29, 1978.

———. "In Spite of His Brief Time, John Paul Left His Own Legacy." *Lewiston Evening Journal*, October 4, 1978.

Cornwell, John. *A Thief in the Night: Life and Death in the Vatican*. New York: Penguin, 1989.

"Coronation of Pope Paul VI." *Caeremoniale Romanum*. Video. https://www.youtube.com/watch?v=KNOedla1cm4.

Coughlan, Robert. *The World of Michelangelo*. New York: Time, 1966.

"Could Popes Have Lived Longer? Papal Health Care Debated." *Eugene Register-Guard*, October 1, 1978.

Coulombe, Charles. *The Vicars of Christ: A History of the Popes*. New York: Citadel, 2003.

"Cousin Predicted Pope's Election." *Argus Press*, August 28, 1978.

Crane, Roger. *The Last Confession*. London: Oberon, 2007.

Daw, Richard W., ed. *Nights of Sorrow, Days of Joy: Papal Transition—Paul VI, John Paul I, John Paul II*. National Catholic News Service, 1978.

Day, James. "The Bridge Builder: Rediscovering Pope John Paul I." *Catholic Exchange*, November 17, 2017. https://catholicexchange.com/bride-builder-pope-john-paul-1/.

"Death and Funeral of Pope John-Paul I—Color." British Movietone. https://www.youtube.com/watch?v=ni_fw-eJv6E.

"Death and Funeral of Pope John Paul I." *Caeremoniale Romanum: Liturgia et Mores Curiae Romanae*, May 6, 2011. Video. https://www.youtube.com/watch?v=voH-OQ7KJ0Q.

Death Certificate of Bortola Tancon. Parish archive, St. John the Baptist of Canale d'Agordo. Death Register n. 17. c. 179r, year 1948. Reference Number 9.

Death Certificate of Giovanni Luciani. Parish archive, St. John the Baptist of Canale d'Agordo. Death Register n. 17. C. 195v, year 1952. Reference Number 1.

"A Death in Rome." *Newsweek*, October 9, 1978.

"The Death of Pope John Paul I." *L'Osservatore Romano*, October 5, 1978, 1.

de Rosa, Peter. *Vicars of Christ: The Dark Side of the Papacy*. New York: Crown, 1988.

de Sales, St. Francis. *Philothea, or An Introduction to the Devout Life*. Rockford, IL: Tan Books and Publishers, 1994.

Diego Lorenzi, don (former personal secretary to Pope John Paul I). Interview with John L. Allen Jr., *Crux*, May 10, 2016.

"The Dolomites." UNESCO World Heritage Convention. https://whc.unesco.org/en/list/1237/.

Donazzon, Renato. *Albino Luciani: Il Papa Degli Umili*. Silea: Piazza Editore, 2010.

Doyle, Kenneth. "The Pope's Security Detail." *The Pilot*, February 19, 2024. https://www.thebostonpilot.com/article.php?ID=182577.

"Easy-Going Style Likely," *Bangor Daily News*, September 4, 1978.

"Elaborate Mourning Plans, Funeral Mapped for Pope." *Pittsburgh Post-Gazette*, August 7, 1978. news.google.com/newspapers?id=ioBIAAAAIBAJ&sjid=020DAAAAIBAJ&pag=710%2C846143.

"The Election of Cardinal Albino Luciani as New Pope." August 26, 1978. https://www.youtube.com/watch?v=ZaSpHn-p1MA.

Falasca, Stefania. *The September Pope: The Final Days of John Paul I*. © 2017, PIEMME; 2020, Libreria Editrice Vaticana. English translation published by *Our Sunday Visitor*, 2021.

Falconi, Marta. "Body of Pope John Paul II Not Embalmed." April 6, 2005. https://www.starnewsonline.com/story/news/2005/04/06/body-of-pope-john-paul-ii-not-embalmed/30778158007/.

Fanning, William. "Papal Elections." In *The Catholic Encyclopedia*, vol. 11. New York: Appleton, 1911. http://www.newadvent.org/cathen/11456a.htm.

Feltes, Victor Fr. "Conclave Accommodations." Pope John Paul I Papacy—Day by Day. https://johnpauli.wordpress.com.

———. "The Conclave Begins." Pope John Paul I Papacy—Day by Day. https://johnpauli.wordpress.com.

———. "The Death and Funeral of Pope John Paul I." Pope John Paul I Papacy—Day by Day. Video. https://johnpauli.wordpress.com/.

———. "Epilogue," Pope John Paul I Papacy—Day by Day. August 6, 2014. https://johnpauli.wordpress.com/.

———. "Faith in Our Mother." Pope John Paul I Papacy—Day by Day. https://johnpauli.wordpress.com.

———. "Greeting the Peacemakers." August 6, 2014. www.johnpauli.wordpress.com.

———. "Inauguration Day September 3." Pope John Paul I Papacy—Day by Day. johnpauli.wordpress.com.

———. "Is the Pope a Friend of Caesar?" Pope John Paul I Papacy—Day by Day. August 6, 2014. https://johnpauli.wordpress.com/2014/09/16/is-the-pope-a-friend-of-caesar-day-22/.

———. "Lessons for Life." Pope John Paul I Papacy—Day by Day. August 6, 2014. https://johnpauli.wordpress.com/2014/09/17/lessons-for-life-day-23/.

———. "Meet the Press." August 6, 2014, https://johnpauli.wordpress.com/.

———. "Pope John Paul I Papacy—Day by Day." August 6, 2014. www.johnpauli.wordpress.com.

———. "Retentions, Reactions, & Regalia." August 6, 2014. www.johnpauli.wordpress.com.

———. "Telling Time." Pope John Paul I Papacy—Day by Day. https://johnpauli.wordpress.com.

———. "To the Ends of the Earth." Pope John Paul I Papacy—Day by Day. https://johnpauli.wordpress.com.

The First Televised Papal Conclave. New York. American Broadcasting Company (ABC). August 25, 1978. https://abcnews.go.com/Archives/video/aug-25-1978-televised-papal-conclave-18702845.

"The First Years of Albino Luciani, Part I" (The Priest). Video. https://www.albino-luciani.com/index.php?id=270&L=3.

"The First Years of Albino Luciani, Part II" (The Bishop). Video. https://www .albi-noluciani .com /index .php ?id =274 &L =3.

"The First Years of Albino Luciani, Part III" (The Cardinal). Video. https://www.albino-luciani.com/index.php?id=272&L=3.

"The First Years of Albino Luciani, Part IV" (The Conclave). Video. https://www.albino-luciani.com/index.php?id=273&L=3.

"The First Years of Albino Luciani, Part V" (The Election). Video. https://www.albino-luciani.com/index.php?id=274&L=3.

Foa, Sylvana. "Devotion Dwindles beyond Papal Wall." *Eugene Register-Guard*, August 19, 1978.

Fondazione Giorgio Cini. "Vittore Branca." https://www.cini.it/en/who-whe-are/staff/vittore-branca.

"Former Italian Prime Minister Aldo Moro Is Found Dead." https://www.history.com/this-day-in-history/aldo-moro-found-dead.

Fornezza, Ettore. Nostalgio di un Sorriso: 33 Giorni Rimasti Nel Cuore. dall'archiviio di mons. Venezia: Associazione Oasi Papa Luciani, 2020.

Foster, Sophie, and Barrie K. Macdonald. "Fiji." Geography and Travel. *Britannica*. https://www.britannica.com/place/Fiji-republic-Pacific-Ocean.

Francesco Taffarel, Msgr. (personal secretary to Bishop Albino Luciani, diocese of Vittorio Veneto, Italy). In discussion with the author, Tarzo, Italy, July 11, 2011.

"Frequently Asked Questions about Embalming." Williams Funeral Homes. October 3, 2022. https://www.williamsfh.com/faqs-about-embalming.

"Fukushima Accident." *Britannica*, May 17, 2024. https://www.britannica.com/event/Fukushima-accident.

Gammarelli DAL 1798. "La Sartoria." Accessed May 19, 2017. https://www.gammarelli.com/.

Garnett, R. "The Alleged Poisoning of Alexander VI." *English Historical Review* 9, no. 34 (1894): 335–39. http://www.jstor.org/stable/548372.

General Secretariat. "How Is a New Pope Chosen?" *United States Conference of Catholic Bishops*. https://www.usccb.org/offices/general-secretariat/how-new-pope-chosen.

Good Morning America, Coverage of Death of Pope Paul VI. New York: American Broadcasting Company (ABC), August 6, 1978. https://www.youtube.com/watch?v=K5hXO0NGV3Q.

Gospel According to St. Matthew, 19:4–5. *New Revised Standard Version with Apocrypha*. New York: Oxford University Press, 1989.

Gospel According to St. Matthew, 19:6. *New American Bible, Revised—Catholic Edition*. United States Conference of Catholic Bishops, 2023. https://bible.usccb.org/bible/matthew/19.

Greeley, Andrew M. *The Making of the Popes 1978: The Politics of Intrigue in the Vatican*. Kansas City: Andrews and McMeel, 1979.

Guernon, Mo. "All Those Years Ago." *Orange County Catholic*, August 11, 2018. https://www.occatholic.com/all-those-years-ago/.

———. "The Forgotten Pope." *America*, October 24, 2011.

———. "Francis: The Resurrection of the People's Pope." *Rhode Island Catholic*, September 24, 2015.

———. "The Paradox of Albino Luciani: Meekness and Strength." Text of speech delivered at the International Conference for the Centenary of Pope John Paul I. New York, October 13, 2012.

———. "Return of a 'People's Pope.'" *Providence Journal*, September 28, 2015. www.providencejournal.com/article/20150928/OPINION/150929436.

———. "The 33-Day Papacy." *St. Anthony Messenger*, April 2016.

———. "We Need Another John Paul I." *Real Clear Religion*, March 13, 2013. https://www.realclearreligion.org/authors/mo_guernon/.

"Hazy Pointers to the Pope's Successor." *Sydney Morning Herald*, August 8, 1978.

"He Was the Perfect Teacher." *Catholic Northwest Progress*, October 4, 1978.

"Heart of Mary, Our Lady of Fatima, Sr. Maria Lucia of Jesus and of the Immaculate Heart, Visionary of Fatima." *Servants of the Pierced Hearts of Jesus and Mary*. 1907–2005 © Recompiled by SCTJM. https://www.piercedhearts.org/hearts_jesus_mary/apparitions/fatima/fatima_lucia_biography.html.

Hebblethwaite, Peter. *In the Vatican*. London: Sidgwick & Jackson, 1986.

———. *The Next Pope: A Behind-the-Scenes Look at the Forces That Will Choose the Successor to John Paul II and Decide the Future of the Catholic Church*. New York: HarperCollins, 2000.

———. *Paul VI: The First Modern Pope*. New York: Paulist, 1993.

———. *Pope John XXIII: Shepherd of the Modern World.* New York: Doubleday, 1985.

———. *The Year of Three Popes*. Cleveland, OH: Collins, 1979.

Hempstone, Smith. "Cardinals Expected to Be Cautious." *Eugene Register-Guard*, August 25, 1978.

"Highlights of the Life of His Holiness John Paul I." Holy See. https://www.vatican.va/content/john-paul-i/en/biography/documents/hf_jp-i_bio_01021997_biography.html.

"His Light, Only for a Moment." *Humilitas*, December 2002.

Hoffmann, Paul. "Papal Conclave Setting Resembles a Monastery." *The Times-News*, August 24, 1979.

———. "Pope John Paul I Promises to Continue 'Ecumenical Thrust.'" *Bangor Daily News* 90, no. 75 (August 28, 1978).

"The Holy See Celebrates 54 Years as Permanent Observer to the United Nations." Permanent Observer Mission of the Holy See to the United Nations. https://holyseemission.org/contents//mission/5ac79b91753bc.php.

"How the Pope Is Elected." *Sydney Morning Herald*, August 8, 1978.

Hyer, Marjorie. "See Hope of Solving Problems: Pope Impresses U.S. Catholics." *Los Angeles Times*, September 1, 1978.

"John Paul, Mender of Fences." *The Age*, August 28, 1978.

"John Paul I." *Britannica*. Updated September 24, 2020. https://www.britannica.com/biography/John-Paul-I.

"John Paul I Inaugurates Reign." *Bangor Daily News* 90, no. 81 (September 4, 1978).

"John Paul I on Love, Part I." The Last Wednesday Audience of Pope John Paul I. Tau Cross Media, September 27, 1978. https://www.youtube.com/watch?v=f-XAWEfvMEk.

"John Paul I on Love, Part II." The Last Wednesday Audience of Pope John Paul I. Tau Cross Media, September 27, 1978. https://www.youtube.com/watch?v=KkO08g6JKGg.

"John Paul I: The Pope of Unity." *Newsweek*, September 4, 1978.

"John Paul I—Timeline of His Life." Eternal Word Television Network, Irondale, AL, 2024. https://www.ewtn.com/catholicism/library/john-paul-i-timeline-24637.

Jones, Alexander, ed. *The Jerusalem Bible*. New York: Doubleday, 1966.

Jones, Kevin J. "The Shortest Papacies of All Time? Pope John Paul I Barely Makes the List." September 18, 2022. https://www.catholicnewsagency.com/news/252309/the-shortest-papacies-of-all-time-pope-john-paul-i-barely-makes-the-list.

Kelly, J. N. D. "John Paul I (1978)." *The Oxford Dictionary of Popes*. Oxford: Oxford University Press, 1986.

Kennedy, John F. "Commencement Address at American University." Speech, American University, June 10, 1963. John F. Kennedy Presidential Library and Museum. https://www.jfklibrary.org/archives/other-resources/john-f-kennedy-speeches/american-university-19630610.

Kivitny, Jonathan. *Man of the Century: The Life and Times of John Paul II*. New York: Henry Holt, 1997.

Klein, Christopher. "10 Grisly Papal Deaths." History, May 5, 2023, https://www.history.com/news/10-grisly-papal-deaths.

Kummer, Regina. *Albino Luciani Papa Giovanni Paolo I: Una Vita per la Chiesa*. Padova: Edizioni Messagero Padova, 2009.

"La Grande Storia/RAI: Giovanni Paolo I Il Papa del Sorriso." https://www.facebook.com/watch/?v=1195316061042114.

La Rosa, Michelle. "Was Pope John Paul I Murdered?" *The Pillar*, October 15, 2021. https://www.pillarcatholic.com/p/was-pope-john-paul-i-murdered.

"L'attivita della Santa Sede 1978." Tipografica Pompei SPA—Pompei (Napoli), 1979.

"A Look Back at the Conclave That Elected Albino Luciani Pope." *La Stampa*, August 25, 2015. https://www.lastampa.it/vatican-insider/en/2015/08/25/news/a-look-back-at-the-conclave-that-elected-albino-luciani-pope-1.35235480/.

Lorenzi, Diego. "Giovanni Paolo I: Nel Ricordo di Don Diego Lorenzi." *Messaggi di Don Orione*. 2000 n. 102.

Luciani, Albino. Date unknown. Photograph (5.JPG). *Foundation Papa Luciani of Canale d'Agordo* (Belluno-Italy).

———. Date unknown. Photograph (84.JPG). *Foundation Papa Luciani of Canale d'Agordo* (Belluno-Italy).

———. Date unknown. Photograph (200.JPG). *Foundation Papa Luciani of Canale d'Agordo* (Belluno-Italy).

———. Date unknown. Photograph (252.JPG). *Foundation Papa Luciani of Canale d'Agordo* (Belluno-Italy).

———. Date unknown. Photograph (285.JPG). *Foundation Papa Luciani of Canale d'Agordo* (Belluno-Italy).

———. Date unknown. Photograph (323.JPG). *Foundation Papa Luciani of Canale d'Agordo* (Belluno-Italy).

———. Date unknown. Photograph (397.JPG). *Foundation Papa Luciani of Canale d'Agordo* (Belluno-Italy).

———. Date unknown. Photograph (687.JPG). *Foundation Papa Luciani Collection of Canale d'Agordo* (Belluno-Italy).

Luciani, Albino. "Fifteen Days in Africa." *Humilitas*, December 2013.

———. "Fifteen Days in Africa." *Humilitas*, March 2014.

———. *Illustrissimi*. Boston: Little, Brown, 1978.

———. "My Meeting with Lucia." Translated by Mother Theresa, OCD. *Humilitas* 24, no. 2 (2013).

———. *A Passionate Adventure: Living the Catholic Faith Today*. Edited and translated by Lori Pieper. New York: Tau Cross Books, 2013.

Luciani, Albino, Marco Ce, and Angelo Scola. *Come il Padre ha Mandato Me, Cosi Io Mando Voi*. Venezia: Marcianum Press, 2007.

Luciani, Patrizia. *Un Prete di Montagna: Gli Anni Bellunesi di Albino Luciani (1912–1958)*. Padova: Edizioni Messagero Padova, 2003.

Luciani, Pia (Pope John Paul I's niece). In discussion with the author. Canale d'Agordo, Italy, July 6, 12, 2011.

———. Letter to author, November 3, 2012.

MacCulloch, Diarmaid. *Christianity: The First Three Thousand Years*. New York: Viking, 2009.

"Madonna di Pietralba Pilgrimage Site." Accessed May 25, 2024. https://www.weinstrasse.com/en/highlights/sights/churches-and-monasteries/madonna-di-pietralba-pilgrimage-site/

Magee, John (personal secretary to Pope John Paul I). In discussion with the author, Cobh, Ireland, February 17, 2010.

———. "Untold Stories of the Last Three Popes." Compact Disc. Lighthouse Catholic Media, NFP, 2008.

Magri, Edward. "Pontiff's Activities Summarized: Pope's Popularity Was Immediate." *Sarasota Herald-Tribune*, September 30, 1978.

"Make Celibacy Optional, Pope Urged by Rice." *Pittsburgh-Post Gazette*, September 1, 1978.

"A Man Who Knew What He Wanted." *Sydney Morning Herald*, August 8, 1978.

"Many Services for the Pope." *Sydney Morning Herald*, August 8, 1978.

"Massive Earthquake Devastates Iran, Killing 15,000 and Destroying Towns." *Harvard Crimson*, September 19, 1978. https://www.thecrimson.com/article/1978/9/19/massive-earthquake-devastates-iran-killing-15000/.

Mauriello, Matthew R., Rev. "Our Lady of Lourdes." University of Dayton. https://udayton.edu/imri/mary/o/our-lady-of-lourdes.php.

Maurus, Rabanus. *Veni, Creator Spiritus* (Come Holy Spirit, Creator Blest). Eternal Word Television Network. Original files by Michael Martin. https://www.ewtn.com/catholicism/library/venicreator-spiritus-come-holy-spirit-creatorblest-11897.

Meyers, John A. "A Letter from the Publisher." *Time*, October 9, 1978.

Miesel, Sandra. "A Quiet Death in Rome: Was Pope John Paul I Murdered?" *Crisis Magazine*, April 1, 2009. https://crisismagazine.com/opinion/a-quiet-death-in-rome-was-pope-john-paul-i-murdered.

Mitchell, Anna. "The Room of Tears." March 23, 2013. https://integratedcatholiclife.org/2013/03/mitchell-the-room-of-tears/.

"Mohamed Siad Barre, President of Somalia." *Britannica*, updated April 8, 2024. https://www.britannica.com/biography/Mohamed-Siad-Barre.

Mohs, Mayo. "After Paul: The Leading Contenders." *Time*, August 21, 1978.

Molinari, Gloria C. "The Conclave: August 25–26, 1978—Memories from the Conclave." 2001. www.papaluciani.com/eng/conclave.htm.

Montalbano, William. "Will the Holy Men Choose Another Like John Paul?" *Montreal Gazette*, September 30, 1978.

Montgomery, Dennis. "111 Cardinals Gather to Select New Pope." *Victoria Advocate*, August 25, 1978.

"Mourning: Thousands View Pope's Body as Vatican Prepares Funeral." *Evening Independent*, September 20, 1978.

Moynahan, Brian. *The Faith: A History of Christianity*. New York: Doubleday, 2002.

Murphy, Francis X. *The Papacy Today*. London: Weidenfeld and Nicolson, 1982.

Musumeci, Robin. "Basilica of St. John Lateran Rome." *Britannica*. https://www.britannica.com/place/Basilica-of-St-John-Lantern.

"New Pontiff a Product of Simple Life." *The Ledger*, August 27, 1978.

"Non-Italians Played Key Role in Election of John Paul I." *Daily News*, August 29, 1978.

Norton, John. "Pope John Paul's Hometown Diocese Begins Work on His Canonization Cause." *Humilitas*. Translated by Lori Pieper. December 2002.

Norwich, John Julius. *Absolute Monarchs: A History of the Papacy*. New York: Random House, 2011.
Nuland, Sherwin B. *How We Die: Reflections on Life's Final Chapter*. New York: Vintage, 1995.
"Obituary: Archbishop Paul Marcinkus." [Archives] February 21, 2006. http://news.bbc.co.uk/2/hi/europe/4737372.stm.
O'Malley, John W. *A History of the Popes: From Peter to the Present*. Lanham, MD: Rowman & Littlefield, 2010.
"One of Bruno Heim's Best." Exarandorum: Fr. Guy Selvester's blog of Ecclesiastical Heraldry. https://exarandorum.com/2013/04/12/one-of-bruno-heims-best/.
Opera Omnia, vol. 7. Translated by Lori Pieper.
Ostling, Richard. "In Search of a Pope." *Time*, August 21, 1978.
"Other Christian Leaders Join Pope in Prayer." *Toledo Blade*, September 3, 1978.
"Our Lady of Fatima." Eternal Word Television Network, Irondale, AL, 2024. https://www.ewtn.com/catholicism/saints/our-lady-of-fatima-423.
Padoan, Udo. "On Pilgrimage with Patriarch Luciani: The Memories of a Pilgrim." *Humilitas* 17, no. 1 (2006).
"Papal History Says the Pope Should Be Italian." *Register-Guard*, August 19, 1978. "The Papal Inauguration Mass of John Paul I." *Caeremoniale Romanum*. September 1978. Video. www.youtube.com/watch?v=6Pjb7mDK4GI&t=3m30s.
"Papal Installation Ceremony." RAI Play. Italiani con Paolo Mieli: Giovanni Paoli I Il Papa del Sorriso. September 1978. https://www.raiplay.it/video/2021/09/Italiani---Giovanni-Paolo-I-il-Papa-del-sorriso-27a1256e-4e15-4eb2-b127-f52c67d084d1.html.
"Papal Interregnum." Eternal Word Television Network, Irondale, AL, 2024. https://www.ewtn.com/catholicism/holysee/interregnum.
"The Papal Liturgy and Pope John Paul I." *Caeremoniale Romanum*. September 1978. Video. www.caeremonialeromanum.com.
"The Patriarch of Venice." *Humilitas* 9, December 1998.
"Paul VI: Helmsman in the Storm." *Sydney Morning Herald*, August 8, 1978.
"Per questo, ho detto, mi chiamero Giovanni Paolo." Fondazione Vaticana Giovanni Paolo i, June 8, 2022. https://www.youtube.com/watch?v=TpWQLJGnfCk.
Perale, Marco. "San Pietro Church." *Belluno Turismo*. https://www.belluno-turismo.it/en/project/s-pietro-church/.
Petri, Lina (niece of Pope John Paul I). Email message to author, February 23, 2024.
———. In discussion with the author, Rome, July 6, 2011.
Pham, John-Peter. *Heirs of the Fisherman: Behind the Scenes of Papal Death and Succession*. Oxford: Oxford University Press, 2004.
Plato. *The Apology of Socrates*. Project Gutenberg, October 4, 2020. https://www.gutenberg.org/ebooks/1656.
"Pontiff 'Great Moral Inspiration,' President Carter Says on Death." *Pittsburgh Post-Gazette*, August 7, 1978.
"Pope Asks Press to Focus on Substance of the Church." *St. Petersburg Times*, September 2, 1978.
"Pope Believed Planning Simple Coronation Rite." *Toledo Blade*, August 29, 1978.

"Pope Helps Free Kidnapped Boy." *The Voice*, September 29, 1978.
"Pope Installed: John Paul I Begins Reign." *The Spokesman-Review*, no. 113, September 4, 1978.
"Pope John Paul Dies of Heart Attack at 65." *Deseret News*, September 29, 1978.
"Pope John Paul Meets Mayor Argan." [Archives] September 25, 1978. Video. www.youtube.com/watch?v=Wnrws5HgcSA.
"Pope John Paul I: 'He Only Had Time to Be Loved.'" *Montreal Gazette*, September 30, 1978.
"Pope John Paul I Dies of Heart Attack." *The Guardian*, September 30, 1978. https://www.theguardian.com/theguardian/2013/sep/30/pope-john-paul-1-death-vatican.
Pope John Paul I. "Angelus." September 3, 1978. In Collection of recordings of the original speeches and statements of Blessed Pope John Paul I of the Archives of the Foundation Papa Luciani of Canale d'Agordo (Belluno-Italy).
———. "Conversation with the Roman Clergy." September 7, 1978. In Collection of recordings of the original speeches and statements of Blessed Pope John Paul I of the Archives of the Foundation Papa Luciani of Canale d'Agordo (Belluno-Italy).
———. "General Audience: 'Faith.'" September 13, 1978. In Collection of recordings of the original speeches and statements of Blessed Pope John Paul I of the Archives of the Foundation Papa Luciani of Canale d'Agordo (Belluno-Italy).
———. "General Audience: 'Hope.'" In Collection of recordings of the original speeches and statements of Blessed Pope John Paul I of the archives of the Foundation Papa Luciani of Canale d'Agordo (Belluno-Italy).
———. "General Audience: 'Humility.'" September 6, 1978. In Collection of recordings of the original speeches and statements of Blessed Pope John Paul I of the Archives of the Foundation Papa Luciani of Canale d'Agordo (Belluno-Italy).
———. "General Audience Address: 'Love.'" September 27, 1978. In Collection of recordings of the original speeches and statements of Blessed Pope John Paul I of the archives of the Foundation Papa Luciani of Canale d'Agordo (Belluno-Italy).
———. "Homily at Mass in Basilica of St. John Lateran." September 23, 1978. In Collection of recordings of the original speeches and statements of Blessed Pope John Paul I of the archives of the Foundation Papa Luciani of Canale d'Agordo (Belluno-Italy).
———. "Homily Delivered at the Initiation Mass." September 3, 1978. In Collection of recordings of the original speeches and statements of Blessed Pope John Paul I of the Archives of the Foundation Papa Luciani of Canale d'Agordo (Belluno-Italy).
———. "Letter to the Bishops of the Episcopal Conference of Argentina." Dicastero per la Comunicazione—Libreria Editrice Vaticana. https://www.vatican.va/content/john-paul-i/fr/letters/documents/hf_jp-i_let_19780920_argentina-cile.html.
———. Remarks to the mayor of Rome. September 23, 1978. In Collection of recordings of the original speeches and statements of Blessed Pope John Paul I of the archives of the Foundation Papa Luciani of Canale d'Agordo (Belluno-Italy).
———. Speech delivered to members of official delegations, September 3, 1978. In Collection of recordings of the original speeches and statements of Blessed Pope

John Paul I of the Archives of the Foundation Papa Luciani of Canale d'Agordo (Belluno-Italy).
———. Speech delivered prior to Sunday Angelus, August 27, 1978. In Collection of recordings of the original speeches and statements of Blessed Pope John Paul I of the Archives of the Foundation Papa Luciani of Canale d'Agordo (Belluno-Italy).
———. Speech delivered prior to Sunday Angelus, September 10, 1978. In Collection of recordings of the original speeches and statements by Blessed Pope John Paul I of the Archives of the Foundation Papa Luciani of Canale d'Argordo (Belluno-Italy).
———. Speech to American bishops making *ad limina* visit. September 21, 1978. In Collection of recordings of the original speeches and statements of Blessed Pope John Paul I of the archives of the Foundation Papa Luciani of Canale d'Agordo (Belluno-Italy).
———. Speech to the diplomatic corps accredited to the Holy See, August 31, 1978. In Collection of recordings of the original speeches and statements of Blessed Pope John Paul I, Archives of the Foundation Papa Luciani of Canale d'Agordo (Belluno-Italy).
———. Speech to the international press corps, September 1, 1978. In Collection of recordings of the original speeches and statements of Blessed Pope John Paul I, Archives of the Foundation Papa Luciani of Canale d'Agordo (Belluno-Italy).
———. Speech to the Sacred College of Cardinals, August 30, 1978. In Collection of recordings of the original speeches and statements of Blessed Pope John Paul I, Archives of the Foundation Papa Luciani of Canale d'Agordo (Belluno-Italy).
———. "Urbi et Orbi." Speech delivered to the Sacred College of Cardinals broadcast on radio and television, August 27, 1978. In Collection of recordings of the original speeches and statements of Blessed Pope John Paul I of the Archives of the Foundation Papa Luciani of Canale d'Agordo (Belluno-Italy).
"Pope Names New 'Camerlengo' to Run Vatican in Papal Transition Period." February 14, 2019. https://www.reuters.com/article/us-vatican-camerlengo/pope-names-new-camerlengo-to-run-vatican-in-papal-transition-period-idUSKCN1Q31ZG.
"Pope Paul Donates His Jeweled Tiara to Poor of World." *New York Times*, November 14, 1964. https://www.nytimes.com/1964/11/14/archives/pope-paul-donates-his-jeweled-tiara-to-poor-of-world.html#:~:text=Estimates%20of%20its%20intrinsic%20value,the%20opinion%20of%20observers%20here.
"Pope Paul VI." *Pittsburgh Post-Gazette*, August 7, 1978.
Pope Paul VI, 1897–1978. http://abcnews.go.com/Archives/video/aug-1978 pope-paul-vi-dies-10502313.
"Pope to Work for World Peace." *Pittsburgh Post-Gazette*, September 1, 1978.
"Pope's Body on View to Visitors." *Sydney Morning Herald*, August 8, 1978.
"The Pre-Papal 'Letters' of John Paul Reviewed Everything from Charismatics to the Beatles." *People Magazine*, September 18, 1978.
"Priest in Agordo and Belluno." *Humilitas* 9, no. 3 (December 1995).
"The Prophecy of St. Malachy." *Our Catholic Faith*. https://ourcatholicfaith.org/prophecy-of-st-malachy/.

"Pulmonary Edema." Mayo Clinic: Disease and Conditions. https://www.mayoclinic.org/diseases-conditions/pulmonary-edema/symptoms-causes/syc-20377009.

"Quotes Reveal Point-of-View." *Toledo Blade*, August 27, 1978.

Redmont, Dennis. "Pope Paul, 80, Dies of Heart Attack." *Pittsburgh Post-Gazette*, August 7, 1978.

Reese, Thomas J. *Inside the Vatican: The Politics and Organization of the Catholic Church.* Cambridge, MA: Harvard University Press, 1996.

———. "The Papal Transition: An Overview." Interview by National Public Radio, April 2, 2005.

"Religion: How Pope John Paul Won." *Time*, September 11, 1978. https://content.time.com/time/magazine/article/0,9171,946069,00.html.

"Rite of Ordination." Roman Catholic Diocese of Syracuse. Accessed September 22, 2024. https://syracusediocese.org/rite-of-ordination.

"Rito della traslazione della salma di papa Giovanni Paolo I Albino Luciani Ottobre 1978 RARISSIMO!!!!" https://www.youtube.com/watch?v=sZICPMqlnQ0&t=50s.

Rocha, Luis Miguel. *The Last Pope*. New York: Penguin, 2006.

Ryan, George. "Why the Papal Conclave of 1271 Was the Longest in History." *uCatholic*, March 29, 2023. https://ucatholic.com/blog/why-the-papal-conclave-of-1271-was-the-longest-in-history/.

"6 Cardinals Mentioned as Successors, Italian Candidates Considered in Lead." *Pittsburgh Post-Gazette*, August 7, 1978.

"The 70th Miracle: Lourdes Healing Officially Declared Supernatural." February 12, 2018. https://www.catholicnewsagency.com/news/37743/the-70th-miracle-lourdes-healing-officially-declared-supernatural.

"St. Peter's Basilica." *New World Encyclopedia*, revised October 14, 2022. https://www.newworldencyclopedia.org/entry/St._Peter%27s_Basilica.

Saxon, Wolfgang. "Giovanni Cardinal Benelli Dead; Was Called Candidate for Papacy." *New York Times*, October 27, 1982. https://www.nytimes.com/1982/10/27/obituaries/giovanni-cardinal-benelli-dead-was-called-candidate-for-papacy.html.

———. "Michele Sindona, Jailed Italian Financier, Dies of Cyanide Poisoning at 65; At the Center of Scandals." *New York Times*, March 23, 1986.

Schneider, Nicholas, OP. "Pilgrimages to Our Lady's Shrines." *Humilitas*, May 2015.

Scola, Angelo. *Uno Sguardo su Albino Luciani*. Venezia: Marcianum Press, 2009.

Scotti, R. A. *Basilica: The Splendor and the Scandal: Building St. Peter's*. New York: Penguin, 2006.

Seabeck, Raymond and Lauretta. *The Smiling Pope: The Life and Teaching of John Paul I*. Huntington, IN: Our Sunday Visitor, 2004.

"The September Pope." *Time*, October 9, 1978. https://time.com/archive/6853830/cover-story-the-september-pope/.

Serafini, Loris. *Albino Luciani: Il Papa del Sorriso*. Padova: Messaggero di Sant'Antonio, 2008.

———. (director, Foundation Papa Luciani and Museum Albino Luciani of Canale d'Agordo). In discussion with the author, Canale d'Agordo, Italy, July 11, 14, and

15, 2011; Gloucester, Rhode Island, October 10 and 11, 2012; New York, October 12, 2012; Canale d'Agordo, Italy, September 6, 7, and 8, 2022.

———. Email message to author, September 15, 2015.

Shapero, Julia. "Belief in God, the Devil Falls to New Low: Gallup—Belief in God and Other Spiritual Entities Is Highest among Those Who Attend Regular Religious Services." Changing America. https://thehill.com/changing-america/respect/diversity-inclusion/4107968-belief-in-god-the-devil-falls-to-new-low-gallup/.

Sheils, Merrill, and Loren Jenkins. "A Man of the People." *Newsweek*, September 4, 1978.

Silvio De Nard, Rev. (pastor, Sacred Heart Parish, East Providence, Rhode Island). In discussion with the author, East Providence, May 14, 2011.

"Simplicity Will Mark Installation of Pope." *Observer-Reporter*, August 29, 1978.

"Sistine Chapel." Musei Vaticani. https://www.museivaticani.va/content/museivaticani/en/collezioni/musei/cappella-sistina/storia-cappella-sistina.html.

Smith, Brixe, Mark Edward Smith, and Stephen Hanley. "Hey Luciani." Single release, Side A. *Beggars Banquet*. United Kingdom, December 1986.

"Solutions Sought by Pope." *Victoria Advocate*, September 1, 1978.

Spackman, Paul. *God's Candidate: The Life and Times of Pope John Paul I*. Herefordshire: Gracewing, 2008.

Sweeney, Jon M. *The Pope Who Quit: A True Medieval Tale of Mystery, Death, and Salvation*. New York: Image, 2012.

"A Swift Stunning Choice." *Time*, September 4, 1978.

Taffarel, Francesco, ed. *Papa Luciani: Un Pensiero Ogni Giorno*. Padova: Edizioni Messaggero, 2008.

"Tears Flow in the Church of the Pope's Hometown." *Montreal Gazette*, September 30, 1978.

Thavis, John. *The Vatican Diaries: A Behind-the-Scenes Look at the Power, Personalities, and Politics at the Heart of the Catholic Church*. New York: Viking, 2013.

Thomas, Gordon, and Max Morgan-Witts. *Pontiff*. New York: New American Library, 1984.

"The Tomb of John Paul I, Vatican Grottoes." https://www.stpetersbasilica.info/Grottoes/JPI/Tomb%20of%20John%20Paul%20I.htm.

Tornielli, Andrea. "Luciani Spoke to Sr. Lucia of Apostasy and the Problems of the Church." *La Stampa*, May 12, 2017. https://www.lastampa.it/vatican-insider/en/2017/05/12/news/luciani-spoke-to-sr-lucia-of-apostasy-and-the-problems-of-the-church-1.34599250/.

Toros, Hilmi "Lead, Oak, Cypress Used for Casket." *Eugene Register-Guard*, August 13, 1978.

———. "Pontiff Makes Use of Throne." *Sarasota Herald-Tribune*, September 14, 1978.

———. "Pope Funeral Set Wednesday; Conclave Soons." *Star News*, October 1, 1978.

———. "Pope: I Am Only a Poor Man." *Tulare Advance-Register* 96, no. 243 (September 29, 1978). https://cdnc.ucr.edu/?a=d&d=TULAR19780929.1.3&e=-------en--20--1--txt-txIN--------.

———. "Pope Paul Passes through 'Door of Death': 100,000 Mourn Pontiff at Simple Requiem Mass." *Eugene Register-Guard*, August 13, 1978.

———. "Pope Paul VI Dies after Heart Attack: Death of 'Pilgrim Pope' Comes while Resting Up from Illness." *Lodi News-Sentinel*, August 7, 1978. lodinews.com/site/about.html.

———. "Reaction in U.S. to the Selection." *Lodi News-Sentinel*, August 28, 1978.

———. "Selection Heavy on Tradition." *Beaver County Times*, August 7, 1978.

"Unfinished Business Will Greet New Pope." *Star News*, October 1, 1978.

United Nations Scientific Committee on the Effects of Atomic Radiation. "Assessments of the Radiation Effects from the Chernobyl Nuclear Reactor Accident." https://www.unscear.org/unscear/en/areas-of-work/chernobyl.html.

"Untiring in His Efforts for Peace—Queen." *Sydney Morning Herald*, August 8, 1978.

"Vatican Medical Care Questioned." *Ottawa Citizen*, October 2, 1978.

"Vatican to Keep Italian Domination after Four Centuries. Speculation Was Growing That Tradition Would End with Pope Paul's Successor." *The Blade*, August 27, 1978.

Vazza, Cesare. "His Light, Only for a Moment." *Humilitas*. Translated by Lori Pieper. December 2002.

"Villot Has Title But Little Say." *Sydney Morning Herald*, August 8, 1978.

Walsh, Michael. *The Conclave: A Sometimes Secret and Occasionally Bloody History of Papal Elections*. Lanham, MD: Sheed & Ward, 2003.

Waters, Harry F. "Cardinal Candidates." *Newsweek*, August 23, 1978.

Watson, Russell, Loren Jenkins, and Elaine Sciolino. "We Have a Pope." *Newsweek*, September 4, 1978.

Weigel, George. *God's Choice: Pope Benedict XI and the Future of the Catholic Church*. New York: HarperCollins, 2009.

———. *God's Choice: Pope Benedict XVI and the Future of the Catholic Church*. New York: HarperCollins e-books, 2009.

———. *Witness to Hope: The Biography of Pope John Paul II 1920–2005*. New York: Harper Perennial, 2001.

"What Are the Three Secrets of Fatima?" Our Pilgrimage Travel Blog. https://joewalshtours.ie/what-are-the-three-secrets-of-fatima/.

"What Changed at Vatican II." *Catholic Register*, October 8, 2012. https://www.catholicregister.org/features/item/15194-what-changed-at-vatican-ii.

"What to See Inside Vatican Museums?" *The Vatican: Tickets & Tours*. Detailed Guide. 2024. https://www.thevaticantickets.com/inside-vatican-museums/.

"Why Are the Popes Buried in Three Coffins?" January 6, 2023. https://dominicanmedia.com.ng/2023/01/06/.

Williams, Leighton Vaughan. "Three Strikes of the Clock: Betting on the Man to Be Pope since 1503." April 18, 2017. https://leightonvw.com/2017/04/18/three-strikes-of-the-clock-betting-on-the-man-to-be-pope-since-1503/.

Willoughby, William F. "Luciani's Early Years Shaped Concern for the Poor." *Bangor Daily News*, August 28, 1978.

Winfield, Nicole. "Conclave's Rituals, Oaths and Secrecy Explained." *San Diego Union-Tribune*, February 16, 2013.

Woodward, Kenneth L. "Choosing a New Pope." *Newsweek*, August 21, 1978.

———. *Making Saints: How the Catholic Church Determines Who Becomes a Saint, Who Doesn't, and Why*. New York: Simon & Schuster, 1996.

———. "The 34 Days of John Paul I." *Newsweek*, October 9, 1978.

"World Mourns Paul VI after Sudden Death." *Sydney Morning Herald*, August 8, 1978.

"World Shocked, Grieved at Death." *Deseret News*, September 29, 1978.

Yallop, David. *In God's Name: An Investigation into the Murder of Pope John Paul I*. New York: Penguin, 1984.

———. *The Power and the Glory: Inside the Dark Heart of John Paul II's Vatican*. New York: Carroll & Graf, 2007.

Index

Note: Photos are indicated by italicized page references.

About the Author

Mo Guernon has been in love with books since checking out his first volume from his local public library as a youngster. Reading and collecting books became a lifelong passion, and writing evolved as an avocation. He is particularly fond of biography, history, religion, philosophy, and literary classics.

For decades the author has been active in numerous Catholic endeavors, including service to the diocese of Providence. His first teaching job was in a Catholic school, and he later served as a Catholic school principal. Guernon taught in public secondary schools and part-time at Bristol Community College in Massachusetts. For several years he lectured at the Robert A. Taft Institute of Government at Rhode Island College.

His professional career also included stints as a consultant to school systems, state government, elected officials, candidates for public office, and nonprofit organizations. In addition, Guernon has been a local elected official and a civic leader.

Besides reading, Guernon relaxes by spending time with his family and friends, visiting historical sites, traveling (especially in Europe), and playing golf. (His aim is to break one hundred someday!)

Guernon earned his EdM in administration, planning, and social policy from Harvard University and his BA in history and English from the University of Rhode Island. He also completed graduate work at Boston College and Providence College in addition to studies in Italy.

He is married to Elizabeth Kelley. The couple has three adult children and four grandchildren.

www.ingramcontent.com/pod-product-compliance
Ingram Content Group UK Ltd.
Pitfield, Milton Keynes, MK11 3LW, UK
UKHW042054130425
457389UK00006B/54